Effective performance of
managerial planning, organizing,
and controlling functions which

Leads to

Either

Effective performance
of individual, group,
and organizational
goals

Or

Ineffective performance
of individual, group,
and organizational
goals

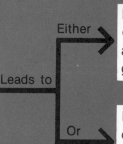

Ineffective performance of
managerial planning, organizing,
and controlling functions which

Leads to

Either

Effective performance
of individual, group,
and organizational
goals

Or

Ineffective performance
of individual, group,
and organizational
goals

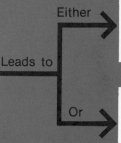

FUNDAMENTALS OF MANAGEMENT
functions, behavior, models

FUNDAMENTALS OF MANAGEMENT

functions, behavior, models

JAMES H. DONNELLY, JR.
Professor of Business Administration
University of Kentucky

JAMES L. GIBSON
Professor of Business Administration
University of Kentucky

JOHN M. IVANCEVICH
Professor of Organizational Behavior and Management
University of Houston

 Third edition   1978

Business Publications, Inc.   Dallas, Texas   75243
Irwin-Dorsey Limited   Georgetown, Ontario   L7G 4B3

ISBN 0-256-02073-6
Library of Congress Catalog Card No. 77–085770

Printed in the United States of America

2 3 4 5 6 7 8 9 0 K 5 4 3 2 1 0 9 8

PREFACE

The purpose of this third edition is the same as its predecessors: to prepare students for managerial careers. Moreover the basic organization of materials to achieve that purpose has not been altered. We continue to believe that introductory management courses at the undergraduate or graduate level should be structured around the contributions of three major schools of management thought in the context of the functions of management. Accordingly the text presents the contributions of the *Classical School*, the *Behavioral School*, and the *Management Science School* using the *planning, organizing*, and *controlling functions* as bases for discussion. It is our contention that theories, concepts, and models found in each of these three schools contribute to the total body of knowledge that comprises management thought.

The practice of using one school as a straw man in promoting another hinders the evolution of a science of management. The style and content of the book, however, does not preclude being critical of the theories, concepts, and models found in the three schools. If managers are to cope effectively with the changes occurring in their environments, they must have an understanding of the lasting contributions of each of the schools. We hope this book will show that the three schools of management are mutually supportive and not separate approaches. It is also implied and illustrated throughout the book that the contributions of the three schools are essential for effective management of all organizations—business/industrial, health care, educational, and governmental.

A significant addition to the revised edition was the inclusion of incidents which we titled "Practical Exercises." The widespread acceptance of these supplemental teaching aids encouraged us to increase their number from 16 to 25. These incidents stress the practical nature of the material covered in the chapter by allowing the student to work through specific situations and decision problems. *Each and every incident* is essentially true and based upon the authors' consulting, training, and personal job experiences. The incidents are set in a variety of different types and sizes of organizations, and include problems of women and minorities and all levels of management. The ones retained from the previous edition received positive student response because of their relevance and ability to stimulate thinking about issues covered in the chapters. In addition to the end-of-chapter exercises, a broad-based, issue-oriented integrative case is included at the end of the last chapter. This case enables the instructor to bring together relevant aspects of the entire book in the context of the case analysis.

In addition to the Practical Exercises, "Management in Action" summaries introduce 11 chapters. These materials report actual managerial applications of concepts and theories presented in the ensuing chapter. Through the identification of actual managerial applications of text materials, the gap between the classroom and the "real world" can be narrowed somewhat. The Management in Action summaries are thus intended to stimulate greater student interest by presenting real-world problems and issues, as well as to supplement the text.

The text material is presented in 17 chapters organized into five parts. The first part, "Management and Managerial Performance," is new and was added in response to reviewers' and adopters' suggestions. Here we develop a concise, conceptual understanding of what management is, how it is undertaken, and why it exists. The purposes of this part are to identify a meaning of management, introduce the three schools of management thought, and establish the importance of effective managerial performance. Chapter 2 was written for this edition to highlight the importance of achieving effective performance and to provide an integrative theme for the remainder of the text.

The second part, "The Classical School of Management," consists of Chapters 3–6. It remains intact, but with the addition of substantially more current information in the chapters on planning (Chapter 4), organizing (Chapter 5), and controlling (Chapter 6). We have made an even greater effort to avoid the impression that the Classical School represents a specific historical period with little relation to contemporary management. Through additional material and revision of existing material, the relevance and importance of effective planning, organizing, and controlling are established more strongly than in previous editions.

Part Three, "The Behavioral School of Management," includes five chapters, 7–11. The topics covered in this section are motivation, work groups, leadership, and organizational change and development. The materials have been updated and upgraded to be consistent with the intended level of discussion. Recent contributions from the burgeoning behavioral science research literature have been incorporated where relevant. The criteria used to include such new topics as behavior modification, path-goal leadership theory, and individual versus group decision making were relevance, increasing applicability, and interest among behavioral scientists and practicing managers.

Part Four, "The Management Science School," has been significantly revised with the addition of a new chapter, 14, on *management information systems* and the elimination of the chapter on PERT/CPM. The section emphasizes *operational management* issues throughout the discussions of decision making (Chapter 13), breakeven and inventory control models (Chapter 15), and linear programming (Chapter 16). Consistent with the previous edition, the chapters are divided into two distinct parts: The first part is completely narrative and discusses the nature of the particular management science model, its advantages and disadvantages. The second part focuses on "Application" and contains an illustrative problem. The purpose of this section is to illustrate the contributions of management science to production and operations management problems.

Finally, Part Five consists of one chapter, "Reality-Centered Management." It is here that a basis for integrating the three schools of management is developed. An "open-system, closed-system" approach is suggested as one way to understand the totality of management thought. The chapter concludes by reopening issues first raised in Chapter 1; that is, what will be the important features of the environment in which future managers will manage.

Numerous other changes and improvements have been made which need not be mentioned here, but taken in total they will, we hope, make this revision better organized and more relevant for the student and a better teaching aid for the instructor. The book is not lengthy yet it contains a vast variety of theories, concepts, models, and examples of actual management applications. Sections of the book can be utilized, depending upon the orientation of the instructor, the objectives of the course, and the role of the introductory course in the curriculum. Some instructors will undoubtedly wish to utilize each "practical exercise" in Parts Two and Three and cover only the narrative parts of Part Four. Others will wish to spend more time on the "Application" sections in Part Four. The book has been developed with these multiple purposes in mind.

The authors wish to acknowledge the contributions of reviewers whose suggestions are reflected throughout this edition. We are especially indebted to David A. Gray, the University of Texas at Arlington, and William G. Ryan, Indiana University at Bloomington. Other reviewers whose contributions should be acknowledged are: Mauritz Blonder, Hofstra University; Arthur H. Boiselle, El Paso Community College; Lyle Brenne, El Paso Community College; Donald R. Burke, Villanova University; Douglas D. Cantrell, Eastern Michigan University; Bernard C. Dill, Bloomsburg State College; Fred C. House, Northern Arizona University; W. Dow Hoyt, San Bernardino Valley College; Jack Kappeler, Platte Tech Community College; John E. Kinney, Jr., Chabot College; Eric A. Larson, Onondaga Community

College; Donald D. Nelson, College of DuPage; L. Richard Oliker, Syracuse University; Charles K. Phillips, Stephen A. Austin University; and Martin H. Wensman, Cerritos College.

In addition to these reviews, the authors benefitted from the suggestions of colleagues and graduate students who used the book in their classes at the Universities of Kentucky and Houston. We particularly wish to thank Roger Blakeney, Lee Bomblatus, Gil Bythewood, Athalia Jones, Bob Keller, Van Miller, Gail Miller, Jim Quick, Skip Szilagyi, and Sam White.

Finally we acknowledge William W. Ecton, Dean of the College of Business and Economics, University of Kentucky, and A. Benton Cocanougher, Dean of the College of Business Administration, University of Houston, for their support of our efforts. The patient, tolerant, and forgiving secretaries were Janie Alexander and Carla Krenek.

January 1978   JAMES H. DONNELLY, JR.
                                                  JAMES L. GIBSON
                                                  JOHN M. IVANCEVICH

CONTENTS

4. The planning function   61

Management in action. Goal-setting and ordering: Priority of goals. Timing of goals. Structure of goals. Measurement of goals. Management by objectives. Forecasting: Sales forecasts. Forecasting approaches. Resource forecasts. Budgeting: Financial budgeting. Two budgeting approaches. Program budgeting. Policy making. Summary. **Practical exercises:** Practical exercises I: MBO Planning in an Occupational Health Division. Practical exercises II: Planning in Fast-Food Stores. Practical exercise III: Problem Identification in a Consumer-Products Firm.

5. The organizing function   95

The principle of specialization of labor. The principle of departmentalization: Output-oriented bases. Internal operations-oriented bases. A final word on departmentalization. The principle of span of control: Span of control and managerial work. Span of control and organizational shape. The principle of unity of command: Chain of command. Unity of command and the staff function. Studies of organizational structure: The Sears, Roebuck study. Porter and Lawler study of attitudes in tall and flat organizations. The Woodward contingency study. Summary. **Practical exercises:** Practical exercise I: Organizational Problems in an Electronic Products Company. Practical exercise II: Reorganizing State Human Resources Agencies. Practical exercise III: The Reorganization of Donzi's Bakery.

6. The controlling function   128

Management in action. Necessary conditions for control. Three types of control. Preliminary control: Preliminary control of human resources. Preliminary control of materials. Preliminary control of capital. Preliminary control of financial resources. Concurrent control. Feedback control: Financial statement analysis. Standard cost analysis. Quality control analysis. Employee performance evaluation. Summary of the controlling function. The classical school in perspective. **Practical exercises:** Practical exercise I: Evaluating Managerial Performance. Practical exercise II: The New Dean. Practical exercise III: Developing a New Product.

PART THREE
The behavioral school

7. Foundations of the behavioral school   161

The human relations approach: The Hawthorne studies. A review and critique of the Hawthorne studies. Human relations modifications of classical organization theory: Division of labor. Scalar and functional

PART ONE

Management and managerial performance

1
THE FIELD OF MANAGEMENT

The purpose of this book is to prepare students for management careers by presenting those concepts and tools that we believe will be useful to the manager *in the future.* We asked ourselves: "What can we do in the present to prepare future managers for the future?" The result is this book. In selecting materials to be included, it was necessary for the authors to make some difficult decisions. The authors' choice was based primarily upon the criterion of "general acceptability." Those topics are included which are regarded by most management scholars and practitioners as constituting the fundamentals of the field.

Accordingly the materials presented here include a variety of theories and opinions which attempt to describe what managers do and should do to be effective. Scholarly research and practical experience are the major sources which we have drawn upon in developing this presentation. Our belief is that one who aspires to become an effective manager can begin by reading, studying, and evaluating fundamental concepts and tools of management.

What is management?

Important work in our society is done by men and women who have such formal titles as president, executive, governor, administrator, chairperson, dean, director, commissioner, superintendent, and officer. Less formal titles include "boss," "whip," and other more imaginative and less flattering ones. These people work in business firms, hospitals, colleges and universities, government and politics, voluntary associations, fraternities and sororities. They are separated by distance, life style, and background, but are bound together by at least one commonality: They all engage in the practice of management. They each face situations and make decisions which differ along some important dimensions, but which are similar along other, equally important dimensions. No doubt a governor makes decisions which touch the lives of many more people than does a college president; and the chief executive of a major publishing firm commands more resources than does a production foreman. But despite these differences, a broad base of similarity exists.

The pervasiveness of the practice of management is widely recognized. McGuire states: "People who don't manage are either too young, too old, or are found in institutions for the incompetent."[1] An overstatement? We think not. If we consider the terms "management" and "manage" in a broad sense, then housewives "manage" their households, school children "manage" their allowances, and we all "manage" our time! These common usages of the terms reflect the practical fact that we all must engage in activities which are intended to allocate scarce means — whether our own or someone else's time, money, energy, or machines — toward numerous, competing, and insatiable ends. The student and housewife share this common problem — neither has enough of anything to accomplish everything. Each of these persons must make choices.

Since nearly everyone manages something, management can be viewed in an all-embracing context. However, this book will concentrate on the process of management as it relates only to a particular, though widespread, instance. We will develop our discussion of management as it arises when the scarce means include *the energies of other people.* Heads of state, executives, administrators, commissioners, directors, foremen, office managers, superintendents, mayors, deans, and academic department chairpersons all share the common problem of having to depend upon others to get the work done. Therefore, they all practice management as it is defined here.

Why study management?

Our concept of management highlights the *importance* and the *content* of management as a field of study. The *importance* of management is based upon the fact that modern society has developed through the creation of specialized institutions and organizations which provide the goods and services it desires. Moreover, these institutions are guided and directed by the decisions of one or more persons who are designated "managers." It is they who allocate scarce resources to alternative and competing ends. Managers, through their skill and judgment, determine the means-end relationships; they have the authority (as granted by society) and the responsibility (as accepted by them) to build or destroy cities, to wage peace or war, to purify or pollute the environment. They establish the conditions for

---

[1] Joseph W. McGuire, "Management and Method," in Joseph W. McGuire, ed., *Contemporary Management: Issues and Viewpoints* (Englewood Cliffs, N.J.: Prentice-Hall, Inc., 1974), p. 1.

the provision of jobs, incomes, products, services, protection, health care, and knowledge. It is difficult to identify anyone in an advanced society who is neither a manager nor subject to the decisions of a manager.

Our concept of management also directs attention to the *content* of the field. The formal study and systematic practice of management focuses on the nature of group effort, various forms of coordination, and the manner of setting, ordering, and measuring goals. The process of management is required whenever two or more persons combine their efforts and resources to accomplish a goal which neither can accomplish by acting alone. The necessity for coordination follows from the fact that the actions of group participants constitute parts of a total task. If one person acts alone to accomplish a task, no coordination is required, but once that person allocates a part of the task to others, the individual efforts must be coordinated in some manner.

To provide the background for understanding some basic management concepts, let us examine how the management process developed in a historical context. We will briefly describe its evolution, with particular attention to the early beginnings of the formal study of management.

The evolution of management

The practice of management is as old as man's history. Throughout time, men have joined with others to accomplish a goal, first in families, later in tribes and other more sophisticated political units. Ancient people constructed pyramids, temples, and ships; they created systems of government, farming, commerce, and warfare. These social achievements were created through the use of management techniques. Professor Claude S. George, Jr., has provided an interesting survey of the management practices of Sumerian temple priests, Egyptian pharaohs, and other functionaries of ancient civilization.[2] He observes that management was quite widespread throughout these civilizations, and that the literature of the times refers to such managerial concepts as planning, staff assistance, division of labor, control, and leadership. But these societies made no effort to accumulate and synthesize knowledge of management practice; what knowledge did exist was passed along from generation to generation or was learned through experience.

Relatively sophisticated management practices emerged during the eras of the Greek and Roman empires. These ancient city-states created organizations to carry on political, commercial, and military

---

[2] Claude S. George, Jr., *The History of Management Thought* (Englewood Cliffs, N.J.: Prentice-Hall, Inc., 1968), pp. 3–26.

activities. As Professor George reports,[3] the Greeks recognized the relationship between efficiency in manual work and standard motions. Through the use of musical accompaniment, the Greeks introduced tempo and rhythm into the work place. The significant writings on the subject were those of Plato, Socrates, Aristotle, Xenophon, and a host of other philosophers. These insightful thinkers espoused principles of logic, economics, government, and science which are the foundations of Western civilization. Roman thinkers also contributed to this early management literature as they documented and analyzed the problems of the Roman Republic and, later, the Roman Empire.

The administration of the far-flung Roman Empire required the application of managerial concepts. As James D. Mooney stated in his analysis of the historical development of management, "The real secret of the greatness of the Romans was their genius for organization."[4] Mooney's opinion is based upon his investigation of the Romans' use of certain principles of organization to coordinate the diverse activities of the Empire. These principles stress the attainment of effective and efficient administration. Whether the fall of the Roman Empire was due to the eventual neglect of these principles is for the historian to decide.

The feudal system which evolved during the Medieval Period was an early experiment in decentralized government organization, and it is all the more interesting when compared to the centralized systems of Greece and Rome. The feudal system introduced the usual problems associated with the management of a decentralized organization, including delegation of authority, decision making, and accountability. The tenor of the times was not conducive to the literary arts; consequently, there is little written word to report the lessons in management to be learned from the feudal era. Niccolo Machiavelli did, of course, provide a treatise on the appropriate use of power. It is perhaps unfortunate that his ideas have been associated with despotism and the cynical use of power when, in fact, he may have provided the first codification of basic managerial thought.

The feudal system ultimately gave way to a recentralization of authority through mercantilism and, eventually, the industrial revolution. With the rise of the factory system and mass production, a need to rationalize the management process soon arose. Most students are well aware of the antecedents to modern manufacturing methods and institutions. It is sufficient to recall that the important developments were both technical and political. The development of steam power and the concept of interchangeable parts combined with a political

---

[3] Ibid., p. 15.

[4] James D. Mooney, *The Principles of Organization* (New York: Harper and Brothers, 1939), p. 63.

philosophy of laissez-faire were the active ingredients of the industrialization of Western civilization. In an industrial society the management of business firms, per se, became the subject of specific analysis. It was during this period that practitioners began to evaluate the potential application of scientific thinking to the management process. They also began to share insights through common associations and writings. Thus, even though the practice of management was present throughout history, the literature of management is barely 200 years old, with the most significant writings appearing in the last 70 years. Historical hindsight permits us to classify this literature on the basis of its primary emphasis.

Three schools of management thought

The literature of management ranges over a wide variety of topics and has been produced by a wide variety of writers. The early writers were practitioners who described their own experiences, from which they generalized to broad principles. They were guided by pragmatic considerations; they wanted to share with others those practices which worked for them. A great deal of what is known about management comes from the autobiographies and memoirs of those who practiced management. On the other hand, there were other writers whose interest in management was (and is) solely scientific. Many social and behavioral scientists view the management of economic, political, military, and service institutions as an extremely important social phenomenon whose very existence justifies its study through scientific inquiry. As scientists using scientific methods, they make no value judgments regarding good or bad management practice; rather, their objective is to understand and to explain the practice of management.

Between the extremes of pragmatism and scientism there are a great number of other writers who have contributed to literature on management. Their professional identifications cover a wide spectrum of knowledge, including engineering, sociology, anthropology, psychology, economics, law, accounting, mathematics, political science, and philosophy. The different points of view represented by these disciplines have been the bases for numerous attempts to provide classification schemes. For example, Harold Koontz and Cyril O'Donnell identify seven schools of management thought: (1) the operational approach, (2) the empirical approach, (3) the human behavior approach, (4) the social system approach, (5) the decision theory approach, (6) the communications center approach, and (7) the mathematical approach.[5]

---

[5] Harold Koontz and Cyril O'Donnell, *Principles of Management*, 5th ed. (New York: McGraw-Hill Book Co., 1972), p. 35.

Others have identified six approaches: (1) managerial accounting, (2) managerial economics, (3) organization theory, (4) human behavior, (5) management science, and (6) industrial engineering.[6] The student can get an intuitive grasp of the kinds of material and subject matter discussed in management literature from the labels that have been used.

Our purpose is not to complicate matters by proposing yet another classification scheme. However, we believe that the discussion of the field of management can proceed quite well by means of a classification scheme that identifies only three schools: the *Classical School*, and *Behavioral School*, and the *Management Science School*. We believe that the ideas and concepts found in each school contribute positively to the total body of knowledge which comprises modern management thought, and that a student of management need not, in fact should not, emphasize one school and ignore the others. All three are mutually supportive; each adds to the total store of management knowledge without detracting from the other two. Through these three schools we can see an evolution of what is known and what should be known about management. At the same time, we have not written a text on the evolution of management thought, although the student of management should recognize and respect the fact that the field of management has historical origins and an extensive body of literature.

The *Classical School* of management is described in the literature that appeared primarily during the pre-World War II period. The writers of this era were seeking answers to quite basic questions. They were practitioners or scientists and engineers employed by business and government. At the most fundamental level these writers were concerned with questions of efficiency, that is, the maximization of output-to-input ratios. The technological insights of engineers were significant as business leaders sought to increase the productivity of workers. The efforts of these engineers led to the development of an extensive body of knowledge regarding plant and machinery design, work methods, materials flow, and the like. The basic orientation of this body of knowledge which was later termed "scientific management," was the application of scientific methods of inquiry to the problems of work and work management. Therefore the use of science to solve pragmatic problems placed management in the same category with engineering and medicine.

The emergence of the Classical School coincided with the creation of large, complex organizations. Persons who had practiced management within these organizations recognized that the management of organizations can be quite different from the management of work.

---

[6] W. Warren Haynes, Joseph L. Massie and Marc J. Wallace, Jr, *Management*, 3rd ed. (Englewood Cliffs, N.J.: Prentice-Hall, Inc., 1975), pp. 4–11.

Literature appeared which sought to explain management in terms of the functions of managers at every level of an organization. Thus the classical writers defined management as the process of coordinating group effort toward group goals. This is the definition used in this textbook. Moreover, through deductive reasoning the classicists identified (1) the *functions* which are necessary for coordination, namely, *planning, organizing, and controlling;* and (2) the *principles* of effective managerial action. The culmination of the Classical School is an elaborate conceptual framework which relates these three basic functions to logically identified subfunctions. Subsequent writers added to and modified the work of the classicists.

The *Behavioral School* has used the concepts of psychology, sociology, anthropology, and other behavioral sciences to extend our knowledge of human behavior in the work environment. The classical writers did not provide in-depth insights into human behavior. This was not due to their ignorance of the importance of the human element, but to their lack of appropriate training. The writers of the Behavioral School have brought their research skills to bear on the *organizing and controlling* functions, beginning with the Hawthorne Studies of the 1920s and continuing with vigorous attempts to evaluate, scientifically, the practical insights of the Classical School.

The literature which we classify as belonging to the Behavioral School has two common characteristics. First, the focal point of the school is human behavior, managerial as well as nonmanagerial, in the context of work organizations. Secondly, the method of inquiry is essentially the scientific method, with emphasis on the discovery of causal relationships. The findings of behavioral research can be blended with the insights of the Classical School to extend our understanding of the fundamentals of management.

The *Management Science School* in one sense is a modern version of scientific management. Its essential feature is sophistication in the use of mathematics and statistics to aid in resolving production and operational problems through *planning* and *controlling.* The literature which we include in the Management Science School, then, focuses on technical (rather than behavioral) problems through the construction of quantitative techniques. The development of the computer has permitted analyses that were previously not possible because of their complexity. The computer has been of tremendous value to the growing importance of the Management Science School.

Our classification of management literature suggests the two main thrusts of management theory and practice since the Classical School. On the one hand there has been emphasis on behavioral problems; on the other hand, but coincidently, there has been emphasis on technical problems. Rather than competing with the Classical School, this two-pronged attack is a natural extension of the earlier work.

Management in the future

At the outset of this chapter we stated that the purpose of this book is to prepare future managers. That purpose is not a modest one! Knowing what the future holds for managers is difficult to discern. Knowing what skills and knowledge will be required to manage in that future is even more difficult. Yet there could not possibly be any more important task than that of preparing today's young people to manage the organizations of tomorrow. But what can be said about the future?

Depending upon which pundit you choose to believe, the future of developed societies is either bright, hopeful, and filled with promise or it is dark, hopeless, and filled with disappointment. On the one hand we are warned that we must make radical changes in the way we work and play because the world's supply of energy will soon be depleted. We are called upon to think of the energy crisis in terms of the moral equivalent of war. We must conserve, we must be more efficient, we must more astutely plan. On the other hand we are told that we must respond to the demands of workers for an improved quality of work life; that employees are turned off by the manufacturing methods which have the greatest potential for being efficient. Mass production, specialization of labor, extensive automation are attacked as creators of working conditions which reduce the opportunities for individual growth and development. It is said that such methods are dehumanizing. Whatever the outcome of this very real dilemma between the opposing forces of efficiency and quality of life, the only certainty is that it will be managers who will make the critical choices.

THE INHERENT DILEMMAS OF MANAGEMENT

Managers have always had to recognize and act on the fact that "there are no solutions, only intelligent choices." If we for the moment ignore the broader environmental forces which will shape tomorrow's societies and concentrate only on the essence of management, we can see that managers have always dealt with dilemmas. John D. Aram notes five dilemmas inherent in any managerial position.[7]

The first of these dilemmas is to integrate the self interests of individuals and the collective interests of the organization. The good of individuals is often in conflict with the good of organization.

Second is the dilemma posed by the need for control and the coincident need for initiative. Managers must obtain adequate performance of specific tasks and duties, yet they must insist upon personal initiative.

Third, the dilemma of adhering to impersonal rules and procedures

---

[7] John D. Aram, *Dilemmas of Administrative Behavior* (Englewood Cliffs, N.J.: Prentice-Hall, Inc., 1976).

and attending to the personal needs of individuals. Rules and procedures exist to reduce favoritism and promote collective well-being, yet individuals have specific needs which often cannot be satisfied through the application of those rules and procedures.

4. Fourth is the dilemma created by the necessity to balance individual needs and group norms. Organizations consist of groups of people working together. These groups exert powerful influences on individuals which often conflict with their wants and desires.

5. The fifth dilemma is related to one above. It focuses, however, on the necessity to adhere to as well as to change group norms. The problem of supporting elements of the status quo while at the same time attempting to change other elements is known to all managers.

Thus without going into any greater detail it is obvious that the necessity to deal with dilemmas is not a recent demand on management. Rather, dilemmas are inherent in the managerial role. Even in placid environments the manager is confronted with choices among alternatives that are "equally attractive or equally unattractive."[8]

THE THREE SCHOOLS OF THOUGHT AND THE FUTURE MANAGER

The most powerful theoretical and practical insights into the nature and problems of future management take into account the entire range of knowledge. The future manager will operate in an environment that is too complicated for easy, one-sided analyses. The manager must be able to blend the concepts, techniques, and models from each of the three schools. To select naively the approach of one of the schools to the exclusion of the others can only compound the problems. The future manager will face diverse and often conflicting demands. The sources of these demands are the many groups which have vested interests in any organization and include employees, customers, suppliers, creditors, owners, clients, patients, students, government officials, and the public at large. The demands of all these groups will seldom, if ever, completely be satisfied by any management decision, a fact which results in the creation of even more dilemmas. In recognition of this fact, managers must often accept "second-best" solutions which rely upon knowledge from all three schools.

Contemporary society is the product of many complex and interrelated forces. No doubt the basic force has been the ability of man to convert scientific discoveries to practical use. Technological innovations in production, distribution, and communication processes have produced irrevocable changes. The associated changes in the nature and composition of society, including organizations and the concen-

---

[8] Ibid., p. 2.

tration of power, are likewise irrevocable, at least in the short run. This means that managers, as the wielders of power, are now and will continue to be called upon to answer to the grantors of that power.

In a traditional society consisting of many small and relatively insignificant firms, the legitimate function of business was to seek a profit through the production of goods and services. The rules of the game were only loosely drawn and seldom given force of law. The marketplace was counted on to provide the brake on the use of power. *Laissez-faire* and *caveat emptor* expressed the prevailing ideology of the times. Society granted considerable freedom to business in exchange for the creation of economic well-being. But, at the turn of the 20th century, the view of society as reflected by its laws was changing.

In the 1930s American society could be described more accurately in terms of large interdependent units than in terms of small independent units. Large firms confronted large unions, with the public interest represented by a large and expanding federal government. The Great Depression of the 1930s was a strong indication that all was not right with the way America did business. The stage was set for the enactment of reform and regulatory legislation that would permanently affect the function of the business manager.

The future manager will recognize full well the legitimate necessity for complying with federal, state, and local legislation designed to regulate the use of economic power. The list of laws and acts will not be catalogued here. At a more subtle level, the manager is now and will continue to be called upon to respond to a host of demands whose legitimacy is now so well established either in law or in practice. These demands find expression in the nebulous and ill-defined phrase, "management's social responsibilities."

That society should have expectations for business that go beyond the provision of goods and services within the framework of legal constraints reflects the ambivalence of society toward business. On the one hand it expects the traditional business functions of providing goods, services, and employment yet it also desires such nontraditional functions as the location of plants in ghettos and in depressed regions. It desires training programs for the hardcore unemployed, yet asks for restraint on price increases in the face of inflation. In the midst of these developments, management must act or not act without the benefit of a clear-cut framework of values.

The resolution of the dilemmas which society imposes will ultimately depend upon managers' value systems. As they confront the conflicting demands in situations where some freedom of choice exists, their system of values will attach relative weights to these demands. That they will err in the minds of some is inevitable; that they must act is likewise inevitable.

Summary and introduction

Thus far we have made a number of points concerning the field of management.

1. We have provided a basis for the importance of management to the workings of society: Society tends to organize its resources through specialized institutions.
2. The process of organizing necessitates some means for coordinating the organization's (group's) activities. This coordinating process is termed management.
3. The literature of management has evolved as the importance of management as a field of study and analysis became more widely accepted.
4. A variety of perspectives and emphases has characterized management literature. We can introduce some clarity by identifying three mutually supportive schools—the Classical, Behavioral and Management Science Schools.
5. Finally, future managers cannot ignore the contributions of any of the three schools if they are to deal effectively with their environment.

With these thoughts established, we now move on to a more fully developed description and analysis of management. In the following chapter a concept of management is developed which explains *what* management is, *why* management exists, and *how* management is undertaken.

Discussion and review questions

1. Explain why management is required to coordinate group effort.
2. What is the significance of the fact that contemporary America is "an organizational society"?
3. Evaluate the concept of management as "getting things done through people."
4. What, in your opinion, are society's ligitimate demands of business firms?
5. What are the features of a value system which suggests that a manager should not fire an elderly employee with 20 years of service but who is no longer able to do his job?
6. What do you understand by the phrase "social responsibilities of management"?
7. What is meant by the statement: "Management is an applied science"?
8. What are the important differences between the three schools of management as you now know them?

9. Apart from the energy shortages and demands for improved quality of worklife, what other environmental forces are likely to be important in the near future?

10. Are the conflicts between individual and organizational needs characteristic of modern society, or are they evident throughout reported history? Explain and illustrate your response.

Additional references

Cheit, E. F., ed. *The Business Establishment.* New York: John Wiley and Sons, Inc., 1964.

Cole, A. H. *Business Enterprise and Its Setting.* Cambridge, Mass.: Harvard University Press, 1959.

Drucker, P. *Management: Tasks, Responsibilities, Practices.* New York: Harper and Row, 1974.

Hanson, A. O. *Executive and Management Development for Business and Government.* Detroit: Gale Research Co., 1976.

Koontz, H. *Toward a Unified Theory of Management.* New York: McGraw-Hill Book Company, 1964.

Likert, R., and Likert, J. G. *New Ways of Managing Conflict.* New York: McGraw-Hill Book Co., 1976.

Linowes, D. F. *Strategies for Survival.* New York: American Management Association, 1973.

McGregor, D. M. *The Professional Manager.* New York: McGraw-Hill Book Company, 1967.

Means, G. *The Corporate Revolution in America.* New York: Crowell-Collier Press, 1962.

Petit, T. *The Moral Crisis in Management.* New York: McGraw-Hill Book Company, 1967.

Stewart, R. *Managers and Their Jobs.* London: Macmillan and Company, 1967.

Walton, C. C. *Ethos and the Executive.* Englewood Cliffs, N.J.: Prentice-Hall, Inc., 1969.

Selected management and related periodicals

Academy of Management Journal

Academy of Management Review

Administrative Management

Administrative Science Quarterly

Advanced Management Journal

Business Horizons

Business Management

California Management Review

Columbia Journal of World Business

Fortune

Harvard Business Review

Human Resource Management

Industrial Engineering

Industrial and Labor Relations
   Review

Industrial Management Review

Journal of Applied Behavioral Science

Journal of Applied Psychology

Journal of Business

Journal of Human Resources

Journal of Management Studies

Management International Review

Management of Personnel Quarterly

Management Review

Management Science

Organizational Behavior and Human
   Performance

Organizational Dynamics

Personnel

Personnel Journal

Personnel Psychology

Public Administration Review

Sloan Management Review

Training and Development Journal

2
THE MANAGER'S JOB

Writers and practitioners of management recognize that the simple question: "What do managers do?" often elicits simple answers.[1] One such answer is: "They manage." Managers are integral aspects of our everyday lives and we take their role for granted. Yet when we try to say more than the obvious, we stumble over our words. If the reader is a college student, he or she can quickly understand the issue by asking the question: "What do students do?" The answer will no doubt be: "They study." Yet we know that the meaning of "student" varies from person to person, from class to class, and from college to college.

The authors' aim is to provide readers a concept of management that will enable them to read with greater understanding the material contained in the remaining chapters. In addition to this immediate benefit, it should provide readers a basis for developing their own concepts of management.

We have chosen to develop a concept of management rather than a definition of management for the following reasons. The word "concept," as usually understood, refers to an abstract idea, or meaning, based upon particular instances. As such, a concept is apt to change and vary depending upon who has the idea and what are the instances. A fundamental aspect of management is that its meaning has changed and will continue to change over time. The word "definition" on the other hand usually suggests a fixed idea. But to suggest that there is a definition of management is to imply that its meaning is relatively fixed. That is simply not the case. The meaning of management is different in the perspectives of the Classical, Behavioral, and Management Science Schools, yet each of these schools has contributed to contemporary meanings and practices of management. Throughout this text the ideas, theories, and research of these three schools will be discussed in the light of contemporary management.

---

[1] Leonard Sayles. *Managerial Behavior* (New York: McGraw-Hill Book Co., 1964), p. 1.

A concept of contemporary management

Let us state what we believe to be a useful concept of contemporary management:

> Management consists of *activities* undertaken by one or more persons to *coordinate* the *activities* of *other persons* to achieve *results* not achievable by any one person acting alone.

This concept draws our attention to a number of key considerations. First, note that the focus of management work is the work of *other persons*; the primary purpose of managerial work is the accomplishment of results through the activities of *other persons.* Second, management does this by *coordinating* the activities of others. Third, managerial work must consider simultaneously two aspects: (1) activities of others, i.e., the work of others and (2) others, i.e. people. This idea is reflected in the often used phrases: "Management is getting *work* done through other *people*" and "management is obtaining organizational objectives with and through people."[2]

The work, or job, of management then must be described and analyzed in terms of those activities which managers undertake to coordinate the work of others. Throughout history the choice of concepts to describe managerial activities has varied depending upon the orientations of writers. Even today the student and practitioner of management can easily be dismayed by the apparent confusion as to what it is that managers do and what words best describe what they do. Regardless of the differences in opinion about the best way to describe what managers do, there is little confusion about what managers are supposed to get done—*they are ultimately responsible for the achievement of results through the specialized efforts of other people, whether individually or in groups or in organizations.*

The necessity of management to coordinate specialized labor was recognized by an early writer, James D. Mooney. He used the simple illustration of two men who "unite their strength to move some object that is too heavy or bulky to be moved by one" to demonstrate that, in some manner, their associated effort must be coordinated.[3] They must lift at the same time, move in an agreed-upon direction, and lower the object at the same time at the agreed-upon place. Contained within that illustration are all the elements of management work: the agreed-upon place for the object to be moved is the result to be obtained; the lifting, moving, and lowering of the object are the activities leading to the results. In this instance the management of the process of lifting and moving the object may be undertaken by one of the men, who says:

[2] Robert F. Pearse, *Manager to Manager: What Managers Think of Management Development* (New York: AMACOM, 1974), p. 11.

[3] James D. Mooney, *Principles of Organization* (New York: Harper and Row Publishers, 1947), p. 1.

"One, two, three, lift!" Or the two men may simply know after repeated practice what and when each must do his part. However it happens, whether explicitly or implicitly, the work must be coordinated to achieve the desired performance.

The example of two men moving an object illustrates the essentials of specialized labor wherever it occurs, whether in business firms, hospitals, universities, or governmental agencies. These organizations include people performing specialized jobs to achieve results that are impossible when done by one person. The advantages of combined efforts have long been the cornerstones of advanced societies.

Modern societies consist of specialized organizations which create the goods and services they desire. These organizations are only more complex and complicated versions of the "two men lifting an object" process. They can consist of literally thousands of individuals dispersed throughout the world performing specialized jobs. Hospitals, business firms, universities, and governmental agencies differ in many aspects, yet they all share the central fact—they must be managed.

Managerial activities

We return then to the question posed earlier: "What do managers do?" We can now ask the question in a slightly different manner: "What do managers do to achieve results through others?" The student and practitioner of management will not find a single, universally-accepted answer to this question; and it would be foolish to believe that such should be the case. The meaning of management changes through time as the society in which it exists changes. The meaning of management in 1980 is different from its meaning in 1880. Yet it is necessary to establish some common understanding to facilitate the development of later material.

As we have seen, managers are concerned with work of other people. These two aspects of managerial work must be taken into account in describing what managers do. In a historical sense the earliest writers described management work almost exclusively in terms of the first aspect, work. These writers, whose ideas we term the Classical School, viewed management in terms of activities required to plan, organize, and control the work of subordinates. Subsequent writers reacted to this apparent overemphasis and placed their emphasis on issues associated with the subordinates, the other people. The ideas of these writers, the Behavioral School, were focussed on such issues as motivating and leading people.

It is possible to combine these two points of view and emphases into a framework for describing managerial work. The framework takes into account the two aspects of managerial work and the purpose of managerial work. We can term all those activities which managers undertake to deal with work of subordinates as *work-related activities*, and those related to subordinates themselves as *person-related activities*. The purposes of these two sets of activities are to plan, organize, and control the activities of others through the achievement of coordinated effort. This framework is depicted in Figure 2-1. The framework reflects a means-ends chain with work- and person-related activities serving as the foundation, and results as the final end. Thus the purpose (end) of managerial activities is planned, organized, and controlled work, which in turn leads to coordinated work, which in its turn leads to results.

FIGURE 2-1
A framework for describing the manager's job

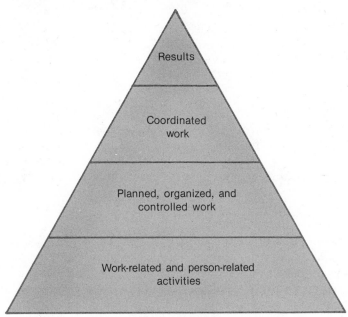

In a practical sense the identification of specific managerial activities is necessary to identify and develop managerial talent. The process of selecting and training managers depends upon first identifying what managers are expected to do and, second, matching skills and knowledge bases with the requirements of the job. For example, one researcher who was attempting to find out how much time managers spent in each managerial activity used the specific activities shown in Table 2-1.

Other writers have described managerial activities in slightly different terms. For example one of the most influential writers on manage-

TABLE 2–1
Specific management activities

Work-related activities

1. Making decisions
2. Solving immediate problems
3. Solving or anticipating long-range problems
4. Delegating assignments to subordinates
5. Processing paperwork
6. Checking company policy
7. Budgetary planning and administration

Person-related activities

1. One-to-one relationships with one's own manager
2. One-to-one relationships with one's peers
3. One-to-one relationships with one's subordinates
4. One-to-one relationships with outsiders
5. Small group meetings as member of one's manager's staff
6. Small group meetings with two or more peers
7. Small group meetings apart from your own or your manager's staff

Source: Adapted from Robert F. Pearse, *Manager to Manager: What Managers Think About Management Development* (New York: AMACOM, 1974), Exhibit 6, pp. 20–21.

ment, Peter Drucker, states that management consists of five basic "operations." According to Drucker, managers: (1) set objectives (work-related activity), (2) organize the work of subordinates (work-related activity), (3) measure performance (work-related activity), (4) motivate and communicate (person-related activity), and (5) develop people (person-related activity).[4] "Every manager does these things—knowingly or not. A manager may do them well, or may do them wretchedly, but always does them."[5]

We could cite numerous other descriptions of managerial activities. And even though the specific terms would differ, the essential two aspects of managers' jobs come down to work and people. They are responsible for the performance of others; more accurately, managers are responsible for the continued improvement of performance.

The management system

As an organization increases in size and complexity, its management adapts by becoming more specialized. Most students are aware of the various modifying adjectives preceding the noun *management*: top management, middle management, first-line management, general

---

[4] Peter Drucker, *People and Performance: The Best of Peter Drucker on Management* (New York: Harper's College Press, 1977), p. 55.

[5] Ibid., p. 55.

management, personnel management, production management, marketing management, and financial management. The history of most ongoing firms can be understood as a process by which the management has, in successive steps, moved from one manager with many subordinates to many managers with many subordinates.

In the "one-manager-many-subordinate firm," the manager performs all the activities necessary to coordinate the work of the subordinates. If the firm is successful so that a larger volume of resources is available for allocation to more goals — more products, wider markets — the manager is confronted with the need to specialize. He or she may decide for example to assign certain activities, such as the marketing of the product, to another person. Or the manager may assign the task of supervising subordinates to another person while continuing to be concerned with the marketing task. Whatever the decision, whether *horizontal specialization* in the first or *vertical specialization* in the second case, the managerial process is now shared, *specialized*, and more complex.

The decision to specialize vertically or horizontally depends upon, in the simplest case, the relative burden imposed by the managerial activities. If, for example, the manager's person-related activities become so time-consuming that the work-related activities go unattended, the decision would be to assign those activities to the supervisor. The result of that decision would be to give the owner-manager more time to devote to work-related activities. On the other hand, if the demands on the manager go beyond his or her ability to deal with work-related activities, the decision would be to hire an expert in marketing, finance, or engineering. The appropriate work-related activities would then be assigned to the new member of the management system.

VERTICAL SPECIALIZATION

One important outcome of vertical specialization is the creation of a *scalar chain*, that is, a chain of command and accountability. The chain of command is termed *hierarchy* because it results in a graded system of authority, with managers located at each point in the vertical chain. Although the terms can differ from organization to organization, it is the general practice to distinguish between *first-line, middle,* and *top management.*

First-line managers coordinate the work activity of others who are not themselves managers. The subordinates may be blue-collar workers, salesmen, clerks, or scientists, depending upon the particular tasks that the subunit must perform, for example, production, marketing, accounting, or research. Whatever the case, first-line managers coordinate the basic work of the organization according to established plans and procedures. They are in daily or near-daily contact with their subordinates. They are ordinarily assigned the task of first-line manager because of their ability to work with people — not only with their own subordinates but also with other first-line supervisors. In contemporary business firms they engage in upward, downward, and lateral relationships. They communicate and interact with their own managers, with their subordinates, and with other first-line managers. The effectiveness of their coordinative efforts will depend as much, if not more, upon their person-related as upon their work-related skills.[6]

Middle managers, unlike first-line managers, coordinate the activity of other managers; yet, like first-line managers, they are subject to the coordinative efforts of a superior. The middle manager coordinates the activity of a subunit of the firm. As shown in the following section, the important characteristics of middle managers are described in terms of horizontal specialization.

Top management of a business firm coordinates the activity of the entire organization through the middle managers. Unlike other managers, the top manager is accountable to no other manager, but instead to the owners of the resources utilized in the business. The form of the enterprise determines the exact manner in which this accountability is exercised. If the enterprise is a corporation, top management reports to the board of directors, which represents the stockholders; top management will report to the partners if it is a partnership; and to the proprietor if it is a proprietorship. Whatever the business form, society grants ultimate authority to the owners of property (resources) utilized in the firm.[7]

The terms used to identify managers at the various hierarchical levels differ from organization to organization. In Table 2–2 we can compare the typically used terms in three types of organizations, business, education, and government. Generally speaking the activities of foremen, chairpersons, and program managers would be similar despite the different terms that are used to identify them. A chairperson in a university could be expected to spend most of the time dealing with the faculty as individuals, as would be the case of foremen and program managers. Similarly we would expect managers, presidents, and secretaries to spend their time being concerned about the work that their organizations are doing in terms of the expectations of owners, students, and taxpayers. At the same time that we can identify similarities in managerial jobs as a function of their level in the hierarchy, we must also recognize that dissimilarities exist. These dis-

---

[6] Eunice C. Coleman and Maureen E. Campbell, *Supervisors: A Corporate Resource* (New York: AMACOM, 1975), pp. 11–15.

[7] See Henry Mintzberg, "The Manager's Job: Folklore and Fact," *Harvard Business Review* (July-August 1975), pp. 49–61, for a report of findings regarding the activities and roles of top managers.

TABLE 2–2
Vertical specialization in three organizational types

	Business	Education	Government
Top-level	Manager	President	Secretary
Middle-level	Superintendent	Vice president	Commissioner
	Supervisor	Dean	Division director
First-level	Foreman	Chairperson	Program manager

similarities arise from the uniqueness of each organization and the environment in which it exists.[8]

In summary the vertical dimension of management can be defined as the process by which the right to act and to use resources within specified limits (authority) is delegated downward. Managers can be described in terms of the extent and limits of authority at their disposal. The delegation of authority also determines differences in the on-job relationships among managers at the same level, that is, horizontal specialization.

HORIZONTAL SPECIALIZATION

The completion of a task requires the completion of a sequence of interrelated activities. As the sequence of activities is identified, and as the responsibility for completing each is assigned to a manager, the managerial process is horizontally specialized. Middle managers are ordinarily responsible for the completion of major subtasks such as those carried on in production, marketing, finance, and personnel. Each manager is at the same level in the hierarchy but each is responsible for completing a different part of the total objective. Middle managers must integrate their own tasks and objectives with other middle managers as well as serve in a pivotal communication position in the vertical hierarchy.

Similarly, a first-line manager is responsible for completing a subpart of the subpart. For example, a production manager will coordinate the activities of first-line managers of the fabrication and the finishing departments. The successful completion of tasks assigned to the subordinates in these two departments, as coordinated by the first-line manager, results in the successful completion of the production manager's task.

The managerial process in contemporary organizations is assigned to numerous persons who have had specialized training and competence

---

[8] Rosemary Stewart, "To Understand the Manager's Job: Consider Demands Constraints, Choices," *Organizational Dynamics* (Spring 1976), pp. 22–32.

to deal with the assigned managerial activities. Descriptive labels promote some degree of understanding of what these persons do and are expected to do. Thus the layman understands, partially, the work of production managers, marketing managers, and personnel managers. There is general understanding of the distinction between top management and first-line management. Yet the specific nature of each managerial task is often unique to the firm within which the task is performed, because of the diversity of business as a social institution and because of the unique character and history of each individual firm.

Managerial and organizational performance

Even though the purpose of management is to facilitate the performance of others, it must be recognized that management is not the only force acting on their performance. In fact management may, in some instances, be the least important influence in determining the extent to which a given group or organization achieves its results. To understand how groups and organizations can fail or succeed despite the best or worst management, we must develop two concepts—*managerial performance* and *organizational performance.*

MANAGERIAL PERFORMANCE

The bases for the following comments are the ideas reflected in Figure 2–2. There we see the now familiar idea that the foci of managerial activities are the activities of others—groups and organizations. The figure shows two immediate outcomes associated with managerial activities—effective and ineffective performance. Thus if managers perform their activities with all the appropriate skill and care, it can be said that they are effective, but if they perform with less than appropriate skill and care, they are ineffective. For example, managers may plan according to the most modern and up-to-date techniques, or they may plan by using incorrect techniques. In the first instance the manager's performance would be termed effective, in the second case it would be judged ineffective.

A recent survey attempted to assess the opinions of American executives on issues related to managerial performance. Questionnaires were mailed to some 6,000 managers in firms of various types and sizes. Some highlights of the study are:

A. In answer to the question of whether managerial performance (termed "executive productivity" in the study) could be improved, 96 percent of the respondents answered "yes."[9]

---

[9] Herman S. Jacobs and Katherine Jillson, *Executive Productivity* (New York: AMACOM, 1974), p. 9.

FIGURE 2–2
Managerial and organizational performance

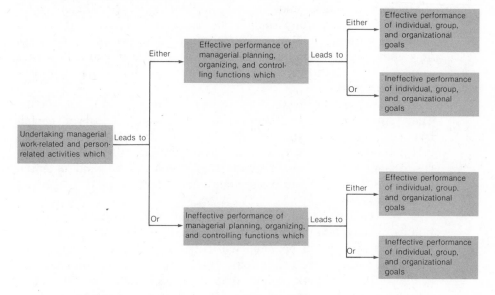

B. In answer to questions concerning specific factors which contribute to ineffective performance, at least 30 percent of the respondents identified one or more of the following factors:[10]
"1. Lack of well-defined organizational or departmental goals and objectives.
2. Ineffective or inefficient operating methods and procedures.
3. Inadequate or ineffective nonmanagerial training or skills development programs.
4. Inadequate managerial leadership
5. Poor supervisor/staff relations at department or lower organizational levels.
6. Poor employee morale."

As is evident, each of these improvement factors can be influenced by management. It is also evident that the first three factors are work-related and the second three are person-related aspects of managerial activities.

The point to be made is that managerial performance can be improved through the application of appropriate skills and knowledge. The development of ability to define goals and select efficient operating methods and procedures is certainly one aim of this textbook. We will also be concerned with providing the reader with bases for improving leadership and motivational skills. Managerial performance is directly related to the ability of managers to perform their jobs. Specifi-

---

[10] Ibid., p. 12.

cally, we can identify at least four areas in which managerial performance can be improved.

Methods of work. Design and implementation of efficient work methods have been proposed by scholars over the years. Setting of work standards through motion and time study, facility layout, and work flow analysis are examples of improving methods of work. There are cases of significant increases in performance following improved methods of work.

In most cases the costs of improving methods of work are moderate. They typically would include the salary and overhead costs of specialists who design and implement the new methods. Investment costs include such items as equipment, tools, and supplies. Thus, from a cost/benefit perspective, methods improvement has good potential because of the moderate costs when compared to capital investment improvements.

There is a drawback to improving methods and it is that an organization can easily "overmethodize." This can result in making the job so simplified that it can be done with little thought. Many employees react negatively to such situations. The boredom and dehumanization of highly routine work is more than some employees can tolerate. A reversal of methodizing is found in what is called job enrichment, which will be discussed in Chapter 8.

Organization of work. No single way to organize work will have positive effects on performance for all types of individuals and in all situations. The different schools of management consider various aspects of organizing. For example, the classical scholar is concerned with hierarchy, formalization, and centralization. On the other hand, behavioral scientists propose decentralized, less structured work organizations.

The manner in which work is organized can influence performance, and the manager's job is to match the appropriate organization with the subordinates, the situation, and the particular tasks to be accomplished. In reality, it appears that multiple structures are appropriate rather than a single structure. An examination of a university, a business firm, or any organization will illustrate that different structural arrangements are used.

Unproductive practices. Since the opportunities for increased performance are diminishing, at least in the areas of substituting machines for people and increased methodization, the importance of minimizing unproductive practices becomes obvious. Generally speaking, there are three sources of unproductive practices. The first is the failure to properly communicate or establish lines of communication between managers and nonmanagers. The second is the disregard shown for such factors as the government, unions, and international competition. Third is the tendency for management to adopt fads or gimmicks to correct major problem areas.

Correction of these three main sources of unproductive practices involves the monitoring of the organization and its activities. Methods of detecting internal and external disturbances are needed. In addition, management needs to develop criteria for evaluating the significance of disturbances that are uncovered. Is the German steel industry a threat to success? What is the result of not complying with air pollution standards? How much money should we expend on executive and nonmanagerial skill and personal development? What types of corrective steps need to be taken? When? How will they be evaluated? These and other questions display why criteria of evaluation are so important in minimizing unproductive practices.

Managing human resources. Improvement in the management of human resources involves the effective utilization of the talent of the organization. It is essentially the application of the idea of full utilization of human resources. Four areas that have the most meaning in utilizing human resources are:

Selection. This involves using valid selection procedures so that employees are properly placed. This applies to hiring employees from outside and to promoting and transferring present employees.

Human resource development. This involves training or providing the knowledge and skills required to improve performance.

Motivation. This practice involves encouraging or otherwise inducing employees to work more effectively. This would include the use of monetary and nonmonetary rewards.

Properly applying managerial functions. This involves utilizing proper planning, organizing, and controlling procedures. Plans are needed as guidelines, organization is necessary to provide a form of structure for completing the work, and controls are needed to monitor progress and make necessary corrections.

The exact procedures used in these four areas for more effectively managing human resources cannot be stated in exact terms. There are few exact answers for managing human resources. The effectiveness of a particular motivation program or plan depends upon a large number of factors. The situation at hand, the people involved, the resources committed to improvement, and the time available are only some of the forces that will affect the success of any management effort to improve human resources.

When questions are asked then about what the manager's job is it seems safe to point to performance improvement. This point has been underscored throughout this chapter. Without adequate performance from the employees, organizational goals cannot be accomplished.

If these goals are not accomplished there is little chance for achieving individual employee goals. The manager must depend on the employees to perform well. This does not mean that the manager just sits idly by and lets events control the situation. The manager needs to search out those factors that have a significant influence on the performance of his or her subordinates. Yet influences other than those under managerial control can affect the work of groups and organizations.

ORGANIZATIONAL PERFORMANCE

Organizational performance refers to the extent to which the goals of others are achieved. As we use the term, it includes the achievement levels, or performance, of individuals, groups, and organizations. The implications of Figure 2-2 are that effective managerial performance does not guarantee organizational performance but does increase the chances.[11] Note that goal accomplishment may be effective or ineffective regardless of whether management is effective or ineffective. The influence of factors other than managerial effectiveness is due to the fact that organizations exist in a larger environment which influences their performances, as shown in Figure 2-3.

The immediate influences — technology, personnel, information, and materials — primarily affect first-level managers. The impact of these influences is not totally beyond their control but it is limited. In fact in many organizations first-level managers have no voice in the selection of personnel and technology that are assigned to them.

The next set of influences consists of larger environmental issues and concerns. All organizations are affected by economic, social, political, and legal circumstances. Governments pass laws almost daily which require business firms to act in ways that may detract from their primary goals. Safety, employment, advertising, and pricing are but a few of the activities which political and legal demands affect. And one cannot help but be aware of the implications of such social changes as the women's liberation movement. These concerns come to the attention of top management primarily. It is the job of managers at this level to serve as linkages between organizations and their environments.

The external environment

The external environment of an organization is a source of many pressures. Some of these potential pressures are shown in Figure 2-3.

---

[11] See Leon Shashua, Arie Melnik, and Yaquov Goldschmidt, "A Quantitative Estimation of Management's Contribution to Output," *Journal of Economics and Business* (Fall 1976), pp. 73–77.

FIGURE 2–3
The environment of management

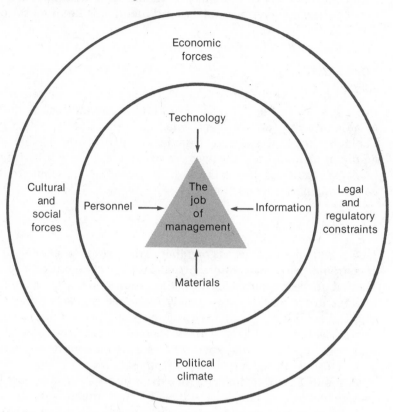

They represent pressure that significantly influences the work of management. The environment is also filled with uncertainties that managers must learn to cope with in reaching planning, organizing, and controlling decisions. The ability to cope with environmental forces such as those presented in Figure 2–3 depends largely on having reliable information. If reliable information about available personnel, legislation, sources of material, technological advances, and the like is not available to the manager, he or she cannot manage effectively. The establishment of marketing research units, executive recruitment committees, attendance at professional meetings, and the development of management information systems to process data are some typical organizational responses to generate reliable information.

Environments can be analyzed in terms of turbulence or stability, complexity or simplicity, or hostility or tranquility among other things. The manager must work with the type of environment that exists for the organization. The specific attributes of an environment have an impact on management activities and decisions because they influence the flow of reliable information into the organization. One way to classify environments is turbulent, hostile, diverse, or technically complex.[12]

TURBULENT

A *turbulent* environment changes regularly. Changes are occurring in such areas as the political, legal, and economic sectors that create some confusion for managers. The confusion results in less than reliable information reaching organizational decision makers. For example, if technological changes are occurring rapidly it is difficult for managers to assess where the industry is going and what are the best advancements being developed.

HOSTILE

A *hostile* environment is one that is risky. Industries in which there is extreme price, promotion, or recruitment competition can be considered to be operating in a hostile environment. For example, two airlines in the Southwest intensely promoted flights between Houston and Dallas. When one airline cut fares, the other cut fares and offered complimentary cocktails. This triggered another round of fare cuts, additional cocktails, and snacks. This environment of promotion and price cutting created a hostile environment.

A hostile environment can also exist if forces such as the government attempt to restrict certain practices for an industry. An oil company may view tighter government control over exploration expenditures as a form of hostility. This hostile action will result in specific policies being followed not only by the company but by other firms in the industry.

DIVERSE

An environment is considered *diverse* if the organization's markets have different needs. For example, a firm operating in Chicago and Detroit may find that the needs of customers in these two markets are similar. However, an organization selling products in Chicago and Argentina will probably have to cope with different customer needs and preferences. The market differences may result in different production, marketing, and promotion activities.

Large organizations such as Tenneco, Inc., and Litton Industries

---

[12] This classification arrangement is suggested by Pradip N. Kdandwalla, *The Design of Organizations* (New York: Harcourt, Brace, Jovanovich, Inc. 1977), pp. 326–40.

operate in a diverse environment because they produce many different products. For example, Tenneco produces food products, automobile parts, aircraft carriers, natural gas, and chemical products. Each of these products uses slightly different technology, materials, personnel, and information. The legal and political constraints impacting each of the products are somewhat different. The government would exercise major control over the construction of an aircraft carrier, while the government and consumer action groups would influence the manufacturing and disposal of chemicals.

TECHNICAL COMPLEXITY

An environment is considered *technically complex* if sophisticated information is needed to make important decisions. The electronics, computer, and nuclear energy industries operate in technically complex environments. Long-range planning, systematic information systems, and technical personnel are characteristics of these industries. Management needs these plans, systems, and personnel to reach effective decisions.

These are four types of environments that exist and have consequences for managers. Of course, all of these environmental features need to be considered together. The environment is not only turbulent or stable but also hostile or tranquil. The important point is that all of the crucial external environmental forces need to be assessed. Some of the important questions that managers can ask to thoroughly assess the environment are the following:

What types of materials are needed? How available are these materials today and tomorrow? Are there substitutes for these materials?

What is the organization's competitive position in the industry? What competition is expected from foreign based corporations?

What legal constraints must be followed? Are these constraints likely to change? Why?

What type of personnel must be recruited? How available are competent personnel? How will these personnel be attracted and retained in the organization?

What is the public image of the firm? How can a favorable image be created?

Is there much technological advancement occurring? Is the technology available to the firm? What types of technology will be needed in five years?

What information is needed to maintain the firm's effectiveness? How should this information be used? Who should process the information?

These questions and their answers can result in some understanding of the environment. From this assessment management can improve their insight about the external environment. Without this insight, decisions are made in a vacuum. It is the external environment components illustrated in Figure 2–3 that introduce uncertainties into the decision-making process. Identifying the properties and features of an organization's environment is needed to properly develop plans, effectively organize the system and jobs, and develop and institute the proper control mechanisms. Each of these necessary processes influences both managerial and organizational performance.

A managerial and organizational performance model

In this concluding section we will summarize much of the foregoing discussion through the use of the model shown in Figure 2–4. In addition to summarizing this chapter it also introduces major ideas which appear throughout the remainder of the text.

Let us begin the description of the model by noting that *managers as individuals* must respond to *organizational goals* in carrying out their *managerial activities*. This conclusion reflects the fact that managers are responsible for the survival and growth of the organization and are accountable to some other part of the *legal, social, economic,* and *political* environment. The managers of business firms are accountable to owners; government administrators are accountable to the taxpayers, and so on. Organizations exist in a society which not only has expec-

FIGURE 2–4
A model of managerial and organizational performance

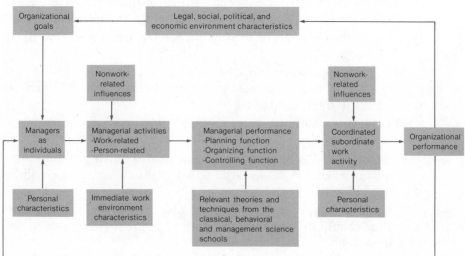

tations for them, but also places constraints on what goals organizations can seek. Thus we see that organizational goals influence the manager, but it is the larger environment that provides the goals.

Managers themselves bring to the job *personal characteristics.* They have abilities, skills, traits, interests, needs, and aspirations, which have been shaped and formed by their experiences. These characteristics will influence the manner in which managers interpret and act on demands exerted by the goals of the organization. The uniqueness of each managerial personality accounts for much of the variation in the way *managerial activities* are carried out. At the same time the more general nature of organizational goals accounts for the continuity and similarity in managerial activity.

Managerial activities are also effected by certain *characteristics of the immediate work environment* as well as certain *non-work-related influences.* Included in the immediate work environment are such factors as the nature of the subordinates' task and the technology available to accomplish that task. For example the managerial activities required to *plan, organize,* and *control* routine tasks with simple, machine-paced technology may be different from those required for a nonroutine task using complex technology. Other work-related factors include the amount of authority delegated to managers and the qualities of the interpersonal relationships between and among managers and their subordinates.

In addition to work-related influences, *non-work-related influences* affect managerial activities. These influences stem from the fact that managers belong to various friendship and interest groups. These groups can exert influence on managers which in turn influence the character of their activity. For example, group pressure can cause managers to emphasize work-related activities at the expense of person-related activities, or vice-versa.

The performance of *planning, organizing, and controlling functions* influences the *work activities of individuals.* The intention of the influence is to achieve coordinated effort, and, thus, high *performance.* Yet as we noted earlier in the chapter, the manager is only one influence factor. Subordinates bring to the job their own unique sets of *personal characteristics* including abilities, interests, and traits. And, much as do managers, they belong to groups which exert *non-work-related influences.* The outcome of these multiple and often conflicting influences is performance which itself becomes an influence on organizational goals and managers as individuals.

Discussion and review questions

1. A supervisor stated in a management training seminar: "I don't understand why we are spending so much time discussing these definitions of

management. As far as I am concerned, management is what my boss says it is." Comment and explain what you think was on this supervisor's mind.

2. From your own work experience, describe a situation which created a conflict between effective completion of a manager's work and people-related activities.

3. The authors believe that classifying managerial activities into two categories, person-related and work-related, is useful for describing and analyzing management. Can you think of alternative categories that would be as useful?

4. What would be some of the early signals that indicate the need to consider vertical specialization? horizontal specialization?

5. Is it true that whenever and wherever one finds a work organization, one will also find a hierarchy of authority?

6. Describe and explain the primary distinctions between the jobs of top management and those of first-line management.

7. Distinguish between organizational and managerial performance. Explain why this distinction is important to know.

8. What criteria could be used to assess managerial performance? Are all of your criteria measurable? What are the problems of subjective measurements?

9. Under what circumstances could the performance of an organization be effective despite ineffective management?

Additional references

Ashford, N. A. *Crisis in the Workplace.* Cambridge, Ma.: MIT Press, 1975.

Cass, E. L., and Zimmer, F. G. *Man and Work in Society.* New York: Van Nostrand Reinhold Co., 1975.

Cyert, R. *The Management of Nonprofit Organizations With Emphasis on Universities.* Lexington, Mass.: Lexington Books, 1975.

Drucker, P. *The Practice of Management.* New York: Harper and Row, 1954.

Elbert, R. J., and Mitchell, T. R. *Organizational Decision Processes: Concepts and Analysis.* New York: Crane, Russak, and Company, 1975.

Emery, D. A. *The Complete Manager.* New York: McGraw-Hill, 1970.

Gowler, D., and Legge, K. (eds.) *Managerial Stress.* New York: Halstead Press, 1975.

Hackman, J. R., and Suttle, J. L. (eds.) *Improving Life at Work.* Santa Monica: Goodyear Publishing Co., 1977.

Jennings, E. E. *Routes to the Executive Suite.* New York: McGraw-Hill, 1971.

Likert, R. *New Patterns of Management.* New York: McGraw-Hill, 1961.

Miles, R. E. *Theories of Management.* New York: McGraw-Hill Book Co., 1975.

Mintzberg, H. *The Nature of Managerial Work.* New York: Harper and Row, 1973.

Newport, M. G. (ed.) *Supervisory Management*. St. Paul: West Publishing Co., 1976.

Ralkich, J. S., Longest, B. B., and O'Donovan, T. R. *Managing Health-Care Organizations*. Philadelphia: W. B. Saunders Co., 1977.

Schulz, R., and Johnson, A. C. *Management of Hospitals*. New York: McGraw-Hill Book Co., 1976.

Spray, S. L. (ed.) *Organization Effectiveness Theory, Research, and Application*. Kent, Ohio: Kent State University Press, 1976.

Steinmetz, L. L., and Todd, H. R., Jr. *First-Line Management*. Dallas: Business Publications, Inc., 1975.

PART TWO

The classical school

3

FOUNDATIONS OF
THE CLASSICAL
SCHOOL

The development of management as a field of study and practice requires answers to important questions. These questions, or issues, define management and explain its relationship to other fields. The body of theory which emerges from these efforts is typically termed "classical theory." Every field of inquiry includes its classical theory. The reader is probably familiar with classical economic theory and classical psychological theory. The chapters in this section present the main ideas of the classical school of management.

Classical management theory is a significant part of contemporary management theories since it provides some important insights into the nature and scope of management. Contributions to management theory by behavioral scientists and management scientists during the past 40 years build upon the ideas of their predecessors. The classical theorists left many questions unanswered, but the reader must not lose sight of the significant fact that they provided answers to many fundamental management questions.

Classical writers defined management in terms of the functions of managers. That is, they studied and wrote about the ways in which managers achieve coordinated group and organizational effort. But classical writers were concerned with more than simply how managers performed their functions, they were also interested in how they *should perform them*. This concern, termed prescriptive, is readily apparent in the ideas of early writers who attempted to discover the "one best way" to do manual tasks. Even today much is written about the best way to *design* a job that will result in the most effective performance.

The classical writers identified three primary functions of management: planning, organizing, and controlling. We first introduced these functions in the previous chapter. The classicists analyzed each of the functions. They attempted to identify each element, or activity,

39

of each function in order to provide the bases for training managers in the correct way to perform each function.

The planning, organizing, and controlling functions can be understood by using an analogy from sailing. The captain of a sailing craft predetermines (plans) the ship's destination. He must also allow for any contingencies that will affect the success of the voyage—for example, weather and water conditions. In anticipation of the future the captain must prepare policies that will guide the ship through the waters. As part of, but separable from, the *planning* function, the captain must predetermine the duties of each member of the ship's company to assure that the crew performs the necessary tasks in the right manner at the right time; that is, the captain must *organize* the crew. Finally, the captain must assure that the ship's passage conforms to the predetermined plan; he must *control* the actual ongoing activities of the ship and the ship's crew. The fact that the captain (manager) performs these three functions continually and without obvious beginning and ending points complicates one's ready understanding of their significance.

FIGURE 3–1
Primary contributors to the classical school

Classical School of Management

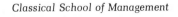

Scientific management (the
management of work)

F. W. Taylor (1856–1915)
Frank (1868–1924) Lillian (1878–
    1972) Gilbreth
H. L. Gantt (1861–1919)
H. E. Emerson (1853–1931)

Classical organization theory (the
management of organizations)

H. Fayol (1841–1925)
J. D. Mooney (1884–1957)
L. Urwick (1891–   )
C. I. Barnard (1886–1961)

In this section of the book, we present the foundations of classical management theory. The remainder of this chapter presents the contributions of scientific management and classical organization theory, beginning first with scientific management. We next combine the ideas of the scientific management approach with the ideas of those who dealt with the problems of *top management* (as distinct from *shop management* which was the focus of scientific management). In Chapters 4, 5, and 6 the basic management functions—planning, organizing and controlling—are discussed.

This presentation of material is based upon the authors' belief that classical management theory consists of two distinct but compatible perspectives in the literature, shown in Figure 3–1. The first is the perspective which focused on the management of work—shop management. This body of literature has been labeled "scientific management," and the label is widely recognized and accepted. The second perspective focused on the management of organizations—the total entity. There is no generally accepted label for this literature; we have chosen to label it "classical organization theory."[1] Therefore, *classical management theory is the blend of scientific management and classical organization theory.*

Scientific management: The management of work

In modern manufacturing the first-level manager is concerned with the day-to-day routine of coordinating the work of specialized labor. Each specialized worker does a job according to a set of rules and procedures designed to assure its completion. The rules and procedures result from analysis of the technical and human requirements of the job and of its relationship to other jobs. The state of the art dealing with work-doing is now highly developed, but this was not so at the turn of the 20th century. The breakthrough occurred when a group of engineers became interested in the techniques of work.

The body of literature which emerged from the efforts of these engineers provides the basis for scientific management, the dominant theme of which is that work-doing and the overseeing of work-doing can be analyzed from a "scientific" point of view. Industrial engineers believed that objective analyses of facts and data collected in experiments should reveal the best way to do the work. Their analyses focused on tasks performed at lower levels in the organization—shoveling, pig-iron handling, and sheet-metal cutting, for example—yet such tasks were crucial to the industrial development of America.

Scientific management was based upon a definite ideology and, as is true of all ideologies, contained implicit assumptions. The ideology, simply put, stated that the cause of industrial conflict was inefficient use of scarce resources.[2] The claimants of the economic pie were continually in conflict because one claimant's share could be increased only at the expense of another's. For example, wages could increase only at the expense of profit. But such is the case only if the

---

[1] This designation is consistent with the usage in Daniel A. Wren, *The Evolution of Management Thought* (New York: The Ronald Press Company, 1972), pp. 463–64.

[2] For a discussion of the historical setting and ideology of scientific management, see Samuel Haber, *Efficiency and Uplift* (Chicago: University of Chicago Press, 1964).

total size of the economic pie is fixed. If the entire supply of economic goods and services is increased through more efficient use of resources, then the shares of the claimants can increase without impinging upon one another.

The proponents of scientific management believed that the economic causes of labor-management disagreements could be eliminated by applying certain physiological and engineering principles to the jobs of blue-collar workers. Thus, at a time of serious social concern for economic growth and resource conservation, scientific management became an important social and economic doctrine. Contained within the doctrine were certain implicit assumptions about the human element. Specifically, scientific management adopted the assumption of classical economic theory that man is basically motivated by his desire for economic betterment. Classical economists believed man is perfectly rational in his choice of means to the end of economic betterment.[3] Thus it followed (according to scientific management) that if managers and workers were taught new methods of work doing which enhanced their chances for economic well-being, they would adopt them.

The implementation of scientific management entailed the adoption of certain methods which would change the ways in which workers and managers had traditionally done their jobs. The major and lasting changes were to be in the ways in which workers had historically done manual work. The suggested changes in the manager's job were minor in comparison.

Major contributions of scientific management

To appreciate fully the importance of scientific management as a philosophy and practice, one must understand the major contributors and the era in which they developed their ideas. We will discuss only four contributors to the scientific management literature, as noted on Figure 3–1. Of these four, the ideas of Frederick W. Taylor will receive most of our attention, since his place in the history of management theory development is well established.

PRINCIPLES OF WORK MANAGEMENT

At the turn of the 20th century, business was expanding, new products and new markets were being created, but labor was in short sup-

---

[3] William F. Whyte, *Money and Motivation* (New York: Harper and Brothers, 1955), pp. 2–3; and James L. Gibson, "Organization Theory and the Nature of Man," *Academy of Management Journal*, vol. 9 (September 1966), pp. 233–45.

ply. To offset labor shortages, two solutions were available: (1) substitute capital for labor or (2) use labor more efficiently. Both approaches reduce labor cost per unit of output and, ordinarily, the average cost. During the last quarter of the 19th century, considerable efforts were made to solve the problem of labor efficiency. Most notable was the work done by the members of the American Society of Mechanical Engineers (A.S.M.E.).

Frederick W. Taylor joined the A.S.M.E. in 1886 and used the organization as a sounding board for his ideas which had started to take shape while he was employed in various steel firms. It was at the Midvale Steel Company that he had observed the phenomenon of "soldiering," men producing far less than their capacities would permit. Taylor believed that this great waste was due to ignorance of what constituted a "fair day's work." There were no systematic studies to determine expected daily output per man (work standards), and the relationship between work standards and the wage system. Taylor's personal dislike for waste caused him to rebel at what he interpreted as inefficient management practice which was based largely on hunch, rule of thumb, conventional wisdom, and ignorance. Taylor believed that ignorance on the part of both management and labor accounted for the great waste of resources.

As a foreman at the Midvale Steel Company, Taylor began an analysis of lathe work. Rather than accept soldiering and ignorance, he began the process of fact gathering and objective analysis which was to be typical of his entire career.[4] He studied the work of an individual lathe worker to discover exactly what the worker did as he performed his task. He identified each element of the worker's job and measured every element that was susceptible to measurement. In short, he was seeking a science of metal cutting. His aim was to provide the craftsman with an objective standard which would define a "fair day's" work.

Taylor sought means for combining the interests of both management and labor to avoid the necessity for "sweat shop" management. He believed that the key to harmony was to discover the "one best way" to perform a task, determine the optimum daily pace of the task, train workers to do the task in the prescribed way and at the prescribed pace, and reward successful completion of the task by using an incentive wage system. Thus, if workers and managers know what is expected and know the positive consequences of achieving mutual expectations, a close harmony between management and labor should

[4] Lyndall Urwick, The Golden Book of Management (London: Newman Neame Ltd., 1956), pp. 72–79, outlines Taylor's career and personal life. Also see Lyndall Urwick and E. F. L. Brech, The Making of Scientific Management (London: Sir Isaac Pitman and Sons, 1951).

result, since the interests of both parties are satisfied: Cooperation should replace conflict.

Consequently, Taylor undertook a series of studies to determine work standards. In some cases, he dealt with physical factors of work. He found, for example, that the optimum weight of a shovel load is 22 pounds and that there is an appropriate shape for each kind of shoveling job. In other instances, he and his associates dealt with the human factor of work. He trained a pig-iron handler to increase his tonnage loaded from 12½ to 47½ long tons per day.

As described by Taylor, there is a science of carrying which relates load weight, load time, and fatigue. The physiological soundness of Taylor's work is not an issue here. The important point is that his analysis of the task of lifting and carrying a 92-pound pig of iron up an inclined plane onto a flatcar suggested the existence of a science that could be used to improve the task. Accordingly, his "law of heavy laboring" states that for each given exertion of energy under load, there must be recuperative time. Taylor applied the "law" to pig-iron handling and believed that a man moving 92-pound pigs can be under load only 43 percent of the time and must rest the remainder of the time. By closely supervising the work of a specially selected pig-iron handler, Taylor and his colleagues produced a remarkable 300 percent increase in production, and the workman's average daily wage increased from $1.15 to $1.85. The method was then learned by a number of workmen, all of whom increased their daily production and their daily wage.

The pig-iron episode illustrates the four principles of "scientific management" which, according to Taylor, are:[5]

First: Develop a science for each element of a man's work which replaces the old rule-of-thumb method.

Second: Scientifically select and then train, teach, and develop the workman, whereas in the past he chose his own work and trained himself as best he could.

Third: Heartily cooperate with the men so as to insure all of the work being done in accordance with the principles of the science which has been developed.

Fourth: There is almost an equal division of the work and the responsibility between the management and the workmen. The management takes over all work for which they are better fitted than the workmen, while in the past, almost all of the work and the greater part of the responsibility were thrown upon the men.

---

[5] Frederick W. Taylor, *Principles of Scientific Management* (New York: Harper and Brothers, 1911), pp. 36–37.

These principles urged managers to take a more systematic approach in performing their coordinative task. Specialization of labor cannot be left to the "invisible hand," as Adam Smith would have it. Rather, the management process requires that initiative be seized by managers to rationalize the process.

The principles define the basic operating characteristics of scientific management as Taylor proposed it. But there was another aspect of scientific management—the essence, according to Taylor. He stated in his testimony before a Special Committee of The House of Representatives that ". . . scientific management involves a complete mental revolution on the part of the working man . . . and it involves the equally complete mental revolution on the part of those on the management's side. . . ."[6] Taylor went on to explain that the mental revolution of which he spoke would shift the emphasis of both management and labor away from the division of economic values and toward increasing the size of the available values.[7] We referred to this earlier in the chapter as the distribution of the economic pie. Taylor viewed scientific management as holding the promise for uplifting the economic well-being of society. But he believed that there could be no scientific management without the mental revolution.

Taylor also proposed that management itself could become more efficient through specialization. In his idea of *functional foremanship*, for example, he proposed that there should be at least eight foremen supervising each worker. Four would be in the planning room (compatible with Taylor's notion that planning and executing are separate processes) concerned with production routing, methods, time and cost, and discipline, while four would be on the shop floor where they would deal with the pace and quality of output and maintenance of machinery. According to Taylor, the economies of specialization could be realized through application to management as well as to labor. However, functional foremanship was never widely adopted in industry.

In the final analysis, Taylor's lasting contributions to management are to be found in the way work is done at the shop level. His experiments with stopwatch studies and work methods stimulated his contemporaries to undertake similar studies in other work contexts. Two important contemporaries were Lillian and Frank Gilbreth.

PRINCIPLES OF WORK SIMPLIFICATION

The Gilbreths, a husband-and-wife team, made significant contributions to the emerging knowledge of scientific management. They

---

[6] Frederick W. Taylor, "Taylor's Testimony before the Special House Committee," ibid., p. 27.

[7] Ibid., p. 30.

combined their talents to produce important breakthroughs in motion study and job simplification. An untrained but insightful engineer, Frank Gilbreth was an apprentice bricklayer in his first job. His observations of skilled bricklayers' motions convinced him that many of the body movements could be combined or eliminated so that the procedure would be simplified and production increased.

Gilbreth's analysis of the sequence and path of basic movements enabled him to reduce the number of motions required to lay exterior brick from 18 to $4\frac{1}{2}$. Craftsmen who used Gilbreth's method were able to increase their production by 200 percent. Economy in the use of human energy, combined with technological improvements such as an adjustable stand to eliminate stooping for the brick and a mortar of proper consistency to eliminate "tapping," resulted in a science of the ancient and honorable craft of masonry.[8] Gilbreth's work was quite compatible and consistent with that of Taylor's as each sought the elusive "one best way" to do a job.

To add precision to his analysis of fundamental hand and arm motions, Gilbreth invented a number of devices. The microchronometer is a clock with a sweep hand which is placed in the field of work being studied. Gilbreth would use a camera to record the work being done against the backdrop to the sweep hand. By such methods, he was able to identify not only the basic motions, but also the time required for each hand and arm movement. The result of his efforts was the identification of numerous distinct movements which he labeled "Therbligs" (Gilbreth spelled backward with transposition of one letter).

PRINCIPLES OF WORK SCHEDULING

A close associate of Taylor at Midvale and Bethlehem Steel was a young graduate engineer, Henry L. Gantt. Like Taylor and the Gilbreths, Gantt dealt with problems of efficiency at the shop floor level, but at the same time he recognized the human element of production work. Gantt's contributions to scientific management are most often recalled in terms of his development of a chart which shows the relationship between work planned and completed on one axis and time elapsed on the other. This chart, referred to as a Gantt Chart, is still used in industry. Yet Gantt's contributions go beyond this.

Unlike Taylor, Gantt believed that wage systems ought to provide a fair remuneration regardless of output. He devised a task-and-bonus system in which a workman received a bonus in addition to his day's wage upon completion of an assigned task. If the workman did not

[8] Claude S. George, Jr., The History of Management Thought (Englewood Cliffs, N.J.: Prentice-Hall, Inc., 1968), p. 97.

complete the task, he was not penalized, but received the day wage. Taylor's differential piecerate system, on the other hand, was a pure incentive plan whereby each worker received a wage based solely on his daily production. There was no guaranteed day wage. Should the worker produce more than the standard output, the piecerate was increased for all units produced.

In other respects, Gantt made unique contributions to the literature of management. He was among the first to recognize that nonmonetary factors such as job security are powerful incentives. His task and bonus plan with its assured daily wage implemented his belief. He argued strongly that a responsibility of management is to train workers to do their jobs. He also agitated for the acceptance of his concept of industrial responsibility whereby industry pursues a service objective rather than a profit objective. Such statements were premature for the times, though they are commonplace today.

In retrospect, Gantt can be understood as a valuable contributor to scientific management. He shared the skeptical orientation of Taylor and the Gilbreths: He, like they, believed that the accepted way of doing things was usually the wrong way. Gantt believed that the best sources of improved efficiency were the work methods of the manager, not of the laborer. He stated that expertise should be the sole criterion for the endowment of authority, and that managers, as the recipients of authority, have the moral obligation to make decisions by scientific methods, not by opinion. Thus Gantt broadened the scope of scientific management by including managerial responsibility as well as managerial methods as appropriate areas for analysis and change.

PRINCIPLES OF EFFICIENCY

The public became aware of Harrington Emerson in 1910, when he testified as an expert witness before the Interstate Commerce Commission that the railroads could save one million dollars per day through the use of the methods and philosophy of scientific management, and thus eliminate the necessity for a requested rate increase. Emerson's ideas are embodied in a set of principles that define the manner in which the efficient use of resources is to be accomplished. His 12 principles implement the basic elements of the scientific management approach. In summary form, they state that the manager should (1) use scientific, objective, and factually based analysis; (2) define the aims of the undertaking; (3) relate each part to the whole; (4) provide standardized procedures and methods; and (5) reward individuals for successful execution of the task.

Emerson's contributions go beyond his 12 principles of efficiency, though they and his testimony before the ICC would have assured his place in management history. In addition to these obvious contributions, Emerson also recognized the positive lessons to be learned from the military's use of formalized staff and advisory positions. In his capacity as one of the first management consultants, he proposed the creation of a strict organization whose activities would be defined by clear statements of goals and purposes. In this respect, Emerson moved away from the traditional scientific management concern for work doing and anticipated many developments of classical organization theory.

Scientific management in retrospect

If it were evaluated in terms of its impact on management practice at the time of its development, scientific management would receive a low grade. Its impact on contemporary management is more pronounced and significant. True, some firms adopted scientific management methods; yet the "mental revolution" which Taylor expected never occurred. Despite the fact that he, the Gilbreths, Gantt, Emerson, and others had provided a substantial, if unorganized, body of knowledge which offered to bring harmony to all participants in economic life, strife between management and labor continued and the methods of scientific management were largely ignored.

One cause of the seeming failure of scientific management is possibly found in the failure of its proponents to understand fully the psychological and sociological dimensions of work. Throughout Taylor's writing one finds the implicit assumption that man is motivated basically by economic considerations, and that when given adequate information, man is able to choose rationally the alternative which maximizes his well-being. This assumption was reinforced by classical economic theory which enjoyed its height of popular acceptance at that time. In the context of the times, such an assumption was credible. Factory workers were by and large first-generation immigrants, ignorant of their surroundings and eking out a living on subsistence wages. Granted the historical justification for the assumption, there was another movement competing with scientific management to bring about industrial harmony, namely, unionism.

The union leaders of the time viewed scientific management as a threat to labor. Taylor's concept of separation of work-doing and work-planning threatened the prerogatives of labor, particularly of craftsmen. Union leaders anticipated the erosion of the importance of labor as each individual worker's contribution diminished. Workers lose control as work becomes more specialized and as each worker is more or less substitutable for any other worker. A second source of threat to unionism was the proposal that wage systems be determined solely by management decision of what constitutes "fair wages" for standard output. This would undercut the attempts of unions to have wages determined through collective bargaining. The conflict between unions and Taylorism was most apparent in 1909, when the federal government introduced an incentive system at the Watertown Arsenal. The union struck and was supported by Samuel Gompers' American Federation of Labor. The period of active antagonism between unionism and Taylorism waned with the entry of America into World War I, when the concern for "efficiency at all cost" gave way to "production at any cost." The latter orientation prevailed throughout the 20s and ended in a crash with the Great Depression.

Classical organization theory: The management of organizations

Scientific management raised questions, undertook analyses, and provided prescriptions which were narrow in scope yet concrete in reality. Issues related to the coordination of large organizations and the managerial roles in these entities are much more complex and abstract. A body of ideas emerged simultaneously with that on scientific management, dealing specifically with these issues. Classical organization theory was affected by the same environmental and cultural conditions which, in turn, affected scientific management. Indeed, as we shall see, the ideology and assumptions so apparent in scientific management are evident in classical organization theory.

The writers in this branch of the Classical School raised two questions: (1) What are the basic principles which should guide the design, creation, and maintenance of an organization structure? and (2) What are the basic functions of management within the organization? An overriding objective, similar to that of sicentific management, was to provide prescriptive guidelines for effective and efficient management.

Major contributions of classical organization theory

Practitioners of management were the major contributors to the literature on classical organization theory. They brought their pragmatic orientation to bear on the problem of coordinating large-scale organizations. In this respect, these writers share the action-oriented background common to writers of scientific management. In this chapter, the work of Henri Fayol, James Mooney, Lyndall Urwick, and Chester Barnard is presented. The reader should keep in mind that the concepts with which these writers dealt are considerably more abstract than those of scientific management.

PRINCIPLES OF MANAGEMENT

Work experience as the managing director of a large coal-mining company in France provided Henri Fayol with the background for his ideas about the managerial process. For 50 years, Fayol practiced and reflected upon the process of coordinating the diverse activities of the organization which he directed. His ideas were first committed to writing and became a part of the literature in 1916, when he contributed to the bulletin of a French industrial association. A more complete statement of his ideas appeared in 1925 with the publication of his book, but it was not until 1929 that the English translation appeared.[9]

Fayol sought to discover principles of management which determine the "soundness and good working order" of the firm. Such principles are flexible and adaptable to circumstances and events. Fayol was not seeking fixed rules of conduct; rather, he sought guidelines to thinking. Deciding upon the appropriateness of a principle for a particular situation is the "art" of management. Fayol believed that any number of principles might exist and described only those which he most frequently applied in his own experience.

Fayol's chief desire was to elevate the status of management practice by supplying a framework for analysis. His framework included a statement of principles and functions. We shall discuss them in that order.

Management principles. Fayol proposed 14 principles which should guide the thinking of managers in resolving concrete problems. To reiterate, Fayol did not expound blind obedience to fixed courses of action; he relied upon managers' "experience and sense of proportion" to guide the degree of application of any principle in any situation. These principles are presented in Table 3–1.

Fayol's principles of management have been much discussed and criticized by management scholars. Any evaluation should take into account the time and place in which they emerged and should be an accurate reflection of Fayol's intent. He stated that the list of principles was not exhaustive, "This list has no precise limits"; the list of principles was not to endure regardless of time and place: "It [the list] seems at the moment especially useful . . . appropriate to concentrate general discussion." The principles do not answer questions of degree or specificity, but Fayol was not suggesting that the principles would relieve management from the responsibility for determining what he termed "the appropriate balance." Indeed, he emphasized

---

[9] Henri Fayol, *General and Industrial Management*, trans. J. A. Conbrough (Geneva: International Management Institute, 1929). All subsequent references in this text are to the more widely available translation by Constance Storrs (London: Pitman Publishing Corp., 1949).

TABLE 3–1
Fayol's principles of management*

1. *Division of work.* Specialization of labor is the natural means by which institutions and societies have progressed and developed. It results in increased productivity through the reduction of job elements required of each worker. Specialization of labor permits large-scale production at minimum cost. Additionally, the cost of training workers is considerably reduced since the content of each job has been greatly narrowed.

2. *Authority and responsibility.* Much confusion exists in current discussions of authority and responsibility. The terms are highly abstract and difficult to define. Fayol recognized this difficulty; he defined *authority* as the "right to give orders and the power to exact obedience." But Fayol went on to distinguish between the *official* authority which derives from holding an office, and *personal* authority which derives from the office holder's own personality, experience, moral worth, and other personal characteristics that enable him to influence the efforts of subordinates.

3. *Discipline.* The essence of discipline, according to Fayol, is obedience to agreements reached between parties in the firm. He believed that clear statements of agreements are necessary, but not sufficient for discipline; he argued that the "state of discipline of any group of people depends essentially on the worthiness of its leaders," leaders who would judiciously apply sanctions in instances of breached discipline.

4. *Unity of command.* Fayol believed that the existence of dual command (two supervisors, one subordinate) causes severe breakdowns in authority and discipline. Consequently he stated that an employee should receive orders from only one superior. He believed that recognition and observance of this principle would eliminate the causes of interdepartmental and interpersonal conflict arising out of jurisdictional issues.

5. *Unity of direction.* Each group of activities having the same purpose should operate under one head and one plan. Fayol observed that this principle should not be confused with the unity-of-command principle. Unity of direction derives from a sound organizational structure which is departmentalized in an appropriate manner; the principle refers to the structure of the organization. Unity of command refers to the functioning of personnel within the structure. Unity of direction does not assure unity of command, but unity of command cannot exist without unity of direction.

6. *Subordination of individual interest to general interest.* This principle states that the whole is greater than the sum of its parts, and that the overall objectives which the group seeks to achieve take precedence over the objectives of individuals.

7. *Renumeration of personnel.* The remuneration of workers and managers for services rendered should be based on a systematic attempt to reward well-directed effort.

8. *Centralization.* Fayol defined centralization as the degree to which the importance of subordinates' roles is reduced. He stated that the degree of centralization should be related to the character of the manager, the reliability of subordinates, and the conditions of the business.

9. *Scalar chain.* The graded chain of authority from top to bottom through which all communications flow is termed the scalar chain. This chain implements the unity-of-command principle and provides for the orderly transmission of information.

10. *Order.* Fayol applied the principle of order to the material and human resources of the firm. This principle states that even as the material instruments of business must be arranged logically and neatly, so must the human instruments.

* This presentation of Fayol's principles is based upon his own discussion in ibid., pp. 19–42.

TABLE 3–1 (continued)

To establish order in the human sphere, the manager must determine the exact nature and content of each job and demonstrate its relationship to the end product and to other jobs.

11. *Equity.* Fayol defined equity as the enforcement of established rules tempered by a sense of kindliness and justice. He believed that employees respond to equitable treatment by carrying out their duties in a sense of loyalty and devotion.

12. *Stability of tenure of personnel.* Fayol had observed that prosperous firms usually had a stable group of managerial personnel. He thus stated as a general principle that top management should implement practices which encourage the long-term commitment of employees, particularly of managers, to the firm.

13. *Initiative.* This principle states that employees must be encouraged to think through and implement a plan of action. Fayol believed that the opportunity to exercise initiative is a powerful motivator. The only limits on personal initiative should be the authority relationship defined by the scalar chain and by the employee's sense of discipline.

14. *Esprit de corps.* Fayol defined *esprit de corps* as unity of effort through harmony of interests. In his view, the most effective means for achieving *esprit de corps* is through unity of command, and through oral rather than written communication. Many approaches to the creation of a sense of unity and harmony exist; Fayol suggested only those methods which seemed important to him.

time and again that the moral character of the manager would determine the ultimate outcome.

Management functions. Fayol elaborated the managerial process by identifying five functions in which managers must engage, as follows:

1. *Planning* includes all those activities of a manager which result in a course of action. The manager should make the best possible forecast of future events that affect the firm and draw up an operating plan that guides future decisions.

2. *Organizing* includes all activities which result in a structure of tasks and authority. This managerial function determines the appropriate machines, material, and human mix which are necessary to accomplish the task.

3. *Commanding* is directing the activities of subordinates. To be successful, Fayol suggests, the manager should set a good example and know thoroughly the personnel and the agreements made between the personnel and the firm. The managers should have direct, two-way communication with subordinates. Furthermore, the manager should continually evaluate the organizational structure and subordinates, and he should not hesitate to change the structure if he considers it faulty, or to fire subordinates if they are incompetent.

4. *Coordinating* activities are those which bind together all indi-

vidual efforts and direct them toward a common objective. Thus Fayol saw coordinating as simply another element of the total managerial process. The concept of management used in this textbook, on the other hand, suggests that coordination is the key element of the process.

5. *Controlling* activities are those which assure that actual activities are consistent with planned activities. Fayol did not expand the concept beyond stating that everything should be "subject to control."

Fayol provides a *means* (the five functions) for viewing the managerial process and *guides* (the principles) for implementing the process. The framework itself lacks logical clarity since it suggests nothing about the primacy of certain principles or the causality among these principles. It did, however, establish a basis for further elaboration by subsequent writers.

PRINCIPLES OF ORGANIZATION

In 1931, James D. Mooney and Alan C. Reiley authored *Onward Industry*, which was revised in 1947 by Mooney and entitled *The Principles of Organization*.[10] This book is a most important part of the literature of classical management thought and, as will be seen, complements Fayol's work while also adding a new dimension.

Mooney viewed management as the technique, or art, of directing and inspiring other men. Organization, on the other hand, is the technique of relating specific duties or functions in a coordinated whole. The interrelationship between the two concepts is immediately apparent when we recognize that the duty of management is to devise an appropriate organization. Mooney's personal experience and his examination of organization in governmental, church, military, and industrial institutions were the bases for a framework of concepts which describes the essential nature of organizations.

The conceptual framework which Mooney used to analyze organizations is based upon logical reasoning. He believed that it is possible to deduce the underlying principles of organization which explain the existence of certain phenomena in all organizations. From his own experience in business and government and his study of other organization types, Mooney observed that a structure of tasks and authority existed in every organization. Although the structure differed from one organization to another in terms of tasks to be done, its key features were the same, namely, a hierarchy of authority and specialized tasks.

These observations led Mooney to believe that natural laws of organizing existed, and it was these natural laws, or principles, which

---

[10] James D. Mooney, *The Principles of Organization* (New York: Harper and Brothers, 1947).

he sought to discover through logic. It is at this point in our discussion of classical organization theory that differences in the use of the term "principles" can be noted. Unlike Fayol who used the term to denote guidelines, Mooney used the term to denote fundamental law, or doctrine. Both usages are acceptable, but understanding classical organization theory is certainly made more difficult as a consequence. The reader should keep in mind the fact that Mooney was seeking to explain the rationale for organized activity; whereas, Fayol had the more modest intent of providing practical guidelines for managing.

Given this background, the principles of organization according to Mooney can be explained, in his terminology, as follows:

1. The first principle of organization is coordination. Note that Fayol defined coordination as one of the five functions of management. Mooney, however, viewed coordination as the primary law which dictates the necessity for organizations coordination, or the coordinative, principle, is the reason for organizing.

2. The necessity for organizing sets in motion other functions, or activities, which in turn are guided by other principles. Scaling the tasks to be performed involves the definition of each task in terms of its duties and responsibilities. That is, Mooney viewed the process of creating the hierarchy to be the natural outcome of the necessity for organizing. The scalar function implements the principle of *authority*, which is derived from, and legitimated by, higher authority—the people (in governments), God (in churches), and private property (in business firms).

3. The scalar process consists of two subfunctions: *delegating authority and defining tasks.* The delegation of authority is guided by the principle of *leadership*, which in Mooney's terms is the personification of authority. Through the delegation of authority, leaders confer authority on subordinates, and so on down the chain. Parallel to the process of delegating is that of defining tasks, termed functional definition. The principle of *specialization* underlies this function. Regardless of organizational type, the necessity exists for people to do different jobs at different times, as Fayol, Taylor, and other classical writers had observed.

Mooney's analysis provides a framework of concepts which he related through logical deduction. From the existence of organizations, he deduced the principles of coordination, authority, leadership, and specialization. Mooney believed that these principles explained the necessity for the organizing function and subfunctions. Yet though his analysis of the organizing function was complete to his satisfaction, there remained the task of synthesizing the totality of classical management theory. Lyndall Urwick undertook this task.

SYNTHESIS OF CLASSICAL MANAGEMENT THEORY

A most important landmark in the literature of management is Lyndall Urwick's *The Elements of Administration*.[11] Urwick combined and synthesized the ideas of Fayol, Mooney, and Taylor into one conceptual framework. It is with Urwick's analysis that scientific management and classical organization theory blend and classical management theory begins to emerge. It provided practitioners and students of management with the basis for understanding the managerial process as it relates to the total enterprise. Its level of abstraction permits broad comprehension, yet it is concrete enough to provide insights into specific managerial functions.

The synthesis of classical management theory is depicted in Figure 3–2. It is based upon Urwick's analysis, but it reflects the authors' interpretation of his work. It combines not only the ideas of Taylor, Fayol, Mooney, and other classical writers, but also Urwick's own analysis of the controlling function. From Taylor, Urwick took the idea that the management process is directed by the principle of scientific investigation. Urwick reemphasized that rigorous analysis, disciplined by the tenets of science, sets management work apart from nonmanagement work. Taylor and others of the scientific management approach had demonstrated that the management of work could be undertaken through the analysis of objective data gathered in the work place itself. Urwick generalized from Taylor's experience and stated the case for scientific analysis as the cardinal principle to govern all management functions.

The management process consists of three functions: planning, organizing, and controlling. These three functions have guiding principles—forecasting, coordination, and command. We have already discussed Mooney's analysis of the organizing function and Fayol's analysis of the planning function; since Urwick adopted them intact, we need not elaborate them again.

The controlling function was analyzed by Urwick chiefly in terms of Fayol's principles. Urwick proposed that controlling entails the application of the principle of command—directing, or supervising, the activity of subordinates. Fayol had previously identified commanding as a single function, but Urwick elevated the concept to the status of a principle. Urwick also derived corollary functions and principles from the function of controlling and the principle of command.

The controlling subfunctions—*staffing, selecting, and placing,* and *disciplining*—relate to the human elements of the organization. In simplest terms, Urwick believed that managers should consider the placement of people into the structure to be separate from the creation

---

[11] Lyndall Urwick, *The Elements of Administration* (New York: Harper and Brothers, 1944).

FIGURE 3–2
Classical management theory

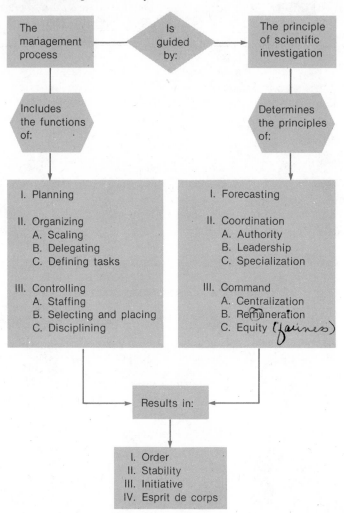

of the structure itself. Yet he recognized that if managers are to be effective, they must pay attention to the controlling function. It was with these concerns that he identified and defined the controlling function.

The staffing function involves the placement of managers into leadership positions and defining their authority and accountability in terms of their abilities. The principle of centralization, as Fayol defined it, requires the delegation of authority on the basis of individual abilities. Selecting and placing managers and nonmanagers alike are determined not only by job requirements but also by the principle of fair remuneration. Thus, a promotion should be awarded for performance, not for personality. The day-to-day supervision of subordinates involves disciplinary activities which are, as Fayol stated, designed to assure compliance with prior agreements. The principle of equity, or fairness, is intended to underlie the disciplining function.

Finally, Urwick included in his synthesis of management theory the intermediate objectives of management: *order*, *stability*, *initiative*, and *esprit de corps*. He believed that to the extent that managers perform their functions with an awareness of appropriate principles, these four ends could be attained.

Urwick's synthesis and integration of scientific management and classical organization theory reflect the essence of classical management theory; it is "that all management principles fit together in a balanced and interrelated framework."[12] Yet, he also recognized that much remains to be done in the routine management of day-to-day operations. Even though the structure is defined and manned, there is room for managerial interpretation of appropriate styles and behavior. Thus, it is necessary to adapt the rather fixed concept of management to take into account the variable nature of human behavior. The first writer to undertake the task of interrelating the nature of organizations and the nature of man was Chester I. Barnard.

ORGANIZATIONS AS COOPERATIVE EFFORTS

The insights of Chester I. Barnard have influenced the development of management thought in significant ways. In fact, his ideas are so pervasive that our efforts to condense and summarize them will surely not do justice to them. Barnard had a background similar to those of Fayol, Mooney, and Urwick. He was a practicing manager, an executive with New Jersey Bell Telephone, where he was president. He also shared his colleagues' interest in analyzing the function he was performing; he wanted to make "sense" of his job and to provide others with the concepts that make sense of management. His ideas were widely circulated in the form of papers, speeches, and books. The most important source of his ideas is *The Functions of the Executive*.[13]

Barnard, who believed that the basic function of the executive is to provide the basis for *cooperative effort*, defined organization as a system of goal-directed cooperative activities. Barnard went on to analyze management's functions to include the formulation of objectives and the acquisition of resources and efforts required to meet the stated

---

[12] Joseph L. Massie, "Management Theory," in James H. March, ed., *Handbook of Organizations* (Chicago: Rand McNally and Co., 1965), p. 413.

[13] Chester I. Barnard, *The Functions of the Executive* (Cambridge: Harvard University Press, 1938).

objectives. This point of view is quite compatible with those of Fayol, Mooney, and Urwick. The new dimension that Barnard introduced was his emphasis on communications as the means for acquiring cooperation. He believed that the system of communication within the organization is the means by which persons are induced to cooperate.

According to Barnard, the degree of employee cooperation depends upon the balance between inducements and contributions. Inducements include the sum total of financial and nonfinancial rewards which accrue to individuals in exchange for their efforts, that is, contributions. The purpose of communication is to provide individuals with the necessary information to evaluate the desired balance. At the same time, Barnard recognized that the communication system is the active process by which authority is implemented. Orders are transmitted downward as superiors seek to acquire certain behavior from their subordinates. He stated that the existence of the formal structure is no guarantee that subordinates will in fact follow orders.

Barnard challenged the wisdom of relying solely upon the authority structure to achieve compliance. Indeed, he stated a position that has become known as the *acceptance theory of authority*. This theory postulates that subordinates will determine whether an order is legitimate, and whether to accept or reject it. They will accept the order only if they can understand it and are able to comply with it. Perhaps more importantly, they will accept it (even if understood) only if the required behavior is consistent with their view of the purposes of the organization *and their own* personal interests.

The ideas of Barnard have been woven into the practice and theory of modern management. It is now generally accepted that the manager must know a great deal about human behavior. As we shall see in subsequent chapters, the analysis of human behavior, singly and in groups, by behavioral scientists has added significant insights; but we must recognize the importance of Barnard as their forerunner.

Contributions of the classical school to the practice of management

The first and foremost contribution of the Classical School was that of identifying management as a distinct element of organized society. The classical writers believed that management, like law, medicine, and other occupations, should be practiced according to principles which managers can learn. Moreover, these principles can be discovered by the application of scientific methods. As Taylor pointed out, manual tasks could be studied and subsequently managed by applying the basic laws of physiology and physics. Mooney made a strong case that the organizing function can be analyzed by applying the fundamentals of deductive logic.

The identification of the planning, organizing, and controlling functions provided the basis for training managers. Many contemporary management textbooks and training courses are based upon these functions. The manner in which management functions are presented and explained often differs, depending upon the particular point of view of the writer or the trainer. Yet, the essence of any listing of management functions is the acknowledgment that managers are concerned with *what* the institution is to be doing, *how* it is to be done, and *whether* it was done.

Contemporary business firms, hospitals, universities, and government agencies have recognized the need to perform these functions. Planning offices, organizational analysis units, and quality control sections can be found in many large organizations. Smaller organizations implement these functions in more general, nonspecialized ways, primarily through the efforts of top management. The essential point is that the Classical School presented a strong case that either managers or their subordinates must perform these functions.

The manner in which planning, organizing, and controlling are implemented should, moreover, not proceed haphazardly. Rather, the manager should practice these functions according to defined principles, or guidelines. The classical writers, beginning with Taylor, identified these principles and argued that they were the bases for managerial work. These principles, according to the classicists, were universal in application; that is to say, they are valid regardless of the institutional setting in which management is practiced.

The contributions of the Classical School go beyond the important work of identifying the management field, its functions, and principles. Many modern management techniques are direct outgrowths of its endeavors. For example, time and motion analysis, work simplification, incentive wage systems, production scheduling, personnel testing, and budgeting are modern management techniques which derive directly from the Classical School. These methods and others are topics of the next three chapters. Suffice to say at this point, the practical contributions of classical writers are many and varied because it was their primary intent to make such contributions.

Discussion and review questions

1. What is the traditional role of classical theory in any field of study, and particularly in management?

2. Why should one study classical management theory? Of what relevance is scientific management to the problems of the 1980s?

3. What is your understanding of the term "ideology" as applied to scientific management?

4. Do you believe that there is "one best way" to perform any task, including the work of a scientist?

5. Compare the concept of the "average worker" to professors' concepts of the "average student."

6. What do the authors mean when they say that classical organization theory dealt with more complex and abstract problems than those which scientific management confronted?

7. Compare the ideologies of classical organization theory and scientific management.

8. What are "principles of management" as Fayol defined and explained them? Compare Fayol's and Mooney's ideas regarding principles.

9. What new dimensions did Barnard add to classical theory?

10. How would a scientist go about testing classical management theory? How would a manager go about applying classical management theory? Which is more important to you personally — testing or applying?

Additional references

Barnard, C. I. *Organization and Management.* Cambridge: Harvard University Press, 1952.

Brandeis, L. D. *Scientific Management and Railroads.* New York: The Engineering Magazine Co., 1911.

Church, A. A. *The Science and Practice of Management.* New York: The Engineering Magazine Co., 1916.

Davis, R. C. *The Principles of Factory Organization and Management.* New York: Harper and Brothers, 1928.

Delmar, D., and Collons, R. D. *Classics in Scientific Management.* University: University of Alabama Press, 1976.

Drury, H. B. *Scientific Management: A History and Criticism.* New York: Longmans, Green and Co., 1922.

Emerson, H. *Efficiency as a Basis for Operations and Wages.* New York: The Engineering Magazine Co., 1900.

————. *The Twelve Principles of Efficiency.* New York: The Engineering Magazine Co., 1913.

Gantt, H. L. *Industrial Leadership.* New Haven: Yale University Press, 1916.

————. *Work, Wages, and Profits.* New York: The Engineering Magazine Co., 1910.

Gilbreth, F. B. *Motion Study.* New York: D. Van Nostrand Co., 1911.

Gilbreth, L. M. *The Psychology of Management.* New York: Sturgis and Walton Co., 1914.

Hoxie, R. F. *Scientific Management and Labor.* New York: D. Appleton and Co., 1915.

4

THE PLANNING FUNCTION

nary function of management is _planning_. Beginning with
or, the classical management writers distinguished between
nd executing, and they argued that managers should plan
onmanagers should execute. This theme was developed by
elaborated further by Urwick. Contemporary management
no longer is concerned with whether managers should plan;
e current focus of attention is on the techniques of planning.
The planning function includes all managerial activities which
determine results and the appropriate means to achieve these results.
Yet more simply, planning is advance thinking as the basis for doing.
In order to analyze the planning function in more specific terms, the
function can be broken down into four distinct, yet interrelated,
phases:

Phase 1 – Establishing goals and their priority.
Phase 2 – Forecasting future events which can affect goal accomplish-
ment.
Phase 3 – Making the plans operational through budgeting.
Phase 4 – Stating and implementing policies which direct activities
toward the desired goals.

Each phase must be undertaken and related to other phases to complete the planning function. The end result is an overall plan which
guides the organization toward predetermined goals. This chapter
presents each phase of planning, and describes some useful managerial
planning techniques.

Goal-setting and ordering

The planning function begins with the determination of future outcomes which if achieved enable the organization to satisfy the expectations of its relevant environment. The environment supplies the
resources which sustain the organization, whether it is a business
firm, a university, or a governmental agency. In exchange for these
resources, the organization must supply the environment with goods
and services at an acceptable price and quality. The increasing interdependence between organizations and their environments has caused
corporate managers to turn more and more to formal planning approaches.[1] Moreover, the evidence is fairly clear that firms which use
formal planning approaches are more profitable than those which do
not.[2] The initial step in planning is the determination of goals. In

---

[1] Thomas H. Naylor, "The Future of Corporate Planning Models," _Managerial Plan-
ning_ (March/April 1976), p. 1.
[2] Zefar A. Malik and Delmay W. Karger, "Does Long-Range Planning Improve Company Performance," _Management Review_ (September 1975), pp. 27–31.

doing so, managers must consider three aspects of goals: *priority,* *timing,* and *structure.*

PRIORITY OF GOALS

Priority of goals implies that at a given point in time, the accomplishment of one goal is relatively more important than others. For example, the goal of maintaining a minimum cash balance may be critically important to a firm having difficulty meeting payrolls and due dates on accounts. Priority of goals also reflects the relative importance of certain goals regardless of time. For example, survival of the organization is a necessary condition for the realization of all other goals.

The establishment of priorities is extremely important in that the resources of any organization must be allocated by rational means. At all points in time managers are confronted with alternative goals which must be evaluated and ranked. Managers of nonbusiness organizations are particularly concerned with the ranking of seemingly interdependent goals. For example, a university president must determine, implicitly or explicitly, the relative importance of teaching, research, and service goals. Of course the determination of goals and priorities is often a judgmental decision and therefore difficult.

The importance of establishing the priority of goals as a basis for allocating resources is widely recognized in public, as well as private management. A primary element in President Jimmy Carter's successful campaign was the promise to institute zero-based budgeting (ZBB) in the federal government. At the core of ZBB is the requirement that all governmental agencies rank the priority of their goals. The growing awareness of limited resources has created increased interest in ZBB as well as other approaches which require managers to rank their sought-for goals.[3]

TIMING OF GOALS

The time dimension of goals implies that the organization's activities are guided by different objectives depending upon the duration of the action; it is traditional to speak of short-run, intermediate, and long-run goals. Short-run goals are those which extend for a period of less than a year; intermediate goals are those covering one to five years; and long-run goals are those extending beyond five years. The relationship between priority and timing of goals is quite close since the long-run goals tend to be stated in terms of "ultimates," that is, those objectives which must be accomplished in order to assure the long-run survival of the organization.

---

[3] Paul J. Stonich, "Zero Base Planning—A Management Tool," *Managerial Planning* (July/August 1976), pp. 1–4.

The timing dimension is reflected in the practice of many organizations to develop different plans for different periods of time. The long-run goal of a business firm could be stated in terms of a desired rate of return on capital, with intermediate and short-run plans stated in terms of objectives which must be accomplished to realize the ultimate goal. Management is then in a position to know the effectiveness of each year's activities in terms of achieving not only short-run but also long-run goals.

In recent years writers and practitioners have adopted the concept of *strategic planning* to refer to the process which ". . . deals with (1) the determination of long-range goals of an enterprise; (2) the selection of courses of action to achieve these goals; (3) the continuous nature of strategic planning; and (4) the allocation of resources to each particular activity."[4] In contrast, short range planning, also termed *functional* or *operational planning,* "is generally concerned with the immediate problems and goals of the enterprise."[5] The responsibility for achieving the objectives of operational plans is that of individual units within the organization. The process of assigning goals to parts of the organization brings us to the third dimension of goals—*structure.*

STRUCTURE OF GOALS

The process of breaking down the firm into units— for example, production, sales, and finance—requires that goals be assigned to each unit. Each unit is then given the responsibility for attaining an assigned goal. The process of allocating goals among various units creates the problem of potential goal conflict and suboptimization, wherein achieving the goals of one unit may jeopardize achieving the goals of another. For example, the production goal of low unit cost achieved through mass production of low-quality products may conflict with the sales goal of selling high-quality, high-markup products. The resolution of this problem is a careful balance of the goal for each unit, with the recognition that the goal of neither unit can be maximized.

The problem of multiple goals can be understood by recognizing a second aspect of goal structure. Many diverse groups have interests in the firm's operation which are potentially in conflict. Thus, at any point in time, stockholders (owners), employees (including unions), customers, suppliers, creditors, and governmental agencies are all concerned with the operation of the firm. The process of goal setting must recognize the relative importance of these interest groups, and the plans must incorporate and integrate their interests. The exact form and

---

[4] Manuel A. Tipgos, "Structuring a Management Information System for Strategic Planning," *Managerial Planning* (January/February 1975), p. 11.

[5] Ibid., p. 11.

relative weight to be given to any particular interest group is precisely the nature of management's dilemma; yet it is precisely management's responsibility to make these kinds of judgments.[6]

The management of the business firm must consider the expectations of the diverse groups because the firm's ultimate success depends upon them. For example, present and potential customers are the ultimate holders of power over the firm. If they are not happy with the price and quality of the firm's product, they withdraw their support (they stop buying), and the firm fails because of lack of funds. Suppliers have the power to disrupt the flow of their materials to express disagreement with the firm's activities. Governmental agencies have power to enforce the firm's accommodation to regulations which, in modern times, are affecting nearly every aspect of the firm's operation.[7] The existence of these interest groups and their power to affect the goal structure of the firm express the reality that the business firm is a social invention; the firm will exist only so long as it satisfies the larger society.

Studies of goals which business managers set for their organizations affirm the difficulty of balancing the concerns of interest groups. These studies also suggest that the more successful firms consistently pursue plans which emphasize the primacy of profit-seeking activities which maximize the stockholder's wealth.[8] This is not to say that successful firms seek only profit-oriented goals, only that such goals are dominant. Evidently such firms are managed by persons whose values stress pragmatic, dynamic, and achievement-oriented behavior,[9] yet tempered by the recognition that business organizations have an increasing responsibility to do what is best for society.[10] The interrelationship among the managers' values, society's needs, and organizational goals has been aptly summarized: "*What to make, what to charge,* and *how to market the wares* are questions that embrace moral as well as economic questions. The answers are conditioned by the personal value system of the decision maker and the institutional values which affect the relationships of the individual to the community."[11]

---

[6] See R. W. Morell, *Management: Ends and Means* (San Francisco, California: Chandler Publishing Co., 1969), pp. 5–30, for a discussion of multiple goals and a suggested hierarchy of goals.

[7] For a complete analysis of the relationship between power and goal setting, see A. D. Newman and R. W. Rowbottom, *Organizational Analysis* (Carbondale, Illinois: Southern Illinois University Press, 1968), pp. 101–8.

[8] George W. England, "Organizational Goals and Expected Behavior of American Managers," *Academy of Management Journal* (June 1967), pp. 107–17; Charles P. Edmonds III and John H. Hand, "What are the Real Long-Run Objectives of Business?" *Business Horizons* (December 1976), pp. 75–81.

[9] George W. England, *The Manager and His Values: An International Perspective* (Cambridge, MA.: Ballinger Publishing Co., 1975).

[10] Rama Krishman, "Business Philosophy and Executive Responsibility," *Academy of Management Journal* (December 1973), pp. 658–69.

[11] Clarence C. Walton, *Ethos and the Executive* (Englewood Cliffs, N.J.: Prentice-Hall, Inc., 1969), p. 192.

MEASUREMENT OF GOALS

Goals must be stated in terms that are understandable and acceptable to those who produce the effort to achieve them. Moreover the evidence is increasing "that specific goals increase [employee and organizational] performance and that difficult goals, if accepted [by the employee], result in better performance than do easy goals."[12] In practice, effective managerial action requires goal setting in every area which contributes to the overall goals. Drucker,[13] has stated that subgoals must be set in at least eight areas, namely, (1) market standing, (2) innovation, (3) productivity, (4) physical and financial resources, (5) profitability, (6) manager performance and responsibility, (7) worker performance and attitude, and (8) public responsibility. Drucker's classification in no way implies relative importance; he is simply pointing out the necessity for considering the entire range of subgoals. The priority of each goal will depend upon the conditions confronting the firm at the particular point in time.

As Drucker observed, "The real difficulty lies indeed not in determining what objectives we need, but in deciding how to set them."[14] The only approach, according to Drucker, is to determine *what* should be measured in each area, and *how* it should be measured. Immediately one can recognize the difficulty of measuring goals in certain areas. How, for example, does one measure employee development or public responsibility? The more abstract the goal, the more difficult it is to measure performance. Additionally, the measurement of abstract goals by quantitative means can lead to the problem of measurement orientation, that is, the tendency to focus attention on the measurement and away from the substance of the goal. Those in academic fields are familiar with this problem in universities and colleges which measure teaching and research accomplishment in terms of quantity of students graduated and articles published.

Nevertheless, effective planning requires goal measurement. A variety of measurements exist for each area:

Profitability measures include the ratios of profits to sales, to total assets, and to capital (net worth). The tendency in recent years has been to emphasize the profit/sales ratio as the important test of profitability,[15] perhaps because both quantities required to calculate this measure are taken directly from the income statement which management generally

---

[12] Gary P. Latham and Gary P. Yukl, "A Review of Research on the Application of Goal Setting in Organizations," *Academy of Management Journal* (December 1975), p. 840.

[13] Peter Drucker, *The Practice of Management* (New York: Harper and Brothers, 1954), and reemphasized in *Management: Tasks, Responsibilities, Practices* (New York: Harper and Row, 1974).

[14] Drucker, *Practice of Management*, p. 64.

[15] Ibid., p. 79; and Neil W. Chamberlain, *The Firm: Micro-Economic Planning and Action* (New York: McGraw-Hill Book Co., 1962), p. 55.

regards as a better test of performance than the balance sheet. However, many managers believe that the true test of profitability must combine the income statement and the balance sheet. Accordingly, such managers would use the profit/net-worth ratio. The arguments for and against the use of either of these two are basically due to differences in point of view as to whether *source* of capital is an important consideration. The profit/total-asset ratio measures the efficiency of management's use of all resources regardless of origin (that is, creditors or owners), whereas the profit/networth ratio measures managerial efficiency only in terms of the use of the owner's contribution.

The resolution of the problem of which profitability measure to select lies in the recognition that the measures are not mutually exclusive. All three can be used to set and evaluate profitability objectives, since each measures a different yet important aspect of the profit structure. However, the problem of the amount of profit remains to be solved, together with certain technical problems derived from the nature of accounting information. With respect to the amount of profit, we should recognize that the functions of profit are (1) to measure effectiveness, (2) to recover one cost element of being in business (return on invested capital), and (3) to provide funds for future expansion and innovation, either through retained earnings or through the capital market at rates made favorable because of the firm's history of profitability. Thus, the minimum profitability is that which assures the continuous stream of capital into the firm, given the inherent risks of the industry in which the firm operates.

Marketing measures must relate products, markets, distribution and customer service objectives. Figure 4–1 shows the matrix of decisions required in the analysis of products and markets. In each existing and potential product, a specified goal must be established for total volume, market share, and profit. Coincidentally, management must develop an organization which will assure that resources are available to achieve the results.

FIGURE 4–1
Marketing planning matrix

	Existing markets	New markets
Existing products	Target Volume Target Share Target Profit	Target Volume Target Share Target Profit
New products	Target Volume Target Share Target Profit	Target Volume Target Share Target Profit

Productivity measures are basically ratios of output to input. Other factors being equal, the higher the ratio, the more efficient is the use of inputs. Usually, productivity measures are related to the output for certain inputs, for example, labor; these have been referred to as ratios of labor productivity. Yet, when different inputs are used together it is quite difficult to identify which output is due to a particular input. Moreover, since the firm exists as an aggregation of resources which must be directed and coordinated to specified ends, the productivity measure should evaluate that which results from the total effort, not the efforts of each part.

Drucker proposes that the ratio of value added to sales and to profit is the superior measure of productivity.[16] Furthermore, he states that the firm's objective should be to increase these ratios, and that units should be evaluated on the basis of these increases. His argument for value added, which he calls contributed value, is that it measures the increase in value of the purchased materials due to the combined efforts of the firm, since value added is equal to the difference between market value and purchased price of materials and supplies. Thus the efficiency of the firm's efforts is measured directly. Furthermore, this measure of productivity could be used for internal comparisons of operating units.

Physical and financial measures reflect the firm's capacity to acquire resources sufficient for its larger objectives. The measurement of objectives in this area is comparatively easy due to the existence of quite a large number of accounting yardsticks which are appropriate for both physical and financial objectives. Rate-of-return measures are appropriate for setting objectives in decisions involving the acquisition of new plants and facilities. Liquidity and solvency measures are available for the measurement of financial objectives. Measures such as the current ratio, working capital turnover, the acid test, accounts receivable and inventory turnover, and debt to equity ratios can be used in setting objectives and evaluating results in the area of financial planning.

Subgoals in the areas of profitability, market standing, productivity, and physical and financial resources are amenable to measurement. Subgoals in areas such as innovation, employee development, and social responsibility are not so easily identifiable and measureable in concrete terms. However, the important point to consider is that, without measurement, subsequent evaluation is necessarily quite inconclusive.

The managers of business organizations are comparatively better able to measure progress toward goals than their counterparts in non-business organizations. With the exception of subgoals such as innova-

---

[16] Drucker, Practice of Management, pp. 71–73.

tion, employee development, and social responsibility, as noted above, business managers not only have straightforward goals, but also have information systems which produce fairly reliable measures of progress toward them. Managers of universities, hospitals, and government agencies are not so fortunate. For example, the dean of a college can measure the number of students enrolled in courses and the number of graduates, but not the *quality* of instruction. Moreover, a hospital administrator can chart patient-days, discharge rates, and cost per patient-day and yet know nothing about the quality of health care patients are receiving. Unlike the business firm, most nonbusiness organizations have no "bottom-line" — that is, profit — indicator of over-all results. Yet the managers of these organizations are continually challenged by students, patients, taxpayers, clients, and other consti-tuents to account for results.

The discussion of setting, ordering, and measuring goals can be sum-marized by referring to Table 4–1. The information contained in the table is based upon an actual organization's experience in goal-setting. This particular firm identified seven goals which management ranked in the order of priority shown in the table. The management also con-sidered it useful to state the goals in more specific terms and also to identify, where relevant, more specific elements of goals; these the management termed *subgoals*. In other organizations different termi-nology can be used; for example, some managers refer to subgoals as objectives. Finally, the table shows the indicators, or measures of goal accomplishment. As noted by one writer, Harold Koontz: "It is impossi-ble to do any effective planning without knowing precisely what end results are sought."[17] This point of view is a major impetus in the development of a widely used management technique termed "Man-agement by Objectives."

MANAGEMENT BY OBJECTIVES

Management by Objectives (MBO) has attracted many proponents since it was first introduced in the early 1950s. Peter Drucker, who in-troduced the concept of MBO, describes it as follows:

> . . . the objectives of the district manager's job should be defined by the contribution he and his district sales force have to make to the sales department, the objectives of the project engineer's job by the contribu-tion he, his engineers and draftsmen make to the engineering depart-ment. . . .
>
> This requires each manager to develop and set the objectives of his unit himself. Higher management must, of course, reserve the power to

[17] Harold Koontz, "Making Strategic Planning Work," *Business Horizons* (April, 1976), p. 38.

TABLE 4–1
Goals and indicators

Goals	Subgoals	Indicator
1. Provide fair return on investment	a. Provide a 15% return on investment	a. Net profits as percent of invested capital
2. Maintain a share of the market	a. Retain 75% of old customers	a. Percent replacement purchases
	b. Obtain 25% of first-time customers	b. Percent initial purchases
3. Develop middle managers for executive positions	a. Develop a merit review system	a. Report submitted on December 1
	b. Send 10 managers to university executive development course	b. Number sent by Jan. 1
4. Be a good corporate citizen	a. Reduce air pollution by 15%	a. By Jan. 1, pollutants to be 125 lbs/hr measured at stack by electrostatic test
5. Provide safe working conditions	a. Automate loading process in Plant B	a. Installation to be 50% complete on January 1
	b. Reduce injuries by 10%	b. Ratio of man-days lost to total man-days
6. Manufacture goods efficiently	a. Increase productivity by 5% through installation of new punching machine	a. Installed by Aug. 1
		b. Ratio of output to total man-hours
7. Maintain and improve employee satisfaction	a. Improve by 15%	a. Ratio of quits to total employees
		b. Attitude survey questionnaire

approve or disapprove these objectives. But their development is part of a manager's responsibility; indeed it is his first responsibility. . . .[18]

Drucker believes that the greatest advantage of MBO is that it allows managers to control their own performance. This self-control is sup-

---

[18] Peter Drucker, *The Practice of Management*, pp. 128–29.

posed to result in stronger motivation to do the best rather than just to get by.

Another slightly different presentation of the basic fundamentals and overall philosophy of MBO is provided by Odiorne:

> . . . a process whereby the superior and subordinate managers of an organization jointly identify its common goals, define each individual's major areas of responsibility in terms of the results expected of him, and use these measures as guides for operating the unit and assessing the contribution of each of its members.[19]

An important factor in Odiorne's viewpoint is for the subordinate and superior to have an understanding regarding the subordinate's major areas of responsibility and what will constitute an acceptable level of performance.

Other well-known management scholars have also written extensively on MBO.[20] Their contentions are similar to those offered by Drucker and Odiorne. Synthesizing the works of these experts enables one to develop a set of three guidelines which provide an understanding of management by objectives:

1. Superiors and subordinates meet and discuss goals (results) for the subordinates which are in line with overall organizational goals;
2. The superiors and subordinates jointly establish attainable goals for subordinates,
3. The superiors and subordinates meet again after the initial goals are established, and evaluate the subordinates' performance in terms of the goals. The essential feature is that feedback on performance is provided the subordinates. The subordinates know where they stand with regard to their contributions to their organizational unit and the firm.

The exact procedures employed in implementing MBO vary from organization to organization or from unit to unit. The anticipated end results, however, will hopefully be the same: (1) improved employee and organizational performance, (2) improved morale and attitudes of the participants, (3) reduced anxiety resulting from ambiguity as to where they stand with their superiors through establishing a direct linkage between individual and organizational objectives.

Many organizations have implemented MBO on a company or de-

---

[19] George Odiorne, *Management by Objectives* (New York: Pitman Publishing Co., 1965), p. 26. Also see George Odiorne, *Personnel Administration by Objectives* (Homewood, Ill.: Richard D. Irwin, Inc., 1971).

[20] See Douglas McGregor, "An Uneasy Look at Performance Appraisal," *Harvard Business Review*, vol. 35 (May-June 1975), pp. 89–94; E. C. Schleh, *Management by Results* (New York: McGraw-Hill Book Co., 1961); and W. J. Reddin, *Effective Management by Objectives* (New York: McGraw-Hill Book Co., 1970).

partmental basis. A number of recent studies report some of the effects of such programs.[21]

A two-part study of a MBO program referred to as "Goal Setting and Self-Control" was undertaken at the Purex Corporation.[22] The result of the research was that after the goal-setting program had been initiated, participants were more concerned about and aware of the firm's goals and future activities. In the initial study it was also found that the goal-setting procedure improved communications and understanding among those involved.

However, the follow-up study showed that many of the participants perceived the program as being an ineffective incentive for improving performance levels. Evidently they had changed their opinions about the program after it had been in operation over a four-year period. Their reasons were:

1. Managers reported that the program was used as a whip.
2. The program increased the amount of paperwork.
3. The program failed to reach the lower managerial levels.
4. There was an overemphasis placed on production.
5. The program failed to provide adequate incentives to improve performance.

Another study was made of the effects of a form of MBO known as "Work Planning and Review."[23] Managers using the "Work Planning and Review" goal-setting program were compared to those operating under the traditional appraisal program. The managers using the goal-setting program expressed significantly more favorable attitudes. Specifically, their attitudes changed in a favorable direction over the one-year study in four areas:

1. Extent to which the managers made use of their abilities and experiences.
2. Ability of the managers to plan.
3. Degree to which the managers were receptive to new ideas and suggestions.
4. Degree to which they felt the goals for which they were aiming were what they should be.

---

[21] The most recent review of these studies appears in Latham and Yukl, "A Review of Research . . . ," pp. 824–45.

[22] Anthony P. Raia, "Goal Setting and Self Control," *Journal of Management Studies*, vol. 2 (September 1965), pp. 34–53; and Anthony P. Raia, "A Second Look at Management Goals and Controls, *California Management Review*, vol. 8 (Summer 1966), pp. 49–58.

[23] Herbert H. Meyer, Emanuel Kay, and John R. P. French, Jr., "Split Roles in Performance Appraisal," *Harvard Business Review*, vol. 43 (January-February 1965), pp. 21–27.

A more recent study dealt with managerial reactions to management by objectives in a large manufacturing firm.[24] The researchers were concerned with the manager's perceptions associated with the MBO approach. The rationale of the program most cited by participants was that the objectives-setting process was intended to link the evaluation of an individual to actual performance rather than to personality or other characteristics. It was found that a majority of the participating managers believed that the most significant advantage of the program was that one was more likely "to know what was expected by the boss." A major problem cited by the managers was that excessive formal requirements were imposed because of the program; that is, the need to process, complete, and update forms, and to provide other data to the coordinator of the program, were major irritants.[25]

The evidence to date, although mixed, indicates that MBO can improve certain performance indicators. For example, Ivancevich reports the results of an MBO program which was implemented in the production and marketing departments of a large organization. In both departments there was sustained increase in the quantity and quality of performance beyond that of other departments not involved in the MBO program.[26]

Despite the evident advantages of MBO, there are several key factors which must be considered in the implementation phase. For example, managers who are about to engage in MBO programs must first be conditioned and psychologically prepared.[27] With the introduction of MBO, changes will often occur in the flow of communications both horizontally and vertically, the intensity of intergroup interaction, and the number of personal contacts between superiors and subordinates. Thus, the dynamic nature of these changes and their impact on the functioning of the organization necessitate complete understanding of MBO by managers, to insure that managerial resistance to implementation and participation is minimal.

Another critical factor in the implementation of MBO programs is

---

[24] Henry L. Tosi and Stephen J. Carroll, "Managerial Reaction to Management by Objectives," *Academy of Management Journal*, vol. 11 (December 1968), pp. 415–26. For other related work, see Stephen J. Carroll and Henry L. Tosi, "The Relation of Characteristics of the Review Process as Moderated by Personality and Situational Factors to the Success of the 'Management by Objectives' Approach," *Academy of Management Journal*, vol. 12 (September 1969), pp. 139–43; and Stephen J. Carroll and Henry L. Tosi, "Goal Characteristics and Personality Factors in a Management by Objective Program," *Administrative Science Quarterly*, vol. 15 (September 1970), pp. 295–305.

[25] Similar conclusions are reached by Carroll I. Stein, "Objective Management Systems: Two to Five Years after Implementation," *Personnel Journal* (October 1975), pp. 525–28.

[26] John M. Ivancevich, "Changes in Performance in a Management by Objective Program," *Administrative Science Quarterly* (December 1974), pp. 563–74.

[27] Henry L. Tosi, Jr., "Management Development and Management by Objectives – An Interrelationship," *Management of Personnel Quarterly*, vol. 4 (Summer 1965), p. 24.

the supportive managerial climate which pervades the organization. Two important conclusions have been cited concerning implementation.[28]

1. Top management must not assume a passive role. The most effective manner to implement MBO is to allow the top-level executives to explain, coordinate, and guide the program. When top managers are actively involved, the philosophy and mechanics of the program filter through and penetrate the entire organization.

2. Improvements are greater in the company where the MBO program is instituted by upper-level executives than in organizations where it is implemented by the personnel department.

Management by objectives is not a cure-all for goal-setting problems, but it is an approach which warrants careful consideration, especially since some evidence of its effectiveness is available.

Forecasting

The critical step in the implementation of goals is that of forecasting the future, the second phase of the planning process. The results of the forecasts are included in budgets which are the major planning documents of the firm. The two basic issues that must be resolved through forecasting are: (1) what level of activity can be expected during the planning period and (2) what level of resources will be available to support the projected activity. The critical forecast upon which all others depend is the sales forecast.

SALES FORECASTS

The projected sales volume of the firm's product or service provides the basis for all other activities. The sales estimate sets the level of production and determines the level and timing of financial resources required to meet the sales volume. Because the sales forecast is so fundamental, we will discuss the methods for forecasting in the context of the sales forecast.

Forecasting is the process of using past and current information to predict future events. There are four widely used methods, each of which requires its own type of data. These methods range in degree

---

[28] John M. Ivancevich, "A Longitudinal Assessment of Management by Objectives," *Administrative Science Quarterly*, vol. 17 (March 1972), pp. 126–38; and John M. Ivancevich, James H. Donnelly, Jr., and Herbert L. Lyon, "A Study of the Impact of Management by Objectives of Perceived Need Satisfactions," *Personnel Psychology*, vol. 23 (Summer 1970), pp. 139–51.

of sophistication from the hunches of experienced managers to econo-metric models.[29]

FORECASTING APPROACHES

Hunches are estimates of future events based upon past sales data, comments by salesmen and customers, and visceral reaction to the "general state of affairs." The hunch approach is relatively cheap and usually effective in firms whose market is stable or at least changing at a predictable rate.

Market surveys of customer intentions provided by the customer or by salesmen in the field can improve the accuracy of sales forecasts. At least, through the means of statistical sampling techniques, the forecaster can specify the range of projected sales and the degree of confidence that he has in his estimates. Of course, one should be very careful to evaluate the reliability of information that goes into the market survey.

Time-series analysis is a third technique of forecasting which, though it is a fairly complex statistical device, is no more effective than the good judgment of the analyst. Time series is nothing more than analysis of the relationship between sales and time, as shown in Figure 4–2. The chart shows points corresponding to the annual sales for each of the years. A straight line is drawn through the points to show that there has been an upward pattern in the sales of the firm during the period.

The short-run question of sales during the first quarter of 1979 cannot be answered in Figure 4–2 if there is seasonality in the firm's sales pattern. If such were not the case, the quarterly sales would be approximately one quarter of the annual sales, but the sales of most firms are seasonal. If a company markets fishing equipment, the sharp-est demand is during the spring and summer months, declining to quite low levels during the fall and winter. The prediction of annual sales can be attempted from the annual data, provided one is willing to make the assumption that conditions which contributed to previous sales levels will prevail in the future. If not, the forecast must include variables other than time in the analysis.

The reader should not be led to believe that time-series analysis is simply the naive projection of trend. It may be in the hands of the un-skilled, but if skilled analysts are supplied with the right information they can confront a whole range of questions. The movement of sales over time is affected by at least three factors: seasonal, cyclical, and

---

[29] Charles W. Gross and Robin T. Peterson, *Business Forecasting* (Boston: Houghton Mifflin, 1976).

FIGURE 4–2
Hypothetical sales-time relationship

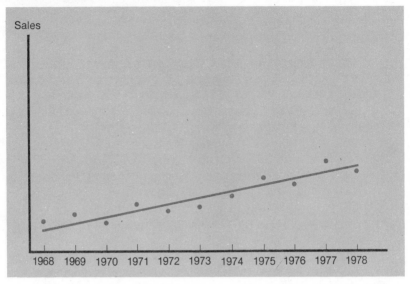

trend; that is, the firm's sales vary in response to seasonal factors, in response to cycles common to business activity generally, and to a trend of long-period duration. The management of a brewery knows that peak sales occur during the summer months, but is also aware of the cyclical nature of beer consumption as beer drinkers shift to liquor when their incomes increase, shifting back when their incomes decline. For long-term planning, the manager must also know something about the trend in beer consumption; consumer tastes change with time and with the introduction of new products. Yet, even the availability of these refinements does not undo the fact that time is the only determinant of sales included in the time-series analyses. Econometric models are means for more systematically evaluating the impact of a number of variables on sales.

Econometric models are applications of multiple-correlation techniques to economic analysis. They permit the forecaster to discover the historical relationship between sales and a number of independent variables. These techniques are the most sophisticated of the methods, yet they offer no hope for the elimination of *all* uncertainty; management judgment is still needed.

The econometric approach begins with identification of those independent variables which would be expected to affect the sales of the firm's product. Among the obvious variables are price, competing products, and complementary products. Variables such as the age of existing stocks of the goods, availability of credit, and consumer tastes are less obvious. Measurements of these variables are obtained for previous years and matched with sales of the product for the same years. An equation is then derived which expresses the historical relationship between the variables. For example, if the sales volume of product Y is found to be related to variables X and Z, and the historical relationship is discovered to be

$$Y = 1.25X - 3.7Z,$$

then the forecaster need only predict the *future* values of X and Z to discover the future sales of Y. Now we see that the *forecast* of Y is derived from the *forecast* of X and Z.

No perfect method exists for projecting future sales. Hunches, surveys, and statistical analyses provide estimates which may or may not be reasonable. The estimates coming from these techniques can be no better than the information which goes into them. As technological breakthroughs in information processing occur, we can expect sales forecasts to become more accurate and consequently better guides for planning. At the present time, however, forecasting requires a great deal of managerial judgment.

RESOURCE FORECASTS

The sales forecast indicates levels of revenues that can be expected if the firm has the product to sell. But in order to have a product to sell, the firm must have the necessary resources. Accordingly, it is necessary to forecast the future availability of major resource components including personnel, raw materials, and capital. The techniques of forecasting resources are the same as those employed to forecast sales—that is, hunches, market surveys, time-series analysis, and econometric models. The only difference is that the analyst is seeking to know the quantities and prices which can be purchased, rather than sold.

The energy shortage which appeared in the early 1970s brought into sharp focus the necessity for resource forecasting. The effects of the shortage were real at every level in the economy, and the early warning signals had apparently gone unheeded. Yet when it was apparent that energy resources would not be available in assumed quantities, managers could respond only reactively. More astute planning would not necessarily have prevented the energy crisis, but it would have enabled managers to respond in more orderly ways.

Thus, the sales forecast, whether for one year or for ten years, is a prediction of the firm's level of activity. At the same time, the prediction is conditioned by the availability of resources, general economic and social events beyond the province and control of management, and by the predetermined goals. The next phase of the planning function is the allocation of resources necessary to sustain the fore-casted level of activity. The principal technique which management uses in this phase of the planning function is the budget.

Budgeting

The third phase of the planning function is the development of bud-gets for each important element of the organization. Budgets are widely used in business and government. A considerable body of literature exists dealing with budgeting techniques.[30] We should recognize the very close relationship between budgeting as a planning technique and budgeting as a control technique. In this section we are concerned only with the preparation of budgets prior to operations. From this perspective, budgeting is a part of planning. However, with the passage of time and as the organization engages in its activities, the actual results are compared with the budgeted (planned) results. This analy-sis may lead to corrective action and this, as we shall see later, is the essence of controlling. The interrelationship between planning and controlling is well illustrated by budgeting techniques.

FINANCIAL BUDGETING

The financial budgeting process implements the income goals of the firm and serves as the chief means for integrating the activities of all the various subunits. Budgeting can be viewed as an important method for coordinating the efforts of the firm.

The complexity of the financial budgeting process is revealed in Figure 4–3. The key position of the sales forecast is evident from the placement of the sales budget; all other budgets are related to it either directly or indirectly. For example, the production budget must specify the materials, labor, and other manufacturing expenses required to support the projected sales level. Similarly, the distribution expense budget details the costs associated with the level of sales activity pro-jected for each product in each sales region. Administrative expenses also must be related to the predicted sales volume. The projected sales and expenses are combined in the financial budgets which consist of pro forma financial statements, inventory budgets, and the capital additions budget.

---

[30] For example: Walter R. Bunge, *Managerial Budgeting for Profit Improvement* (New York: McGraw-Hill Book Co., 1968); Francis C. Dykeman, *Financial Reporting Systems and Techniques* (Englewood Cliffs, N.J.: Prentice-Hall, 1969); J. Brooks Heckert and James D. Wilson, *Business Budgeting and Control* (New York: Ronald Press Co., 1967).

FIGURE 4–3
The financial budgeting process*

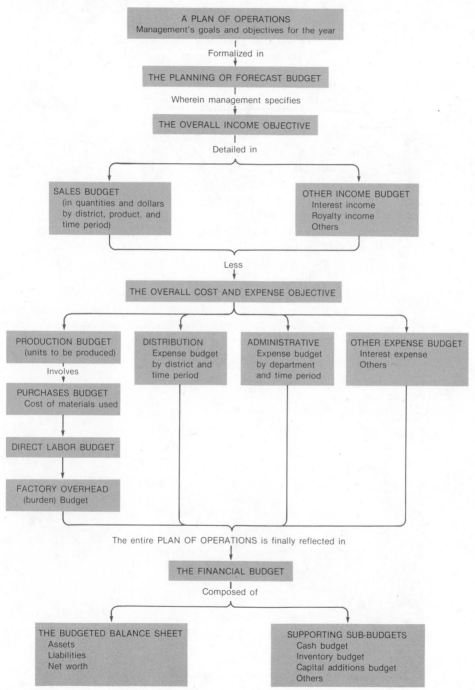

* Glenn A. Welsch, *Budgeting: Profit Planning and Control*, 2d ed., © 1964, p. 50. Reprinted by permission of Prentice-Hall, Inc., Englewood Cliffs, N.J.

TWO BUDGETING APPROACHES

The usefulness of financial budgets depends mainly on the degree to which they are flexible to changes in conditions. The forecasted data are based upon certain premises or assumptions regarding the future. If these premises prove wrong, the budgets are inadequate. Two principal means exist to provide flexibility, namely, variable budgeting and moving budgeting.

Variable budgeting provides for the possibility that actual output deviates from planned output. It recognizes that certain costs are related to output (variable costs), while others are unrelated to output (fixed costs). Thus, if actual output is 20 percent less than planned output, it does not follow that actual profit will be 20 percent less than that planned. Rather, the actual profit will vary depending upon the quite complex relationship between costs and output. Figure 4–4 demonstrates a hypothetical situation.

The relationships shown in Figure 4–4 take the form of the familiar break-even model. The point to be made here is simply that profit varies with output variations, but not proportionately. Table 4–2 shows a variable budget which allows for output variations and which demonstrates the behavior of costs and profits as output varies.

Variable budgeting requires adjustments in all supporting budgets for completeness. The production, distribution, and administrative budgets must likewise allow for the impact of output variation.

Moving budgeting is the preparation of a budget for a fixed period,

FIGURE 4–4
The relationship between profit and output

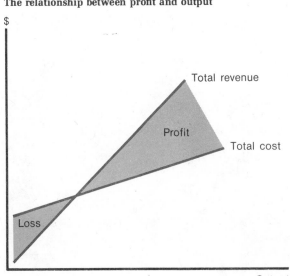

TABLE 4–2
A hypothetical variable budget

Output (units)		1,000		1,200		1,400		1,600
Sales @ $5.00		$5,000		$6,000		$7,000		$8,000
Variable costs @ $3.00	$3,000		$3,600		$4,200		$4,800	
Fixed costs	1,000		1,000		1,000		1,000	
Total costs		4,000		4,600		5,200		5,800
Planned profit		$1,000		$1,400		$1,800		$2,200

say, one year, with periodic updating at fixed intervals, say, one month. For example, the budget is prepared in December for the next 12 months, January through December. At the end of January, the budget is revised and projected for the next 12 months, February through January. In this manner, the most recent information is included in the budgeting process. Premises and assumptions are constantly being revised as management learns from experience.

Moving budgets have the advantage of systematic reexamination, but the disadvantage of becoming costly to maintain. Budgets are important instruments for implementing the objectives of the firm; on the other hand, they must be kept in perspective and viewed as competing with other demands for managerial time.

PROGRAM BUDGETING

A recent development in public administration employs the planning concepts described in this chapter, that is, that plans and budgets should be devised in terms of goals. The development of program budgeting, or PPB, in government began with the attempts of Secretary of Defense McNamara to prepare the 1963 budget of the Department of Defense in a manner which reflected the expected cost of each departmental objective. This effort was in contrast with the historical practice of preparing budgets by objects of expenditure—personnel, operating expenses, and capital improvement expenditures.[31] The traditional governmental budgeting process did not reflect the goals of the department and therefore did not permit rational allocation of resources among those goals.

From those beginnings in the Department of Defense, the concepts of program budgeting spread throughout the federal government as well as state and local governments. For example, Kentucky, Michigan, and Pennsylvania are among the states which have adopted some vari-

---

[31] See Leonard Merewitz and Stephen H. Sosnick, *The Budget's New Clothes* (Chicago: Markham Publishing Co., 1971), for a more detailed description of program budgeting.

ant of the program budgeting approach. It is not possible to develop a complete description of PPB here. The important point is to recognize that the logic of planning from goals to resource allocation is well established in business management, yet that logic has only recently been adopted in public management.

Policy making

The principal means by which management implements plans is through policy making, the fourth phase of planning. *Policies are statements which reflect the basic objectives of the entity and which provide the guidelines for carrying out action throughout the entity.*[32] Policies, like plans, are both specific and general, abstract and concrete, short-run and long-run.

Policy making is an important management tool for assuring that action is goal oriented. Policies explain *how* the goals are to be achieved; they thus direct the behavior of persons in the firm. The interrelation among the managerial functions is reflected in the nature of policies. As we shall see, managerial *control* includes specification of action before the fact, and policies serve this end.

Effective policy making requires recognition of the many dimensions and characteristics of policies. Ziegler[33] has suggested the following characteristics as important for creating effective policies:

1. *Flexibility.* A policy must strike a reasonable balance between stability and flexibility. Conditions change and policies must change accordingly. On the other hand, some degree of stability must prevail if order and a sense of direction are to be achieved. There are no rigid guidelines to specify the exact degree of requisite flexibility; only the judgment of management can determine the balance.

2. *Comprehensiveness.* A policy must be comprehensive to cover any contingency if plans are to be followed. The degree of comprehensiveness depends upon the scope of action controlled by the policy itself. If the policy is directed toward very narrow ranges of activity — for example, hiring policies — it need not be as comprehensive as a policy concerned with public relations.

3. *Coordinative.* A policy must provide for coordination of the various subunits whose actions are interrelated. Without coordinative direction provided by policies, each subunit is tempted to pursue its

---

[32] M. Valliant Higginson, *Management Policies I, AMA Research Study 76* (New York: American Management Association, 1966).

[33] Raymond J. Ziegler, *Business Policies and Decision Making* (New York: Appleton-Century-Crofts, 1966).

own goals. The ultimate test of any subunit's activity should be its relationship to the policy statement.

4. *Ethical.* A policy must conform to the canons of ethical behavior which prevail in society. The manager is ultimately responsible for the resolution of issues which involve ethical principles. The increasingly complex and interdependent nature of contemporary society has resulted in a great number of problems involving ethical dimensions which are only vaguely understood.

5. *Clarity.* A policy must be written clearly and logically. It must specify the intended aim of the action which it governs, define the appropriate methods and action, and delineate the limits of freedom of action permitted to those whose actions are to be guided by it.

The ultimate test of the effectiveness of a policy is whether the intended objective is attained. If the policy does not lead to the goal, it should be revised. Thus, policies must be subjected to reexamination on a continual basis.

Summary ⨯

The planning function is the fundamental managerial activity. It consists of four distinct phases, or subfunctions: *goal setting, forecasting, budgeting,* and *policy making.* We have seen that planning can have any time dimension ranging from the short run to long run. We have also surveyed some of the more important forecasting and budgeting techniques. Readers should not assume, however, that they have now surveyed the entire range of problems and issues associated with planning. At the same time, they should recognize that the essence of management is planning, and that all other functions are derived from planning.

The manager who successfully practices the planning function recognizes that much of the task consists of asking the appropriate questions. Table 4–3 suggests the basic ones; other, more specific, questions might well be posed. Yet the fundamental questions are appropriate regardless of the type and size of the organization. Such questions lead to the development of means by which the four phases of the planning function are implemented, and the means will vary depending upon the answers to the question. We can readily appreciate the fact that the planning function will be undertaken differently in IBM as compared to a neighborhood grocery store, or in the Department of Health, Education, and Welfare as compared to a county health department. There are no universally applicable planning approaches, but the necessity for "advance thinking as a basis for doing" is universal.

TABLE 4–3
Key managerial planning issues

Planning phase	Key managerial decisions
Goal setting	1. What goals will be sought? 2. What is the relative importance of each goal? 3. What are the relationships among the goals? 4. At what point in time should each goal be achieved? 5. How can each goal be measured? 6. What person or organizational unit should be accountable for achieving the goal?
Forecasting	1. What are the important variables which bear on the successful achievement of goals? 2. What information exists regarding each variable? 3. What is the appropriate technique for forecasting the future movement of each important variable? 4. What person or organizational unit should be accountable for the forecasts?
Budgeting	1. What resource components should be included in the budget? 2. What are the interrelationships among the various budgeted components? 3. What budgeting technique should be used? 4. Who or what organizational unit should be accountable for the preparation of the budget?
Policy making	1. What policy statements are necessary to implement the overall plan? 2. To what extent are the policy statements comprehensive, flexible, coordinative, ethical, and clearly written? 3. Who or what organizational units should authorize and prepare policy statements? 4. Who or what organizational units are to be affected by the policy statements?

Discussion and review questions

1. Discuss the bases for the statement that planning is the essential management function.

2. A manager is overheard saying: "Plan? I never have time to plan. I live from day to day just trying to survive." Comment.

3. It it accurate to say that since planning involves goal setting and goal setting involves value judgments, planning is the implementation of the manager's value system?

4. The three major areas of goal-setting in universities are teaching, research, and public service. Discuss and explain the potential conflict among these goals from the perspective of a professor.

5. What factors do you believe account for the popularity of MBO as a planning technique? Explain why it often fails to achieve many of the hoped-for results.

6. Do you believe that MBO provides employees greater opportunity to be innovative and creative? Or does it reduce the possibility of these outcomes by providing management with the information to pinpoint accountability for unachieved objectives?

7. Describe potential conflicts between the goals of a production department and the goals of a sales department.

8. Is it true that the planning function is only as good as the underlying forecasts?

9. The budgeting process in government is often described in political terms; to what extent is the budgeting process in business also a political process?

10. How would you measure the results of programs designed to meet a firm's social responsibilities?

11. Do you believe that the *basic* purpose of a business firm is to provide goods or services at a profit?

12. Illustrate the misuse of policy statements from your own experience.

13. What is the only valid test of the appropriateness of a policy?

Additional references

Ackoff, L. R. *A Concept of Corporate Planning.* New York: John Wiley and Sons, Inc., 1970.

Ansoff, H. I., Declerck, R. P., and Hays, R. L. (eds). *From Strategic Planning to Strategic Management.* New York: John Wiley and Sons, 1976.

Anthony, R. N. *Planning and Control Systems.* Boston: Harvard University, Graduate School of Business, Division of Research, 1965.

Baur, R. A., and Fenn, D. H. *The Corporate Social Audit.* New York: Russell Sage Foundation, 1972.

Bierman, H., and Smidt, S. *The Capital Budgeting Decision.* New York: The Macmillan Co., 1966.

Branch, M. C. *Planning: Aspects and Applications.* New York: John Wiley and Sons, Inc., 1966.

England, G. W. *Personal Value Systems of Managers.* Minneapolis: Industrial Relations Center, University of Minnesota, 1973.

Ewing, D. W. *The Human Side of Planning.* New York: The Macmillan Co., 1969.

Glueck, W. F. *Business Policy.* New York: McGraw-Hill Book Co.. 1972.

Henry, H. W. *Long-Range Planning Practices in 45 Industrial Companies.* Englewood Cliffs, N.J.: Prentice-Hall, Inc., 1967.

Hughes, C. L. *Goal Setting: Key to Individual and Organizational Effectiveness.* New York: American Management Association, 1965.

Ishikawa, A. *Corporate Planning and Control Model Systems.* New York: New York University Press, 1975.

Kastens, M. L. *Long-Range Planning for Your Business.* New York: AMACOM, 1976.

Kolasa, B. J. *Responsibility in Business*. Englewood Cliffs, N.J.: Prentice-Hall, Inc., 1972.

LeBreton, P. P., and Henning, D. A. *Planning Theory*. Englewood Cliffs, N.J.: Prentice-Hall, Inc., 1961.

McConkey, D. D. *MBO for Nonprofit Organizations*. New York: AMACOM, 1975.

Paine, F. T., and Naumes, W. *Strategy and Policy Formation*. Philadelphia: W. B. Saunders Co., 1974.

Payne, B. *Planning for Company Growth*. New York: McGraw-Hill Book Co., 1963.

Pyhrr, P. A. *Zero-Base Budgeting, A Practical Management Tool for Evaluating Expenses*. New York: John Wiley and Sons, Inc., 1973.

Raia, A. P. *Managing by Objectives*. Glenview, Ill.: Scott, Foresman and Co., 1974.

Steiner, G. A. *Managerial Long-Range Planning*. New York: McGraw-Hill Book Co., 1963.

Sweet, F. H. *Strategic Planning*. Austin, Tex.: University of Texas, Bureau of Business Research, 1964.

Thompson, S. *How Companies Plan*. New York: American Management Association, 1962.

Warren, E. K. *Long-Range Planning: The Executive Viewpoint*. Englewood Cliffs, N.J.: Prentice-Hall, Inc., 1966.

Weber, J. A. *Growth Opportunity Analysis*. Reston, Va.: Reston Publishing Co., 1976.

PRACTICAL EXERCISE I
MBO Planning in an Occupational Health Division

The Commissioner of Health of a large midwestern state had initiated a MBO planning system in the State Health Department. The system had been used for four years, but he believed that many division directors had as yet not fully understood the system. The steps in the system included a discussion and agreement with each division director regarding the mission of division. The "mission statement," as it is termed, specifies the relationship between the division's activities and the department's mission, which is to protect and promote the physical well-being of the citizens of the state. After the division's mission is stated, each division director prepares an "MBO Statement of Objectives" in April prior to the beginning of each fiscal year. This statement is the basis for discussions between the commissioner and each division director. The results of the discussion are approval of the objectives and allocation of funds to achieve the objectives.

Late in April, the Commissioner asked his executive assistant to meet with John Pasada, recently appointed Director of the Division of Occupational Environment. Pasada had prepared his MBO statement without benefit of the training sessions held three years earlier since he was not then the director. And he evidently had not consulted either his staff or the files to obtain any information about what was expected. He had prepared and submitted the MBO Statement in the correct format (Exhibit 1), but as the Commissioner stated: "Those objectives have nothing to do with preventing occupational disease and health hazards. . . ." He instructed the executive assistant to go to Pasada and explain to him the necessity for rewriting the objectives.

The executive assistant dutifully made an appointment with Pasada and told him that he would have to rewrite his objectives: "The basic problem is that you do not specify the extent to which what you are doing—investigating, inspecting, providing, etc.—has anything to do with what you want to get done—prevention of occupationally-related disease and injury. The purpose of the MBO system is to enable

EXHIBIT 1 MBO Statement. Division of occupational environment

General objectives in order of priority	Specific subobjectives to be accomplished	Target dates for general and subobjectives	Resource requirements for general objectives
1. Investigate the occupational health problems in 3,112 priority industries and reduce the worker exposure to health hazards in these industrial establishments		1. June 30.	1. $424,914
	a. Recruit and train personnel.	a. Dec. 31.	
	b. Organize and staff five regional offices.	b. Dec. 31.	
	c. Conduct 3,112 industrial hygiene inspections of work places containing potential health hazards, including industrial hygiene field studies of 100 deficient industrial establishments, and 50 followup compliance inspections.	c. June 30.	
2. Inspect 50% of radiation sources for compliance with State Board of Health Regulations		2. June 30. Progress to be measured at six months.	2. $134,330
	a. Reduce X-ray exposure index by 10% by the inspection of 1,800 machines with necessary corrective actions.	a. June 30. Progress to be measured at six months.	
	b. Analyze 4,000 environmental samples for excesses of the maximum permissible concentrations, with necessary corrective actions.	b. June 30. Progress to be measured at six months.	
	c. Inspect 120 radioactive material licenses, and take necessary corrective actions.	c. June 30. Progress to be measured at six months.	
3. Provide industrial hygiene services to 220 coal mines to evaluate worker exposure to health hazards.	a. Service 168 mines: 1. Collect and analyze 4,200 respirable dust samples. 2. Conduct 2,520 noise exposure evaluations. 3. Collect and analyze 100 mine fungus samples. b. Provide engineering and consultative service to 52 mines for analysis and evaluation of specific dust or noise control methods.	3. June 30. Progress to be evaluated quarterly, 10% first quarter, 30% each remaining quarter.	3. $152,094

#	Objective / Action	Target Date	Amount
4.	Reduce the worker exposure to lead, free silica dust, asbestos, carbon monoxide, and cotton dust in 200 industrial establishments.	June 30.	$162,408
a.	Conduct industrial hygiene field studies of 17 selected Target Health Hazard industries each month.	June 30.	
b.	Conduct 50 follow-up compliance inspections.	June 30.	
5.	Initiate a Radiation Certification Program for implementation of Act passed by 1976 Legislation.	June 30. Progress to be measured quarterly.	$31,403
a.	Complete drafting of radiation machine user certification regulations for submission to State Board of Health for adoption.	June 30. Progress to be measured quarterly.	
b.	Complete first draft of laser and microwave regulations.	June 30. Progress to be measured at six months.	
6.	Fifty percent conversion of radiation data management to computer systems.	June 30. Progress to be measured at six months.	$15,113
a.	Complete transfer of X-ray data management to computer system.	June 30. Progress to be measured at six months.	
b.	Initiate computer system for environmental surveillance by completing a data form adaptable to computer input requirements.	June 30. Progress to be measured at six months.	
c.	Initiate a radioactive material licensing computer system.	June 30. Progress to be measured at six months.	
7.	Conduct ten training sessions to certify mining personnel in dust and noise measurement techniques, in accordance with the Federal Ccal Mine Health and Safety Act.	June 30. Progress to be evaluated monthly. (One session per month beginning the third month.)	$ 2,200
a.	Train 200 miners to qualify for certification in measurement techniques.		

the department to tell the Governor and the taxpayers what we are getting done with the money they provide. If your investigations and inspections do not make a difference in the incidence of occupational disease and injury, then you should not be doing these things."

Mr. Pasada thought for a moment and responded: "Look, I do not know what my predecessor was telling you or the commissioner, but I can assure you that there is no way of knowing whether what we are doing here makes any difference. The state of scientific knowledge does not permit us to be able to relate the impact of certain working conditions on health. And even if we could, the level of potential funding would not enable us to assure that the conditions in plants, factories, and mines remain as they were when our inspector approved them. The best we can do is to say what we will be doing, and you will simply have to take my word for it that working people's health will be better off."

The executive assistant related the discussion to the Commissioner. He responded: "If Pasada wants any money to run that division, he damn well better revise the general objectives in his MBO statement to reflect the extent to which the incidence and prevalence of occupational disease and injury will be decreased as a result of his efforts."

Questions for analysis:

1. If you were John Pasada, what would be your reaction to the Commissioner's threat?
2. If Pasada is correct in saying that it is not possible to know the relationship between what his division does and the incidence of occupational disease and injury, can you think of similar situations in business organizations?
3. Is the MBO system as used in the State Health Department conducive to the development of joint goal-setting?

PRACTICAL EXERCISE II
Planning in Fast-Food Stores

After serving 20 years in the U.S. Public Health Service, Dr. Joseph Skaggs retired and invested his savings in five fast-food stores. The stores were patterned after the successful Kentucky Fried Chicken national chain. The five stores were previously owned by a small-town banker who had aspirations, at one time, of recreating the Kentucky Fried Chicken success story. When it became apparent that such was not to be the case, he sold the business to Dr. Skaggs.

Dr. Skaggs' preinvestment research convinced him that the five stores could be more profitable than they had been simply through the application of basic management principles and techniques. To begin with, he believed that the previous owner's practice of allowing the five store managers to run their operations without any central direction was a mistake. He reasoned that even though the stores were spread throughout the state, thus precluding day-to-day supervision, coordinated effort should be attempted. At the same time, he did not want to jeopardize the initiative of the store managers by strapping them into rigid rules and procedures. He decided that the best way to introduce "good management" into the system was by beginning with the essential management function – planning.

The concept of planning which Dr. Skaggs presented at his first meeting with the five store managers was based upon his experience in public health administration. The planning concept, termed POAR, is explained as follows: POAR is an acronym which is formed from the four elements of a plan: Problem, Objectives, Activities, Resources. Accordingly the planners, the five store managers in this instance, were instructed to prepare annual plans of action for each problem that they identified in their respective stores. The plans would subsequently be the bases for allocating funds and reporting progress.

The store managers agreed with Dr. Skaggs that greater emphasis on planning should result in greater awareness of what needed to be done to make all the stores more profitable. They also accepted the legitimacy of Dr. Skaggs' right to expect them to follow his direction. Yet they were somewhat skeptical that POAR was applicable to business planning. They asked Dr. Skaggs to explain the concept by using an example. He responded by showing them the following plan for a family-planning program that he had developed during his public health career:

1. Problem Identification
   a. Desired Situation
      All 2,500 women residing in the county, and in the child-bearing age, should be provided family-planning services.
   b. Present Situation
      At present, 500 women are receiving family-planning services either through public or private clinics and physicians' offices.
   c. Specific Problem
      The problem is the difference between the desired situation and the present situation; therefore, the problem is to provide family-planning services to 2,000 women.
2. Objective
   By the end of the fiscal year 1,500 women will have received family-planning services from either public or private sources.

3. Activities
   In order to achieve the objective, the following activities will be required:
   a. Conduct 100 weekly clinics with an estimated 30 patients per clinic for a total of 3,000 patient-visits.
   b. Arrange physician office visits for 100 patients.
   c. Conduct 10 family-planning classes for teachers in 7th-12th grades, reaching approximately 250 teachers and, subsequently, 5,000 school children.
   d. Disseminate information to community and civic groups by giving 20 formal presentations.
4. Resources
   The projected cost of the plan is the total of each activity cost:
   a. Clinic cost.......................... $2,000.
   b. Office visit cost................. 500.
   c. Classes............................ 100.
   d. Information dissemination... 200.
           Total cost.................... $2,800. .

After examining the above example, one of the store managers stated that POAR may be appropriate for health management, but he failed to see its relevance for business management.

Questions for analysis:
1. What would be your response to the store manager concerning the appropriateness of POAR?
2. Do you believe that POAR is appropriate as a format for planning in a fried-chicken store?
3. Do you agree that Dr. Skaggs should have initiated the planning function as he did?

PRACTICAL EXERCISE III
Problem Identification in a Consumer-Products Firm

The top management of a large consumer-products company was preparing for its annual planning session. It was at these sessions that the management identified the company's significant problems, set priorities, and provided guidelines and policies for the preparation of detailed plans. In advance of these sessions, the manager of each of the functional departments was instructed to define the single significant problem facing the company from the perspective of that function. The top management would devise a set of company problems from those provided by the functional managers and place the problems in order of priority.

The seven functional departments of the company were: production, personnel, sales, staff development and training, finance, legal counsel, and engineering. Each of these functions consisted of subunits and operated on annual plans which developed from the planning session.

The problems which were presented for discussion are summarized as follows:

Production: The major problem from the perspective of the production manager was the excessive downtime of machine-paced operations. The amount of downtime was 20 percent more than the previous year. The cause of the problem was the necessity for more intensive preventive maintenance to stay within quality control tolerances imposed by more restrictive consumer protection laws passed by the state legislature.

Personnel: The manager of the personnel department stated that the major company problem was the excessive number of grievances which went to the departmental level for arbitration. The personnel manager indicated that the settlement of grievances at that level was inappropriate as a general rule and reflected the inability of first-line managers to deal with personnel problems.

Sales: The sales manager stated that the major problem was the spiraling cost of product distribution. The company's distribution system was based upon regional warehouses connected to production facilities by a fleet of trucks. The rising cost of fuel was driving up the delivered cost of products in addition to disrupting delivery schedules—all of which indicated the necessity for increasing the delivered price to customers who already were disgruntled by price increases in the previous year.

Staff development and training: The manager of this department stated that the major problem was the inability of first-line supervisors to deal effectively with their subordinates. The problem grew out of the company's affirmative response to equal opportunity laws which required the employment of persons formerly considered marginal. For the most part, these new employees required intensive skill training and close supervision. Moreover, they tended to be particularly sensitive to criticism. The problem required a significant expenditure of resources to train supervisors to manage with greater sensitivity.

Finance: According to the finance department, the company must move to reduce its reliance on short-term debt to meet current obligations. The financial manager stated that the company's cash flow was seriously unbalanced, the major cause being the company's liberal credit terms and, subsequently, unpredictable collections from customers.

Legal counsel: The chief legal officer stated that the company must either meet the recently legislated air quality standards or be brought under injunction. The company's principal source of power was coal. The air quality standards required the removal of air pollutants through the use of filter mechanisms, but at heavy expense to the company.

Engineering: The engineering department's manager stated that the company's significant problem was the high turnover of engineers for better-paying jobs with other companies. He stated that salaries must be upgraded or else the company would face the continued drain of engineering talent.

Questions for analysis:

1. In what order of priority would you place these problems?
2. Is there any basis for interrelating the problems, that is, is each a separate, unrelated problem?
3. Once problems are identified, what information is needed for subsequent planning decisions?

5

THE ORGANIZING
FUNCTION

The planning function refers to managerial activities which determine, in advance, goals and the means for achieving them. In a practical sense the determination of means involves an assignment of tasks to people who must then complete their work in a coordinated manner. The requirement for a coordinated effort derives from the fact that overall goals and tasks are subdivided into subgoals and subtasks. These, in turn, must be accomplished in definite ways and sequences to accomplish the overall goals and tasks.

The purpose of the organizing function is *to achieve coordinated effort through the design of a structure of task and authority relationships*. The two key concepts in the above sentence are *design* and *structure*. Design, in this context, implies that managers make a conscious effort to predetermine the way in which work is done by employees; structure refers to relatively stable relationships and aspects of the organization. The term "anatomy" is often used synonymously with structure.[1] This term is used to distinguish the structure, or anatomy, of an organization from the processes of an organization.[2]

When viewed in rather abstract terms, the organizing function is the process of breaking down the overall task into individual assignments and then putting them back together in units, or departments, along with a delegation of authority to a manager of the unit, or department. Thus, we can describe the organizing function in terms of *dividing* tasks, *departmentalizing* tasks, and *delegating* authority. But when we move from an abstract discussion of the organizing function to its concrete, practical application, simplicity is soon replaced by complexity.

The classical school of management attempted to deal with the complexity of the organizing function by stating certain "principles of organization." Here we will apply these principles in the context of the four fundamental problems of organizing:

1. What should determine the nature and content of each job? The principle of specialization of labor addresses itself to this problem.
2. What should determine the nature and content of each job? The principle of departmentalization suggests bases for grouping jobs.
3. What should determine the size of the groups? The span-of-control principle provides guidelines for solving this issue.
4. How should authority be distributed? The unity-of-command principle is relevant to this issue.

---

[1] Pradip N. Khandwalla, *The Design of Organizations* (New York: Harcourt Brace Janovich, Inc., 1977), pp. 17–19.

[2] James L. Gibson, John M. Ivancevich, and James H. Donnelly, Jr., *Organizations: Behavior, Structure, Processes* (Dallas: Business Publications Inc., 1976).

The principle of specialization of labor

Probably the most important single principle in an analysis of the classical approach to organizational design is specialization of labor. This principle affects everyone every day. For example, in the construction of a single-family home, a number of divisions of work occur in every phase of construction. The workers perform tasks within a specialized framework, and include bricklaying specialists, electrical specialists, plumbing specialists, and carpentry specialists. Each performs a narrow range of duties. The overall task of building the home is too large for any one group of specialists to handle within a reasonable period of time. The "jack of all trades" has moved aside for the "master" of a specialized task in home construction.

The narrow work capacity of one group of specialists (for example, plumbers) is one of many reasons why high degrees of division of labor are popular in the classical management approach. The overall production efficiencies generated by dividing labor are viewed as beneficial. This belief is certainly not new and is still accepted as valid.

The gains derived from narrow divisions of labor can be calculated in purely economic terms. Figure 5–1 shows this relationship. As the job is divided into ever smaller elements, additional output is obtained; but more men and capital must be employed to do the smaller jobs. At some point, the costs of specialization (labor and capital) begin to

FIGURE 5–1
The economics of specialization

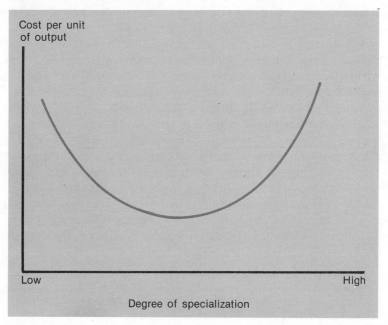

Cost per unit of output

Low   High

Degree of specialization

outweigh the increased efficiency of specialization (output), and the cost per unit of output begins to rise.

The problem of determining the appropriate degree of specialization becomes more difficult as the task becomes more abstract and less amenable to measurement. Nevertheless, the principle of specialization states that one must investigate the potential for gains due to specialization.

The end results of implementing the specialization-of-labor principle are job descriptions which define the depth and scope[3] of each job. The depth reflects the relative freedom that the job holder has in planning and controlling assigned duties. Ordinarily, one expects the depth of a job to increase as one moves up in the levels of the organization. An obvious contrast can be drawn between the work of the chief executive and the work of an assembly-line worker. But there can also be differences in job depth among persons at the same level. For example, a maintenance man has considerably more job depth than does a lathe worker. The scope of a job refers to the length of time of the job cycle; that is, the more often the job is repeated in a given time period, the more limited is its scope. We can expect to find differences in job scope among jobs at the same level and at different levels in the organization.

The writers of the Classical School of management went to great lengths in the application of specialization of labor to manual tasks. Taylor and the Gilbreths were instrumental in the development of analyses termed motion and time study. We have earlier alluded to this development in the context of goal clarity; here the emphasis is on the design of particular jobs, particularly those which involve expenditures of physical, rather than mental, energy. According to the classical writers, the work of lathe operators, assemblers, ironworkers, bricklayers, and similar occupations can be broken down into separable and discrete hand, eye, and body movements. These movements, termed Therbligs, are defined in Table 5–1.

The identification of Therbligs led the classical writers to believe that high degrees of specialization could be achieved in many different settings.[4] Their calculations of the net benefits to be derived from specialization did not include certain cost factors which have, more recently, been identified by the writers of the Behavioral School. The costs of overspecialization include excessive monotony, boredom, and fatigue which in turn can induce absenteeism, turnover, and shoddy workmanship. As we will see in Chapter 8, the contemporary

---

[3] Alan C. Filley, Robert J. House, and Steven Kerr, *Managerial Process and Organizational Behavior* (Glenview, Ill.: Scott, Foresman and Co., 1976), pp. 214–16.

[4] The design of individual tasks is an ongoing activity in most modern organizations. See Carl F. Lutz and Albert P. Ingraham, "Design and Management of Positions," *Personnel Journal* (April 1972), pp. 234–40.

TABLE 5–1
The basic hand movements of manual work

Therblig	Objective
1. Grasp	To gain control of an object
2. Position	To line up, orient, or change position of a part
3. Pre-position	To line up part or tool for use in another place
4. Use	To apply tool
5. Assembly	To assemble parts or objects
6. Disassemble	To separate objects
7. Release load	To release a part or object
8. Transport empty	To reach for something
9. Transport loaded	To change location of an object
10. Search	To seek to find an object
11. Select	To locate an object from a group of objects
12. Hold	To hold object in fixed position and location
13. Unavoidable delay	To wait for other body member or machine as a part of the work movement
14. Avoidable delay	To wait for other body member or machine not a part of the work movement
15. Rest for fatigue	To remain idle as a part of the cycle to overcome fatigue
16. Plan	To determine course of action
17. Inspect	To determine quality of item

Source: Adapted from Marvin E. Mundel, "Motion and Time Study," *Industrial Engineering* (Englewood Cliffs, N.J.: Prentice-Hall, Inc., 1955), pp. 296–98.

thinking in management is that while the very essence of work in organizations requires the division of labor, the calculation of the optimum degree of specialization must include psychological as well as economic costs and benefits.[5]

The principle of specialization of labor guides managers in determining the content of individual jobs. From a different perspective, the principle also guides them in determining how jobs should be grouped together, the principle of departmentalization.

The principle of departmentalization

The managerial problems associated with departmentalization are directly related to the degree to which individual jobs have been specialized. That is, the number of ways to group jobs increases with the number of different (specialized) jobs. Moreover, as Adam Smith observed some 200 years ago, the extent of specialization is limited by the extent of the market. Thus, the owner-manager of a small-town

---

[5] Jon L. Pierce and Randall B. Dunham, "Task Design: A Literature Review," *Academy of Management Review*, October 1976, pp. 83–97.

clothing store specializing in men's clothing and employing three persons has little difficulty determining the way jobs should be grouped, as compared to the management of Sears, Roebuck and Co.

In general, the bases for grouping jobs can be classified into two major categories: (1) outputs and (2) internal operations. In terms of concepts developed in the discussion of the planning function these two categories could be termed (1) goals or outcomes, and (2) means, or activity bases. Thus jobs could be grouped according to common goals regardless of activities or jobs could be grouped according to activities regardless of goals.[6] These two general categories of bases for departmentalization are elaborated below.

OUTPUT-ORIENTED BASES

The three commonly used output-oriented bases are product, client, and geographic.

Product departmentalization involves the grouping together of all activities necessary to manufacture a product or product line. As the

FIGURE 5–2
Departmentalization along product lines

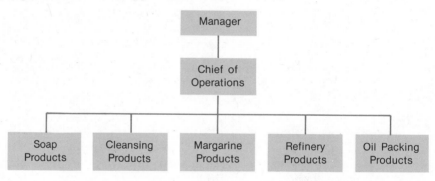

organization grows in size, it becomes difficult for managers to coordinate the activities of the expanding product lines. One commonly adopted strategy is to establish departments based upon products. The grouping of activities along product lines permits the utilization of the specialized skills of those people affiliated with a particular product or product line. An example of this type of departmentalization is presented in a partial organization chart, Figure 5–2.

Customer departmentalization is the grouping of activities based

[6] See Luther Gulick, "Notes on the Theory of Organization," in Luther Gulick and Lyndall F. Urwick, eds., *Papers on the Science of Administration* (New York: Columbia University, 1947), pp. 15–30, for the classical discussion of the departmentalization bases.

FIGURE 5–3
Departmentalization along customer lines

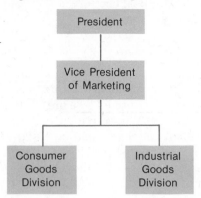

upon the customers served. For example, a company may have two sales departments that deal with two major groups of customers. One department may service the general public, while the other may be designed to provide goods to an industrial group of customers. The customer departmentalization design is presented in Figure 5–3.

Geographical departmentalization, grouping activities according to location, is popular in organizations that have physically dispersed markets to serve. The assumption is that if markets are widely dispersed, an improved cost-and-profit situation will result if all activities affecting a product or product line in a specific geographical region are grouped together. Figure 5–4 illustrates an example of geographical departmentalization.

The first classification for grouping work — that is, product, customer, and geography — is oriented toward factors which are external to the

FIGURE 5–4
Departmentalization along geographical lines

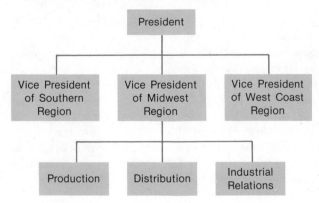

actual operations of the firm. For example, the customer is a factor "out there" in the market. The geographical territory is also "out there," as is the distribution of the product.

INTERNAL OPERATIONS-ORIENTED BASES

Two bases in this category are discussed: functional and process. *Functional departmentalization* is used when organizations are designed on the basis of the operations performed by a unit. For example, in a food-processing firm, all job-related activities involved in recruiting and selecting management trainees might be assigned to the personnel department, all marketing-related activities to the marketing department, and all activities concerned with the actual production of goods would be grouped in the production department. The functional organization design is used extensively in manufacturing firms. Figure 5–5 illustrates the design.

FIGURE 5–5
Departmentalization along functional lines

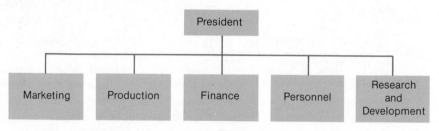

Process departmentalization is the grouping of jobs according to technical operations. For example, the manufacturing of a product may include cutting the materials on a lathe, heat-treating the materials, and finally painting the product. The same type of technical division of work may be found in an office of a business administration department at a college. A number of typists may be assigned specific duties to perform. One types manuscripts; another typist is concerned with correspondence; and the third handles the telephone and the typing of classroom materials. In Figure 5–6, the division of work along process lines is presented.

The bases for departmentalization are generally identifiable in any organizational setting. In Table 5–2 four bases are identified in four organizational settings. There we see, for example, that the equivalent to the Pontiac Division of General Motors (product bases) are patient-care in hospitals, degrees in universities, and safe drinking water in a public health agency. The only basis not shown is geographic; this basis becomes relevant only if the organization is dispersed with offices and facilities in different locations.

FIGURE 5–6
Departmentalization along process lines

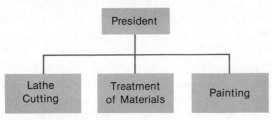

TABLE 5–2
Comparison of departmental bases in four organizational settings

	Organizational settings			
Basis	*Business*	*Hospital*	*University*	*Public health*
Function	Manufacturing	Surgery	Teaching	Engineering
Process.............	Assembly	Diagnosis	Evaluation	Inspector
Product............	Pontiac	Patient-care	Degree	Safe drinking water
Customer..........	Military	Children	Graduate	Residential

A FINAL WORD ON DEPARTMENTALIZATION

The methods cited above for dividing work are not exhaustive; there are many other ways. Furthermore, in large organizations a number of different methods of dividing work are used at the same time. For example, at the upper levels of management, the vice presidents reporting to the president may represent different product groups. At the level directly below the vice presidents, the managers may be part of a particular function. At the next level in the organization, there may be a number of different technical classifications. This approach is illustrated in Figure 5–7.

The principle of departmentalization specifies the general objective to be followed in grouping activities, but the basis actually chosen is a matter of balancing advantages and disadvantages. For example, the advantage of departmentalizing on the basis of customers or products is that of bringing together under the control of a single manager all the resources necessary to make the product and/or service for the customers. Additionally, the specification of goals is considerably easier when the emphasis is on the final product. Yet, at the same time, the ease of goal identification and measurement can encourage the individual departments to pursue their own goals at the expense of company goals; we referred to this possibility in the discussion of goal structure and the problem of suboptimization in Chapter 4. A second disadvantage of product and customer departmentalization is that the task of coordinating the activities tends to be more complex. Reporting to the unit manager are the managers of the various functions (production, marketing, and personnel, for example) whose diverse but interdependent activities must be coordinated.

Departmentalization based upon internal operations (function and process departments) has advantages as well as disadvantages. The primary advantage is that such departments are based upon specific skills and training; and activities assigned to the department emphasize the skills which individual members bring to the job. The managerial task of coordinating the activities of process departments is con-

FIGURE 5–7
Organizational design using mixed departmentalization

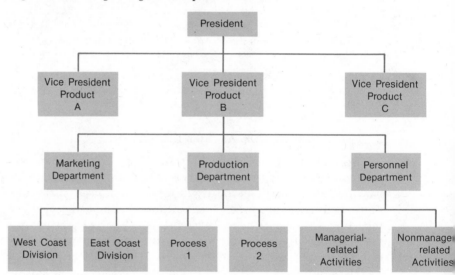

siderably less complex than in the product department because of the similarity of the subordinates' tasks. At the same time, the disadvantages of process departments must be recognized, the principal disadvantage being the difficulty of providing job depth for the managers of such groups. Since process departmentalization involves breaking up a natural work flow and assigning parts of this flow to different departments, each departmental manager must coordinate the task with those of other departmental managers. As shown in Figure 5–6, the president must necessarily limit the freedom of the managers of each of the three process departments in order to coordinate their activities.

The relative advantages of the alternative departmentalization bases can be evaluated in terms of three criteria:[7]

1. Which approach (basis) permits the maximum use of special technical knowledge?
2. Which provides the most efficient utilization of machinery and equipment?
3. Which provides the best hope of obtaining the required control and coordination:

These three criteria represent the essential thinking of the Classical School regarding the choice of bases. But as Walker and Lorsch state, they fail to recognize the complex trade-offs between them. Whereas the classical writers left it to managerial judgment to determine these trade-offs, contemporary writers are turning to researchers for help. Yet even if the combination of judgment and research leads to the correct bases for departmentalization in a given situation, the question of size of each group, or department, must be confronted; this is the question of span of control.

The principle of span of control

The span-of control principle concerns the number of subordinates who report to a supervisor. The number of persons who report to a supervisor has two important implications. First, it is influential in determining the complexity of individual managers' jobs; all things equal, it is easier to manage six persons rather than ten. Second, the span of control determines the shape, or configuration of the organization; the fewer the number of people reporting to a supervisor, the larger the number of managers required. Each of these two issues is discussed next.

SPAN OF CONTROL AND MANAGERIAL WORK

An early classical writer applied deductive reasoning to the span-of-control issue.[8] He demonstrated that, as the number of subordinates reporting to a manager increases arithmetically, the number of potential interpersonal interactions between the manager and the subordinates increases geometrically.

As Graicunas explained, the manager can relate directly to each

---

[7] Arthur H. Walker and Jay W. Lorsch, "Organizational Choice: Product versus Function," in Jay W. Lorsch and Paul R. Lawrence, eds., *Studies in Organization Design* (Homewood, Ill.: Richard D. Irwin and the Dorsey Press, 1970), p. 39.

[8] A. V. Graicunas, "Relationships in Organization," in Gulick and Urwick, eds., *Papers on the Science of Administration*, pp. 183–87.

individual subordinate (direct single) or to each possible group of subordinates (direct group). Moreover, it is possible for subordinates to
relate to each other (cross). For example, a manager (M) is assigned two
subordinates (A and B). The total number of relationships is six, as
shown in Figure 5–8. But if only one more subordinate (C) is assigned
to the manager, the total number of potential relationships increases
from 6 to 18, as shown in Figure 5–8.

FIGURE 5–8
Potential relationships among a manager and two/three subordinates

A manager (M) and two subordinates (A and B)		A manager (M) and three subordinates (A, B, and C)	
Direct single........	1. $M \rightarrow A$	Direct single........	1. $M \rightarrow A$
	2. $M \rightarrow B$		2. $M \rightarrow B$
			3. $M \rightarrow C$
Direct group	3. $M \rightarrow A$ with B	Direct group	4. $M \rightarrow A$ with B
	4. $M \rightarrow B$ with A		5. $M \rightarrow A$ with C
			6. $M \rightarrow B$ with A
			7. $M \rightarrow B$ with C
			8. $M \rightarrow C$ with A
			9. $M \rightarrow C$ with B
			10. $M \rightarrow A$ with B and C
			11. $M \rightarrow B$ with A and C
			12. $M \rightarrow C$ with A and B
Cross.................	5. $A \rightarrow B$	Cross.................	13. $A \rightarrow B$
	6. $B \rightarrow A$		14. $A \rightarrow C$
			15. $B \rightarrow A$
			16. $B \rightarrow C$
			17. $C \rightarrow A$
			18. $C \rightarrow B$

To demonstrate the impact of increasing the manager's span of control, Graicunas devised a formula which can be used to calculate the
total number of potential relationships for any number of subordinates.
The formula is as follows:

$$C = N \left[\frac{2^N}{2} + N - 1 \right].$$

In this formula, C designates the total potential contacts and N the
number of subordinates reporting directly to the manager. Table 5–3
clearly shows the geometric increase in the number of possible relationships if the number of subordinates increases arithmetically.

The recognition that potential managerial effectiveness is limited as
the number of subordinates increases has led others to propose definite
limits on the span of control. For example, Davis distinguishes between

TABLE 5-3
Potential relationships with variable
number of subordinates*

Number of Subordinates	Number of Relationships
1	1
2	6
3	18
4	44
5	100
6	222
7	490
8	1,080
9	2,376
10	5,210
11	11,374
12	24,708
18	2,359,602

* From Harold Koontz and Cyril O'Donnell, *Principles of Management*, 5th ed. (New York: McGraw-Hill Book Co., 1972), p. 253.

two categories of span of control, an *executive span* and an *operative span*.[9] It is Davis's contention that the executive span includes the middle and top management positions in an organization. The span for managers at these levels should vary from three to nine, depending upon the nature of the managers' jobs and responsibilities and the rate of growth of the company, among other factors. The operative span applies to the lowest level of management. Davis proposes that the operative span can be effective with as many as 30 subordinates.

Another classical writer, Urwick, contends that managers should have a limited span of control because man in general has a limited span of attention.[10] That is, a limit exists as to the number of other people or objects to which a person can attend at the same time. Urwick recognizes that, though managers with ten subordinates can be involved with over 5,210 contacts, they typically do not enter into every potential contact in the course of a day. However, if only a portion of the potential 5,210 relationships actually occurs in a day, there is a definite limit on their time. Based upon his interpretation of span of control and the potential relationships, Urwick proposes that the ideal span for top management is four, but that at other supervisory levels the number may be eight to twelve.

[9] Ralph C. Davis, *Fundamentals of Top Management* (New York: Harper and Row, 1951).

[10] Lyndall F. Urwick, "The Manager's Span of Control," *Harvard Business Review*, (May-June 1956), pp. 39-47.

SPAN OF CONTROL AND ORGANIZATIONAL SHAPE

The span of control has important implications for the shape of an organization. For example, assume that a company has 48 nonmanagers and the span of control is 8. There would be six supervisors directing the workers and two senior supervisors directing three supervisors, each. This type of structure is illustrated in Figure 5–9 where there are three levels of management: president, senior supervisor, and supervisor.

If the same number of workers (48) were supervised by two superiors, an organization with only two managerial levels could be structured. The organizational design resulting from widening the span

FIGURE 5–9
Narrow span of control

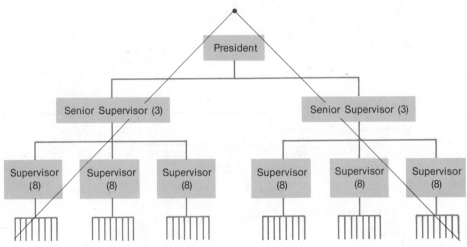

of control to 24 is presented in Figure 5–10. By increasing the span of control from 8 to 24, one level of management and six managerial positions were eliminated from the organization.

The relatively flat organization which results from wide spans of control shortens the communication channel from top to bottom. It also fosters more general supervision since, as noted earlier, the managers will not be able to devote as much time to each individual employee. In contrast, narrow spans of control foster close supervision, but at the cost of lengthened communication channels and increased cost.

The classical view of the span-of-control principle is flexible in specifying the exact span. Both Davis and Urwick recognize that the optimum span depends upon a number of considerations. A latter-day

FIGURE 5–10
Wide span of control

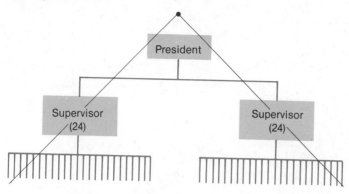

statement of the principle recognizes that the optimum span is related to at least the following considerations:[11]

1. The competence of both the superior and the subordinates.
2. The degree of interaction between the units or personnel being supervised.
3. The extent to which the supervisor must carry out nonmanagerial responsibilities, and the demands on his or her time from other people and units.
4. The similarity or dissimilarity of the activities being supervised.
5. The incidence of new problems in a unit.
6. The extent of standardized procedures.
7. The degree of physical dispersion of subordinates.

Depending upon the relative importance of each of these factors, the optimum span of control could vary quite considerably. Classical management theory leaves unanswered the manner in which the optimum can be determined for any particular situation. Such determination had to await the development of more sophisticated analyses than were available to the classicists. It is fair to say, however, that the tendency in classical theory is toward a narrow span of control, because the emphasis in classical literature is on stability and predictability.

The principle of unity of command

One of the most fundamental relationships presented in the classical approach to organizational design is that existing between superior and subordinate. The classical interpretation of unity of command can be

---

[11] Harold Steiglitz, *Organization Planning* (New York: National Industrial Conference Board, 1966), p. 15.

described easily once the concept of chain of command is understood. The chain-of-command relationship is viewed as a series of superior-subordinate relationships. Starting at the top of the organization with the president and progressing down to the unskilled employee, the managerial chain of command is viewed as a pyramid. Figure 5–11 depicts the chain of command in a hypothetical managerial hierarchy.

FIGURE 5–11
Chain of command

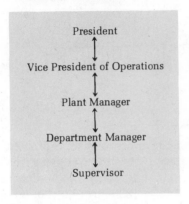

CHAIN OF COMMAND

The chain of command is the formal channel which determines authority, responsibility, and communications. It is postulated that because of the complexity of these phenomena, no individual should be subject to the direct command of more than one superior, as defined by the principle of unity of command. Thus, in a simplistic way, unity of command stresses that a subordinate is delegated authority and decision-making power from, and communicates with, one superior.

The classical management reasoning for advocating the unity-of-command principle is that receiving commands from two or more superiors is likely to bring about confusion and frustration. According to the classicists, which superior's command should be followed poses a frustrating and confusing dilemma for the subordinate.

The unity-of-command principle is *directly related* to the authority principle which specifies that an unbroken chain of command must be instituted from top to bottom. At the same time, the classicists recognized the need for providing the opportunity to bypass the formal chain when conditions warrant. Fayol had this in mind when he proposed that a subordinate should be empowered to communicate directly with a peer outside the chain, provided that the appropriate superiors approve beforehand the circumstances which permit the crossovers. Figure 5–12 shows a bridge between F and G which D and

FIGURE 5–12
Fayol's bridge

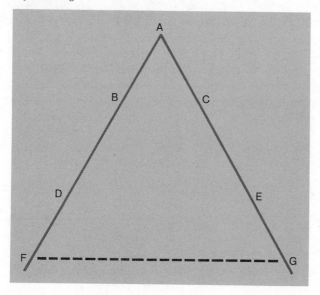

E have approved. Under special circumstance, F and G may communicate directly without going through channels, yet neither F nor G would be accountable to anyone but their immediate superiors — in this case, D and E.

UNITY OF COMMAND AND THE STAFF FUNCTION

The classicists also invoked the unity-of-command principle to guide the use of staff personnel. An important point in examining organizational design in terms of the classical theory is to distinguish between line and staff. Many different definitions of line and staff can be found in the management literature. Perhaps the most concise and least confusing definition is one which defines *line* as deriving from operational activities in a direct sense — creating, financing, and distributing a good or service, while *staff* is viewed as an advisory and facilitative function for the line.[12] The crux of this viewpoint of line and staff is the degree to which the function contributes directly to the attainment of organizational objectives. The *line functions* contribute directly to accomplishing the firm's objectives, while *staff functions* facilitate the accomplishment of the major organizational objectives in

---

[12] Our choice of this particular distinction is arbitrary. For a complete discussion of various line-staff conceptualizations, see Robert T. Golembiewski, *Organizing Men and Power: Patterns of Behavior and Line-Staff Models* (Chicago: Rand McNally and Co., 1967).

an indirect manner. Figure 5–13 illustrates a line-and-staff organizational design.

Assuming that the organization depicted in Figure 5–13 is a manufacturing firm would enable one to conclude which of the positions are line and which are staff. Using the criterion that the line function contributes directly to the firm's objectives would lead to the conclusion that the marketing and production departments perform activities directly related to the attainment of a most important organizational goal—placing an acceptable product on the market. The activi-

FIGURE 5–13
A line-and-staff design

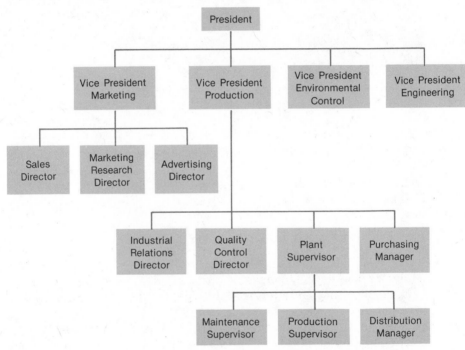

ties of the managers of environmental control and engineering are advisory in nature. That is, they are helpful in enabling the firm to produce and market its product, but do not directly contribute to the process. Thus they are considered to be staff departments in this particular firm.

The unity-of-command principle quite clearly defines the appropriate role of the staff specialist in the organization: The staff advises and provides information, but has no authority over the work of a particular line manager's subordinates. To place a subordinate under the jurisdiction of a staff official as well as a line manager would violate the span-of-control principle and weaken the chain of command.

Studies of organizational structure

The outcome of the series of managerial decisions relating to dividing work, departmentalization, and delegating authority is an organization structure. The classical writers initiated interest in determining the relative advantages and disadvantages of different structures. Theorists and researchers have contributed a great number of studies which attempt to evaluate alternative organization designs. Three of these studies are reviewed in this section.

THE SEARS, ROEBUCK STUDY

Worthy studied the morale of over 100,000 employees at Sears, Roebuck and Company during a 12-year period.[13] He was concerned with determining the morale of Sears's employees with respect to six major factors of their work environment: (1) the company in general, (2) the local organization, (3) the local management, (4) immediate supervision, (5) fellow employees, and (6) job and working conditions.

The results of Worthy's research are basically the following:

1. The more complex the organizational structure, the greater the probability that poor management-employee relationships will result.
2. Dividing work into fewer and fewer units and dividing departments into subdepartments often results in low output and low morale. Those groups that contribute consistently to the organization (for example, salesmen) and display the highest morale are those that complete entire tasks.
3. Overfunctionalization requires close and constant supervision at the work level to maintain production. A consequence of closely supervising employees is rigid control systems which negatively affect morale and productivity.
4. Overfunctionalization does not allow personnel to operate except in closest coordination with others, and the system is often so complex that this coordination cannot occur spontaneously.
5. The overly complex, overly functionalized organizational structure typically requires the type of leader who uses pressure as a supervisory device.

---

[13] James C. Worthy, "Organizational Structure and Employee Morale," *American Sociological Review* (April 1950), pp. 169–79.

Next, Worthy compared and contrasted various unit structures at Sears. The implication of his analysis is that organizations with fewer levels and wider spans of control yield a less complex organizational structure. The wide span of control literally forces management to delegate authority. In addition to delegation, the flattening technique (widening span of control) requires a trained management team, shortens communication networks, and shortens the administrative distance between the levels of management. According to Worthy, the executives at Sears found that the flatter organization structure with maximum decentralization develops self-reliance, initiative, and decision-making abilities. Worthy's conclusions imply that the flatter structure is the best way to design an organization.

PORTER AND LAWLER STUDY OF ATTITUDES IN TALL AND FLAT ORGANIZATIONS

A study conducted by Porter and Lawler concentrated upon the job attitudes of managerial personnel in tall and flat organization structures.[14] They utilized a questionnaire to ascertain the attitudes of managers in the tall and flat structures. Over 1,900 managers participated in this study. The major findings of this investigation are briefly summarized as follows:

1. In firms employing fewer than 5,000 employees, managerial attitudes were more positive in the flat than in the tall organization structure.
2. In firms employing more than 5,000 employees, the managers in the tall organization structure generally reported more positive attitudes.
3. Thus, reviewing their findings, Porter and Lawler conclude that there is no clear overall superiority of a flat organization structure over a tall organization structure.

The conclusions of Worthy support contentions regarding the advantages of the flat structure over the tall structure. The Porter and Lawler research, however, prevents one from making sweeping generalizations that a flat organization structure produces more favorable attitudes.

A recent review of over 50 relevant studies reaffirms the inconclusive relation of organization structure to employees' attitudes and behaviors.[15] The review notes that attempts to discern simple cause-

[14] L. W. Porter and E. E. Lawler, "The Effects of Tall versus Flat Organization Structures on Managerial Job Satisfaction," *Personnel Psychology* (Summer 1964), pp. 135–48. pp. 135–48.

[15] L. L. Cummings and Chris J. Berger, "Organization Structure: How Does it Influence Attitudes and Performance?" *Organizational Dynamics* (Augumn 1976), pp. 34–49.

and-effect relationships are bound to fail; nevertheless, some conclusions appear justified, among these being:

1. Job satisfaction tends to increase as one moves up in the hierarchy.
2. Recognition, achievement, and prestige become more important sources of satisfaction as one moves up the hierarchy.
3. No consistent differences in satisfaction exist between line and staff personnel.
4. Managers' job satisfaction increases as their span of control increases.
5. Top management in tall organizations and lower-level management in flat organizations experience more satisfaction than their counterparts.

Despite these conclusions, the relation of organization structure to employee satisfaction and performance is far from completely understood. The tendency in contemporary research and practice is to specify *contingencies*. Much work is now being devoted to studying factors such as technology, environmental uncertainty, and personnel characteristics which condition the relationship between organization structure and performance. An important initial study of this nature was completed by Woodward.

THE WOODWARD CONTINGENCY STUDY

An important study of organization structures was conducted by Joan Woodward.[16] She and research associates studied 100 firms in Great Britain. All the firms manufactured goods and offered them for sale, but the nature of their markets and market share goals differed considerably.

By a combination of research methods various kinds of information were collected. Some of the information obtained for each firm was:

1. History, background, and objectives of the firm.
2. Information on the manufacturing processes and methods employed.
3. Forms and routines through which the firm was organized and operated.
4. Organization chart.
5. Labor structure and cost.
6. Qualifications of managers.
7. Assessment of the success of the firm in their respective industries.

Woodward developed a system for classifying firms as above average, average, and below average in success. In constructing the

---

[16] Joan Woodward, *Industrial Organization: Theory and Practice* (London: Oxford University Press, 1965).

success criterion, such factors as the state of the industry in which the firm operated (for example, new and expanding, old and contracting), the percentage of the total volume of the industry the firm contributed, five-year profit figures and investment figures, the fluctuation of the firm's shares on the Stock Exchange, the reputation of the firm, the salaries it paid, and the union opinion about the firm were some of the items considered.

The researchers became aware of the many variations in manufacturing methods utilized by the firms studied. This led to classifying the firms into three groups.[17]

1. Unit and small-batch (for example, a job shop).
2. Large-batch and mass production (for example, an auto assembly plant).
3. Long-run process production (for example, a chemical manufacturing plant).

The three groupings suggested differences in technological complexity of operations. The simplest technology involved the production of goods for a single customer in the form of unit or small-batch manufacturing operations. The middle range of technological complexity involved the production of large batches of goods on a mass-production scale, while the highly complex technology included the production of goods utilizing interrelated processes.

The relatively successful firms using process and small-batch technology had similar organization structures. They tended to be relatively nonspecialized, product and customer based, with wide spans of control, and decentralized. The successful firms using mass-production technology, however, were more specialized, function- and process-based, with narrow spans of control and with centralized authority.

In the final analysis, Woodward's research findings suggest that although there is no one best way of structuring an organization, there seems to be a particular form of structure most appropriate for each technology. The firms engaged in large-batch production appear to operate more successfully if they are organized along classical lines. However, firms in the other two classifications are more successful if a less classical orientation is utilized.

Summary

The classical approach emphasizes the design of the formal structure of the organization to achieve coordinated effort. Various principles of management such as division of labor, span of control, unity of com-

---

[17] Woodward, *Industrial Organization*, p. 39.

mand, departmentalization, and authority provide the cornerstones of the classical approach. It is generally concluded that the main emphasis of classical organization theory is upon the structure of the organization, and that the prescribed design is similar to the bureaucratic structure.

The bureaucratic organization, as described by Max Weber, is a highly structured, formalized, and impersonal organization.[18] Weber, writing at the same time as the classical management theorists, stated that the bureaucracy is the most effective form of organization for achieving goals such as production efficiency. He recognized that the degree of bureaucratization varied widely in practice; but he proposed that certain characteristics define the most effective organization, which he termed the "ideal" type, as follows:

1. A clear division of labor exists, so that each task to be performed by employees is systematically established and legitimatized by formal recognition as an official duty.
2. The functions within the organization are officially arranged in a hierarchial manner. That is, a chain of command from the top down is established. This is referred to in the management literature as the *scalar chain.*
3. The actions of employees are governed by rules and procedures which are formally prescribed and which are utilized in a uniform manner in every situation.
4. The officials of the bureaucracy apply the rules and procedures as impersonally as is humanly possible. The "people" element is given consideration after the entity itself.
5. Employment in the bureaucracy is based upon rigid selection criteria which apply uniformly and impersonally to each candidate applying or being considered for a position. The criteria for selection are based upon objective standards for the job which have been established by the officials of the organization.

Examination of these five characteristics shows that they are similar in many ways to classical organization principles.

When research evidence is examined, it appears that the classical approach to organization design is not perfectly applicable to all situations and organizations. The limited amount of research evidence does not allow conclusive statements to be made concerning which type of design is best for a particular organization. The research studies available in the management literature suggest that the type of managerial and nonmanagerial personnel, the type of work being performed, the size, and the production processes of the organization are some vari-

---

[18] Max Weber, "The Essentials of Bureaucratic Organization: An Ideal-Type Construction," in Roberton K. Merton, et al., eds., *A Reader in Bureaucracy* (Glencoe, Ill.: The Free Press, 1952), pp. 18–27.

ables that should be given more than passing attention in designing an organization. When management experts more clearly specify the significant organizational factors influencing the success of a particular design, they will be in a better position to design effective organizations.

Discussion and review questions

1. What objectives do managers seek through the organizing function, and what are the indications that they have achieved them?
2. In what specific ways are the organizing and planning functions interrelated? What kinds of work would you expect to find in a unit titled "Organization Planning"?
3. Use the classical organizing principles to describe and evaluate an organization to which you belong. For example, describe and evaluate the formal structure in terms of division of labor, bases of departmentalization, span of control, and unity of command.
4. What are the bases of departmentalization in the college in which you are enrolled? What alternative bases might be used to group faculty together? Which one is the "best"?
5. How does the manager know that he has designed the right organization structure?
6. A critic of capitalism states that the cost of specialization of labor is alienation from the work place. Is he correct? If he is, so what? What is the alternative?
7. How can the use of staff personnel conflict with the unity-of-command principle? How could such conflicts be resolved?
8. What is the relationship between Taylor's "functional foremanship" and the use of staff?
9. What is the meaning of bureaucracy to a political scientist?
10. Is it true that all organizations have some of the characteristics of bureaucracy? Moreover, can it be argued that "bureaucracy" is necessarily a poor form of organization?
11. Classical organization theory proposed that stability and predictability are appropriate objectives of organization. Do these objectives conflict with creativity and innovativeness?

Additional references

Baker, A. W., and Davis, R. C. *Ratios of Staff to Line Employees and Stages of Differentiations of Staff Functions.* Columbus: Ohio State University, Bureau of Business Research, 1954.

Bowers, D. *Systems of Organization.* Ann Arbor: University of Michigan Press, 1976.

Brown, A. *Organization of Industry.* Englewood Cliffs, N.J.: Prentice-Hall, Inc., 1947.

Dale, E. *Organization.* New York: American Management Association, 1967.

————. *Planning and Developing the Company Organization Structure.* New York: American Management Association, 1952.

Dale, E., and Urwick, L. F. *Staff in Organization.* New York: McGraw-Hill Book Company, 1960.

Davis, R. C. *The Fundamentals of Top Management.* New York: Harper and Brothers, 1951.

Downs, A. *Inside Bureaucracy.* Boston: Little, Brown. 1967.

Famularo, J. J. *Organizational Planning Manual.* New York: American Management Association, 1970.

Fox, W. M. *The Management Process.* Homewood, Ill.: Richard D. Irwin, Inc., 1963.

Frank, H. E. *Organization Structuring.* New York: McGraw-Hill Book Co., 1971.

Hall, C. L. *The Management Guide.* Standard Oil Company of California, Department of Organization, 1948.

Holden, P. E., Fish, L. S., and Smith, H. L. *Top-Management Organization and Control,* New York: McGraw-Hill Book Company, 1941.

Jaques, E. *A General Theory of Bureaucracy* New York: Halsted Press, 1976.

Klein, L. *New Forms of Work Organization.* New York: Cambridge University Press.

Mahler, W. *Structure, Power and Results.* Homewood, Ill.: Dow-Jones, Inc., 1975.

Pfiffner, J. M., and Sherwood, F. P. *Administrative Organization.* Englewood Cliffs, N.J.: Prentice-Hall, Inc., 1960.

PRACTICAL EXERCISE I
Organizational Problems in an Electronic Products Company

The plant superintendent and the personnel manager of a large electronic products manufacturing facility were discussing current problems. It was their practice to meet at least twice a month to "review the situation," particularly with respect to personnel. The plant had been opened less than a year ago and the management had spent the better part of its time recruiting and training employees. The superintendent believed that sufficient time had been spent in gearing up the plant and that it was now time to begin to expect that problems would be the exception, rather than the rule. He specifically was concerned with the high levels of downtime, scrappage, labor cost, and absenteeism.

The personnel manager argued for more patience. She stated that the new employees had not had sufficient time to develop the basis for understanding and relating to one another. "Nonsense," replied the plant manager. "We have organization charts, job descriptions, and policy manuals. There is no reason for the work to go undone or half done if the people are trained to do it. And they are trained because you trained them!"

The personnel manager could agree with most of the superintendent's comments. She had to agree that the employees were trained. But she went on to suggest that the existence of a formal structure does not assure that employees will behave in the correct manner. She persuaded the superintendent of the wisdom of using an employee opinion questionnaire to determine the extent to which employees understand the organization.

The opinion questionnaire was completed by all 600 employees, managers and nonmanagers alike, on company time. It included approximately 100 questions dealing with a variety of issues concerning the organization structure. The responses to the questionnaire were tabulated by the personnel manager's staff and a summary was prepared for discussion with the plant superintendent.

Some highlights of the summary are as follows:

1. Thirty-five percent of the nonmanagerial employees stated that they very often felt that there is day-to-day uncertainty concerning the goals of their job.
2. Twenty percent of the nonmanagerial employees stated that they often had difficulty getting necessary job-related information from their supervisors.
3. Twenty percent of the managerial personnel believed that there was seldom enough communication between their units and those with which they came in contact.
4. Forty percent of the nonmanagerial personnel believed that strict enforcement of rules and procedures usually prevented appropriate action.
5. Thirty percent of the managerial personnel believed that they seldom had authority commensurate with their responsibility.
6. Twenty percent of the managerial personnel believed that coordination was rarely achieved through planning.

The plant superintendent read the summary report and stated: "How is it possible for people to believe these ways? After all, we have all kinds of documents, procedures, and policies which define our organization structure. The only explanation that I can accept is that they simply haven't been told."

Questions for analysis:

1. What would be your response to the superintendent if you were the personnel manager?
2. Do you, as the personnel manager, believe that the evidence from the opinion survey warrants a critical analysis of the organization structure? Why?
3. How would the superintendent know that the organization structure of the plant is the best one?

PRACTICAL EXERCISE II
Reorganizing State Human Resources Agencies

The governor of a southeastern state had pledged during his campaign to reorganize state government. The purpose of the reorganization was to simplify the structure, eliminate overlapping functions, and, consequently, obtain more effective and efficient delivery of governmental services. The governor ran a successful race and was sworn into office.

Within a few weeks after taking office, the governor set in motion the process that would result in reorganization. One of the first areas to be reorganized was human resources. The state agencies which previously were concerned with a range of activities directed toward the health and welfare of people included the Departments of Health, Economic Security, Mental Health, Child Welfare, Handicapped Children, Veterans Affairs, and Aging. The combined budgets of these agencies totaled nearly $650 million and represented one half of the total state budget. By executive order, the governor placed all of these and other smaller agencies into a single unit, named the Department for Human Resources. The new organization was to be headed by a Secretary who was also named by the governor with the issuance of the executive order. He also named the commissioners of the five bureaus of the new department.

One of the first acts of the Secretary was to issue the following directive to the bureau commissioners:

> The executive order reorganized several formerly independent agencies into a Department for Human Resources. That executive order defined the new department as composed of the Bureaus for Health Services, Social Services, Manpower Services, Social Insurance, and Administration and Operations. The internal structure of each of these bureaus was not specified. The executive order only outlined the board function of these larger units and allocated various organizational entities from the former agencies to the respective bureaus. The executive order did not define the organizational structure inside these units to allow the commissioners to assist in the development of this organizational refinement. This paper outlines the steps, procedures, checkpoints, and expectations of the Secretary for Human Resources with regard to that organizational refinement.

TASK I. *Inventory of Present Situation* (Due September 24)

The executive order defined the broad purpose of the bureaus of the department and transferred organization subunits of the former agencies into the Department for Human Resources and placed them within the various bureaus. The Human Resources commissioners are directed to prepare an inventory of:

A. *Outline of Mission*

The executive order outlines the overall function of each bureau. Discussion between the secretary and each of the commissioners has amplified that definition of organizational purpose. Each commissioner should now commit to paper the purpose of his bureau as he now understands it, with specific reference to any issues on which there is still confusion and on which further discussion with the secretary is required.

B. *Organizational Resources*

Each commissioner should inventory the organizational units that have been transferred from the former Human Resources agencies to his bureau. The subunits of each of these organizational units, so transferred, should be identified. Each commissioner should identify any organizational units that were not transferred into his bureau that should have been to fulfill the *intent* of the executive order. Each commissioner should identify organizational units or subunits that were transferred into his bureau that should not have been so transferred in accordance with the *intent* of the executive order.

C. *Available Resources*

Each commissioner should present to the secretary a list of his field offices, personnel, and other nonmonetary resources that will affect the eventual development of refined organizational structures. Special note should be taken of personnel within the bureaus that have particularly high levels of competence and will have to be considered for appointment as division directors or other officials of major responsibility within each bureau.

TASK II. *Organization Principles and Alternative Structures* (Due October 8)

Following a discussion between the secretary and each commissioner on the Task I products, each commissioner should prepare the following:

A. *Mission Statement*

Each commissioner should prepare a proposed detailed mission statement for his bureau. These mission statements should reflect refinement in the statement of purpose resulting from discussions with the secretary. The secretary will review these documents to assure that responsibilities do not overlap and that the potential for confusion has been minimized. Upon adoption by the secretary, these mission statements will be the formal basis for subsequent policy and organizational refinement.

B. *Organizational Principles*

Each commissioner should prepare a statement of proposed organizational principles. These organizational principles will guide the development of the organizational structure in each bureau. The organizational principles should reflect the mission of each bureau rather than the overall responsibility of the Department for Human Resources.

C. *Alternative Structures*

Since any organizational structure may be subdivided according to four different rationales — programmatic functions, clientele, activity, and geography — there are four alternatives available for consideration at each level of an organizational hierarchy. The results or implications, both positive and negative, of each reasonable alternative should be presented for the consideration of the Secretary.

Note: Just as the department is functionally divided between program areas of income maintenance, health services, social services, and manpower services, each bureau may be further divided according to any of the four rationales we have defined. The organizational outline or alternatives presented by each commissioner should include all reasonable alternatives and should include them to all levels of organizational hierarchy for which there will be formal structure within each bureau.

Since the Department for Human Resources was designed to acquire and benefit from important programmatic and informational interaction across bureau lines, no recommendation should be presented until all alternatives for all bureaus have been reviewed in light of interbureau relationships. That is, the development of the internal organizational structure of a bureau is not a purely internal question, it is dependent upon the alternative chosen for the other bureaus. This particular factor will be most important in the Bureau for Administration and Operations which must be designed to reflect and support the organizational structure of all program bureaus.

TASK III. *Organizational Recommendations* (Due October 22)

After consideration of all alternatives presented on October 8, and after adequate discussion between the secretary and each of the commissioners individually, and the executive staff of the department collectively, a formal, detailed organizational recommendation will be prepared by each commissioner for submission to the secretary.

Questions for analysis:

1. Assume that you are a management consultant employed by the Secretary to assist him in the work of organizing the Department for Human Resources. As a consultant, what would you be looking for in the reports which each of the bureau commissioners would submit in response to the directive?

2. As a consultant, what would be your advice to the Secretary in his discussions with the commissioners regarding the missions of each bureau?

3. Again, as a management consultant, how would you advise the Secretary to proceed in the evaluation of the proposed alternative structures?

PRACTICAL EXERCISE III
The Reorganization of Donzi's Bakery

Only six months after graduating from the state university, Pete Donzi had to take over his father's bakery business because his dad passed away unexpectedly. Donzi's Bakery Corporation was started as a small store on the South Side of Chicago in 1961. By 1970 Joe Donzi, the owner, had bought eight other bakery stores, owned ten trucks which delivered bakery products to industrial plants throughout the city and the suburbs, and employed about 120 people.

Joe literally ran his business out of his back pocket. Pete had wanted his dad to become more systematic and businesslike in running the company. Pete had continually attempted to convince his dad that an organization chart was needed so that the authority and responsibility of each person in a crucial position were clarified. Joe argued that by not having a chart he was able to give the people assignments that had

EXHIBIT 1

Organization chart for Donzi's Bakery as of summer 1973

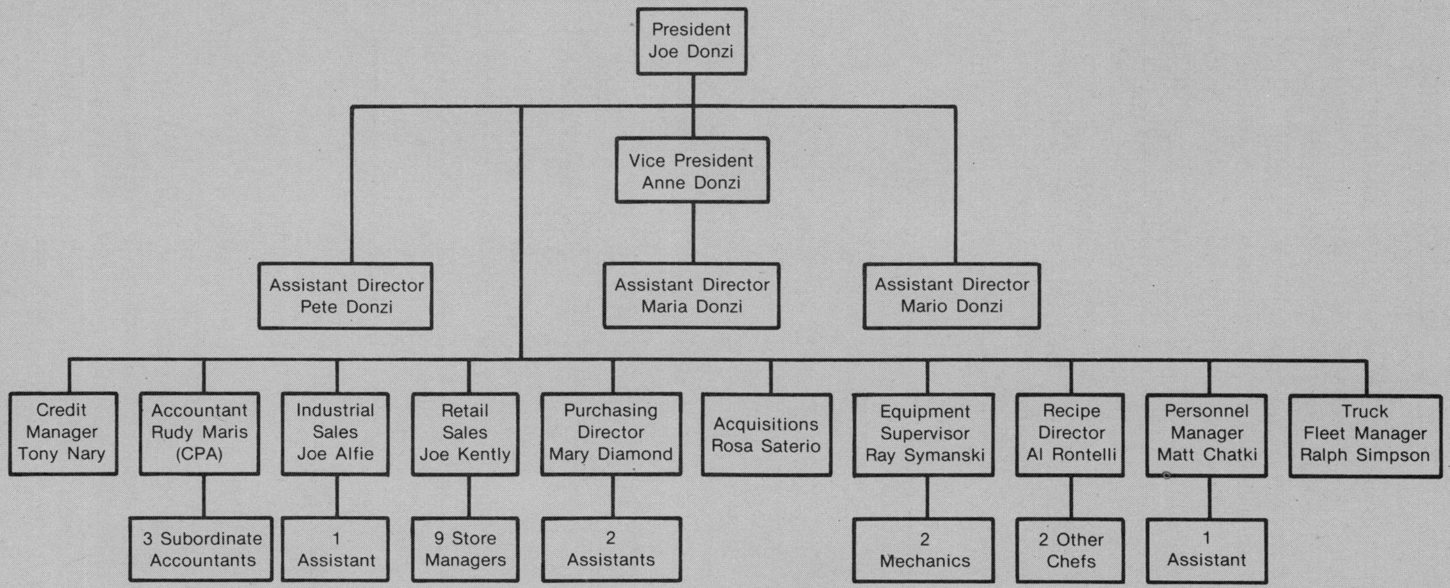

President
Joe Donzi

Vice President
Anne Donzi

Assistant Director
Pete Donzi

Assistant Director
Maria Donzi

Assistant Director
Mario Donzi

Credit
Manager
Tony Nary

Accountant
Rudy Maris
(CPA)

Industrial
Sales
Joe Alfie

Retail
Sales
Joe Kently

Purchasing
Director
Mary Diamond

Acquisitions
Rosa Saterio

Equipment
Supervisor
Ray Symanski

Recipe
Director
Al Rontelli

Personnel
Manager
Matt Chatki

Truck
Fleet Manager
Ralph Simpson

3 Subordinate
Accountants

1
Assistant

9 Store
Managers

2
Assistants

2
Mechanics

2 Other
Chefs

1
Assistant

to be accomplished on short notice. This flexibility is what Joe believed was a key to his success in the bakery business. A formal organization chart would restrict his style and not allow him to cope with changes in the environment and in the capabilities of his employees.

Despite his dad's resistance Pete, during his summer vacation in 1973, developed an organization chart. The chart is shown in Exhibit 1. The dominant and key person in the entire operation was Joe. He was the decision maker, problem solver, and disciplinarian in the company. Joe's wife, Anne, and his three children, Pete, Maria, and Mario, were given key positions in the company.

When Joe died the family had to decide what to do with the business. They all decided that Pete was the best qualified to succeed Joe as president. They also agreed to give Pete complete control of the organi-

EXHIBIT 2
Organization chart for Donzi's Bakery as of January 1975

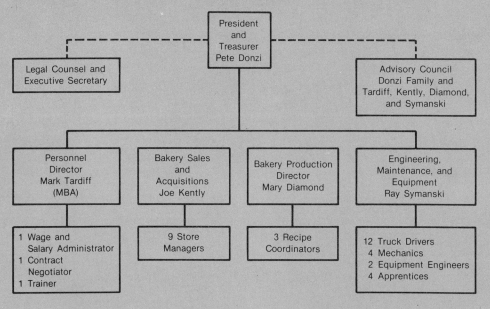

zation. This freedom would allow Pete to do whatever he thought was best for the organization.

One of the first jobs Pete undertook was to improve the organizational design of his company. He examined closely the organization chart which he had constructed in the summer of 1973. He found that his span of control as president, if he followed this design, would be 13. This he felt was too large and would not enable him to operate as a president should. It was his belief that a president should delegate authority, and should be involved in providing guidance and overall direction to the company. He certainly did not want to abdicate his decision-making responsibility, but he wanted to develop some key subordinates. Pete assumed that he would need competent subordinates to take advantage of growth opportunities in the next ten years.

The organizational design Pete established after taking over the business is shown in Exhibit 2. He believed that his new organizational design was contingency oriented in that it faced the realities of the bakery industry. That is, it placed the most knowledgeable and promising people in four, key, line positions; it reduced his span of control; it increased the administrative distance between the president and the line-operating employees; and it removed family members from line positions that he felt irritated almost everyone in the company. Of course, Pete felt that his family would be hurt by his reorganization, and he began to prepare an explanation of why this was the way the business had to be operated.

Questions for analysis:

1. Compare and contrast the two organization charts—Exhibits 1 and 2.
   a. Is there a reduction in the president's span of control in Exhibit 2? Explain.
   b. Is Pete correct in his assumptions about administrative distance?
   c. What kind of positions would the family assume under the Exhibit 2 arrangement?
   d. Why might some of the family members be hurt by Pete's reorganization?
2. Is the organizational design of Exhibit 1 taller than that reflected in Exhibit 2? Why?
3. What behavioral problems could a recent college graduate expect in introducing a specific organizational design change like the one illustrated in this case?

6

THE CONTROLLING FUNCTION

pulls them to pieces for a much more thorough inspection. The contents and the packaging are closely examined for defects. The seriousness of the defects are assessed on a 100-point scale. The more serious problems receive 100 demerits, while a relatively minor defect will score between 10 and 1. Items examined are returned to the production department to be fixed, reassembled, or repackaged.

"The department is so effective that Western Electric's customers (most of whom are members of the Bell Telephone System) do not examine the company's products before accepting delivery, thus eliminating the need to hire some 10,000 additional employees. The quality assurance specialists are also able to identify design and engineering problems that can easily be missed by a quality control inspector."

* Source: American Management Association, *Management in Practice* (November/December 1975), p. 1.

The third distinct function comprising the management process as identified and analyzed in classical theory is that of controlling.[1] This function includes *all activities which the manager undertakes in attempting to assure that actual operations conform to planned operations.* We can see that control was the emphasis of scientific management. The development of standard methods was the result of concerted efforts by Taylor, the Gilbreths, and others to implement managerial control. They recommended a complete separation of duties between workers and managers, with workers executing tasks in consistent and uniform ways as defined by management.

The control function was discussed in considerable detail by Urwick, who synthesized the previous work of Fayol, Mooney, and Taylor to arrive at a framework for analyzing the controlling function. According to Urwick, the desired effect of managerial control is a *stable* work force which pursues its prescribed (planned) activities with a spirit of *initiative* and a *sense of unity.* The means to these ends include staffing the firm with competent managers, and selection and placement of qualified workers, augmented by the use of rewards and sanctions. The classicists emphasized impersonal means for control, but they stressed that the competence of managers crucially determines the outcome of control efforts.

---

[1] William G. Ouchi, "The Relationship Between Organization Structure and Organizational Control," *Administration Science Quarterly* (March 1977), pp. 95–113, reestablishes the uniqueness of the control function as distinct from the organizing function.

The plan of this chapter is to present the controlling function in terms of three primary topics. First, we will describe the conditions which must be present in order to realize the objectives of the controlling function. In a simplistic sense, managerial control is effective when standards can be established for the variables that are to be controlled, when information is available to measure the established standards, and when managers can take corrective action whenever the actual state of the variable deviates from its desired, or standard, state. Second, we will provide a basis for classifying and understanding managerial control procedures. This classification scheme is then used to discuss the third topic: managerial control procedures. Contemporary management practice utilizes a number of different procedures which derive from the ideas of the Classical School and it is these *practical* applications which receive our most extended attention.

Necessary conditions for control

The implementation of control requires three basic conditions: (1) *Standards must be established,* (2) *information* which indicates deviations between actual and standard results must be available, and (3) *action* to bring about correction of any deviations between actual and standard must be possible. The logic is evident: Without standards, there can be no basis for evaluating the effectiveness of actual performance; without information there can be no way of knowing the situation; without provision for action to correct deviations, the entire control process becomes a pointless exercise.

Standards are derived from goals and have many of the characteristics of goals. Like goals, they are targets; to be effective, they must be clearly stated and logically related to the larger goals of the unit. Standards are the criteria against which future, current, or past actions are compared. They are measured in a variety of ways, including physical, monetary, quantitative, and qualitative terms. The various forms which standards can take will be made clear in subsequent discussions of control methods.

Information which reports actual performance and which permits appraisal of the performance against standards must be provided. Such information is most easily acquired for activities which produce specific and concrete results; for example, production and sales activities have end products which are easily identifiable and for which information is readily obtainable. The performance of legal departments, research-and-development units, and personnel departments is quite difficult to appraise because the outcomes of such activities are difficult to measure.

Managerial actions to correct deviations are stimulated by the discovery of the need for action and from the ability to implement the desired action. People responsible for taking the corrective steps must know that they are indeed responsible and that they have the assigned authority to take the action. Unless the job and position descriptions include specific statements which clearly delineate these two requirements, the control function will surely fall short of its objective.

The control function, then, involves the implementation of methods which provide answers to three basic questions, namely: What are the planned and expected results? By what means can the actual results be compared to planned results? What corrective action is appropriate from which authorized person? Let us go on to describe more specifically the relationship between controlling, planning, and organizing by identifying three major types of control.

Three types of control[2]

The control function can be broken down into three types on the basis of the focus of control activity. Figure 6–1 describes the three types.

FIGURE 6–1
The controlling function

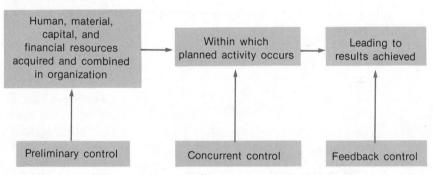

Preliminary control focuses on the problem of preventing deviations in the quality and quantity of resources used in the organization. Human resources must meet the job requirements as defined by the organization structure; employees must have the capability, whether physical or intellectual, to perform the assigned tasks. The materials must meet acceptable levels of quality and must be avail-

---

[2] In this section we identify *feedback* control as a separate type. Many students will recognize that feedback can also be viewed as part of the broader concept of control where it refers to the information which reports results to the manager.

able at the proper time and place. In addition, capital must be on hand to assure the adequate supply of plant and equipment. Finally, financial resources must be available in the right amounts and at the right times. Methods exist which enable management to implement preliminary control. Some of these are described in this chapter.

Concurrent control monitors actual ongoing operations to assure that objectives are pursued. The principal means by which concurrent control is implemented are the directing or supervisory activities of managers. Through personal, on-the-spot observation, managers determine whether the work of others is proceeding in the manner defined by policies and procedures. The delegation of authority provides managers with the power to use financial and nonfinancial incentives to affect concurrent control. The standards guiding ongoing activity are derived from job descriptions and from policies which result from the planning function.

FIGURE 6–2
A simple feedback control system

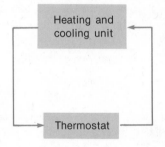

Feedback control methods focus on end-results. The corrective action, if taken, is directed at improving either the resource acquisition process or the actual operations. This type of control derives its name from the fact that historical results guide future actions. An illustration of feedback control is a thermostat, which automatically regulates the temperature of a room by constantly measuring actual temperature and comparing it with the desired temperature. Figure 6–2 shows feedback control applied to the temperature example. Since the thermostat maintains the preset temperature (goal) by constantly monitoring the actual temperature, future results (temperature) are directly and continually determined by actual results (again, temperature). The feedback methods employed in business include budgets, standard costs, financial statements, and quality control.

At this point, the three types of control can be described and distinguished by examining the focus of corrective action. As shown in Figure 6–3, preliminary control methods are based upon information

FIGURE 6–3
The three types of control as distinguished by focus of corrective action

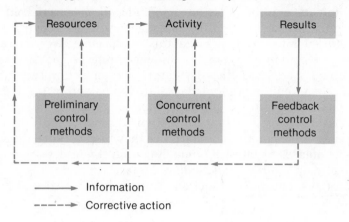

which measures some attribute or characteristic of resources; the focus of corrective action is directed, in turn, at the resources. That is, the variable measured is the variable acted upon. Similarly, concurrent control methods are based upon information related to activity, and it is activity that is acted upon. However, the focus of corrective action associated with feedback control is not that which is measured—results. Rather, resources and activity are acted upon.

The distinction between preliminary, concurrent, and feedback enables us to classify certain of the more widely used control techniques as shown in Table 6–1. The ten techniques are presented in the remainder of this chapter and our emphasis will be on standards, information, and corrective action as appropriate for each technique.

TABLE 6–1
Control types and techniques

Types of control	Control techniques
Preliminary control	Selection and placement Staffing Materials inspection Capital budgeting Financial budgeting
Concurrent control	Direction
Feedback control	Financial statement analysis Standard cost analysis Quality control procedures Employee performance evaluation

Preliminary control

Preliminary control procedures include all managerial efforts to increase the probability that future actual results will compare favorably with planned results. From this perspective, we can see that policies are important means for implementing preliminary control, since policies are guidelines for future action. Yet we want to distinguish between *setting* policies and *implementing* them. Setting policy is included in the planning function, whereas implementing policy is a part of the control function. Similarly, job descriptions are aspects of the control function since they predetermine the activity of the jobholder. At the same time, however, it is necessary to distinguish between *defining* and *staffing* the task structure. The former is a part of the organizing function, and the latter of the controlling function.

PRELIMINARY CONTROL OF HUMAN RESOURCES

The organizing function defines the job requirements and predetermines the skill requirements of the jobholders. These requirements vary in the degree of specificity depending upon the nature of the task. At the shop level the skill requirements can be specified in terms of physical attributes and manual dexterity. On the other hand, the job requirements of management and staff personnel are more difficult to define in terms of concrete measurements.

Preliminary control is effected through procedures which include the selection and placement of managerial and nonmanagerial personnel.[3] We should distinguish between those procedures which are designed to obtain qualified subordinate managers (staffing) and those which are designed to obtain qualified nonmanagers and operatives (selection and placement). The basic procedures and objectives are essentially the same; yet classical theory makes the distinction because of its emphasis upon managerial competence as the fundamental determiner of the organization's success.

The candidates for positions must be recruited from inside or outside the firm and the most promising applicant selected from the list of candidates. The selection decision is based upon the congruence of the applicant's skills, personal characteristics, and the job requirements. The successful candidate must be trained in methods and procedures appropriate for the job—a managerial responsibility that is

---

[3] This phase of preliminary control is an aspect of personnel management. See Leon C. Megginson, *Personnel: A Behavioral Science Approach to Administration* (Homewood, Ill.: Richard D. Irwin, Inc., 1972); Paul S. Greenlaw and Robert D. Smith, *Personnel Management* (Scranton, Pa.: International Textbook Co., 1970); John B. Miner and Mary G. Miner, *Personnel and Industrial Relations* (New York: The Macmillan Co., 1973).

clearly defined in classical theory by Taylor. Most modern organizations have elaborate procedures for providing training on a continual basis.

PRELIMINARY CONTROL OF MATERIALS

The raw material which is converted into the finished product must conform to standards of quality. At the same time, a sufficient inventory must be maintained to insure a continuous flow to meet customer demands. The techniques of inventory control are discussed in a later chapter; at this point, we should only be concerned with the quality of incoming materials.

In recent years numerous methods have been devised which use statistical sampling to control the quality of materials by the inspection of samples rather than of the entire lot. These methods are less costly in terms of inspection time, but there is the risk of accepting defective material if the sample does not happen to contain any of the defectives.

A complete discussion of statistical sampling is beyond the scope of this text, but the essence of the procedure can be explained easily.[4] Suppose, for example, that management sets a standard 3 percent level of defective items as the maximum that it will accept from the supplier. The material is then inspected by selecting a random sample and calculating the percentage of defective items in that sample. The decision that must then be made, based on the sample, is whether to accept or reject the entire order, or to take another sample. Errors can be made in sampling so that a lot is accepted when in fact it contains more than 3 percent defectives, or a lot is rejected when in fact it contains less than 3 percent defectives. The control system will be constructed based upon a careful balancing of the relative costs of these two types of errors.

The characteristics of materials preliminary control are illustrative of control systems which are quite routine. The decision to accept or reject materials recurs frequently and must be made on a fairly routine basis. The standard is easily measured and information (the sample) is readily available. The decision to accept or reject (or take another sample) is based upon straightforward instructions; given the sample results, the decision is automatic. The inspector's instructions may read: "If sample defectives are equal to or less than 3 percent, accept the lot; if sample defectives are equal to or more than 5 percent, reject the lot; if sample defectives are between 3 and 5 percent, take another

---

[4] See Lloyd A. Knowler, *Quality Control by Statistical Methods* (New York: McGraw-Hill Book Co., 1969); Eugene L. Grant, *Statistical Quality Control* (New York: McGraw-Hill Book Co., 1952); Acheson J. Duncan, *Quality Control and Industrial Statistics* (Homewood, Ill.: Richard D. Irwin, Inc., 1959).

sample." If a second sample is required, the inspector's actions will be determined by another set of instructions.

PRELIMINARY CONTROL OF CAPITAL

The acquisition of capital reflects the need to replace existing equipment or to expand the firm's productive capacity. Capital acquisitions are controlled by establishing criteria of potential profitability which must be met before the proposal is authorized. Such acquisitions are ordinarily included in the *capital budget,* which is an intermediate and long-run planning document that details the alternative sources and uses of funds. The decisions to be made by the manager, which involve the commitment of present funds in exchange for future funds, are termed *investment decisions;* and the methods which serve to screen investment proposals derive from economic analysis.[5] In this section a number of methods in widespread practice will be discussed. Each of these methods involves the formulation of a standard which must be met in order to accept the prospective capital acquisition.

The payback method. The simplest and apparently most widely used method is the payback method. This approach calculates the number of years needed for the proposed capital acquisition to repay its original cost out of future cash earnings. For example, a manager is considering a machine which will reduce labor costs by $4,000 per year for each of the four years of its estimated life. The cost of the machine is $8,000 and the tax rate is 50 percent. The additional after-tax cash inflow from which the machine cost must be paid is calculated as follows:

Additional cash inflow before taxes (labor cost savings)		$4,000
Less additional taxes:		
Additional income	$4,000	
Less depreciation ($8,000 ÷ 4)	2,000	
Additional taxable income	$2,000	
Tax rate	.5	
Additional tax payment		1,000
Additional cash inflow after taxes		$3,000

---

[5] The analysis of investment opportunities is a highly developed topic in financial management. See Adolph E. Grunewald and Erwin E. Nemmers, *Basic Managerial Finance* (New York: Holt, Rinehart, and Winston, 1970); Curtis W. Symonds, *Basic Financial Management* (New York: American Management Association, 1969); Harold Bierman and Seymour Smidt, *The Capital Budgeting Decision* (New York: The Macmillan Co., 1972); William R. Park, *Cost Engineering Analysis* (New York: John Wiley & Sons, Inc., 1973); Arnold C. Harberger, *Project Evaluation* (Chicago: Markham Publishing Co., 1973).

After additional taxes are deducted from the labor savings, the payback period can be calculated as follows:

$$\frac{\$8,000}{\$3,000} = 2.67 \text{ years.}$$

The proposed machine will repay its original cost in two and two thirds years; if the standard requires a payback of at most three years, the machine would be deemed an appropriate investment.

The payback method suffers many limitations as a standard for evaluating capital resources. It does not produce a measurement of profitability and, more importantly, it does not take into account the time value of money, that is, it does not recognize that a dollar today is worth more than a dollar at a future date. Other methods can be employed which include these important considerations.

Rate of return on investment. One alternative which produces a measure of profitability and which is consistent with methods ordinarily employed in accounting is the simple rate of return. Using the above example, the calculation would be as follows:

Additional gross income..		$4,000
Less depreciation ($8,000 ÷ 4)...	$2,000	
Less taxes...	1,000	
Total additional expenses...		3,000
Additional net income after taxes...................................		$1,000

The rate of return is the ratio of additional net income to the original cost:

$$\frac{\$1,000}{\$8,000} = 12.5\%.$$

The calculated rate of return would then be compared to some standard of minimum acceptability, and the decision to accept or reject would depend upon that comparison.

The measurement of the simple rate of return has the advantage of being easily understood. It has the disadvantage, however, of not including the time value of money. The discounted rate of return method overcomes this deficiency.

Discounted rate of return. A measurement of profitability which can be used as a standard for screening potential capital acquisitions, and which takes into account the time value of money, is the discounted rate of return. This method is similar to the payback method, in that only cash inflows and outflows are considered. The method is

widely used because it is considered the "correct" method for calculating the rate of return.[6] It proceeds as follows, based upon the above
example:

$$\$8,000 = \frac{\$3,000}{(1+r)} + \frac{\$3,000}{(1+r)^2} + \frac{\$3,000}{(1+r)^3} + \frac{\$3,000}{(1+r)^4};$$
$$r = 18\%.$$

The discounted rate of return (r) is 18 percent, which is interpreted to
mean that an $8,000 investment which repays $3,000 in cash at the
end of each of four years yields a return of 18 percent.

The rationale of the method can be understood by thinking of $3,000
inflows as cash payments received by the firm. In exchange for each of
these four payments of $3,000, the firm must pay $8,000. The rate of
return, 18 percent is the factor which equates future cash inflows and
present cash outflow.[7]

PRELIMINARY CONTROL OF FINANCIAL RESOURCES

An adequate supply of financial resources must be available to
assure the payment of current obligations arising from current operations. Materials must be purchased, wages paid, interest charges and
due dates met. The principal means of controlling the availability and
cost of financial resources is budgeting—particularly cash and working
capital budgets.[8]

These budgets anticipate the ebb and flow of business activity when
materials are purchased, finished goods are produced and inventoried,
goods are sold, and cash received. This cycle of activity, the operating
cycle, results in a problem of *timing* the availability of cash to meet

---

[6] Eugene F. Brigham, "Hurdle Rates for Screening Capital Expenditure Programs,"
Financial Management (Fall 1976), pp. 17–26.

[7] The time value of money is explicitly considered in the method in the following
way: If we remember that 18 percent is the rate of return and that there are four distinct
and separate future receipts of $3,000, we can see that $8,000 is the *present value* of the
future proceeds.

$2,542 = present value of $3,000 to be received in 1 year
     or $2,542 × (1.18) = $3,000
2,155 = present value of $3,000 to be received in 2 years
     or $2,155 × (1.18)² = $3,000
1,826 = present value of $3,000 to be received in 3 years
     or $1,826 × (1.18)³ = $3,000
1,547 = present value of $3,000 to be received in 4 years
     or $1,547 × (1.18)⁴ = $3,000
$8,070 = Total present value, error due to rounding.

[8] Yair E. Ogler, *Cash Management* (Belmont, Calif.: Wadsworth Publishing Co., Inc.,
1969); William J. Vatter, *Operating Budgets* (Belmont, Calif.: Wadsworth Publishing
Co., Inc., 1969); Colin Park and John W. Gladson, *Working Capital* (New York: The
Macmillan Co., 1963); Walter Rautenstrauch and Raymond Villers, *Budgetary Control*
(New York: Funk and Wagnalls, 1968).

the obligations. The simple relationship between cash and inventory is shown in Figure 6–4. As inventories of finished goods increase, the supply of cash decreases while materials, labor, and other expenses are incurred and paid. As inventory is depleted through sales, cash increases. Preliminary control of cash requires that cash be available during the period of inventory buildup and be used wisely during periods of abundance. This requires the careful consideration of alternative sources of short-term financing during inventory buildup and of alternative short-run investment opportunities during periods of inventory depletion.

To aid in the process, attention is given by managers to certain financial ratios. For example, the standard may be in terms of the current ratio (the ratio of current assets to current liabilities) and a minimum and a maximum are set. The minimum ratio could be set at 2:1 and the maximum at 3:1, a practice which recognizes the cost of both too little and too much investment in liquid assets.[9] The control would be in terms of corrective action when the actual current

FIGURE 6–4

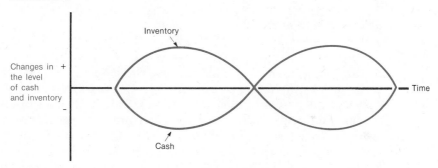

ratio deviates from the standard. Other financial ratios which contribute to control of financial resources include the acid test ratio, inventory turnover, and average collection period. These ratios are discussed in greater detail in the section on feedback control methods.

Concurrent control

Concurrent control consists primarily of actions of supervisors who *direct* the work of their subordinates. *Direction* refers to the acts of managers which they undertake (1) to instruct subordinates in the

---

[9] H. Stephen Grace, Jr., and M. K. Rajaraman, "Cash Management: An Optimal Control Approach," *Journal of Economics and Business* (Spring 1975), pp. 254–60.

proper methods and procedures and (2) to oversee their work to assure that the work is done properly.

Direction follows the formal chain of command since the responsibility of each superior is to interpret for subordinates the orders received from higher echelons. The relative importance of direction depends almost entirely upon the nature of the tasks which are performed by subordinates. The foreman of an assembly line which produces a component part requiring relatively simple manual operations may seldom engage in direction. On the other hand, the manager of a research-and-development unit must devote considerable time to direction. Research work is inherently more complex and varied than manual work, thus requiring more interpretation and instruction.

Directing is the primary activity of the first-line supervisor, but every manager in an organization engages at some time in directing employees.[10] Directing employees is guided by the stated goals and policies of the organization as reflected in the planning function. It is apparent that as a manager moves up the hierarchy the relative importance of directing diminishes as other functions become relatively more important. For example, the chief executive officer will devote considerably more time to the planning and organizing functions and subfunctions.

The scope and content of the direction phase varies, depending upon the nature of work being supervised, as noted above. We can also distinguish a number of other factors which determine differences in the form of direction. For example, if we recognize that direction is basically the process of personal communication, then we can see that the amount and clarity of information are important factors. Subordinates must receive sufficient information to carry out the task and must understand the information that they receive. On the other hand, too much information and too much detail can be damaging. We should also recognize that the manager's mode and tone of expression greatly influence the effectiveness of direction.

The tests of effective direction are related to the characteristics of effective communication. To be effective, a directive must be reasonable, intelligible, and appropriately worded, and consistent with the overall goals of the organization.[11] Whether these criteria are met is not the manager's decision to make, rather it is the subordinate who decides. Many managers have assumed that their directives were straightforward and to the point, only to discover that their subordinates failed to understand or to accept them as legitimate.

The process of direction includes not only the manner in which directives are communicated, but also the mannerisms of the person who directs. This understanding was recognized by an early writer

[10] Theo Haiman and Raymond E. Hilgert, *Supervision Concepts and Practices of Management* (Cincinnati: South-Western Publishing Co., 1972), p. 287.

[11] Ibid., pp. 289–92.

in the field of management who noted that direction "involves face-to-face leadership."[12] Whether the supervisor is autocratic or democratic, permissive or directive, considerate or inconsiderate has implications for the effectiveness of direction as a concurrent control technique. But this understanding cannot be fully developed here; a later chapter delves deeply into leadership behavior as related to performance of individuals and groups. It is apparent, however, that the expected supervisory behavior must be compatible with the manager's style.[13]

At this point we simply must establish that direction involves day-to-day overseeing the work of subordinates. As deviations from standards are identified, managers take immediate corrective action through demonstrating and coaching their subordinates to perform their assigned tasks appropriately.

Feedback control

The distinguishing feature of feedback control methods is focusing attention upon *historical* outcomes as the bases for correcting *future* actions. For example, the financial statements of a firm are used to evaluate the acceptability of historical results and to determine the desirability of making changes in future resource acquisitions or operational activities. In this section we outline four feedback control methods which are widely used in business; they are: financial statement analysis, standard cost analysis, quality control, and employee performance evaluation. Our objective is to demonstrate the general features of feedback control techniques through these four examples.

FINANCIAL STATEMENT ANALYSIS

A principal source of information from which managers can evaluate historical results is the firm's accounting system. Periodically, the manager receives a set of financial statements which usually includes a balance sheet, an income statement, and a sources and uses of funds statement. These statements summarize and classify the effects of transactions in terms of assets, liabilities, equity, revenues, and expenses—the principal components of the firm's financial structure.[14]

---

[12] Ralph C. Davis, *The Fundamentals of Top Management* (New York: Harper and Brothers, 1951), p. 709.

[13] Cortlandt Cammann and David Nadler, "Fit Control Systems to Your Managerial Style," *Harvard Business Review* (January/February 1976), pp. 65–72.

[14] See John N. Meyer, *Financial Statement Analysis* (Englewood Cliffs, N.J.: Prentice-Hall, Inc., 1969); S. Winston Korn and Thomas Boyd, *Accounting for Management Planning and Decision Making* (New York: John Wiley and Sons, 1969); Leopold A. Bernstein, *Financial Statement Analysis* (Homewood, Ill.: Richard D. Irwin, Inc., 1974).

A detailed analysis of the information contained in the financial statements enables management to ascertain the adequacy of the firm's earning power and its ability to meet current and long-term obligations; that is, the manager must have measures of and standards for profitability, liquidity, and solvency. The various measures of profitability were discussed in Chapter 4. The planning discussion described the various profitability measures and presented arguments for each. Whether the manager prefers the rate of return on sales, on owner's equity, or on total assets, or a combination of all three, it is important to establish a meaningful norm — one that is appropriate to the particular firm, given its industry and stage of growth. An inadequate rate of return will negatively affect the firm's ability to attract funds for expansion, particularly if a downward trend over time is evident.

The measures of liquidity reflect the firm's ability to meet current obligations as they become due. The widest known and most often used measure is the ratio of current assets to current liabilities. The standard of acceptability depends upon the particular firm's own operating characteristics. Bases for comparison are available from trade associations which publish industry averages. A more rigorous test of liquidity is the acid test ratio, which relates only cash and near cash items (current assets excluding inventories and prepaid expenses) to current liabilities.

The relationship between current assets and current liabilities is an important determinate of liquidity. Equally important is the composition of current assets. Two measures which indicate composition and which rely upon information found in both the balance sheet and income statement are the accounts receivable turnover and the inventory turnover. The accounts receivable turnover is the ratio of credit sales to average accounts receivable. The higher the turnover, the more rapid is the conversion of accounts receivable to cash. A low turnover would indicate a time lag in the collection of receivables, which in turn could strain the firm's ability to meet its own obligations. The appropriate corrective action might be a tightening of credit standards or a more vigorous effort to collect outstanding accounts. The inventory turnover also facilitates the analysis of appropriate balances in current assets. It is calculated as the ratio of cost of goods sold to average inventory. A high ratio could indicate a dangerously low inventory balance in relation to sales with the possibility of missed sales or production slowdowns; conversely, a low ratio might indicate an over-investment in inventory to the exclusion of other, more profitable, assets. Whatever the case, the appropriate ratio must be established by the manager based upon the firm's experience within its industry and market.

Another financial measure is solvency, the ability of the firm to meet its long-term obligations—its fixed commitments. The solvency measure relates the claims of creditors and owners on the assets of the firm. An appropriate balance must be maintained—a balance which protects the interests of the owners, yet does not ignore the advantages of long-term debt as a source of funds. A commonly used measure of solvency is the *ratio of net income before interest and taxes to interest expense.* This indicates the margin of safety and, ordinarily, a high ratio is preferred. However, a very high ratio combined with a low *debt-to-equity ratio* could indicate that management has not taken advantage of debt as a source of funds. The appropriate balance between debt and equity depends upon a great number of factors; and the issue is an important topic in financial management. But, as a general rule, one can say that the proportion of debt should vary directly with the stability of the firm's earnings.

The ratios discussed above are only suggestive of the great number and variety of methods used to evaluate the financial results of the firm. Accounting as a tool of analysis in business management has a long history predating scientific management.[15] Our point here is that financial statement analysis as a part of the management process is clearly a feedback control method.

STANDARD COST ANALYSIS

Standard cost accounting systems date from and are considered a major contribution of the scientific management era. A standard cost system provides information that enables management to compare actual costs with predetermined (standard) costs. Management can then take appropriate corrective action or assign the authority to take action to others. The first use of standard costing was affecting control over manufacturing costs; but, in recent years, standard costing has been applied to selling, general, and administrative expenses. Here we discuss standard manufacturing costs.

The three elements of manufacturing costs are direct labor, direct materials, and overhead. For each of these, an estimate must be made of the element's cost per unit of output. For example, the direct labor cost per unit of output consists of the standard usage of labor and the standard price of labor. The standard usage derives from time studies which fix the expected output per man-hour; the standard price of labor will be fixed by the salary schedule appropriate for the kind of work necessary to produce the output. A similar determination is

---

[15] A. C. Littleton, *Accounting Evolution to 1900* (New York: Russell and Russell, 1966).

made for direct materials. Thus, the standard labor and standard materials costs might be as follows:

Standard labor usage per unit..	2 hours
Standard wage rate per hour	$3.00
Standard labor cost (2 × $3.00)...	$6.00
Standard material usage per unit	6 pounds
Standard material price per pound...	$ .30
Standard material cost (6 × $.30)	$1.80

The accounting system produces information which enables the manager to compare incurred costs and standard costs. For example, if during the period covered by the report, 200 units of output were produced, the standard labor cost is $1,200 (200 × $6.00) and the standard material cost is $360 (200 × $1.80). Assume that the actual payroll cost for that same time period was $1,500 and the actual material cost was $400. That is, there was an *unfavorable labor variance* of $300 and an *unfavorable material variance* of $40. Management must determine the reasons for the variances and decide what corrective action is appropriate.

Assuming that the standards are correct, the manager must analyze the variance and fix the responsibility for restoring the balance between standard and actual costs. It is obvious that if actual labor cost exceeds standard cost, the reason for the difference is found in labor usage and labor wage rates. Either actual labor usage exceeded standard labor usage or actual wage rates exceeded standard wage rates, or some combination of both. Suppose that, in this example, the accountant reports the actual payroll consisted of 450 actual hours at an average wage rate of $3.33. The questions management must resolve are now narrowed to two: What happened during the period to cause output per man-hour to go down (to produce 200 units of output should require 400 labor hours); and why was the average wage rate more than the standard wage rate. The answers to these questions are found in the resources and activity stages of the cycle (see Figure 6–3).

Similar analyses are made to discover the causes for the unfavorable material variance. The first step is discovering the relationships between actual and standard usage and between actual and standard price. As with the labor, the manager may find actual material usage exceeded that specified by standard; and/or the manager may find the actual price exceeds the standard price. Once the cause is isolated, the analysis must proceed to fix responsibility for corrective action.

The analysis of manufacturing overhead variances is considerably more complicated than that for labor and material. A complete discussion would carry us far afield.[16] Suffice to say that it is necessary to isolate the causes through comparisons with standards and budgets.

QUALITY CONTROL ANALYSIS

Quality control uses information regarding attributes and characteristics of output to ascertain whether the manufacturing process is "in control," that is, producing acceptable output. To make this determination, the manager must specify the product characteristic that is considered critical. This may be weight, length, consistency, or defects. Once the characteristic is defined, it must be measured.

For an example, consider one problem of a manufacturer of peanut butter: maintaining a minimum quantity of peanut butter in each container, say, 12 ounces. One approach would be to weigh each container when it is filled—that is, 100 percent of the output could be inspected. An alternative is to inspect samples of output to make inferences about the process based upon the sample information. This latter approach is termed *statistical quality control.* This method makes use of statistical sampling theory, and since the amount of time devoted to inspection is reduced, the cost of inspection is also reduced.

EMPLOYEE PERFORMANCE EVALUATION

No doubt the most important and difficult feedback control technique is performance evaluation. It is important because the most crucial resource in any organization are the people. As so often said, "People make the difference." Effective business firms, hospitals, universities, and governments are staffed by people effectively discharging their assigned duties. Evaluation is difficult because the standards for performance are seldom objective and straightforward; many managerial and nonmanagerial jobs do not produce outputs which can be counted, weighed, and evaluated in objective terms.

Certain jobs, particularly those analyzed by the scientific management writers, produce physical units of output. Assembly line workers, manual laborers, and clerical workers, for example, produce outputs which can be evaluated in terms of acceptable quantity and quality. But in many instances the work of individuals is not so well-defined. Consequently a considerable part of the evaluation process is based

---

[16] The reader can consult any text in cost accounting and managerial accounting for discussions of standard cost analysis. For example, see: Charles T. Horngren, *Accounting for Management Control* (Englewood Cliffs, N.J.: Prentice-Hall, Inc., 1974); Gerald Crowningshield and Kenneth Gorman, *Cost Accounting* (Boston: Houghton Mifflin, 1974); Nicholas Dopuch, Jacob G. Birnberg, and Joel Demski, *Cost Accounting* (New York: Harcourt, Brace, Jovanovich, Inc., 1974).

almost exclusively on the judgment of the evaluators, usually managers or a management team.[17]

A second complicating factor is that most jobs must be evaluated in terms of more than one standard, or criterion. Thus, even in a simple case, a worker may produce an acceptable quantity of output but of unacceptable quality. College professors in major universities are expected to perform in at least three areas: teaching, research, and public service. Moreover, not only will individuals perform at different levels of acceptability across each criterion, but their performance will vary through time.[18] Thus an employee, whether a blue collar worker or a college professor, may perform one job aspect effectively, but not other aspects. That same individual's performance will also change, for better or worse, over time. It is no surprise that personnel evaluation is often the most difficult control mechanism to develop and implement.

Finally it must be recognized that employees react to performance evaluation in different ways. The primary purpose of performance evaluation is to improve job performance.[19] But the opposite can occur if employees do not believe the process to be fair and equitable and related to their job performance. If employees believe that their evaluations reflect managers' biased personal opinions, they are apt to respond in a variety of behaviors that result in negative job performance. Such behaviors would include excessive absenteeism, tardiness, restricting of output, and even sabotage of plant, equipment, and products. That is, unlike physical resources, human resources react to the process of control itself. Each of us has experienced this phenomenon at some time. If you are a student, you can certainly recall instances when your reaction to an examination that you considered unfair caused you to lose interest in the course, or even to stop going to class.

Managers have no responsibility that is more important and difficult than that of evaluating subordinates. The importance of this responsibility has produced many thoughtful discussions of alternative evaluation methods.[20] Although the specifics of each method vary, the general features are the same: performance standards must be established for each job, information which measures the extent to

---

[17] Alan L. Patz, "Performance Appraisal: Useful But Still Resisted," *Harvard Business Review* (May/June 1975), pp. 74–80, reviews appraisal methods for jobs which are intrinsically subjective in nature.

[18] Abraham Korman, *Organizational Behavior* (Englewood Cliffs, N.J.: Prentice-Hall, Inc., 1977), p. 352.

[19] Richard M. Steers, *Organizational Effectiveness* (Santa Monica, Calif.: Goodyear Publishing Co., 1977), p. 146.

[20] See L. L. Cummings and Donald P. Schwab *Performance in Organizations: Determinants and Appraisal* (Glenview, Ill.: Scott, Foresman and Co., 1973) for a definitive source.

which these standards are achieved must be acquired, and corrective action must be undertaken.

In an ideal sense performance standards should derive from the planning function wherein the goals of the organization are specified. The standards should reflect the contribution that each employee is to make to achieve the organizational goals. The information must be provided by the organizing function; such information would flow to the appropriate manager in a timely manner. Directing, the principal concurrent control technique, is the major source of information for evaluating employee performance; a prime managerial responsibility is to acquire objective perceptions of subordinates' job performance. The corrective actions which are available include retraining or reassigning an employee to a different job. Alternatively it may involve changing the job to conform more nearly to the skills and abilities of the employee.

Finally, we must note that performance evaluation also involves rewarding employees for effective job performance. In many, but not all, organizations salary increases and promotions are based upon performance evaluation. Yet, as observed by recent wirters, the ability to reward for performance depends upon the organization's ability to measure the appropriate job behaviors.[21] Thus we return again to the point made in our discussion of the planning function (Chapter 4); without objective, measurable goals and derived performance standards, managers cannot know with assurance the extent to which the organization and its employees are achieving what it and they have set out to accomplish.

Summary of the controlling function

The controlling function consists of the development of techniques which bring about planned-for results. The discussion is conveniently summarized in Table 6–2. There the techniques are compared in terms of standards, information, and corrective action relevant for each one. The table also brings into focus the relationship between the planning function as a source of standards and the organizing function as a source of information. The overriding managerial responsibility is to integrate the three functions into a coherent management process which enables the organization to achieve the levels of performance expected by the elements of society which sustain it.

---

[21] Edward K. Lawler III and John G. Rhode, *Information and Control in Organizations* Pacific Palisades, Calif.: Goodyear Publishing Co., Inc., 1976), p. 34.

TABLE 6–2
Summary of the controlling function

Technique	Standards	Information	Corrective action
1. Job description	Job specifications – skills, experience, education bearing on job success	Test scores, credentials, background data	Hire/no hire; remedial training
2. Selection	Job specifications – skills, experience, education bearing on job success	Test scores, credentials, background data	Place/no place; remedial training
3. Materials inspection	Percent or number defective within tolerance limits	Sampling of inputs	Accept, reject; or retest
4. Capital budgeting	Simple rate of return; payback period; discounted rate of return	Projected cost, revenue, and engineering data over the life of the asset	Accept, reject
5. Financial budgeting	Requirements arising out of the forecasting step of planning	Projected cost, revenue, and engineering data over the planning period	Accept, reject; revise
6. Direction	Required job behavior in terms of end results	Plans and job specifications	Change plans and/or job specifications; train, fire people
7. Financial statement analysis	Relative data found in trade, banking, and rule-of-thumb sources	Balance sheet, income statement	Revise inputs; revise direction
8. Standard cost analysis	Standard times/usage from engineering studies	Cost accounting system	Revise inputs; revise direction
9. Quality control	Percent or number defective consistent with marketing strategy	Sampling procedures	Revise inputs; revise direction
10. Employee performance	Job-related performance criteria	Managerial observation; self-reports	Retrain, replace personnel; change assigned jobs

The classical school in perspective

This chapter concludes our discussion of the Classical School. In a very general sense, classical writers believed that the performance of business firms, governmental agencies, churches, military units — indeed, all instances of consciously organized group endeavor — could be improved through the application of fundamental management principles and techniques. These principles, or guidelines, were derived primarily from the writers' personal experiences as managers, but also from logical deduction. In retrospect, a major contribution of the classical writers was to popularize management as a field of scientific inquiry.

The analyses of Taylor, the Gilbreths, Fayol, Mooney, Urwick, and others produced a conceptual framework for analyzing and practicing the managerial process. That framework defines the managerial process as consisting of three functions—planning, organizing, and controlling. Whether these three functions completely describe management is more a matter of definition than conceptualization. For example, one might well argue that the managerial process consists of planning, organizing, staffing, directing, coordinating, reviewing, and controlling. It all depends upon the definitions of the concepts. We have chosen to present the classical interpretation of management in terms of only three major concepts; we believe that they are sufficient, can be understood, and adequately represent the classical framework. Moreover, as we have tried to show, the Classical Management School contributed much more than a lengthy list of functions which the aspiring manager could commit to memory.

Identifying the primary management functions as planning, organizing, and controlling does not end the discussion. Rather, it simply initiates further discussion about how managers do and should perform each function. Moreover, it is necessary to understand the interrelationships among and within the functions. At the highest level of abstraction, we know that the practice of management is a continual process of determining what should be done (planning), how it should be done (organizing), and whether it was done (controlling). Yet one should not infer that the process is as simple as the statement which described it. The discovery of the interrelationships between and among these three functions is the continuing challenge to students, teachers, and practitioners of management.

At this point in our discussion of management fundamentals, a foundation for meeting this challenge has been developed. What remains is to build on this foundation by considering the contributions of the Behavioral School and the Management Science School. It is reasonable to state that the classical writers did not take into account the potential contributions of these schools if, for no other reason, than that they had not been fully developed. The significant advances in psychology, sociology, anthropology, statistics, and mathematics have occurred in the past 60 years. We shall, in the remainder of this book review the impact of these advances on the study and practice of management.

Discussion and review questions

1. It is said by some management experts that the term "control" should not be used in the management literature: These experts argue that control implies some loss of freedom and individuality and that such im-

plications should be avoided. Do you agree with these experts, and what is your reasoning?

2. Illustrate the relationship between goals, policies, and standards in the context of an organization in which you are a member.

3. Why are preliminary and concurrent control procedures so widely used in universities, hospitals, governmental agencies, and other nonmarket institutions?

4. The term "cybernetics" was coined by modern system theorists such as Nobert Wiener. As an extra-classroom exercise, research this term and relate it to the chapter discussion of feedback control procedures.

5. Some management writers have argued the point that the creation of organization structures is basically a form of the controlling function and not a separate managerial function. What would be your response to this argument?

6. A number of standards have been discussed as measures of investment profitability. These measures include the payback period, the rate of return, and the discounted rate of return. If only one measure is "correct," why do others exist in management practice?

7. Financial managers state that financial ratios are similar to other statistical data in the way that they can be used, or misused, to prove a point. How can the nonfinancial expert, such as a plant superintendent, know whether his financial expert is misusing such ratios to press for his own point of view in an executive decision?

8. Under what circumstances would the use of feedback control procedures be inappropriate?

9. The concept of "responsibility accounting" has received much attention in the accounting literature. Research this concept in terms of its relationship to the chapter discussion of necessary conditions for effective managerial control.

10. "Performance evaluation would be a simple task if it weren't for the fact that people are involved." Comment on this statement.

11. Directing is a crucial aspect of control, and information received (the perceived performance of subordinates) and sent (orders and instructions) is a key element of directing. What abilities and traits do you believe are associated with effective directing?

Additional references

Chruden, H. J. *Personnel Management.* Cincinnati: South-Western Publishing Co., 1972.

Duncan, A. J. *Quality Control and Industrial Statistics.* Homewood, Ill.: Richard D. Irwin, Inc., 1965.

Emery, J. C. *Organizational Planning and Control Systems: Theory and Technology.* New York: Macmillan, 1969.

Gardner, F. V. *Profit Management and Control.* New York: McGraw-Hill Book Co., 1955.

Hamner, W. C., and Schmidt, F. L. *Contemporary Problems in Personnel.* Chicago: St. Clair Press, 1974.

Jerome, W. T. *Executive Control – The Catalyst.* New York: John Wiley and Sons, Inc., 1961.

King-Scott, P. *Industrial Supervision.* London: Sir Isaac Pitman and Sons, Ltd., 1969.

Koontz, H. *Appraising Managers as Managers.* New York: McGraw-Hill Book Co., 1971.

Lawler, E. E., III, and Rhode, J. G. *Information and Control in Organizations.* Pacific Palisades, Calif.: Goodyear Publishing Co., 1976.

Livy, B. *Job Evaluation: A Critical Review.* New York: Halsted Press, 1975.

Martindell, J. W. *The Appraisal of Management.* New York: Harper and Row, 1962.

Newman, W. H. *Constructive Control.* Englewood Cliffs, N.J.: Prentice-Hall, Inc., 1975.

Pigors, P., and Myers, C. A. *Personnel Administration.* New York: McGraw-Hill Book Co., 1973.

Rose, T. G. *Top Management Accounting.* London: Sir Isaac Pitman and Sons, Ltd., 1958.

Rose, T. G., and Farr, D. E. *Higher Management Control.* New York: McGraw-Hill Book Co., 1957.

Sartain, A. Q., and Baker, A. W. *The Supervisor and His Job.* New York: McGraw-Hill Book Co., 1972.

Terry, G. R. *Supervisory Management.* Homewood, Ill.: Richard D. Irwin, Inc., 1974.

PRACTICAL EXERCISE I
Evaluating Managerial Performance

Steven Patrick was anxiously awaiting the Monday morning staff meeting to begin. He had only recently been promoted to corporate Director of Personnel and today he would present an idea to the rest of the corporate staff. This morning would be the first time that he had initiated a new idea. In the past six months since Steven took the new job and began attending the meeting, he had remained silent except when responding to a direct question from one of the other corporate-level managers.

The staff meeting convened and its chairperson, the Executive Vice-President, called upon Steven to present his idea. "As you know," said Steven, "the Personnel Division has the responsibility for developing procedures to evaluate the performance of line managers throughout the company. We view this responsibility in terms of the larger issue of developing the skills and abilities of line managers. Historically this company has relied upon the evaluation by superiors but I would like to suggest that the real source of information about how managers perform is their subordinates. As a company, we have not attempted to obtain information from the people who report to each manager. Many companies, including some of our competitors, attempt to obtain information from subordinates.

"I am proposing that we consider a procedure for obtaining information that will enable us to know the strengths and weaknesses of each manager as viewed by those who report to him or her. The procedure is relatively simple: Each manager will meet with his people. A trainer from the Personnel Division will also be present at this initial meeting. The manager must assure his people that the purpose of the meeting is to obtain their cooperation in a process which will help him become a better manager. Any subordinate must feel free to refuse to take part in the process.

"Once the manager has met and explained what is going on, one of my trainers will meet with each subordinate who has agreed to participate and have the subordinate complete a questionnaire. The

152

specific questions to be included in the questionnaire will relate to the manager's performance of assigned activities, including his or her manner of dealing with people. Each subordinate will rate the manager on each activity on a numerical scale, and explain to the trainer the basis for the rating. To protect the subordinates from any real or imagined threat for participating, the responses will remain anonymous when reported to the manager. Only the trainer will know the source of any comments.

"After the trainers have obtained information from the subordinates, they will meet with each manager. The managers will be given all of the information and they will discuss it with the trainer. The purpose of this session and others to follow is to prepare a plan which will enable each manager to take corrective action. The corrective action can range from a simple change in the manager's behavior if, unknowingly he or she has been relating to people in objectionable ways to a training program designed to develop the manager's skills and knowledge.

"Let me conclude my remarks by saying that we in Personnel believe that this procedure will provide valuable information to our managers. It will also be possible to take the corrective action necessary to improve the performance of line managers. The only unresolved issue is that of standards. We will obtain numerical ratings for each manager, but we will have nothing to compare them to except those of other managers. If this group accepts the feasibility of this plan, our next step is to develop standards for managerial performance. I believe that is the responsibility of top management, as represented by this group."

Questions for analysis:

1. What would be your reaction as a line manager to Steven's plan? Would you consider it threatening? Why?
2. Do you see any problems in a procedure that attempts to obtain data for performance evaluation *and* personal development?
3. How would you go about obtaining the performance standards if you were Steven? What type of control does Steven's plan represent?

PRACTICAL EXERCISE II
The New Dean

The College of Business, Midwestern State University, was made up of five academic departments: accounting, economics, finance, management, and marketing. Each department was headed by a chairman who reported to the dean of the College of Business. The faculty numbered approximately 50, and they were evenly distributed among the five departments. The 2,500 students enrolled in the college were required to "major" in one of the five departments as a part of the requirements for the Bachelor of Business Administration (B.B.A.) degree. The course work in the student's major comprised one third of the total required course work; the remaining two thirds were taken in other departments in the college and the university. In a general sense, the College of Business was typical of those in any land-grant state university.

In 1977, the dean of the college retired after serving in that post for 26 years. He was, at the time of his retirement, the senior member of the college faculty; he had hired all of the 50 members of the faculty and he had appointed each of the five chairmen. During the 26 years of his tenure, the retiring dean had managed the college in a highly autocratic style. He personally hired and fired faculty members, determined their salaries and promotions, and defined the course requirements for each of the departmental majors. He would arrive at his decisions, announce them to the five department chairmen, and expect them to carry out his decisions. With the passage of time, those professors who disagreed with the dean's management style would resign and go elsewhere.

The president of Midwestern State University moved very quickly to replace the retired dean. The procedures required the president to appoint a search committee which would screen candidates and make recommendations to the president. The search committee was formed from the faculty of the College of Business as well as from other parts of the University. The committee reviewed the credentials of a number of candidates and brought many of them to the campus for interviews. It reached a decision and recommended to the president that he offer the appointment to a youthful and successful business executive. The executive had a Ph.D. degree from a prestigious university, but rather than go into teaching he had opted for a business career. The committee's recommendation was accepted by the president. On July 1, 1977, the new dean of the College of Business moved into his office.

One of the first acts of the new dean was to meet with the college's five department chairmen. After inviting each of them to remain as chairmen, he stated that he intended to manage the College of Business according to fundamental management principles. In a sense, he said, "I believe that we should practice what we teach." The dean explained that he was primarily concerned with establishing management procedures for controlling the teaching function of the college. "How do we know," he asked, "whether we are teaching the appropriate subject matter? How do we know whether the professors are actually teaching the subject matter they are assigned? How do we know whether students have learned the subject matter, or, for that matter, how do we know whether the students have received any benefit from their courses? Finally, how do we know which professors are doing the most effective job in the classroom?"

The dean stated that he fully appreciated the fact that the faculty of the college engaged in activities other than teaching. He anticipated that the faculty would continue to engage in research and service activities. "I want us to submit all of our activities to the same set of questions that I have posed about teaching, but, for the moment, I only want to concentrate on teaching." The dean stated that he believed that teaching was the appropriate activity for which to initiate control procedures because of the existence of tangible standards. Research and service activities were less tangible, according to the dean, and therefore less amenable to the development of standards. But as far as the dean was concerned, the teaching function lent itself to the development of standards for which information either was or could be made available, and corrective action could be taken whenever necessary.

The dean directed each of the chairmen to prepare a draft statement which analyzed the most suitable procedures for obtaining answers to the questions he had posed. He stated that he wanted each chairman to appoint a committee of key departmental faculty members to work with him in the preparation of the analysis. He reasoned that college-wide procedures could be devised to meet each department's needs, only after department-level analyses had been completed. The draft statements were to be available for the dean's review within a month.

After this first meeting, the dean was approached by the chairman of the economics department. "Look," he said, "I and my colleagues in the department want to work with you in constructive ways. But quite frankly, I haven't the slightest idea about how to do what you have asked. We economists are not business types, and when you say that you are going to use management fundamentals to control the teaching functions, I don't know what you mean. All that I ever did as chairman was to tell the faculty what the dean said they were to teach. If you want me and a committee of economists to analyze and evaluate procedures for controlling our teaching, you are going to have to be much more specific."

Questions for analysis:

1. What should be the dean's response to the chairman of the economics department?

2. If you, as the dean, were to meet with the faculty of the economics department to explain your intentions, what should you be saying?

3. Assume the role of one of the chairmen and prepare an analysis of how preliminary, concurrent, and feedback control procedures can be utilized in controlling the teaching function.

PRACTICAL EXERCISE III
Developing a New Product

The plant manager of a major electronics manufacturer called a meeting with his immediate subordinates to discuss and decide whether to go into full-scale production and marketing of a new product, a miniature thermostat. The miniature thermostat, MT, had been in the developmental process for the past three years, and the manager believed that it was time to make a decision. The meeting was to be attended by the marketing manager, the production superintendent, the purchasing manager, and the plant cost accountant. The plant manager instructed each official to bring appropriate information and be prepared to make a final decision regarding the MT.

Prior to the meeting, the plant manager noted the following facts concerning the MT.

1. Developmental efforts had been undertaken two years ago in response to the introduction of a similar product by a major competitor.
2. Initial manufacturing studies had indicated that much of the technology and know-how to produce the MT already existed in the plant and its work force.
3. A prototype model had been approved by Underwriter's Laboratory.
4. A pilot production line had been designed and installed. Several thousand thermostats had already been produced and tested.
5. Market projections indicated that the trend toward miniaturization of components such as thermostats was likely to continue.
6. The competitor who had introduced the product was successfully marketing it at a price of $0.80 each.
7. The cost estimates derived by the cost accountant over the past two years consistently indicated that the firm could not meet the competitor's price and at the same time follow its policy of marking up all products to 14 percent of the selling price.

Because of his concern for the cost of the MT, the plant manager asked the cost accountant to brief the group at the outset of its meeting. The accountant's data are shown below:

	Actual costs	Standard costs
Direct labor	$0.059	$0.052
Direct material	0.340	0.194
Manufacturing overhead (438% of standard direct labor)	0.228	0.228
Total manufacturing cost	$0.627	$0.474
Spoilage (10%)	0.063	0.047
Selling and administrative costs (40% of direct labor and overhead)	0.115	0.112
Total cost per MT	$0.805	$0.633
Required price to achieve 14% markup on selling price	$0.936	$0.736

The accountant noted for the group that the firm would not be able to manufacture and sell the MT for less than $0.805 each, given present actual costs. In fact, to meet their markup objective would require a selling price of approximately $0.94 each, but that would be impossible since the competitor was selling the same product for $0.80. She explained that if the MT could be manufactured at standard costs, the product could compete successfully with the competitor's thermostat.

The marketing manager stated that the MT was an important product and that it was critical for the firm to have an entry in the market. He maintained that in a few years the MT would be used by all major customers; he also stated that competition had already moved into the area with a strong sales program. He added that he personally did not place too much reliance on the cost estimates because the plant had so little experience with full-scale production of the MT.

The manufacturing superintendent stated that he was working with engineers to develop a new method for welding contacts and that if the technique proved successful, direct labor cost would be reduced significantly. This would have a cumulative effect on cost since overhead, spoilage, and selling and administrative expenses are based on direct labor. He also believed that with a little more experience, the workers could reach standard times on the assembly operations. He stated that much progress in this direction had been made in the past four weeks.

The purchasing manager stated that material costs were high because the plant did not procure materials in sufficient quantity. She stated that with full-scale production, material costs should reduce to standard.

Questions for analysis:

1. If you were the plant manager, what would be your decision regarding the MT?
2. If you decided to manufacture the MT, would your decision indicate that the standard of 14 percent markup is not valid?
3. What is the cost of the MT? What concept of cost would be appropriate for basing pricing decisions?

PART THREE

The behavioral school

Foundations of the behavioral school
Motivation
Work groups
Leadership
Organizational change and development

7
FOUNDATIONS OF
THE BEHAVIORAL
SCHOOL

As noted in previous chapters, early approaches to management were built on the notion that if the industrial engineer could properly design a job and if management could devise the right kind of incentive, then productivity would be maximized. The industrial psychologist was supposed to aid the whole process by properly selecting and training workers. As is readily apparent the entire approach was very impersonal. Therefore, it is not surprising that a school of thought developed which challenged some of the established classical theories. While this school has been described in several ways, we shall call it the *Behavioral School of Management*.[1] Its first branch may be identified as the "human relations" approach, and became popular in the 1940s and early 1950s. The second branch was the "behavioral science" approach, which came into popular use in the early 1950s and today receives much emphasis in the literature on management. Both branches and important characteristics of each are illustrated in Figure 7–1. Both will be discussed in this chapter, in which we shall touch briefly upon the foundations of the Behavioral School of Management.

The human relations approach

Human relations writers brought to the attention of management the important role played by individuals in determining the success or failure of an organization. They dealt with the task of compensating for some of the deficiencies in classical theory. Basically, the human relations approach accepted the major premises of the Classical School.

---

[1] Some writers describe this school as the "human relations" or "neoclassical" school and distinguish it from the behavioral science school, which they consider as part of "modern" management theory. However, in this text the human relations and behavioral science theories will be examined under the general heading of the Behavioral School of Management.

FIGURE 7-1

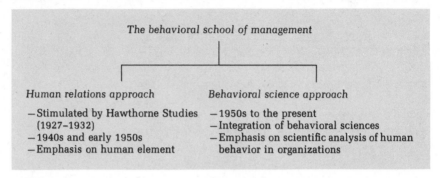

However, it showed how these premises should be modified because of differences in individual behavior and the influence of work groups upon the individual, and *vice versa*. Thus, human relations theory concentrated on the *social* environment surrounding the job, whereas classical writers were concerned mainly with the *physical* environment. For the student of management, the human relations movement has left a wealth of important ideas, research findings, and values about the role of the individual in an organization. Let us examine some of these contributions.

THE HAWTHORNE STUDIES

The human relations approach began when a group of sociologists from Harvard University was invited to conduct studies at the Chicago Hawthorne Plant of Western Electric.[2] The researchers originally set out to study the relationship between productivity and physical working conditions.

The general progression of the research at Hawthorne can be grouped in four phases.[3] However, it should be noted that each of the last three developed as an attempt on the part of the researchers to answer questions raised by the previous phase. The four phases were:

1. Experiments to determine the effects of changes in illumination on productivity.
2. Experiments to determine the effects of changes in hours and other working conditions (for example, rest periods, refreshments) on productivity (The Relay Assembly Test Room Experiment).

---

[2] For a complete account of these studies, see Fritz J. Roethlisberger and W. J. Dickson, *Management and the Worker* (Boston: Harvard University Press, 1939).

[3] Paul R. Lawrence and John A. Seiler, *Organizational Behavior and Administration* (Homewood, Ill.: Richard D. Irwin, Inc., 1965), p. 165.

3. Conducting a plant-wide interview program to determine worker attitudes and sentiments.
4. Determination and analysis of social organization at work (The Bank Wiring Observation Room Experiment).

Experiments in illumination. In the first series of experiments a group of workers were chosen and placed in two separate groups. One group was exposed to varying intensities of illumination. Since this group was subjected to experimental changes, it was termed the *experimental* group. Another group, called the *control* group, continued to work under constant intensities of illumination. Surprisingly, the researchers found that as they increased the illumination in the experimental group, both groups increased production. When the researchers decreased the intensity, output continued to rise for both groups. Finally, the illumination in the experimental group was reduced to that of moonlight. Then, and only then, was there a significant decline in output. The researchers concluded that illumination in the work place had little or no effect on the productivity of the two groups.

Relay assembly test room experiment. In the second phase of the study, several persons volunteered to work under controlled conditions isolated from the other workers. Several changes were made in the conditions of the job (for example, refreshments, work-place temperature) with little effect on productivity. In another phase, a group of women employees was placed together in an isolated part of the assembly department. The experimental group was given a special group incentive as a wage payment. In this case, output increased for each operator.

Overall, the relay assembly test room experiment was designed to determine the effect of changes in various job conditions on group productivity. The researchers concluded that these factors had little or no effect.

Employee interviews. After the first two phases, the researchers concluded that their attempt to relate physical conditions of the job to productivity did not produce any significant results. They therefore postulated that the *human element* in the work environment apparently had a significantly greater impact on the rate of productivity than the technical and physical aspects of the job. The researchers summarized this as follows:

> In brief, the increase in the output rate of the girls in the Relay Assembly Test Room could not be related to any change in their physical conditions of work, whether experimentally induced or not. It could, however, be related to what can only be spoken of as the development of an organized social group and a peculiar and effective relation with its supervisors.[4]

---

[4] Ibid., p. 173.

On the basis of their extensive interview program, the researchers proposed the premise that the work group as a whole determined the production output of individual group members by enforcing an informal norm of what a fair day's work should be.

Bank wiring observation room experiment. In order to test the premise formulated at the conclusion of the interview program, the researchers decided to conduct a final experiment. The procedure in this part of the study was similar to that in the relay assembly test room procedure, except that nine males who assembled terminal banks for telephone exchanges were used.

In this experiment, an attempt was made to determine the effect of a group piecework incentive pay plan. The assumption was that the workers would seek their own economic interests by maximizing their productivity and that faster workers would pressure the slower ones to improve their efficiency. However, the researchers found that pressure was actually a form of social behavior. In order to be accepted in the work group, the worker had to act in accord with group norms and not be a "rate buster" by overproducing, or a "chiseler" by underproducing. The group defined what constituted a day's work, and as soon as they knew that they could reach this output level, they slacked off. This process was more marked among the faster than the slower workers.

The researchers concluded that the work group set the fair rates for each of its members. They found no relationship between productivity and intelligence, dexterity, and other skills. They concluded that the wage incentive plan was less important in determining an individual worker's output than group acceptance and security.

A REVIEW AND CRITIQUE OF THE HAWTHORNE STUDIES

Probably the major contribution of the Hawthorne studies is that they generated a great deal of interest in human problems of the work place. They were also the catalyst for a number of future studies of human behavior in organizational settings. They started managers and others interested in management problems thinking about the worker as a social being with a set of needs.

The Hawthorne studies have been widely criticized by some behavioral scientists because of the lack of scientific objectivity used in arriving at conclusions. Some critics feel that there was bias and preconception on the part of the Harvard researchers. One writer developed a detailed comparison between the conclusions drawn by the researchers and the evidence they presented, and found that their conclusions were almost entirely unsupported.[5] He asked the question

---

[5] Alex Carey, "The Hawthorne Studies: A Radical Criticism," *American Sociological Review*, (June 1967), pp. 403–16.

". . . how it was possible for studies so nearly devoid of scientific merit, and conclusions so little supported by evidence, to gain so influential and respected a place within scientific disciplines and to hold this place for so long."[6]

Other criticisms have also been leveled at the Hawthorne studies.[7] For example:

1. The Hawthorne researchers did not give sufficient attention to the attitudes that people bring with them to the work place. They did not recognize such forces as class consciousness, the role of unions, and other extraplant forces on attitudes of workers.
2. The Hawthorne plant was not a typical plant because it was a thoroughly unpleasant place in which to work.
3. The Hawthorne studies look upon the worker as a means to an end, not an end in himself. They assume acceptance of management's goals and look on the worker as someone to be manipulated by management.

Although they have been criticized, the Hawthorne studies had a significant impact on management practice, teaching, and research. An obvious one was that the assumptions of classical writers began to be questioned. Subsequent studies of the behavior of workers confirmed this criticism and led to revised assumptions about human nature.[8] Behavioral scientists began attacking the "dehumanizing" aspects of the scientific management approach and bureaucratic forms of organization. There were a great number of training programs undertaken to teach foremen how to better understand people and groups in the work situation. With this, the pendulum began to swing away from the supposed depersonalized view of classical management to a more personalized view (some would say overpersonalized). Consequently, the worker, rather than the job or production standards, became the focus.

While we do not hold up the Hawthorne studies as a model in the application of scientific methodology to problems of human behavior, it does represent a pioneering effort in such studies. If it did nothing else, it stimulated an interest in the human problems of management. It was a beginning in bringing new, people-oriented insights to the attention of managers. Although the assumptions and methods of human relations and behavioral science are not the same, it was the human relations branch that provided the impetus for the present-day behavioral science emphasis in management theory.

---

[6] Ibid., p. 403.

[7] Henry A. Landsberger, *Hawthorne Revisited* (Ithaca, N.Y.: New York State School of Industrial and Labor Relations, Cornell University, 1958).

[8] Elton Mayo, *The Social Problems of an Industrial Civilization* (Cambridge, Mass.; Harvard University Press, 1945).

Human relations modifications of classical organization theory

The human relations approach to management regarded the classical principles of organization as given. However, an attempt was made to modify classical doctrine by injecting the human element either through individual behavior or through the influence of the work group. Let us examine these modifications of classical organization theory.[9]

DIVISION OF LABOR

The division of labor received a great deal of attention from human relations writers. Special attention was given to the social isolation of workers and their feelings of anonymity, resulting from insignificant jobs and lack of feeling of task completion because of negligible contributions to the final product.

Human relations writers generally assumed that, as the division of labor increased, the need arose for motivating and coordinating the activities of others. Thus a large volume of their writing focused upon the consequences of dividing work into smaller and smaller units. The emphasis of many of these writers is on procedures that can be used to minimize some of the negative consequences (for example, boredom, fatigue) of the division of labor.

SCALAR AND FUNCTIONAL PROCESSES

The human relations writers believed that the scalar and functional processes are sound, but break down once the human element enters the picture. They believed that the classical writers assumed perfection in the delegation and functionalization processes, but that human problems result through imperfections in the manner in which these processes are handled.

For example, too much or not enough delegation may discourage managerial action; or the failure to delegate sufficient authority, or an unequal delegation of authority and responsibility, may cause frustration for the subordinate. These and other human relations implications of the scalar and functional processes were examined and discussed by human relations writers.

STRUCTURE

The human relations writers were quick to point out that human behavior can disrupt the best-laid structural arrangements. Once the

---

[9] William G. Scott, "Organization Theory: A Reassessment," *Academy of Management Journal* (June 1974), pp. 242–254.

human element is considered, much of the neatness and the logical relationships set forth in the formal structure are changed. They also noted the internal frictions that can develop among people who perform different functions. One of the often-mentioned areas of friction was that between line and staff functions. The human relations writers offered prescriptions for the management of conflict within the organization structure. Two of the most frequently mentioned prescriptions were participation and better communication. The latter, however, was not necessarily a new prescription since classical writers such as Fayol, Mooney, and Barnard also discussed communications.

SPAN OF CONTROL

The human relations writers believed that it was not possible to reduce the problem of span of control to an accurate ratio. They were concerned with the various situational factors that affect span of control, believing that the key determinants were individual differences in managerial abilities, the kind of people and the type of function supervised, and the effectiveness of communication between superior and subordinate.

Another problem relating to span of control examined by human relations writers was the type of organization structure which developed. In other words, is a tall structure with a short span of control or a flat structure with a wide span of control more appropriate for good human relations? Here again they concluded that the answer is situational; that is, because of differences in the people or the organization, one is sometimes more effective than the other.

In addition to modifying the principles of organization, human relations writers also focused attention on the informal work group, which the classical writers did not fully recognize. By informal groups we mean natural formations of people in the work situation, not specified in the formal organization. The Hawthorne studies stimulated interest in the study of groups in the work situation. Human relations writers, and later behavioral science writers, began to examine the underlying characteristics and roles of work groups.

The behavioral science approach

The behavioral science approach to management began to appear in the early 1950's. It was at this time that the Foundation for Research on Human Behavior was established. The goals and objectives of this organization were to promote and support behavioral science research in business, government, and other types of organizations. The work of this Foundation encouraged managers and researchers to look at the behavioral science approach. We shall define the behavioral science approach to the study of management as follows:

> . . . the study of observable and verifiable human behavior in organizations, using scientific procedures. It is largely inductive and problem centered, focusing on the issue of human behavior, and drawing from any relevant literature, especially in psychology, sociology and anthropology.[10]

There were many things about the classical management and human relations approaches that bothered advocates of the behavioral science approach. For example, they recognized that managers did indeed plan, organize, and control but believed that viewing management solely in this way led mainly to descriptions of what managers do rather than an analysis and understanding of what they do.

Many individuals also believed what while the economic man model of the classical writers was an oversimplification, the "social man" model of the human relations approach was likewise oversimplified. We shall see later that the emphasis of the behavioral science approach has shifted more and more to the nature of work itself and the degree to which it can fulfill man's needs to use skills and abilities.

Finally, advocates of the behavioral science approach were bothered by the fact that both practitioners and scholars had accepted without scientific validation so much of the management theory that preceded them. They wanted to test theory against reality and see what was successful and unsuccessful. Their scientific approach has added greatly to the earlier body of knowledge, since they provided a means to test the earlier theories. Through their work some aspects of the classical approach have been modified while others withstood the test of scientific validation. Because of the emphasis on the behavioral sciences and on science itself, let us examine each of these briefly.

THE BEHAVIORAL SCIENCES

First we must distinguish between the social sciences and the behavioral sciences. The term "social sciences" usually refers to six disciplines: anthropology, economics, history, political science, psychology, and sociology. When we use the term "behavioral sciences," we refer to the disciplines of psychology, sociology, and anthropology.

Psychology is the study of human behavior. There are many branches of general psychology which have provided concepts and theories useful to the study of management, for example, social psychology, which deals with behavior as it relates to other individuals. It studies how groups and individuals influence and modify each

---

[10] Alan C. Filley, Robert J. House, and Steven Kerr, *Managerial Process and Organizational Behavior* (Glenview, Ill.: Scott, Foresman, and Company, 1976), p. 16.

other's behavior. *Organizational psychology* is a relatively new branch which deals with man's behavior and attitudes within an organizational setting. It studies the effect of the organization upon the individual and the individual's effect upon the organization. It is easy to see that these areas of psychology have direct relevance to the field of management.

Of all the behavioral sciences, psychology has probably played the biggest role in influencing management thought and practice. Psychologists have shown that people have a great variety of needs which they attempt to satisfy at work. In the next chapter in this section, we shall see that these include social and psychological as well as economic needs.

Sociology attempts to isolate, define, and describe human behavior in groups. It strives to develop laws and generalizations about human nature, social interaction, culture, and social organization.

One of the major contributions of sociologists to management thought has been their focus on small groups, which are often treated in the management literature as the informal components of organizations. Sociologists also have an interest in formal organizations, which they approach as the study of bureaucracy, focusing on bureaucratic behavior as well as the structural relationships in bureaucratic organizations. Sociologists have provided managers with knowledge regarding leader and follower roles and the patterns of power and authority in organizations.

Anthropology examines all the behaviors of man which have been learned, including all of the social, technical, and family behaviors which are a part of the broad concept of "culture." This is the major theme of cultural anthropology, the science devoted to the study of different peoples and cultures of the world, and is a key concept in the behavioral sciences. In fact, the ways in which individuals behave, the priority of needs they attempt to satisfy, and the means they choose to satisfy them are functions of culture.

While psychology and sociology have had a greater impact in shaping management thought, cultural anthropology has made significant contributions regarding the impact of culture on organizations. In the future, as firms expand their activities overseas, anthropology will undoubtedly provide managers with valuable insights as they attempt to perform the functions of planning, organizing, and controlling in different cultural environments.

SCIENCE AND HUMAN BEHAVIOR

The scientific approach has much to offer to the study of human behavior. First, it has been used successfully in many other fields such as the physical sciences. In addition, it has produced information about human behavior that has become established knowledge. The greatest advantage of the scientific approach has been summarized as follows:

> The scientific approach has one characteristic that no other method of attaining knowledge has: self-correction. There are built-in checks all along the way to scientific knowledge. These checks are so conceived and used that they control and verify the scientist's activities and conclusions to the end of attaining dependable knowledge outside himself.[11]

The one word that best describes this approach is objectivity. It forces the researcher or manager to be as objective as possible. Most writers agree that there is no single scientific method, but rather several methods that scientists can and do use. Thus, it is probably better to say that there is a *scientific approach*.

CHARACTERISTICS OF THE SCIENTIFIC APPROACH

While only an "ideal" science would exhibit all of the following characteristics, they nevertheless are the hallmarks of the scientific approach.[12]

1. The procedures are public. This means that a scientific report contains a complete description of what was done, to enable other researchers in the field to follow each step of the investigation as if they were actually present.

2. The definitions are precise. The procedures used, the variables measured, and how they were measured must be clearly stated. For example, if we were examining motivation among employees in a given plant, it would be necessary to define what we mean by motivation and how we measured it (for example, number of units produced, number of absences).

3. The data collecting is objective. Bias in collecting data as well as in the interpretation of results has no place in science. Objectivity throughout is a key feature of the scientific approach.

4. The findings must be replicable. This enables any researcher in the field to test the findings or results of a study by attempting to reproduce them.

5. The approach is systematic and cumulative. This relates to one of the underlying purposes of science, to develop a unified body of knowledge. Thus, a major purpose of the behavioral science approach to management is to develop an organized system of verified propositions about human behavior in organizations.

---

[11] Fred N. Kerlinger, *Foundations of Behavioral Research* (New York: Holt, Rinehart, and Winston, Inc., 1973), p. 6.

[12] Bernard Berelson and Gary A. Steiner, *Human Behavior: An Inventory of Scientific Findings* (New York: Harcourt, Brace and World, Inc., 1964), pp. 16–18.

6. The purposes are explanation, understanding and prediction. Every scientist wants to know "why" and "how." If one determines "why" and "how" and is able to provide proof, one can then predict the particular conditions under which specific events (behavior in this case) will occur. Prediction is the ultimate objective of behavioral science, as it is of all science.

These six characteristics exhibit the basic nature of the scientific approach. The objective, systematic, and controlled nature of the scientific approach enables others to have confidence in research outcomes. What is important is the overall fundamental idea that the scientific approach is a controlled rational process.

METHODS OF INQUIRY USED BY BEHAVIORAL SCIENTISTS

Just as other scientists have certain tools and methods for obtaining information so does the behavioral scientist. These are usually referred to as research designs. In broad terms, there are three basic designs used by behavioral scientists: the experiment, the sample survey, and the case study.[13]

The experiment. An investigation that can be considered an experiment must contain two elements: manipulation of some variable by the researcher and observation or measurement of the results. There are several different forms which an experiment can take, but we shall not examine them here.[14] An example of a simple experiment might be one in which management is trying to determine the effect of increases in piece rates on quantity of production. Since they probably already have measures of present levels of productivity, they would have a "before" measure with which to compare the results. Their first step would be to assign workers randomly to two groups. The experimental group would have its rates altered while the control group would continue working under the existing rates. After a period of time (for example, six months), the output of both groups would be compared with their productivity before the experiment began. This might give some idea as to the effect of a higher piece rate on this one performance indicator. This experiment is an oversimplification used for illustrative purposes. Obviously, there would have to be provisions made to keep the results from being distorted (for example, workers being aware that they are participating in an experiment). However, this example does illustrate the two major elements of an experiment, manipulation of some variable by the researcher (piece rates) and observation or measurement of the results (productivity).

---

[13] Ibid., pp. 18–27.

[14] The interested reader should consult Kerlinger, *Foundations of Behavioral Research*, chaps. 17–21.

Obviously, practical aspects often preclude experimentation in an ongoing organization. As a result, some of the findings of behavioral scientists which are being applied in the field of management have resulted from experimental studies outside organizations.

The sample survey.   In this type of study, the collection of data is from a limited number of subjects which are assumed to be representative of an entire group. For example, suppose we decide to study college students. This is the group or "population" we are concerned about. We then select a sample of this group and collect some measures on particular characteristics in which we are interested (for example, attitudes toward big business). It should be clear that there are certain kinds of questions such as the attitudes of college students toward big business that can only be answered by a sample survey. However, it is often necessary to develop provisions to study changes in attitudes over time to improve the usefulness of the findings.

The case study.   Unlike the sample survey which attempts to measure one or more characteristics in many people, usually at one point in time, the case study attempts to examine numerous characteristics of one person or group, usually over an extended time period. A behavioral scientist who spends time living with a mountain tribe or working with a group of blue-collar workers will usually report the results in the form of a case study (for example, the key factors and incidents leading up to a strike).

While this method is extremely valuable in answering questions concerning development (for example, factors leading up to the strike) and for exploratory purposes, its major limitation is that the ability to generalize from it is uncertain, since the results are usually based on a sample of one instance. Perhaps, in another firm, the same incidents may not result in a strike. A case study, therefore, usually does not prove or disprove anything.

Contributions of the behavioral school to the practice of management

The Behavioral School gained much attention during the 1960s and 1970s. An underlying rationale of the school is that since a manager must "get work done through others," management is really applied behavioral science because a manager must know how to motivate, be a leader, and understand interpersonal relations and the operation of groups, among other things. Therefore, the logic is that future managers must be prepared in these behavioral areas. While we would argue that management is more than solely applied behavioral science, the basic assumption of the behavioral science approach that managers must know how to deal with people appears valid.

One of the vital tasks performed by managers is decision making. To make decisions they must have possible alternatives from which to choose, authority to implement the alternative, and information. This last factor is our concern in this section. Managers need two kinds of information: First, they must have facts about the particular system, the people and machines involved, and the cost. Second, they need theory to aid in explaining what will happen if one variable is altered, and they must know how the different variables are related to each other.

If the Behavioral School is to be useful to managers in improving performance, it must suggest to them what to do in problem situations, provide them with a description of their environment, or provide them with a framework on which to rely in problem-solving situations. In other words, it must provide managers with guides for defining a problem correctly, problem solving, explanation of behavior, and control of variables. In order to be useful, it must make them better practitioners.

This section of the book should in no way be viewed separately from the Classical School. Early management writers identified management as a process consisting of the functions of planning, organizing, and controlling and provided insights into the nature and demands of these tasks. The question the reader should ask is, "How can the behavioral sciences help a manager better perform these tasks?"[15] The behavioral science approach should be regarded as an addition to the person-related activities of the functions of *organizing* and *controlling*. The sole purpose in presenting the behavioral material in the following chapters is to provide readers with knowledge from the behavioral sciences that will make them better managers. Since the functions of management include organizing and controlling, the findings of the behavioral scientists must assist them in performing these functions. Otherwise they would be of little value to managers and would have no place in this text.

While the Behavioral School has not yet produced an integrated body of knowledge, it has provided much useful information for practitioners and students of management. In subsequent chapters of this section, we shall examine such behavioral topics as motivation, leadership, groups, organizational design, and organizational change and development. In doing so, we will draw upon material from the behavioral sciences. While the disciplines may differ, the material will, for the most part, have a common thread. It will have been arrived at through the use of the methods described in this chapter for gaining knowledge in the behavioral sciences.

---

[15] A reference on this subject is Edwin B. Flippo, "The Underutilization of Behavioral Science by Management," in Joseph W. McGuire, ed., *Contemporary Management* (Englewood Cliffs, N.J.: Prentice-Hall, Inc., 1974), pp. 36–41.

Discussion and review questions

1. The Hawthorne studies are considered to be a landmark in studying behavior within organizations. One behavioralist has commented that the Hawthorne studies are so complex that there is something in them for almost everyone. Do you agree?

2. Why do you believe that some managers and workers think that human relations applied to an organization is nothing more than manipulation?

3. Is the behavioral approach applicable to industrial organizations? Health care institutions?

4. Assume that a supervisor has asked you to study the problem of worker motivation. You have decided to use the scientific approach. What are some questions you would need to answer before you could begin to study?

5. Why is it impossible to control for all variables in a study that takes place in an ongoing organization?

6. What is the human relations approach?

7. Do behavioral scientists assume that such concepts as division of labor, scalar and functional processes, structure, and span of control are outdated and not applicable to the modern worker? Explain.

8. A sales manager was overheard saying the following: "I've got enough to do *planning* the work of my sales force, *organizing* their activities and routes, and *controlling* their actions and expenses. I haven't got the time to mess around with that behavioral science stuff. Besides that theory business belongs in school, I can't use it in my world." Is the sales manager right? Of what value is theory to the practicing manager?

9. A popular magazine offers the following title on its front page: "Thirty-Five Days as a Blue-Collar Worker in South Chicago." Upon reading the article you find that it is actually a case study by a reporter who spent 35 days as a steelworker in a large steel plant in South Chicago. Evaluate the study method based upon what you know about the characteristics of the scientific approach in the behavioral sciences and the methods of inquiry used by behavioral scientists.

10. Does the behavioral approach result in better performance than the classical approach? Explain.

Additional references

Argyris, C. *Integrating the Individual and the Organization.* New York: Wiley and Sons, 1964.

Barnard, C. I. *The Functions of the Executive.* Boston: Harvard University Press, 1938.

Connor, P. E. "Research in the Behavioral Sciences: A Review Essay," *Academy of Management Journal,* 15 (1972), pp. 219–228.

Cyert, R. M., and March, J. G. *A Behavioral Theory of the Firm.* Englewood Cliffs, N.J.: Prentice-Hall, Inc., 1963.

Gibson, J. L., Ivancevich, J. M., and Donnelly, J. H. *Organizations: Behavior, Structure, Processes.* Dallas, Tex.: Business Publications, Inc., 1976.

"Hawthorne Revisited: The Legend and the Legacy," *Organizational Dynamics,* 3 (Winter 1975), pp. 66–80.

Helmstadter, G. C. *Research Concepts in Human Behavior.* New York: Appleton-Century-Crofts, Inc., 1970.

Leavitt, H. J. *Managerial Psychology.* Chicago: The University of Chicago Press, 1972.

Leavitt, H. J., Dill, W. R., and Eyring, H. B. *The Organizational World.* New York: Harcourt Brace Jovanovich, Inc., 1973.

Mayo, E. *The Human Problems of Industrial Civilization.* New York: Macmillan and Company, 1933.

Miles, D. Q. "Managing Human Relationships among Organizations: Theory and Practice," *Organizational Dynamics,* 3 (Spring 1975), pp. 35–50.

Miles, R. E. *Theories of Management: Implications for Organizational Behavior and Development.* New York: McGraw-Hill, 1975.

Ritti, R. R. and Funkhouser, G. R. *The Ropes to Skip and the Ropes to Know.* Columbus, Ohio: Grid, Inc., 1977.

Roethlisberger, F. J. *Management and Morale.* Boston: Harvard University Press, 1941.

Schein, E. H. *Organizational Psychology.* Englewood Cliffs, N.J.: Prentice-Hall, Inc., 1970.

8

MOTIVATION

Motivation is concerned with the "why" of human behavior, what it is that makes people do things. Why does Harry have frequent run-ins with the boss, or why does Dianne work so much harder than Jim? These questions can be partially answered with an understanding of human motivation. An understanding of motivation is a necessity for the student of management and it is an area which receives a great deal of attention in the Behavioral School.

The nature of motivation

Before examining the elements of motivation, it is vital that we clearly understand exactly what the term means. Berelson and Steiner define motivation as "all those inner striving conditions described as wishes, desires, drives, etc. . . . It is an inner state that activates or moves."[1]

More specifically, the term motivation has often been called an intervening variable.[2] Intervening variables are internal and psychological processes which are not directly observable and which, in turn, account for behavior.[3] Thus, motivation is an intervening variable for it cannot be seen, heard, or felt, and can only be inferred from behavior. In other words we can only judge how motivated a person is by observing his behavior; we cannot measure it directly because it is unobservable. This means that we must first operationally define what motivation is, since we can only measure presumed indicators of motivation. For example, if one student consistently achieves higher grades than other students with similar intelligence we might infer that he or she is highly motivated. If a typist completes more purchase orders with no more errors than other typists with comparable skills we might infer that the typist is motivated. However, note that in each case we did not measure motivation directly; we observed a presumed indicator of motivation (grades and purchase orders completed) and made inferences from our observations.

MOTIVATION AND BEHAVIOR

Psychologists generally agree that all behavior is motivated, and that people have reasons for doing the things they do or for behaving in the manner that they do. In other words, all human behavior is designed to

---

[1] Bernard Berelson and Gary A. Steiner, *Human Behavior: An Inventory of Scientific Findings* (New York: Harcourt, Brace, and World, 1964), p. 239.

[2] E. Tolman, *Behavior and Psychological Man* (Berkeley, Calif.: University of California Press, 1958), pp. 115–29.

[3] Fred N. Kerlinger, *Foundations of Behavioral Research* (New York: Holt, Rinehart, and Winston, Inc., 1973), p. 40.

achieve certain goals and objectives. Such goal-directed behavior re-
volves around the desire for need satisfaction.

As shown in Figure 8–1, an unsatisfied need is the starting point in
the process of motivation. It is a deficiency of something within the
individual and provides the spark which begins the chain of events
leading to behavior. An unsatisfied need causes tension (physical or
psychological) within the individual, leading the individual to engage
in some kind of behavior (seek a means) to satisfy the need, and thereby
reduce the tension. Note that this activity is directed toward a goal;
arrival at the goal satisfies the need, and the process of motivation is
complete. For example, a thirsty person *needs* water, is *driven* by thirst,
and *motivated* by a desire for water in order to satisfy the need. Thus,
the continuous process begins with an unsatisfied need and ends with
need satisfaction, with goal-directed behavior as a part of the process.

FIGURE 8–1
The process of motivation

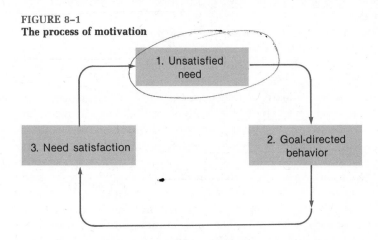

The importance of understanding the relationships between motivation and behavior was underscored by McGregor. He proposed that
managers usually assume that employees are motivated by one of two
ways.[4] The traditional way, or view was referred to as Theory X. This
view suggested that in order to motivate subordinates, managers assumed that they needed to coerce, control, and threaten. These managerial actions were needed because employees:

    a.   inherently disliked work.
    b.   disliked responsibilities for decision making.
    c.   had little ambition and wanted job security above all.

---

[4] Douglas McGregor, *The Human Side of Enterprise* (New York: McGraw-Hill Book
Co., 1960).

Thus, Theory X if believed by a manager would result in practices that were authoritarian and directive. These practices resulted because managers made some assumptions about how and why subordinates behave.

The opposite of Theory X is called *Theory Y*. It was McGregor's belief that Theory Y was a reasonable alternative to the more traditional Theory X approach. The manager using Theory Y assumed that employees were:

a. not lazy and wanted to do challenging work.
b. interested under proper conditions in accepting responsibility.
c. interested in displaying ingenuity and creativity.

An analysis of McGregor's Theory X and Theory Y distinction displays a traditional and a behavioral approach to motivation. The differences lie in the assumptions each manager makes about the needs of their subordinates. If workers are assumed to have Theory X needs, management will create tighter controls and use coercion to motivate better performance. On the other hand, if Theory Y assumptions are made about subordinates, managers would probably be involved in helping create an environment under which a full range of needs can be fulfilled.

Individual needs and motivation

As we have already mentioned, unsatisfied needs are the starting point in the process of motivation. These needs may be classified in different ways. Many of the early writers on management emphasized monetary incentives as prime means for motivating the individual. These writers were influenced by the classical economists of the 18th and 19th centuries who placed emphasis on man's rational pursuit of economic objectives and believed that economic behavior was characterized by rational economic calculations. Today, many psychologists agree that while money is obviously an important motivator, people seek to satisfy other than purely economic needs. In fact, Freud was the first psychologist to hypothesize that much of man's behavior may not even be rational, but that it may be influenced by needs of which the individual is not aware.

While most psychologists agree that man is motivated by the desire to satisfy many needs, there is a wide difference of opinion as to what these needs and their relative importance are. Most, however, take the pluralistic view, emphasizing many different types of needs the satisfaction of which is a key determinant of behavior. Let us now examine one of the most widely adopted theories of human motivation.

THE NEED HIERARCHY

Maslow's need hierarchy theory has enjoyed widespread acceptance particularly in the writings of behavioralists. His theory of motivation stresses two fundamental premises:

1. Man is a wanting animal whose needs depend on what he already has. Only needs not yet satisfied can influence behavior. In other words, a satisfied need is not a motivator.
2. Man's needs are arranged in a hierarchy of importance. Once one need is satisfied, another emerges and demands satisfaction.

Maslow hypothesized five levels of needs. These needs are (1) physiological, (2) safety, (3) social, (4) esteem, and (5) self-actualization.[5] He placed them in a framework referred to as the hierarchy of needs because of the different levels of importance indicated. This framework is presented in Figure 8–2.

Maslow states that if all of a person's needs are unsatisfied at a particular time, satisfaction of the most predominant needs will be more pressing than the others. Those which come first must be satisfied before a higher level need comes into play, and only when they are sufficiently satisfied are the next ones in line significant. Let us briefly examine each need level.

Physiological needs. This category consists of the primary needs of the human body such as food, water, and sex. Physiological needs will dominate when all needs are unsatisfied. In such a case, no other needs will serve as a basis for motivation. As Maslow states, "a person who is lacking food, safety, love, and esteem would probably hunger for food more strongly than for anything else."[6]

Since these types of situations probably do not arise often these days, particularly in the United States, the important needs, at least from a managerial standpoint, would appear to be those higher in the hierarchy.

Safety needs. With the physiological needs met, the next higher level assumes importance. Safety needs include protection from physical harm, ill health, economic disaster, and avoidance of the unexpected. From a managerial standpoint, safety needs manifest themselves in attempts to insure job security and attempts to move toward greater financial support. For example, in the early days of labor unions, the primary demands which unions presented to management

---

[5] Less described, and hence not as well known are the cognitive and aesthetic needs hypothesized by Maslow. Examples of cognitive needs are the need to know or to understand, and the manipulation of the environment as the result of curiosity. The aesthetic needs are satisfied by moving from ugliness toward beauty. Maslow did not include them in the formal hierarchy framework. Abraham H. Maslow, *Motivation and Personality* (New York: Harper and Brothers, 1954), pp. 93–98.

[6] Ibid., p. 82.

consisted of monetary increases. In recent times, however, many unions are making demands on management for such things as fringe benefits and job security, with less emphasis on increases in pay.

Social needs. These needs are related to the social nature of people and their need for companionship. This level in the hierarchy is the point of departure from the physical or quasiphysical needs of the two

FIGURE 8–2
Hierarchy of needs

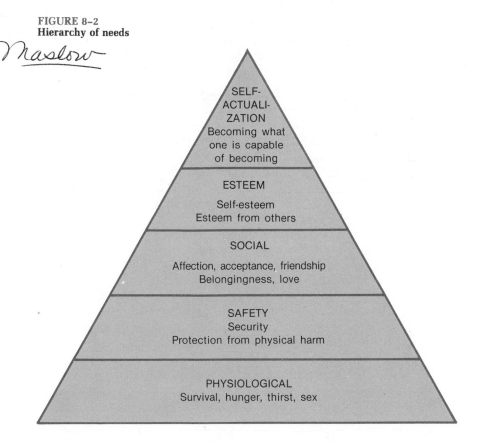

previous levels. Nonsatisfaction of this level of need may affect the mental health of the individual.

Esteem needs. These needs consist both of the need for the awareness of importance to others (self-esteem) and the actual esteem from others. Esteem from others must also be felt as warranted and deserved. Satisfaction of these needs leads to a feeling of self-confidence and prestige.

Self-actualization needs. Maslow defines this need as the "desire to become more and more what one is, to become everything one is capable of becoming."[7] This means that the individual will fully realize the potentialities of talents and capabilities.

Obviously, as the role of an individual varies so will the external aspects of self-actualization. In other words, whether the person is a college professor, corporate manager, parent, or athlete, the need is to be effective in that particular role. Maslow assumes that satisfaction of the self-actualization need is possible only after the satisfaction of all other needs. Moreover, he proposes that the satisfaction of the self-actualization need will tend to increase the strength of that need. Thus, when people are able to achieve self-actualization they will tend to be motivated by increased opportunities to satisfy that need.[8]

MANAGEMENT'S USE OF THE NEED-HIERARCHY MODEL

The need-hierarchy model is widely accepted and referred to by practicing managers. It is easy to comprehend, has a great deal of "commonsense" validity, and points out some of the factors that motivate people in business and other types of organizations. Most organizations in the United States have been extremely successful in satisfying lower-level needs. Through the wages or salary they receive, individuals are able to satisfy the physiological needs of themselves and their families. Organizations also aid in satisfying security or safety needs through both salary and fringe benefit programs. Finally, they aid in satisfying social needs by allowing interaction and association with others on the job. In one way, all of this may have created a future problem for management. Since human behavior is primarily directed toward fulfilling unsatisfied needs, how successful a manager is in the future in motivating subordinates may be a function of the ability to satisfy their higher-level needs.

While Maslow's need hierarchy does not provide a complete understanding of human motivation or the means to motivate people, it does provide an excellent starting point for the student of management. We shall use it in this chapter as the foundation for an understanding of motivation in organizations.

Nonsatisfaction of needs

Unsatisfied needs are the starting points for the understanding of motivation. Many times an individual is unsuccessful in attempts to satisfy needs. In order to improve our understanding of motivation, it is necessary to explore what happens when needs are not satisfied.

---

[7] Ibid., p. 92.

[8] Maslow, A. H., *Motivation and Personality* (New York: Harper & Row, 1970), p. 81.

As noted previously, unsatisfied needs produce tensions within the individual. (The reader is encouraged to think of these unsatisfied needs as occurring at any level in the need hierarchy. An unsatisfied social need can produce as much tension as an unsatisfied physiological need such as hunger.) These unsatisfied needs motivate the individual to behavior which will relieve the tension. When the individual is unable to satisfy needs (and thereby reduce the tension), frustration is the result. The college male who plots conscientiously for half a semester to secure a date with a co-ed in his management class only to have her refuse is an example of an individual who would probably be quite frustrated. His goal of getting a date, the attainment of which would have brought the satisfaction of several needs, has been blocked. Reactions to frustration will vary from person to person. Some people will react in a positive manner (constructive behavior), and others in a negative manner (defensive behavior).

CONSTRUCTIVE BEHAVIOR

The reader is undoubtedly familiar with the constructive adaptive behavior in which a person engages when faced with frustration in attempts to satisfy needs. An assembly-line worker frustrated in attempts for recognition because of the nature of the job may seek recognition off the job by winning election to leadership posts in fraternal or civic organizations. In order to satisfy social and belonging needs, a worker may conform to the norms and values of a group which bowls together on week-ends. Finally, the college male mentioned previously may settle for a date with a less desirable co-ed or attend a party without a date but with some friends. Each of these is an example of constructive adaptive behavior which individuals employ to reduce frustration and satisfy needs.

DEFENSIVE BEHAVIOR

When individuals are blocked in attempts to satisfy their needs, they may evoke one or more defense mechanisms instead of adopting constructive behavior to solve problems. All of us employ defense mechanisms in one way or another because they perform an important protective function in our attempts to cope with reality. In most cases, they do not handicap the individual to any great degree. Ordinarily, however, they are not adequate for the task of protecting the self. As a result, adults whose behavior is continually dominated by defensive behavior will usually have great difficulty in adapting to the responsibilities of work and of other people.

What happens when needs are not satisfied is difficult to understand and is still being investigated by psychologists. However, there are some general patterns of defensive behavior which have been identified, some of the most common being:

Withdrawal. One obvious way to avoid reality is to withdraw or avoid those situations which will prove frustrating. The withdrawal may be physical (leaving the scene), but more than likely will be internalized and manifested in apathy. Workers whose jobs provide little in the way of need satisfaction may "withdraw" and this is reflected by excessive absences, latenesses, or turnover.

Aggression. A very common reaction to frustration is aggression. In some cases, there may be a direct attack on the source of the frustration. However, this may often not be possible (for example, to fight the boss). Unfortunately, all too often the aggression is directed toward another object or party. This is known as *displacement*. For example, a supervisor may displace aggression on a subordinate production worker who, in turn, may displace his aggression on his wife.

Substitution. This occurs when the individual puts something else in the place of the original object. An employee frustrated in attempts to be promoted may substitute achieving leadership status in a work group whose objectives are to resist management policies.

Compensation. When a person goes overboard in one area or activity to make up for deficiencies in another, this defense mechanism is being evoked. A superior who has a disagreeable personality may overcompensate with attempts to practice good "human relations" with subordinates.

Repression. Many times the individual will repress a situation and a problem in order to keep frustration down. At times repression is an almost automatic response whereby the individual loses awareness of incidents that would cause anxiety or frustration if allowed to remain at the conscious level of the mind. Thus an unpleasant situation with a superior may be quickly "forgotten" by a subordinate.

Regression. When confronted with frustration, some individuals will revert back (regress) to childlike forms of behavior in their attempts to avoid the unpleasant reality. In the work situation, this often manifests itself in some form of horseplay.

Projection. This involves attributing one's own feelings to someone else. A subordinate may dislike a superior for some particular reason and attempt to make the superior appear ineffective whenever possible. The subordinate will attempt to justify this by saying, "My boss never liked me from the moment I got here."

Rationalization. This occurs when an individual presents a reason for behavior which is less ego-deflating or more socially acceptable than the true reason. An example of this defense mechanism is perceiving one's own poor performance as the result of obsolete equipment rather than personal deficiency.

Since every person relies to some extent on defense mechanisms, this kind of behavior is difficult to eliminate completely in organizations. In fact, it performs a useful role in maintaining mental health. However, its occurrence may be minimized if managerial decisions provide conditions under which employees experience minimum frustration. In addition, a manager who understands such behavior will have greater empathy with superiors and subordinates, and will realize that an individual's behavior may not be a true indication of the person, since defense mechanisms may hide the true personality.

We can summarize what has been said thus far about motivation in the model presented in Figure 8–3. The diagram indicates that an unsatisfied need results in tensions within the individual and motivates a search for ways to relieve the tension. The diagram indicates that, if one is successful in achieving a goal, the next unsatisfied need

FIGURE 8–3
A motivation model

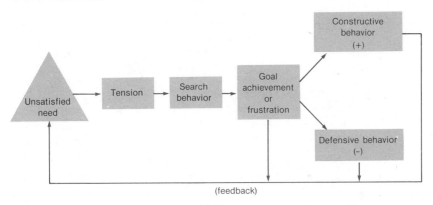

(feedback)

emerges. If, however, attempts are met with frustration, one either engages in constructive behavior (note the plus sign to indicate its adaptive/positive nature), or resorts to defensive behavior (indicated with a minus sign because of its often negative effects). In either case, the person returns to the next unsatisfied need which emerges.

Personality, behavior, and motivation

In the previous section a conceptual framework illustrating the relationship between needs and motivation was introduced. It is obvious that this is a general behavioral model which does not consider individual differences in motivation and behavior; otherwise, based on this model, one should be able to predict behavior. The reader should see that this is not possible: Given similar needs, different people react in different ways, not only in the goals they select and the means they choose to achieve them, but also in their reactions to frustration. Evidently there is some element missing in our explanation of motivation. This important element is the individual personality. Though each of us may be motivated to fulfill similar kinds of needs, the particular patterns of behavior we choose will differ from those of others because of our personalities.

The term personality means many things to behavioral scientists. We shall define it as the general sum of traits or characteristics of an individual. Personality is a conglomerate of forces within the individual.

DETERMINANTS OF PERSONALITY

A person is like all other people, and yet like no other person. One of the unique areas of a person's development is the personality. In order to understand how personality relates to motivation and behavior, we must first examine the determinants of personality.

The formation of the human personality is influenced by the mutual interaction of many factors. While the list could be unending, experts agree that there are four general categories of influencing factors.[9]

Constitutional determinants. These are inborn characteristics which the individual inherits. For example, different genetic structures result in varying potentials for learning, energy, activity, and tolerance for frustration. Age is also an important constitutional determinant of personality. These characteristics influence an individual's needs and expectations.

Group membership determinants. Individuals within any culture are exposed to the beliefs, values, and mores of the culture in different ways. These are usually transmitted through the various groups (for example, family, education, religion) with which they come into contact. The relationships which individuals develop are likely to have a lasting influence on their personalities and ways of viewing life.

Role determinants. In a sense, role determinants of personality can be considered a special class of group membership determinants. Each of us has a number of different roles which we play at different times. The roles an individual plays to fulfill a given position are determined by the group within which the position exists. For example, the roles of a husband and wife are determined by the cultural environment within which the positions exist, while the roles of a military officer and a college professor are determined by their reference groups. While it is incorrect to accept a person's behavior in a particular

---

[9] Clyde Kluckhohn and Henry A. Murray, *Personality* (New York: Alfred A. Knopf, Inc., 1956), chap. 2.

situation (for example, a college professor's behavior in the classroom or on campus) as representative of the total personality, the roles which people play everyday have a great influence upon their personalities.

Situational determinants. Situational determinants of personality include the unique factors which influence an individual's personality. For example, a student who is undecided which functional area of business to major in while at college may have in the first management course a dynamic, persuasive bank executive as a guest speaker. While this event may not directly and immediately alter the student's personality, it may put into motion events which will be decisive in influencing his personality.

While each of the determinants discussed has an important influence on personality development, it is necessary to recognize their interdependence rather than considering them as isolated factors. In other words, it is incorrect to view a single determinant as the cause of personality. Instead, the personality of an individual is conditioned by several mutually interdependent and interacting variables and must be viewed as a dynamic system.

PERSONALITY AND MOTIVATION

In our earlier discussion of motivation, we constructed a motivational model which indicated that most behavior is directed toward satisfying an unsatisfied need, and that whenever need satisfaction is blocked, the individual experiences frustration. We saw that the individual may react to frustration either by engaging in some kind of constructuve behavior to solve the problem or evoking one or more defense mechanisms. Now that we have discussed personality, how does this important determinant of behavior fit into the motivation process? Personality differences influence the process of motivation in the following ways.[10]

Strength of needs. The strength and importance of various needs will differ from one individual to another depending on the individual's personality. For example, some people have strong esteem needs which lead them to seek different kinds of employment or buy a whole different range of products than people whose esteem needs are not as strong.

Aspiration level. Aspiration levels differ among individuals depending upon the strength of their needs. One individual may not be satisfied until reaching a position of power and influence in an organi-

---

[10] Max D. Richards and Paul S. Greenlaw, *Management: Decisions and Behavior* (Homewood, Ill.: Richard D. Irwin, Inc., 1972), pp. 149–53. Also see an earlier edition, *Management Decision Making* (1966), pp. 112–15.

zation, while another may be quite satisfied in a middle management position.

Types of behavior.   Although individuals may experience the same needs, the strategies or types of behavior which an individual utilizes to achieve need satisfaction are a function of personality. For example, one person may satisfy esteem needs by gaining on-the-job recognition from superiors, while another may satisfy the same need by striving to become a repsected member of a professional or peer group. The need is the same but the behavior used to satisfy it differs.

Reaction to frustration.   How a person reacts to nonsatisfaction of needs is also a function of personality. Personality differences affect the types of situations which cause frustration, the degree to which defense mechanisms are evoked, and the kinds of defense mechanisms that are employed. For example, one individual frustrated in attempts to move up in an organization may instead seek leadership positions in external political or civic organizations (constructive behavior), while another individual experiencing the same frustration might engage in sabotage activities against the organization (defensive behavior).

In this section, we have presented a motivational model based upon the need-hierarchy framework. We have also noted that both motivation and behavior will vary from person to person as a result of differences in personality.

Other models of motivation

Before leaving the subject of motivation, let us examine two other widely discussed models of motivation which are especially useful for students of management because they are specifically concerned with motivation in the work situation.

HERZBERG'S TWO-FACTOR MODEL

This approach to motivation was first advanced by Frederick Herzberg who based his theory on a study of need satisfactions and on the reported motivational effects of these satisfactions on 200 engineers and accountants. It is often referred to as the "two-factor" theory of motivation.[11]

In this study, Herzberg and his associates asked these subjects to think of times when they felt especially good, and times when they felt especially bad about their jobs. Each employee was then asked to

---

[11] See Frederick Herzberg, B. Mausner, and B. Snyderman, *The Motivation to Work* (New York: John Wiley and Sons, Inc., 1959).

describe the conditions which led to these particular feelings. It was found that the employees named different kinds of conditions which caused each of the feelings. For example, if recognition led to a good feeling about the job, the lack of recognition was seldom indicated as a cause of bad feelings.

Based on this research, Herzberg reached the following two conclusions:

1. Some conditions of a job operate primarily to dissatisfy employees when they are not present. However, the presence of these conditions does not build strong motivation. Herzberg called these factors *maintenance* factors since they are necessary to maintain a reasonable level of satisfaction. He also noted that many of these have often been perceived by managers as factors which can motivate subordinates, but that they are, in fact, more potent as dissatisfiers when they are absent. He concluded that there were ten maintenance factors, namely:

a.	Company policy and administration.	f.	Salary.
b.	Technical supervision.	g.	Job security.
c.	Interpersonal relations with supervisor.	h.	Personal life.
d.	Interpersonal relations with peers.	i.	Work conditions.
e.	Interpersonal relations with subordinates.	j.	Status.

2. Some job conditions build high levels of motivation and job satisfaction. However, if these conditions are not present, they do not prove highly dissatisfying. Herzberg described six of these factors as *motivational* factors or satisfiers:

a.	Achievement.	d.	The work itself.
b.	Recognition.	e.	The possibility of personal growth.
c.	Advancement.	f.	Responsibility.

In summary, the maintenance factors cause much dissatisfaction when they are not present, but do not provide strong motivation when they are present. On the other hand, the factors in the second group lead to strong motivation and satisfaction when they are present, but do not cause much dissatisfaction when they are absent.

The reader has probably noted that the *motivational factors* are job-centered; that is, they relate directly to the job itself, the individual's performance of it, its responsibilities, and the growth and recognition obtained from it. *Maintenance factors* are peripheral to the job itself and more related to the external environment of work. Another important fiinding of the study is that when employees are highly motivated, they have a high tolerance for dissatisfaction arising from the peripheral factors. However, the reverse is not true.

The distinction between motivational and maintenance factors is similar to what psychologists have described as *intrinsic* and *extrinsic* motivators. Intrinsic motivators are part of the job and occur when the employee performs the work. The opportunity to perform a job with intrinsic motivational potential is motivating because the work itself is rewarding. Extrinsic motivators are external rewards that have meaning or value after performing the work or away from the work place. They provide little, if any, satisfaction when the work is being performed. Pay, of course, is a good example of what Herzberg classifies as a maintenance factor and what some psychologists call an extrinsic motivator.

Criticisms of the Herzberg model. One limitation of Herzberg's original study and conclusions is that the subjects consisted of engineers and accountants. The fact that these individuals were in such positions indicates that they had the motivation to seek advanced education and expect to be rewarded for it. The same may not hold true for the nonprofessional worker. In fact, some testing of Herzberg's model on blue-collar workers showed that some of the factors considered as maintenance factors by Herzberg (pay, job security) are considered by blue-collar workers to be motivational factors.[12]

Another limitation of Herzberg's work has been cited by Vroom.[13] He believes that Herzberg's inference concerning differences between dissatisfiers and motivators cannot be completely accepted, and that the differences between stated sources of satisfaction and dissatisfaction in Herzberg's study may be the result of defensive processes within those responding. Vroom points out that people are apt to attribute the causes of satisfaction to their own achievements, but more likely to attribute their dissatisfaction to obstacles presented by company policies or superiors than to their own deficiencies.

Another group of writers believe that the two-factor theory is an oversimplification of the true relationship between motivation and dissatisfaction as well as between the sources of job satisfaction and dissatisfaction.[14] They reviewed several studies which showed that one factor can cause job satisfaction for one person and job dissatisfaction for another. They concluded that further research is needed to be able to predict in what situations worker satisfaction will produce greater productivity.

---

[12] Michael R. Malinovsky and John R. Barry, "Determinants of Work Attitudes," *Journal of Applied Psychology* (December 1965), pp. 446–51. For a discussion of other alternative interpretations of the two-factor theory and the research support for the various interpretations, see N. King, "Clarification and Evaluation of the Two-Factor Theory of Job Satisfaction," *Psychological Bulletin* (July 1970), pp. 18–31., and D. A. Ondrack, "Defense Mechanisms and the Herzberg Theory: An Alternate Test," *Personnel Psychology* (March 1974), 79–89.

[13] Victor H. Vroom, *Work and Motivation* (New York: John Wiley and Sons, Inc., 1964), pp. 128–29.

[14] R. J. House and L. A. Wigdor, "Herzberg's Dual-Factor Theory of Job Satisfaction and Motivation: A Review of the Evidence and a Criticism," *Personnel Psychology* (Winter 1967), pp. 369–89.

Since his original study, Herzberg has cited numerous and diverse replications of the original study which support his position.[15] These subsequent studies were conducted on professional women, hospital maintenance personnel, agricultural administrators, nurses, food handlers, manufacturing supervisors, engineers, scientists, military officers, managers ready for retirement, teachers, technicians, and assemblers; and some were conducted in other cultrual settings — Finland, Hungary, Russia, and Yugoslavia. However, other researchers who have used the same research methods employed by Herzberg have obtained results different from what his theory would predict,[16] while several others using different methods have also obtained contradictory results.[17]

This discussion indicates that Herzberg's theory has generated a great deal of controversy. Therefore readers should view this theory not as a panacea for all motivation problems in organizations, but as a starting point which they can use when attempting to develop their own approaches to motivation in the work situation.

Even after considering the legitimate criticisms, few would argue that Herzberg has not contributed substantially to our thinking on motivation at work. He certainly has extended Maslow's ideas and made them more applicable to the work situation. Finally, he has drawn attention to the critical importance of job-centered factors in work motivation which previously had been given little attention by behavioral scientists. This insight has resulted in an increased interest in *job enrichment*, an effort to restructure jobs so as to increase worker satisfaction.

Comparison of Herzberg's and Maslow's models.   There is much similarity between Herzberg's and Maslow's models. A close examination of Herzberg's ideas indicates that what he is actually saying is that some employees may have achieved a level of social and economic progress in our society such that the higher-level needs of Maslow (esteem and self-actualization) are the primary motivators. However, they still must satisfy the lower-level needs for the maintenance of their current state. Thus, we can see that money might still be a motivator for nonmanagement workers (particularly those at a minimum wage level) and for some managerial employees. In addition, Herzberg's model adds to the need hierarchy model because it draws a distinction

---

[15] Frederick Herzberg, *Work and the Nature of Man* (Cleveland: World Publishing Co., 1966).

[16] Donald P. Schwab, H. William DeVitt, and Larry L. Cummings, "A Test of the Adequacy of the Two-Factor Theory as a Predictor of Self-Report Performance Effects," *Personnel Psychology* (Summer 1971), pp. 293–303.

[17] Marvin D. Dunnette, John P. Campbell, and Milton D. Hakel, "Factors Contributing To Job Satisfaction and Job Dissatisfaction in Six Occupational Groups," *Organizational Behavior and Human Performance* (May 1967), pp. 143–74; C. L. Hulin and P. A. Smith, "An Empirical Investigation of Two Implications of the Two-Factor Theory of Job Satisfaction," *Journal of Applied Psychology* (October 1967), pp. 396–402.

between the two groups of motivational and maintenance factors, and
points out that the motivational factors are often derived from the job
itself. Figure 8–4 compares the two models.

THE EXPECTANCY MODEL OF MOTIVATION

A model of motivation has been developed by Vroom that expands
upon the work of Maslow and Herzberg.[18] The Vroom model views
motivation as a process governing choices. Thus, if an individual has
a particular goal, in order to achieve the goal, some behavior must be

FIGURE 8–4
A comparison of the Maslow and Herzberg models*

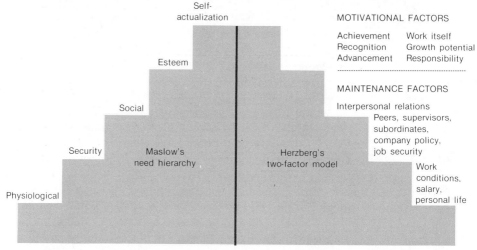

* Also see Keith Davis, *Human Behavior at Work* (New York: McGraw-Hill Book Co., 1977), p. 53.

performed. The individual, therefore, weighs the likelihood that
various behaviors will achieve the desired goal, and if certain behavior
is expected to be more successful than others, that type of behavior
will likely be selected.

An important contribution of Vroom's model is that it explains how
the *goals* of individuals influence their *effort* and that the behavior
individuals select depends upon their assessment of the probability
that the behavior will successfully lead to the goal. For example, all
members of an organization may not place the same value on such job
factors as promotion, high pay, job security, and working conditions.
In other words, they may rank them differently. Vroom believes that
what is important is the perception and value the individual places
upon certain goals. Suppose that one individual places high value on

[18] Vroom, *Work and Motivation.*

salary increases and perceives superior performance as instrumental in reaching that goal. According to Vroom, this individual will strive toward superior performance in order to achieve the salary increases. On the other hand, another individual may value a promotion and perceive political behavior as instrumental in achieving it. This individual, therefore, is not likely to emphasize superior performance to achieve the goal. The reader is now encouraged to think of this in terms of student motivation, where one student has the goal of an A grade and another the goal of a C grade in a particular course. How might their respective efforts and behaviors in the course vary?

In summary, Vroom emphasizes the importance of individual perceptions and assessments of organizational behavior. What is important here is that what the individual perceives as the consequence of a particular behavior is far more important than what the manager (or professor) believes the individual should perceive.[19]

Since the expectancy model is relatively new there are few tests of its validity.[20] It is certainly more abstract than the Maslow and Herzberg models, and, as such, it may be some time before it is of any practical use to a manager. However, despite the lack of tested validity it would seem that the expectancy model adds additional insight into the study of motivation at work since it attempts to explain how *individual goals* influence *individual effort*. Note that the common thread running through each of the three models discussed in this chapter is that behavior is goal directed. Thus, the process of motivation as it was presented earlier in the chapter (Figure 8–1) serves as the cornerstone of the Maslow, Herzberg, and Vroom models of motivation.

Management programs designed to increase motivation

Behavioral scientists have called attention to a number of programs that may be able to motivate workers so that better performance is the

---

[19] Using Vroom's terminology, the behavior of an individual is based upon the strength (*valence*) of the desire for achieving a particular outcome. This is related to perception of how the *first-level* outcome (for example, superior performance, extensive outside reading) is associated with the *second-level* outcome (for example, promotion, an A grade). The individual's perception of this relationship is called *instrumentality*. Finally, *expectancy* is the probability that a particular action will lead to a first-level outcome. It differs from instrumentality in that it relates efforts to first-level outcomes where instrumentality relates first- and second-level outcomes to each other. Thus, Vroom's model is often referred to as the Expectancy/Valence Model.

[20] See V. H. Vroom, "Organizational Choice: A Study of Pre- and Post-Decision Processes," *Organizational Behavior and Human Performance* (August 1966), pp. 212–25; and J. Galbraith and L. L. Cummings, "An Empirical Investigation of the Motivational Determinants of Task Performance: Interactive Effects Between Instrumentality — Valence and Motivation — Ability," *Organizational Behavior and Human Performance* (August 1967), pp. 237–57. For a critical review of field research on expectancy theory predictions of employee performance, see H. G. Heneman III, and D. P. Schwab, "Expectancy Theory Predictions of Employee Performance: A Review of the Theory and Evidence," *Psychological Bulletin* (July 1972), pp. 1–9.

result. Three programs that have been beneficial to some managers are job enrichment, tying pay to job performance, and behavior modification. While others could be cited, the three discussed here appear to be among the most publicized.

JOB ENRICHMENT

The "quality of life" at work is currently receiving much attention from practicing managers, behavioralists, government officials, and union leaders. There is a current wave of interest in humanizing jobs by job enrichment. It appears that many workers are becoming increasingly dissatisfied and frustrated by routine, mechanically paced tasks and are reacting negatively with output restrictions, poor quality work, absenteeism, high turnover, and by pressing for higher wages, expanded fringe benefits, and greater participation in decisions which directly affect their jobs. Earlier we discussed the Herzberg motivational model. In recent efforts, he has gone farther and attempted to increase employee motivation by actually including the motivational factors in a job. This practical contribution of Herzberg is a motivational technique known as *job enrichment* and has been supported by many as a solution to the problem of the "quality of life" at work. He first reported the successful application of his approach in the case of stockholder correspondents employed by a large corporation.[21] Job enrichment as Herzberg describes it,

> . . . seeks to improve both task efficiency and human satisfaction by means of building into people's jobs, quite specifically, greater scope for personal achievement and recognition, more challenging and responsible work, and more opportunity for individual advancement and growth. It is concerned only incidentally with matters such as pay and working conditions, organizational structure, communications, and training, important and necessary though these may be in their own right.[22]

In another series of experiments, Herzberg studied five British firms to determine, among other things, the generality of his original findings.[23] The five studies covered widely different business areas and company functions as well as many types and levels of jobs. The five groups were laboratory technicians in a research and development department, sales representatives, design engineers, production foremen on shift work, and engineering foremen on day work. There were three main features to the study:

---

[21] Frederick Herzberg, "One More Time: How Do You Motivate Employees?" *Harvard Business Review* (January–February 1968), p. 53.

[22] William J. Paul, Jr., Keith B. Robertson, and Frederick Herzberg, "Job Enrichment Pays Off," *Harvard Business Review* (March–April 1969), p. 61.

[23] Ibid.

1. The maintenance factors were held constant. This means that no deliberate changes were made in pay, security, and other maintenance factors, because the researchers were only interested in determining gains which were brought about through change in job content.
2. An "experimental" group was formed for whom the specific changes in job content were made, and a "control" group was formed whose job content remained the same.
3. The fact that the studies were being done was kept confidential. This was done to avoid the well-known tendency of people to behave differently when they are aware that they are part of a study.

The researchers sought to measure job satisfaction and performance for both groups over the study period, which generally lasted one year. Performance measures were specific to the group concerned and, in addition, were determined by the local management of the participating company.

How were the jobs in the experimental group "enriched"? Rather than examine all five groups, let us review the program of action devised and implemented for the sales representatives.

> Sales representatives were no longer obliged to write reports on every customer call. They were asked simply to pass on information when they thought it appropriate or request action as they thought it was required.
> Responsibility for determining calling frequencies was put wholly with the representatives themselves, who kept the only records for purposes such as staff reviews.
> The technical service department agreed to provide service "on demand" from the representatives; nominated technicians regarded such calls as their first priority. Communication was by direct contact, paperwork being cleared after the event.[24]

Following the changes in job content of the sales representatives, there resulted an increase in sales of 19 percent over the same period of the previous year for the experimental group. In the control group, sales declined during the study period by 5 percent. The equivalent change for both groups the previous year had been a decline of 3 percent.

The content of the jobs in the remaining four groups was "enriched" in a fashion similar to that for the sales representatives. The specific changes are not detailed here. However, it is necessary to note that similar positive results were found for each of the other four types of jobs when specific changes were made in the job content of the workers

---

[24] Ibid., p. 66.

in each "experimental" group. The researchers concluded among other things that "tasks have to be motivational—that is, the more they draw upon the motivators, the more likely they are to produce an effective contribution to business objectives."[25]

Herzberg emphasizes the importance of differentiating between *job enrichment* and *job enlargement*. He views job enrichment as providing the employee with an opportunity to grow psychologically and mature in his job, while job enlargement merely makes a job structurally larger by increasing the number of tasks.

The core dimensions of jobs. Building on the work of Herzberg, Hackman and others have identified five core dimensions which if present provide enrichment for jobs.[26] Hackman, after conducting research on many different occupations, concludes that these core dimensions are often not found in many managerial and blue-collar jobs. He also states that there are large individual differences in how employees react to core dimensions. Not all employees want or can benefit from enriched jobs.

Variety. The first core dimension is variety in the job. Variety allows employees to perform different operations using several procedures and perhaps different equipment. Jobs that are high in variety often are viewed as challenging because they require the use of the full range of an employee's skills.

Task identity. The second core dimension, task-identity, allows employees to perform a complete piece of work. Overspecialized jobs tend to create routine job duties. This results in a worker performing one part of the entire job. There is a sense of loss or of nonaccomplishment in doing only a part of a job. Thus, broadening the task to provide the worker with a feeling of doing a whole job is what is meant by task identity.

Task significance. The amount of impact that the work being performed has on other people is called task significance. This impact may be within the organization or outside in the community. The feeling of doing something worthwhile is important to many people. For example, an employee may be told by a respected supervisor that she has done an outstanding job that has contributed to the overall success of the department. The task has significance because it is recognized by a superior.

Autonomy. The fourth core dimension, autonomy, refers to the idea that employees have some control over their job duties and work area. This seems to be an important dimension in stimulating a sense

---

[25] Ibid., p. 77.

[26] J. Richard Hackman, Greg Oldham, Robert Janson, and Kenneth Purdy, "A New Strategy For Job Enrichment," *California Management Review* (Summer 1975), pp. 57–71 and J. Richard Hackman and Greg Oldham, "Development of the Job Diagnostic Survey," *Journal of Applied Psychology* (April 1975), pp. 159–70.

of responsibility. The popular practice of management by objectives discussed in Chapter 4 is one way of establishing more autonomy because it provides employees with an opportunity to set work and personal goals.

Feedback. The fifth core dimension, feedback, refers to information that workers receive on how well they are performing. People in general have a need to know how they are doing. They need this feedback frequently so that necessary improvements can be made.

Diagnosing jobs. These five core dimensions are what Hackman and his associates believe need to be modified to accomplish job enrich-

FIGURE 8–5
Profiles of core dimensions for two jobs

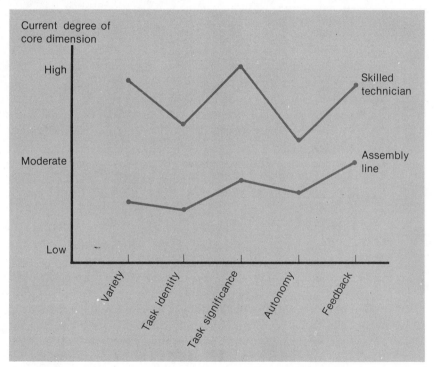

ment. They suggest that organizations can study jobs to determine the quantity and quality of the core dimensions for each job. Hackman and Oldham developed the Job Diagnostic Survey (JDS) to measure each dimension.[27] By measuring the core dimensions the weak dimensions can be identified and perhaps modified.

Profiles of two jobs are presented in Figure 8–5. One job is that of a skilled technician, while the other is an assembly line position. By

[27] Hackman and Oldham, "Development of the Job Diagnostic Survey."

use of the JDS, worker opinions, and managerial opinions, a job's core dimensions can be studied in depth. The weak dimensions can be pinpointed and managerial attention to these problem areas can result in job enrichment. Not all jobs can be enriched in each core dimension. This constraint, however, should not stop managers from attempting to search further for methods to improve the total job or a specific core dimension.

The Hackman approach to job enrichment attempts not only to profile jobs but to examine the employee's readiness for enrichment and the special problems that may hinder any job redesign. The employee who does not have a need for autonomy and feedback may not respond favorably to any job enrichment attempt. Thus the employee's need strength is an important factor in developing the most appropriate job enrichment strategy.

One special problem of job enrichment that needs to be considered is how the program can be continued after it is started. How far will management go in each core dimension area? What is the limit of autonomy that management is willing to build into the job? If management is reluctant to continually diagnose and modify the job enrichment program, further improvement will be difficult. The management team needs to consider the following questions when reviewing job enrichment:

1. Can the employee accept more responsibility?
2. Can the employee work with more autonomy?
3. Is management able to accept changes in jobs that may result in more worker autonomy and more feedback?

Organizational applications of job enrichment. One attempt to implement job enrichment occurred at Saab-Scania in the 1960s.[28] The engine assembly group was organized as a team. Each team consisted of employees who assembled the entire engine and were in charge of their work area. There was no mechanical assembly line. Each team was able to control its own work pace and team arrangement. Workers rotated job duties to minimize boredom. Following this team arrangement, Saab-Scania reported increased productivity, higher job satisfaction, reduced turnover, and fewer work stoppages.

An attempt to enrich jobs was built into a General Foods pet-food plant that opened in 1971.[29] The new plant management established work teams of seven to fourteen employees. Teams were given large amounts of autonomy and frequent feedback. There was also a high

---

[28] Noel M. Tichy, "Organizational Innovations In Sweden," *The Columbia Journal of World Business* (Summer 1974), pp. 18–27.

[29] Richard E. Walton, "How To Counter Alienation In The Plant," *Harvard Business Review* (November–December 1972), pp. 70–81.

degree of variety built into each job. Most routine work was mechanized. The five core dimensions appear to have been provided to a large extent.

Preliminary results indicate that the pet-food plant compared favorably to more traditionally operated plants. Productivity was greater and absenteeism and turnover were less in the pet-food plant. It has been suggested that the positive results may have occurred because the pet-food facility was new. These results began to weaken in 1977, as reported in the Management in Action description presented at the beginning of this chapter.

The Non-Linear Systems experiment offers a caution to advocates of job enrichment.[30] The firm manufactured digital electrical measuring instruments. Management replaced an assembly line with teams of three to twelve employees. Managers of each team provided minimal supervision. The teams decided how the instruments would be produced. Work could be rotated and the pace controlled by the team. Each group was also responsible for resolving conflicts and handling disciplinary problems.

The first set of findings at Non-Linear revealed increased productivity and morale. Over a period of years, however, productivity and quality began to suffer. The teams were not able to make quick decisions because there was little structure within the units. The team members became dissatisfied. After approximately four years of experimenting, the firm reverted to its previous managerial practices.

These three experiences suggest that the implementation of job enrichment principles can be successful in some situations but not in others. There is also the question of how long performance improvements can continue. This is an important issue in the General Foods example. Job enrichment should not be viewed as a universally desirable program. Some workers and managers cannot operate effectively under job enrichment conditions. Therefore, both worker and managerial reactions need to be considered by managers before implementing job enrichment.

PAY AND JOB PERFORMANCE

Research evidence indicates that in some cases pay can be used to motivate employee performance.[31] In order for a pay plan to motivate, it must (1) create a belief that good performance leads to high levels of pay, (2) minimize the negative consequences of good performance,

---

[30] Erwin L. Malone, "The Non-Linear Systems Experiment in Participative Management," *Journal of Business* (January 1975), pp. 52–64.

[31] The best available discussion of pay and performance appears in Edward E. Lawler III, *Pay and Organizational Effectiveness* (New York: McGraw-Hill, 1971).

and (3) create conditions so that desired rewards other than pay are seen to be related to good performance.[32]

One procedure for creating the belief that pay is related to performance is to relate pay directly to job performance and to make this relationship clear to everyone. Several studies have attempted to determine whether this is typically done in organizations. It appears that pay is not very closely related to performance in many organizations that supposedly have merit salary programs. Lawler reports that pay seems to be more closely related to job level, seniority, and other non-performance factors.

Overall, research findings suggest that many organizations do not do a very good job of relating pay to performance. This conclusion applies to both managers and nonmanagers. It is surprising that in the managerial ranks, where no unions exist, pay is not related to performance. This may mean that pay is not a very powerful motivator.

Relating pay to performance. Managers use numerous methods in their attempt to relate pay to performance. Campbell, Dunnette, Lawler, and Weick in a survey of personnel practices reported high dissatisfaction with pay programs.[33] It seems that many plans are disliked because they are implemented poorly or because they are not well suited for a particular job.

Lawler has developed a list of different types of incentive pay plans and offers an effectiveness rating for each on three separate criteria.[34] First, each plan is rated in terms of how effective it is in creating the perception that pay is tied to performance. Second, the plans are evaluated in terms of minimizing negative side effects, such as disruptive competition, conflict, and grievances. Third, each plan is rated in terms of whether it contributes to the perception that important rewards other than pay (e.g., feelings of worth and increased responsibility) result from good performance. The ratings Lawler proposes range from +3 to −3, with a +3 indicating that the plan is effective with regard to the criterion, while −3 indicates that the plan is a failure.

The Lawler ratings indicate that no one plan is the answer to all pay problems. Each company has problems associated with its pay plans that could be minimized by using the best approach for the situation. It is necessary to analyze the foregoing criteria and such factors as the nature of the job being done, cost-of-living increases, seniority, and actual performance if pay is to have any motivational value. The most difficult part of the necessary analysis is the measure-

[32] Ibid.

[33] John P. Campbell, Marvin D. Dunnette, Edward E. Lawler III and Karl E. Weick, Jr., *Managerial Behavior, Performance and Effectiveness* (New York: McGraw-Hill, 1970), pp. 51–59.

[34] Lawler, *Pay and Organizational Effectiveness.*

TABLE 8-1
Ratings of selected pay-incentive plans

	Type of plan	Performance measure	Tie pay to per-formance	Minimize negative side effects	Tie other rewards to per-formance
Salary	Individual plan	Productivity	+2	0	0
		Cost effectiveness	+1	0	0
		Superiors' rating	+1	0	+1
	Group	Productivity	+1	0	+1
		Cost effectiveness	+1	0	+1
		Superiors' rating	+1	0	+1
	Organizationwide	Productivity	+1	0	+1
		Cost effectiveness	+1	0	+1
		Profits	0	0	+1
Bonus	Individual plan	Productivity	+3	−2	0
		Cost effectiveness	+2	−1	0
		Superiors' rating	+2	−1	+1
	Group	Productivity	+2	0	+1
		Cost effectiveness	+2	0	+1
		Superiors' rating	+2	0	+1
	Organizationwide	Productivity	+2	0	+1
		Cost effectiveness	+2	0	+1
		Profits	+1	0	+1

Source: Edward E. Lawler III, *Pay and Organizational Effectiveness* (New York: McGraw-Hill, 1971) pp. 164–65.

ment of performance. The criteria to measure performance must be valid, equitable, and accepted.

A note of caution. In many jobs it is difficult to develop valid, equitable, and accepted measures of performance. Therefore, it is difficult to relate pay to performance. For example, measures of college teaching effectiveness are quite controversial. No widely accepted objective measure of college teaching performance exists, although subjective peer or student measures are often used.

In other situations too much emphasis may be placed on objective measures of performance. If only objective measures are used in determining pay increases, then the employee may emphasize only these and disregard others that are also important. Management must balance the objective and subjective evaluations of performance.

Another important issue involved in tying pay to performance is that of the amounts. Motivating high performers may cost a lot of money. A company that cannot afford large increases may not want to use pay to motivate exceptional performance. Moreover, some individuals are not motivated by even large increases in pay. Management

needs to determine what value employees place on pay before tying
pay increases to performance.

In summary, behavioralists suggest that before pay is used to
motivate good performance, management needs to consider a number
of issues. They are:

1. Methods of measuring individual job performance,
2. The subjective-objective mix for evaluating job performance,
3. The size of pay rewards for high performers,
4. The preferences of the employees,
5. The length of time between performance and a pay reward (e.g.,
    the longer the time, the more difficult it is to show that pay is
    tied to performance).

BEHAVIOR MODIFICATION

A method for improving employee productivity which has emerged
in recent years is behavior modification. This method is based largely
on the theory and research of B. F. Skinner[35] who emphasizes the
effect of environmental influences on behavior.

Skinner distinguishes between respondent and operant behavior.
Respondent behavior is the type that occurs because of some prior
stimulus. It is unlearned, instinctive behavior. One does not learn to
sneeze or to cough. Operant behavior, on the other hand, must be
learned.

The fundamental difference between respondent and operant behavior can be further illustrated by the relationship between response
and the environment. In respondent behavior the environment acts on
the person and there is a response. The doctor taps a knee and the leg
moves — respondent behavior. However, the patient must first call the
doctor for an appointment — operant behavior.

In studying this distinction, Skinner introduced the concept of
operant conditioning. In Skinner's theory operant behavior is based
on or is contingent on a response. Thus, learned behavior operates on
the environment to produce a change. If the behavior causes a change,
then Skinner states that this environmental change is contingent upon
the behavior. For example, being permitted to drive across a toll bridge
is contingent upon inserting the proper change in a coin meter. If the
proper change is inserted, the green light will flash and the gate will
go up. The behavior is inserting the coin, and the consequence is the
gate going up.

Over the years, scientific experimentation has produced information

---

[35] B. F. Skinner, *Contingencies of Reinforcement* (New York: Appleton-Century-
Crofts, 1969).

needed to implement behavioral modification programs in organizations. Three specific strategies have emerged from this work—*positive reinforcement, negative reinforcement, and punishment*. The strategies can and are used singly or in various combinations to improve performance.

Positive reinforcement refers to an increase in the frequency of a response which is followed by a positive reinforcer. These reinforcers are often called rewards. For example, an employee repeatedly produces large quantities of parts because he is paid on a piece-rate basis. Something is reinforcing the behavior to produce the large quantities. In this example, pay is the positive reinforcer (reward) that increases the frequency with which the worker produces large quantities.

Negative reinforcement refers to an increase in the frequency of a response which is brought about by removing a disliked event immediately after the response occurs. An example would be an employee who has a supervisor who continually nags about producing more units. By producing more, the worker causes the supervisor to stop nagging. The removal of the nagging supervisor results in more production.

Punishment is the introduction of something disliked or the removal of something liked following a response which decreases the frequency of that response. A worker may tell the supervisor that she has discovered a way to reduce machine downtime. The supervisor publically reprimands her for wasting time working on stupid projects like this and to get back to work. The actions of the supervisor are punishment-oriented because they are disliked and will probably reduce the tendency of the worker to be creative.

Management literature indicates that the positive reinforcement strategy is the most widely used for motivating employees to better performance. Some companies have used money, praise, recognition, or even tokens to be redeemed later, as positive reinforcers.[36]

Organizational applications of behavior modification.[37] Emery Air Freight has used positive reinforcement as a behavior modification strategy. Under the direction of Edward J. Feeney, a vice president at the time of the introduction of behavior modification at Emery, the company reported a saving of $2 million over a three-year period. Feeney developed what he called a *Performance Audit* for identifying performance-related behaviors and strengthening them with positive reinforcement.

An audit was conducted to find the job behaviors that were most closely linked to profit. The strategy was to tell individuals who were

---

[36] An excellent summary of some organizationally based behavior modification programs appears in W. C. Hamner and E. P. Hamner, "Behavior Modification on the Bottom Line," *Organizational Dynamics* (Spring 1976), pp. 2–21.

[37] Ibid.

responsible for profit-oriented behaviors how they were doing. This *feedback* was a part of learning for the employees. They found out for the first time on a regular basis how they were doing and what the company thought about their work.

The Emery program is kept simple in each unit. First, the audit identifies the key performance behaviors. Second, management establishes a realistic goal and gives the employees frequent feedback on how they are performing. Third, improved performance is strengthened by positive reinforcement such as praise and recognition. The main thrust of the Emery program is to provide timely feedback and to use positive reinforcement that is contingent upon performance improvement.

B. F. Goodrich Chemical Company utilized a positive reinforcement program. One production section in a B. F. Goodrich plant in Ohio was not performing well. After identifying some problems, the production manager introduced a positive reinforcement program. The program provided cost, scheduling, and goal accomplishment information directly to the first-line supervisors once a week. Daily meetings were also held to discuss how each group in the section was doing. This program allowed the supervisor and subordinates to look at the performance of the group on a regular basis. Illustrative charts were developed that showed achievements in terms of sales, cost, and production as compared to goals.

The evaluation of this program by company representatives indicated that production increased over 300 percent in five years. Costs of production went down. The company believed that these impressive results were largely the result of providing the supervisors and employees with feedback about their performance.

Criticisms of behavior modification. Despite impressive results from behavior modification, there are many critics of this approach.[38] Some of the major criticisms of behavior modification are:

It is coercive.

It is bribery.

It is dependent upon extrinsic reinforcers.

It requires continual reinforcement.

One means to avoid coercion is to have employees participate in the development of the reinforcement program. Participative behavior modification programs are certainly possible.

In some programs, tokens are used to reward employees for not being absent or for performing well. The critics charge that this is an illicit use of rewards, and also that it demeans the persons receiving them.

---

[38] Fred L. Fry, "Operant Conditioning in Organizational Settings: Of Mice or Men," *Personnel* (July–August, 1974), pp. 17–24.

They point out that tokens are sometimes used in mental institutions for patients who display socially acceptable behavior, and argue that they ought not to be applied to normal employees in a work setting.

Some critics object that reinforcement leads to a dependence upon reinforcers. This could result in extrinsic reinforcers always being required in order to secure acceptable performance. The issue here is whether enough extrinsic reinforcers can be found to continue the program. If the same reinforcers are used over and over again, they become boring and lose their effect.

The final criticism focuses on the necessity for continual reinforcement. To be successful, behavioral modification requires that supervisors monitor closely the performance of their subordinates and reward continually each instance of desired behavior. Yet in many organizations managers simply do not have sufficient time to devote to such close supervision.

Behavior modification, like the use of a good pay plan, or job enrichment, will work in some organizations but not in others. The evidence of success is not overwhelming, but it does appear promising. Of course, failures are usually not as widely publicized as successes. It appears that Skinner's ideas may be used by some managers to obtain some degree of performance improvement. So far, however, there is no indication that behavior modification will become the cornerstone of motivation programs in a majority of organizations.

Summary

We have examined motivation, an area of prime importance in the Behavioral School. Motivation is closely related to individual needs and to personality. A knowledge of these behavioral concepts provides managers with insight into the complex area of human motivation.

We have also examined three management techniques—job enrichment, pay, and behavior modification—whose supporters believe can lead to many positive consequences if utilized correctly. The authors do not contend that any of these techniques is free of limitations for managers. There are also many additional techniques not discussed in this text for lack of space. We do not mean to imply by omission that those other techniques will not result in positive performance improvements if they are utilized.

One final comment is in order: The reader should note that discussions of motivation techniques such as job enrichment, pay and performance, and behavior modification, stress the necessity to adapt the techniques to each situation. The special and unique characteristics of each organization must be considered; for example the needs of managers and subordinates vary in strength and intensity. We shall see in following chapters that advocates of behavioral science approaches emphasize the appropriate matching of techniques to situations.

Discussion and review questions

1. Why do some writers claim that if management enriches the job's core dimensions, a worker may become more motivated?

2. Are there any differences between expectancy theory and behavior modification?

3. The manager of a fast-food restaurant was overheard saying, "I believe that money is the best of all possible motivators. You can say what you please about all that other nonsense, but when it comes right down to it, if you give a guy a raise, you'll motivate him. That's all there is to it." In light of what we have discussed in this chapter, advise this restaurant manager.

4. Think of a situation from your personal experiences in which two individuals reacted differently to frustration. Discuss each situation and the reactions of the two individuals. Can you give a possible explanation why the two individuals reacted differently?

5. Some critics of job enrichment and behavior modification programs state that most of the declared successes are based on faulty measurements or short periods of time. A proper evaluation over a longer period of time would show less positive results with these behaviorally oriented programs. Comment.

6. Can the job of a manager be validly measured so that pay can be more closely tied to performance?

7. In this chapter it was emphasized that managers must be familiar with the fundamental needs of man in order to motivate employees successfully. Select two individuals with whom you are well acquainted. Do they differ, in your opinion, with respect to the strength of various needs? Discuss these differences and indicate how they could affect behavior. If you were attempting to motivate those persons, would you use different approaches for each? Why?

8. Can a student's "job" be enriched? Assume that your professor has asked you to consult with him about applying the "two-factor" motivation model in your class. You are to answer two questions for him: (1) Can you apply this approach to the classroom? Why? and (2) If so, differentiate between maintenance and motivational factors and develop a list of motivational factors your professor can use to "enrich" the student's job.

9. Assume that you have just read Vroom's thoughts on how the *goals* of individuals influence their *effort* and that the behavior the individual selects depends upon his assessment of the probability that the behavior will successfully lead to the goal. What is your goal in this management course? Is it influencing your effort? Do you suppose another person in

your class might have a different goal? Is his or her effort (behavior) different from yours? If your professor was aware of this, could it be of any value to him?
10. What is the difference between intrinsic and extrinsic rewards? What types of rewards are used in job enrichment, pay, and behavior modification programs?

Additional references

Fein, M. "Motivation For Work," in R. Dubin, ed. Handbook of Work, Organization and Society. Chicago: Rand McNally, 1976.

Hackman, J. R., and Suttle, J. L., eds. Improving Life At Work. Santa Monica: Goodyear Publishing, 1977.

Herzberg, F. "Motivation-Hygiene Profiles." Organizational Dynamics (Fall 1974): 18–29.

Herzberg, F. "The Wise Old Turk," Harvard Business Review (September–October, 1974): 70–80.

Kazdin, A. E. Behavior Modification In Applied Settings. Homewood, Ill.: The Dorsey Press, 1975.

Lawler, E. E. III. Motivation In Work Organizations. Monterrey, Calif.: Brooks/Cole, 1973.

Luthans, F., and Kreitner, R. Organizational Behavior Modification. Glenview, Ill.: Scott, Foresman and Co., 1975.

Meyer, H. "The Pay-For-Performance Dilemma," Organizational Dynamics (Winter 1975): 39–50.

Pedalino, E., and Gamboa, V. "Behavior Modification and Absenteeism: Intervention In One Industrial Setting," Journal of Applied Psychology (1974): 694–698.

Schaefer, S. D. The Motivation Process. Cambridge, Mass.: Winthrop Publishers, Inc., 1977.

Schrank, R. "Work In America: What Do Workers Really Want?" Industrial Relations (1974): 24–29.

Steers, R. M., and Porter, L. W. Motivation and Work Behavior. New York: McGraw-Hill, 1975.

PRACTICAL EXERCISE I
A Frustrated Nurse

Nanci Green is a licensed practical nurse at Michael's Hospital. She has worked for six years in various jobs at the hospital and is considered a dedicated and exceptional nurse. Her supervisor, Toni Jones, has noticed that Nanci has been moody and irritable for the past few months. Apparently Nanci has been frustrated because she would like to be promoted to a more challenging and better paying position. However, all better nursing positions at Michael's demand the RN (registered nurse) degree as a requirement.

Every supervisor at Michael's believes that Nanci would make an excellent registered nurse. However, she has expressed little interest in going to school to earn the required degree. In fact Nanci believes that her work experience is sufficient to allow her to be promoted. She has even considered resigning and finding a job in another occupation. This drastic action is not compatible with her desire to be a nurse, which has been her career goal for years.

There is no chance that Nanci can be given a promotion without earning the degree. This is a legal requirement of the collective bargaining agreement that the nurses have with the hospital. Therefore, Toni is considering what she can do to motivate Nanci to go on to school and obtain the RN degree. The nursing director has instructed Toni to do whatever is necessary to get Nanci to go to school.

Questions for analysis:
1. What goal of Nanci's is being blocked by not having the RN degree?
2. What should Toni do to help motivate Nanci to go on to school?

PRACTICAL EXERICSE II
John Sloane

Since he was in between his sophomore and junior years in college, Jeff Bailey considered himself very fortunate to land a summer job in the stock transfer department at one of the largest stockbrokers in his home town. The job would provide him with some spending money for his junior year but perhaps also give him some practical work experience. Since he was a business administration major he thought this might be especially valuable.

His job consisted of the following: When a purchase order for securities was received, it was typed on a purchase order form which consisted of four different colored carbon copies. The form was pulled apart and each colored carbon went to a specific department in the firm. Jeff's group received the pink copy. Jeff sat at a long table with five other men. The forms would come in batches, and his task was to look up the closing price of the security for the previous day, multiply it by the number of shares purchased, and write the total figure on the form. It was not necessary to be precise; it was only an estimate, since stock prices fluctuated. On a busy day the forms would pile up. If they were not completed by the end of the day, the group had to work overtime until all work was completed. The job wasn't much of a challenge, Jeff thought, but at least it gave him spending money.

After his first week on the job Jeff learned that two of his coworkers were students like himself; two others were attending a local university part-time in the evening while working during the day. The other was John Sloane. John had been employed by the firm for 37 years in various clerical jobs and had been doing his present job for over five years. He knew his job so well that, unlike the others, he did not consult a list to identify the prices of securities. He had the approximate prices committed to memory. Jeff heard that Sloan was paid $140 per week, twice the amount he was making. Sloane stayed by himself mostly and rarely talked with other members of the group.

Jeff worked well with the group and they often went to lunch together and to dinner on the nights when overtime was necessary. One night, on returning early from dinner, Jeff saw John Sloane stuffing a large batch of purchase forms into his coat pocket in the cloak room. Jeff didn't say anything but was embarrassed. John Sloane said nothing.

A few days later when the two were alone John confided in Jeff that he did it occasionally when work piled up in order to get home at a reasonable time. He said, "What difference does it make? By the time it shows up it might be two or three months and they can't trace it to any department. Besides there are three other carbon copies floating around the company. Believe me, kid, this company doesn't give a damn about you or me so don't give them an inch more than you have to."

Jeff never said anything about his conversation with Sloane. During the summer he became pretty friendly with John and found him to be a likeable person.

As he sat on the plane returning to school in the fall, Jeff thought about John Sloane. Actually he didn't know really what to think about John—whether to like him or dislike him, respect him or not respect him. Frankly, he was puzzled.

Questions for analysis:

1. Assume you had just been hired as head of the stock transfer department and were made aware of John Sloane's behavior. In terms of what you have just read in the chapter, can you provide a possible explanation for his behavior?
2. What do you believe are the causes of John Sloane's behavior?
3. Can anything be done to motivate John Sloane in a positive direction? Explain.

PRACTICAL EXERCISE III
Motivating Different Individuals

Below are brief descriptions of several individuals. Assume that you are their manager. Select from the following the strategy that you feel would be most likely to motivate each person to improved performance. Explain your reasons for selecting it.

a. An individual incentive plan.
b. Recognition for achievement.
c. A salary increase.
d. Threat of demotion or discharge.
e. Additional status (for example, bigger office, title, carpeting in office, secretary).
f. A group profit-sharing plan.
g. Job enrichment.
h. Additional fringe benefits.
i. More participation in management decisions.
j. More freedom of action (that is, less supervision).

1. Jim Hammer is a marketing representative for a large pharmaceutical firm. His job involves calling on medical doctors to promote the firm's line of prescription drugs. He is 27 years old, married with one child, and holds a college degree in business administration. He has been with the firm five years and earns $15,700 annually.

2. Barbara Oldec is head pediatrics nurse at a large public hospital. She is 29 years old, married with two children, and is currently pursuing a master's degree. She has a reputation among staff physicians as an extremely competent nurse. Her yearly salary is $12,000.

3. John Ekard is vice president of operations for one of the nation's largest fast-food franchisers. He is 51 years old, divorced, and has

three children—two attend college and one is married. He has been with the company for nine years and earns a salary of $52,500 per year. He is among a group of top-level executives in the company who share in company profits through a bonus system.

4. Dave Noe is a part-time employee for a large supermarket chain. He is 26 years old, an Air Force veteran, and has worked for the firm before entering and after being discharged from the service. He is a highly valued employee and earns approximately $4.50 per hour. He also attends a local university and is presently completing the final 12 hours for a degree in business administration.

5. Marie Glass is assistant director of market development for a new space industry firm. She is 25 years old, single, bright, witty, and energetic. She exemplifies the "new woman." Her annual salary is $14,000. She has just completed her master's degree.

6. Bill Porter is assistant manager of a low-priced restaurant which is part of a 14-unit chain. He is 25 years old, single, and has three years of college. He works six days each week and earns $150 per week. He receives about $4,000 per year from a family inheritance.

7. Betty Harris is the administrative assistant to the dean of a liberal arts college. She is 31 years old, single, and has had one year of secretarial training. Her duties involve counseling students on degree requirements, supervising registration, and keeping student records. She earns $9,500 per year. She has been at the college for 12 years where she began as a typist.

8. John Richards is a research chemist for one of the nation's largest chemical companies. He joined the firm four years ago upon graduating from a leading university. He is 26 years old and his present annual salary is $13,500 per year. He is getting married in two months.

9. Sam Wilson supervises the 16-man night cleaning crew in a large office building. He has been supervisor for two years, being promoted to his present job after performing various cleaning jobs for 11 years. He is 44 years old, married, and has two children. He earns $10,000 per year. Three days each week he holds a part-time job on the cleaning crew at a local hospital. During the baseball season he works Sundays at the local stadium when the home team is playing.

10. Dr. Thomas Pryor is professor of history at a well-known university. He is well recognized in his field of American history, having published several articles in respected professional journals and written one well-recognized text. However, he has not written anything during the past four years. He is a full professor with tenure, earning the top salary in his department, $25,000. He is 40 years old, married, and has three children under ten years of age. His interest and enthusiasm for teaching appear to have declined during the last two years, and his excellent teacher ratings by students have also begun to decline slightly.

9

WORK GROUPS

MANAGEMENT IN ACTION*

Until recently, executives who sat on the compensation committees of even the largest U.S. corporations were not given to making waves. However, today's typical compensation committee is much more active and independent than it traditionally has been. Instead of simply reacting to proposals it usually takes the lead. It calls on experts from both inside and outside the firm for fact-finding and advice. For example, the committee often hires an outside consulting firm to review everything the company is doing in the field of compensation as compared with what its competitors are doing, and also to design new plans that will more effectively motivate and reward its executives. In some cases the committee calls in leading firms like McKinsey & Co. or Booz, Allen & Hamilton, Inc., to evaluate a new plan.

A compensation committee usually meets formally no more than four times a year, but the decisions it makes are very crucial. Companies like Thiokol, Mobil, Olin Corporation, and Squibb expect their compensation committees to be on top of problems, to keep up with the activities of competitors, and to be aware of the latest Internal Revenue Service rulings. The job of these committees is to decide whether or not a compensation plan for managers is reasonable and will tie an executive's pay to performance. The committees must always try to maintain an equitable balance between the interests of management and of shareholders.

Passing judgment on the quality and equity of a compensation plan is difficult for any committee. In most instances the committee must attempt to evaluate how well various members of the management team are performing their jobs. This, of course, makes the job of a committee member challenging and extremely difficult.

* A more detailed discussion of compensation committees is found in "The Men Who Set Your Salary," *Duns Review* (February 1977), pp. 75–76, 78.

Few managers question the existence of work groups. This chapter is concerned with the general concept of groups in all types of organizations. Beginning with the famous Hawthorne studies of the 1920s, behavioral scientists have paid special attention to the processes occurring within groups which affect individuals and organizations. Thus, any presentation of a behavioral approach to management would certainly be incomplete if the reader were not provided with a framework for understanding the nature and characteristics of work groups.

The purpose of this chapter is to provide (1) a classification of the different types of work groups; (2) some explanation of methods utilized to study work groups; (3) some knowledge about the reasons for formation and development of work groups; (4) an understanding of some of the characteristics of groups; and (5) some insights into the results of group membership.

An appropriate definition of the term "work group" is essential to an analysis of the way in which behavioral scientists discuss groups in the management literature. The list of elaborate definitions proposed by individuals studying work groups is endless. However, a concise definition is as follows: A work group is a collection of employees (managerial or nonmanagerial), sharing certain norms, who are striving toward member need satisfaction through the attainment of a group goal(s).

Students often ask why work groups should be studied in a management text. There are, of course, many different answers which can be provided. Some of the more relevant responses are:

1. The formation of work group(s) is inevitable and ubiquitous. Consequently, no matter how rewarding or satisfying it is to work in a particular organization, it is almost certain that work groups will be formed. Thus it is in management's interest to understand what happens within work groups because they are found throughout the organization.
2. Work groups strongly influence the overall behavior and performance of members. To understand the forces of influence exerted by the group requires a systematic analysis.
3. Group membership can have both positive and negative consequences as far as the organization is concerned. If managers are to avoid the negative consequences generated by work groups, it behooves them to learn about groups.

These three answers are typical of the numerous explanations provided when writers are attempting to justify their discussion of work groups. The common thread found in most answers is that groups exist and are a force which affect the attitudes and behaviors of employees. This is the most obvious and pragmatic reason for the study of groups; no further justification or explanation is needed.

Classification of groups

Every organization has technical requirements which arise from its stated goals. The accomplishment of these goals requires certain tasks to be performed, and employees are assigned to groups to perform these tasks. In addition, other types of groups form which are not the result of deliberate design. Accordingly, we can identify two broad classes of groups in organizations—formal and informal groups.

Most employees will be members of a group based on their positions in the organization. These formal groups are the departments, units, etc. that the organization forms to do the work of the organization. The demands and processes of the organization lead to the formation of these groups.

On the other hand, whenever employees associate on a fairly continuous basis there is a tendency for groups to form whose activities may be different from those required by the organization. These informal groups are natural groupings of people in the work situation in response to social needs. In other words, they do not arise as a result of deliberate design but rather evolve naturally. While this distinction is convenient for our discussion later in the chapter on specific types of groups in organizations, both formal and informal groups exhibit the same general characteristics. Thus, throughout the chapters we should use the term work group unless otherwise specified.

The influence of informal groups over employee behavior and performance was spelled out in the famous Hawthorne studies. In the bank wiring room portion of the study, a group of workers were observed for approximately three months. This group had specific norms for level of output and other aspects of job behavior. The group decided to produce two units a day and to finish the second unit exactly at quitting time. Any group member who tried to speed up the work to change the two-unit norm was ridiculed. These behaviors existed despite the fact that the group had the capability to produce more and despite the existence of what management believed was a good pay incentive plan.

The point of the Hawthorne example is not that informal groups are disruptive to managers. Rather, it illustrates the powerful influence that groups can exert over their members. Both formal and informal groups can exert powerful influence forces. This influence can be economic, social, psychological, or even physical.

Techniques for studying groups

Behavioral scientists believe that managers must continually acquire vital knowledge about factors such as characteristics of group structure, the impact of groups on the attitudes of members, and how the membership influences phenomena like group culture and attractiveness. The methods typically suggested by behavioral scientists have, in most instances, proved successful in studying group behavior in a laboratory setting. The college classroom, management development seminar, or boys' day camp are often used as settings for investigating group phenomena. These settings are not exactly similar to a company office or production department work area, an internal revenue service office, or an emergency room in a hospital, but many perceptive insights are provided by laboratory group behavior studies. For example, the flow of communication and personal interaction, the emergence of leaders, and the exercise of pressure upon members are some of the phenomena that can be examined in laboratory settings.

Several methods for studying group behavior are proposed in the behavioral literature. Two methods, developed over two decades ago yet continually discussed in the contemporary literature, are Bales's interaction analysis and Moreno's sociometric analysis.

BALES'S INTERACTION ANALYSIS

R. F. Bales developed what is called the interaction analysis to obtain work group behavior data by observing directly what is occurring within a group. He studied groups attempting to reach a decision (for example, solving a business case). After studying groups in the laboratory setting, Bales concluded that group behavior can be classified as task oriented and human-relations oriented. He proposed that through group interaction a number of task and human-relations reactions occur in both positive and negative forms.[1]

Bales observed the interactions and recorded the group discussion that occurred in leaderless groups attempting to analyze a case in human relations. He identified 12 categories of interactions which occurred within the groups as they attempted to resolve the case. The 12 categories were briefly described as follows:[2]

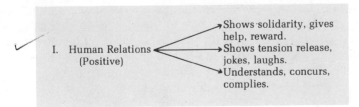

I. Human Relations (Positive) → Shows solidarity, gives help, reward. → Shows tension release, jokes, laughs. → Understands, concurs, complies.

[1] R. F. Bales and F. L. Strodbeck, "Phases in Group Problem Solving," *The Journal of Abnormal and Social Psychology* (October 1951), pp. 485–95. For a complete discussion of the interaction analysis, see R. F. Bales, *Interaction Process Analysis: A Method for the Study of Small Groups* (Cambridge, Mass.: Addison-Wesley, Inc., 1950).

[2] Ibid.

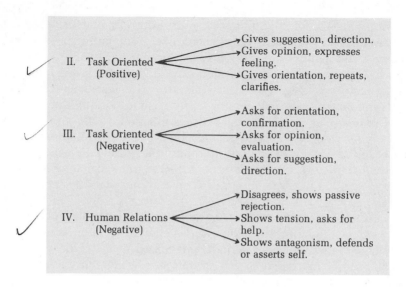

II.   Task Oriented ← Gives suggestion, direction.
      (Positive)   Gives opinion, expresses
                         feeling.
                         Gives orientation, repeats,
                         clarifies.

III. Task Oriented ← Asks for orientation,
      (Negative)   confirmation.
                         Asks for opinion,
                         evaluation.
                         Asks for suggestion,
                         direction.

IV.   Human Relations ← Disagrees, shows passive
      (Negative)   rejection.
                         Shows tension, asks for
                         help.
                         Shows antagonism, defends
                         or asserts self.

After the group case-solving sessions, members completed a questionnaire concerning their reactions, their satisfactions, their relations to each other, and their opinions about their discussion group. From the questionnaire answers and from observation, Bales developed an interaction profile of satisfied and dissatisfied case-solving groups using his 12-category descriptive system.

Another procedure developed by Bales for understanding of work group behavior and interaction is the who-to-whom matrix. Bales tabulated the number of discussions between individuals, who initiated the discussion, and who addressed discussion to the group as a whole.

Bales found that the patterns of discussion varied under different circumstances. For example, groups with no designated leader generally tend to have more equal participation than groups with designated leaders of higher status. It was also found that the size of the group is an important factor affecting within-group discussion patterns. The leader in groups larger than five tends to speak considerably more to the group as a whole than to specific members. All other members tend to speak more to specific individuals than to the group as a whole. As groups increase in size, a larger and larger proportion of the activity tends to be addressed to the leader, and a smaller and smaller proportion to other members. In effect, the communication pattern tends to "centralize" around the leader.

In addition to tracing communication patterns, Bales also studied the roles of group members. Specifically, he investigated the roles of the best idea person, best guidance person, best liked, and scapegoat.

The individual who had the best ideas and gave the most guidance was classified as the group task specialist, while the best-liked person was viewed as the group human relations specialist.

By using these two classifications, Bales introduced an interesting analysis of what can happen if, for example, the human relations specialist attempts to take over the group from the task specialist. This type of internal struggling can disrupt the activities and overall performance of the group. The implication of this part of the Bales analysis is that groups work more effectively with two members filling the two separate leader roles.

Bales's interaction analysis furnishes a valuable technique for analyzing small-group functioning in laboratory settings. The findings and insights of his research provide managers with insights about communication patterns, roles, and the status systems within work groups. Thus, although it would be extremely difficult, if not impossible, to perform interaction analysis in a real world organization setting, the laboratory-based findings provide needed knowledge about groups. The vital questions regarding what makes a group "tick," what is the pattern of group communications, and who is the task leader and human relations leader can be coped with more effectively if research findings similar to those of Bales are available to managers.

MORENO'S SOCIOMETRIC ANALYSIS

The sociometric-analysis method of studying work group behavior and structural characteristics involves the use of self-reports from group members. These reports indicate the preference and repulsion patterns of group members. Based on the expressed choices of members, this method provides insights about the leaders and status hierarchy of the group and about communication patterns to those interested in such phenomena.[3]

For the purpose of understanding the complex communication patterns and interactions of groups, Moreno asked group members whom they liked and disliked within the group,[4] enabling him to gain knowledge about group relations. From the data collected by interview and/or questionnaire, Moreno was able to construct a *sociogram*.

The *sociogram* is a diagram which illustrates the interpersonal relationships existing within a group. Figure 9–1 presents a simple sociogram based upon feelings of attraction reported by a group of workers. The line from Nick to Jim represents an expressed choice by Nick. That is, Nick likes to work with Jim. The Jim-to-Nick lines shows

---

[3] J. L. Moreno, "Contributions to Sociometry to Research Methodology in Sociology," *American Sociological Review* (June 1947), pp. 287–92.

[4] J. H. Jacobs, "The Application of Sociometry to Industry," *Sociometry* (May 1954), pp. 181–98.

FIGURE 9–1
Sociogram patterns of attraction

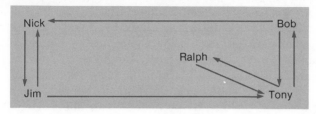

that Jim likes to work with Nick. This is a mutual-choice pair (Nick to Jim and Jim to Nick). The relationship reported between Bob and Nick, however, is a single choice pattern: Bob likes to work with Nick. The same type of procedure can be used to depict rejections, that is, asking with whom someone dislikes working would show rejection choices.

The sociometric procedures recommended by Moreno have value for managers. For example, if managers can identify the leader(s) of a group, they may be able to work with the leader(s) in bringing about change. Of course, many factors such as the type of change being introduced, the group's past relations with management, and the influence of the leader within the group would be critical to the success of dealing with work group leaders.[5]

Formation and development of work groups

An explanation of the reasons for group formation can center around a number of factors which may be physical economic, and socio-psychological. All of these factors can be viewed as categories of determinants for group formation.

LOCATION

When people are put in close proximity to each other, there is a tendency for them to interact and communicate with each other. If workers are not able to do this on a fairly regular basis, there is less tendency to form the group.[6] This is not to say that workers must

---

[5] For an excellent discussion of some of the limitations of sociometric analysis (for example, inadequate attention to the selection of sociometric criteria), see Gardner Lindzey and Edgar F. Borgatta, "Sociometric Measurement," in Gardner Lindzey, ed., *Handbook of Social Psychology* (Reading, Mass.: Addison-Wesley, Inc., 1954), pp. 405–48.

[6] Dorwin Cartwright and Ronald Lippett, "Group Dynamics and the Individual," *International Journal of Group Psychotherapy* (January 1957), p. 88.

communicate hourly or even daily before a work group forms. Instead, it should be obvious that some degree of interaction and communication is necessary.

In organizations, a typical procedure is to locate workers in similar occupations together. For example, in the construction of a home, the bricklayers perform their jobs in close proximity to each other. The same situation exists in offices where secretaries are located next to each other.[7]

ECONOMIC REASONS

In some cases, work groups form because individuals believe that they can derive more economic benefits on their jobs if they form into groups. For example, individuals (strangers) working at different stations on an assembly line may be paid on a group incentive basis. Whatever the particular group produces determines the wages for each member. Because of the interest of the workers in their wages, they will interact and communicate with each other. By working as a group instead of as individuals, they may perceive and actually obtain higher economic benefits.

Another example of the economic motive for work group (informal) formation might be a nonunion organization, where the workers might form a group to bring pressure against management for more economic benefits. The group members would have a common interest — increased economic benefits — which would lead to group affiliation.

A number of older workers may form a work group because of economic motives, such as the administration and payment of their pensions after retirement. Assuming that they want to handle discussions of the pension plan outside the jurisdiction of their union (if they are in a unionized plant), they will be considered a work group (informal).

SOCIO-PSYCHOLOGICAL REASONS

Workers in organizations are also motivated to form work groups so that certain needs can be more adequately satisfied. The safety, social, esteem, and self-actualization needs can be satisfied to some degree by work groups.

Safety. Work groups protect members from outside pressures such as demands by management for better quality and quantity of production, insistence that they punch the clock on time, and recommendations for changing individual work area layouts. By being members of a

---

[7] William G. Scott and Terence R. Mitchell, *Organization Theory* (Homewood, Ill.: Richard D. Irwin, Inc., 1976), p. 171.

group, individual employees can become involved in group activities and openly discuss these management demands with fellow workers who usually support their viewpoint. Without the group to lean on when various management demands are made, employees often assume that they are standing alone facing management and the entire organization. This "aloneness" leads to a degree of insecurity.

The interactions and communications existing between members of a work group serve as a buffer to management demands. Another form of safety need satisfaction occurs in instances when an employee is new and is asked to perform a difficult job task over an extended period of time. The employee may not want to continually contact the supervisor for help in correctly performing the job, and therefore depends largely upon the group. This reliance can certainly be interpreted as providing the new employee with a form of security need satisfaction. New employees are often very concerned with performing well so that they can continue on the job. Thus, continually requesting help from the supervisor is thought of by some new employees as indicating that they are not able to handle the job. Consequently they turn to the group for help so that their new position is not threatened. Whether the supervisor believes that continual requests for help are a sign of inability to perform the job is not the main issue. The important point is how new workers perceive their situation and job security.

Social? Employees often join work groups because of their need for affiliation. The basis of affiliation ranges from wanting to interact with and enjoy other employees to more complex desires for group support of self-image.[8] A management atmosphere which does not permit interaction and communication suppresses the desire of employees to feel a sense of belongingness.

The desire to belong and to be a part of a group points up the intensity of social needs. An excellent discussion of the social needs of Americans is offered by Schein. He discusses the concern which was voiced about the behavior of United States prisoners of war in North Korea, when there were few escapes and numerous instances of apparent collaboration. Schein suggests that one of the reasons for the situation was the manner in which prisoners were treated.[9]

In the North Korean POW camps, officers were separated from enlisted men. Groups were systematically broken up and prisoners were regularly transferred between barracks to forestall the development of groups. The fact that groups could not be formed on a continuing basis could explain the low escape rate: Because the men could not get organ-

---

[8] David R. Hampton, Charles E. Summer, and Ross A. Webber, *Organization Behavior and the Practice of Management* (Glenview, Ill.: Scott, Foresman and Company, 1973), p. 215.

[9] Edgar Schein, "The Chinese Indoctrination Program for Prisoners of War," *Psychiatry* (May 1956), pp. 149–72.

ized, they could not make escape plans. Also, they could not develop the trust in each other that is so essential for escape. Without the required trust, the social need was greatly undermined, as was the morale of the prisoners.

Schein's discussion of POWs certainly has implications for managers in organizations. Work groups appear to satisfy an individual's social needs. The group affiliation enables the individual to identify and to deal with the environment, whether a POW camp or a business organization. Research findings indicate that employees who are isolated from each other because of plant layout report that their jobs are less satisfying than those of group members who are able to socialize on the job.[10]

Esteem Some employees are attracted to a work group because they perceive themselves as gaining prestige by being in the group. In an organization, a particular group may be viewed by employees as being a top-notch work group. Consequently, membership in the elite group bestows prestige upon the members which is not enjoyed by nonmembers. This prestige is conferred on members by other employees (nonmembers), and this often leads to more gratification of the esteem need. By sharing in the activities of a high-prestige work group the individual identifies more closely with the group. This form of identification is valued highly by some employees.

Self-actualization The desire of individuals to utilize their skills to maximum efficiency and to grow and develop psychologically on the job is interpreted as the self-actualization need. Employees often believe that rigid job requirements and rules do not enable them to satisfy this need sufficiently. One reaction to rigid requirements, rules, and regulations is to join a work group, which is viewed as a vehicle for communicating among friends about the use of a job-related skill. The jargon utilized and the skill employed are appreciated by the knowledgeable group members. This appreciation can lead to a feeling of accomplishing a worthwhile task. This feeling, and other similar feelings which are related to a belief that one is creative and skillful, often lead to more satisfaction of the self-actualization need.

DEVELOPMENT OF WORK GROUPS

The development of work groups is distinctly related to learning—learning to work together, to accept each other, and to trust each other. These phases are referred to as the maturation of a group.[11] Bass has succinctly presented a four-phase group development process which

---

[10] Elton Mayo, *The Human Problems of an Industrial Civilization* (Boston: Graduate School of Business Administration, Harvard University, 1946), pp. 42–52.

[11] Warren G. Bennis and Herbert A. Shepard, "A Theory of Group Development," *Human Relations* (Summer 1963), p. 415–57.

points out clearly some of the problems and frustrations inherent in group development.[12]

Bass
4-phase
group
development
process

① **First phase: Mutual acceptance.** Employees are often hampered by their mistrust of each other, of the organization, and of their superiors. They are fearful that they do not have the necessary training or skill to perform the job or to compete with others. These feelings of insecurity motivate employees to seek out others in the same predicament and to express their feelings openly. A group results, and the mistrust is significantly reduced. Thus, after an initial period of uneasiness and learning about the feelings of others, individuals begin to accept each other.

② **Second phase: Decision making.** During this phase, open communication and expression of thoughts concerning the job are the rule. Problem solving and decision making are undertaken. The workers trust each other's viewpoints and beliefs; they develop strategies to make the job easier, to help each other perform more effectively.

③ **Third phase: Motivation.** The group has reached maturity and the problems of its members are known. It is accepted that it is better for the group to have cooperation instead of competition from the members. Thus, the emphasis is on group solidarity in the form of cooperating with each other so that the job is more rewarding both economically and socio-psychologically.

④ **Fourth phase: Control.** The group has successfully organized itself, and members contribute according to their abilities and interests. The group exercises sanctions when control is needed to bring members into line with the group's norms.

The structures and processes which are found in work groups develop over a period of time. The motivation or control of members' behavior is not an overnight occurrence. The four phases of development show that a learning process is involved. Performance and motivation of group members depend on individual learning and on the degree to which the group coordinates the efforts and desires of members. The degree of maturity of the group will have important implications for the perceived and actual level of satisfaction derived by belonging to the group.

Specific types of groups in an organization

Both managers and nonmanagers belong to a number of different groups within the organization. The membership in groups often

[12] The discussion of the development of groups is based largely upon Bernard Bass, *Organizational Psychology* (Boston: Allyn and Bacon, Inc., 1965), pp. 197–98. A number of alterations were made by the authors. Also see J. Stephen Heiner and Eugene Jacobson, "A Model of Task Group Development in Complex Organizations and A Strategy of Implementation," *Academy of Management Review* (October 1976), pp. 98–111.

overlap.[13] In some instances, individuals are members of a group because of position in the organization. However, through the contacts they make in the group, they begin to affiliate with some of its members on an informal basis.

Earlier, a general distinction was made between formal and informal groups. Another more specific and descriptive classification system used to describe groups is the command, task, interest, and friendship framework.[14] Command and task groups are *formal* groups because they are defined by the organization structure; interest and friendship groups are not defined by the organization structure and are *informal* groups.

COMMAND GROUP

The command group is specified by the organization chart. The subordinates who report directly to a given supervisor make up a command group. The relationship between the department manager and the three foremen in a machine shop is spelled out in the organization chart. As the span of control of the department manager increases, his command group increases in size.

TASK GROUP

A number of employees that work together to complete a project or job are considered a task group. A manufacturing or office work process that requires a great deal of interdependency is an example of a task group. Assume that three office clerks are required for (1) securing a file of an automobile accident claim; (2) checking the accuracy of the claim by contacting persons involved; and (3) typing the claim, securing the required signatures of those involved, and refiling the claim.

The activation of the file and the steps required before the claim is refiled constitute required tasks. These activities create a situation in which three clerks must communicate and coordinate with each other if the file is to be handled properly. Their activities and interactions facilitate the formation of the task group.

INTEREST GROUP

In discussing the economic determinant of group formation, an example of older workers grouping together to present a united front was

---

[13] Rensis Likert, *New Patterns of Management* (New York: McGraw-Hill Book Company, 1961), chap. 8.

[14] This is the widely used and insightful framework offered by Leonard R. Sayles, "Research in Industrial Human Relations," *Industrial Relations Research Association* (New York: Harper and Row, 1957), pp. 131–45.

cited. This type of group can be viewed as an interest group, for the members have joined together to achieve some objective such as an equitable pension payment. The members of the group may or may not be members of the same command or task group.

When the desired objective has been achieved or is thought to be within reach, the interest group might disband. Thus, this type of group typically exists for a shorter period of time than other types of groups.

FRIENDSHIP GROUP

In the work place, employees, because of some common characteristic such as age, ethnic background, political sentiment, interest in sports, or desire to drink coffee in the lounge at 10:30 A.M., often form a friendship group. These groups often extend their interaction and communication to off-the-job activities. For example, they get to know each other in the work place because of friendship and then bowl together, or attend sporting events together, or take their families on picnics.

If an individual's affiliation patterns are reviewed, it becomes readily apparent that managerial and nonmanagerial personnel belong to many different and occasionally overlapping groups. Membership in command and task groups is designated by the formal organization, which specifies who will be the superior and who will be the subordinate in the command group. The flow of work specified by management and the job description designate the composition of command and task groups.

The membership patterns of interest and friendship groups are not tightly controlled by the organization. However, managerial actions such as laying out a work area, allowing workers to take coffee breaks at a specified time, and demanding a certain level of productivity influence the interaction and communication patterns of employees, causing individuals to affiliate with each other so that interest and friendship groups emerge.

COMMITTEES: SPECIAL KINDS OF GROUPS

The use of committees in organizations is very common.[15] Committees are actually task groups established for such purposes as:

a. exchanging views and information;
b. recommending action;
c. generating ideas;
d. making decisions.

---

[15] Rollie Tillman, Jr., "Problems in Review: Committees on Trial," *Harvard Business Review* (May–June 1960), pp. 6–12; 162–72.

Committees can achieve each of these purposes. However, a group of individuals may have difficulty in making decisions. Thus, the fourth purpose cited is hard to achieve in a committee. Behavioral scientists recommend that a committee be kept relatively small, since size affects the quality of a group's decision.[16] Increasing a committee's size tends to limit the extent to which members want to or can communicate. As size increases, a growing number of members seem to feel threatened and less willing to participate actively. This perceived threat can lead to increased stress and conflict. Of course these type of outcomes do not encourage the generation of good committee decisions.

The committee chairperson. In most committees a chairperson is expected to provide proper direction. Ordinarily successful committees have chairpersons who understand group processes. The group's objectives and purpose are clear, the members are encouraged to participate, and he or she knows how to keep the committee moving toward the objectives without becoming constrained by endless debates, conflict, and personality clashes.

A committee chairperson must follow a fine line. A chairperson who is too loose may lose the members' respect. On the other hand, a tightly controlled committee may alienate all the members. The chairperson needs to be directive without alienating the membership. A dominating chairperson will not usually acquire the group's acceptance. Without group acceptance the chairperson is a leader without a group.

The behavioralists have studied committees and formulated guidelines that can aid committee chairpersons. Some of these are:[17]

1. Be a careful listener and listen with an open mind.
2. Allow each member to voice opinions and do not place your opinions above others.
3. Get everyone involved in the committee's activities.
4. Display an active interest in the purpose of the committee and the ideas of the membership.
5. Help the committee focus on the task at hand and the progress being made.

Committee members. There is the image that a committee is a group cooperating to reach an objective. This image is not often the case, and what is found in some committees is negative competition and a general lack of cooperation. The chairperson is an important person in creating a cooperative atmosphere. Behavioral studies indicate that in

---

[16] A. C. Filley, "Committee Management Guidelines From Social Science Research," *California Management Review* (Fall 1970), pp. 13–21.

[17] G. M. Prince, "How To Be A Better Chairman," *Harvard Business Review* (January-February 1969), pp. 98–108.

cooperative groups as distinguished from competitive groups one finds:

  a. stronger motivation to accomplish the task;
  b. more effective communication;
  c. more ideas generated;
  d. more membership satisfaction; and
  e. more group productivity.

These findings suggest that when cooperation prevails, rather than negative competition, there are generally positive results. Communication, satisfaction, and productivity are generally all more positive in the cooperative committee. Thus, the importance of the chairperson and what he or she must do should not be underestimated.

Characteristics of work groups

The creation of an organization structure results in characteristics such as specified relationships between subordinates, superiors, and peers, leaders assigned to positions, communication networks, standards of performance, and a status rank order according to the position an individual is filling. The logic behind these formally established characteristics is that, if the organization is to accomplish its goals, retain its personnel, and project a favorable image to the public, it must have structure and a favorable work atmosphere (that is, the employees must enjoy going to work to some extent). Work groups have characteristics which are similar to those of formal organizations and include standards of conduct, communication systems, and reward and sanction mechanisms.[18] These and other characteristics of groups are discussed below.

THE EMERGENT LEADER

As a group attempts to complete some objective and the individual members begin to know each other, members begin to fill one or more of the many group roles. One of the most important roles is that of the group leader. The leader is accepted by the group members and emerges from within. In the formal organization, the leader is appointed.

The leaders in the formal organization are followed and obeyed because employees perceive them as possessing power and influence to reward or punish them for not complying with requests. The formal leaders possess the power to regulate the formal rewards of the mem-

---

[18] Leonard R. Sayles and George Strauss, *Human Behavior in Organizations* (Englewood Cliffs, N.J.: Prentice-Hall, Inc., 1966), pp. 90–100.

bers of a work group. On the other hand, informal group leaders do not possess this power.

The informal leader emerges from within and serves a number of facilitating functions. First, any group of individuals that does not have a plan or some coordination becomes an ineffective unit. The individuals are not directed toward the accomplishment of goals, and this leads to a breakdown in group effectiveness. The leader serves to initiate action and provide direction. If there are differences of opinion on a group-related matter, the leader attempts to settle the differences and move the group toward accomplishing its goals.

Second, some individual must communicate the group's beliefs about policies, the job, the organization, the supervision, and other related matters to nonmembers. The nonmembership category could include members of other groups, supervisory personnel, and the union. In effect, the group leader communicates the values of the group.

A number of research studies have been made on the personal characteristics of group leaders, which can be summarized as follows:

1. The leadership role is filled by an individual who possesses the attributes which the members perceive as being critical for satisfying their needs.
2. The leader embodies the values of the group and is able to perceive these values, organize them into an intelligible philosophy, and verbalize them to nonmembers.[19]
3. The leader who is able to receive and decipher communication relevant to the group and effectively communicate important information to group members can be thought of as an information center.[20]

STATUS IN A GROUP

Managers in an organization are accorded status because of position in the hierarchy; that is, the top management group of the firm has more prestige or status than middle managers in the organization, while middle managers have more prestige or status than lower-level managers. The basic cornerstone of status in the formal organization is a comparative process. The top-level positions embody more authority, responsibility, power, and influence, and thus are accorded more status. In effect, a status hierarchy emerges with the top-level positions listed first and the lower-level positions listed last.

In an informal group a similar type of status system develops. For many different reasons, individuals are accorded status by the group in

[19] Scott and Mitchell, *Organization Theory*, pp. 175–82.
[20] Ibid.

which they interact and communicate. The individuals performing in leadership roles possess prestige because of their role. Consequently they are ranked by group members as being at a particular level in the group-status hierarchy.

There are a number of other factors which influence the status systems developed in groups. The seniority of a member is a factor which many groups consider to be important. A worker having more seniority is often thought of as being "organizationally intelligent," which means that person knows how to adapt to the demands of supervisors, subordinates, or peers. This ability to adjust is an important status factor with group members.

The skill of an individual in performing a job is another factor related to status. An individual who is an expert in the technical aspects, managerial or nonmanagerial, of the job is given a high status ranking in some groups. This type of status does not mean that the individual actually utilizes the skill to perform more efficiently, but that the group members perceive this skill in the individual.

Thus the status system in a work group is formed on the basis of such factors as leadership, seniority, and skill. These and other factors are weighted differently by each type of work group; the varying amount of importance placed on them affects the status system.

WORK GROUP NORMS AND CONTROL

A norm is an agreement among the group membership as to how members in the group should behave.[21] The more an individual complies with norms, the more that person accepts the group's standards of behavior. The teen-age girl who dresses exactly like her friends at school is being influenced by the group norm concerning dress behavior.

Work groups also utilize norms to bring about job performance that is acceptable to the group. In the work place a number of different production-related norms are evident. The following are typical: (1) Don't agree with management in its campaign to change the wage structure; (2) present a united front to the supervisor concerning the displeasure of the group about the firing of Mr. Jones; (3) resist the suggestions of the new college graduate assigned to the group's work area; (4) do not produce above the group leader's level of production; (5) help members of the group to achieve an acceptable production level if they are having difficulty and if you have time; and (6) don't allow the union steward to convince you to vote for his favorite union presidential candidate in the upcoming election.

---

[21] Joseph A. Litterer, *The Analysis of Organizations* (New York: John Wiley and Sons, Inc., 1973), p. 96.

Three specific social processes bring about compliance with group norms,[22] namely, group pressure, group review and enforcement, and the personalization of norms.

① **Group pressure.** The process of group pressure is clearly illustrated by Asch in a series of experiments[23] in which he was concerned with studying how social forces constrain opinions and attitudes. Asch utilized groups of college students to conduct a "psychological experiment" in visual judgment. The experimenter informed the members of the group that they would be comparing the lengths of lines. Two sets of cards, similar to those presented in Figure 9–2, were used for each comparison. The individuals had to choose the line on the second card that matched the line on the first card in length. These comparisons were made a number of times.

FIGURE 9–2

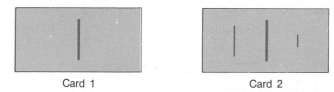

Card 1   Card 2

Prior to the actual visual observation of the lengths of lines on various sets of cards, the experimenter "rigged" the results. He informed all but one member of the group that they should choose on the third comparison a line that did not match the length of the line shown in the first card of the set. The reaction of the uninformed member in each group of students was observed and recorded.

The results of the Asch experiments showed that when individuals were confronted with only one other group member who was giving incorrect responses, they continued to stick with their correct answer. When the opposition (those giving incorrect answers) was increased to two, the group pressure influence became noticeable: The uninformed group members accepted the incorrect answer 13.6 percent of the time. Under the group pressures provided by three incorrect responses, the uninformed members gave incorrect responses 31.8 percent of the time.

This experiment illustrates how group pressures and support for one's viewpoint are related. If individuals stand alone, they are inclined to succumb to group pressures; but when they find their attitude supported by even one group member, they resist pressure to change.

Individuals who value their group membership highly and who

[22] Ibid., pp. 245–47.

[23] Solomon E. Asch, "Opinions and Social Pressures," *Scientific American* (November 1955), p. 31–35.

satisfy some combination of personal needs by being a part of a group allow group pressures to influence their behavior and performance. This premise leads to a second type of group process designated here as group review and enforcement.

2. **Group review and enforcement.** When individuals become members of a group, especially task groups, they quickly become aware of group norms. The group position on such matters as production, absenteeism, and quality of output is communicated. The group members then observe the actions and language of new members to determine whether the group norms are being followed.

If individual members, both oldtimers and newcomers, are not complying with generally accepted norms, a number of different approaches may be employed. A "soft" approach would be a discussion between respected leaders and those persons deviating from the norm. If this does not prove effective, more rigid corrective action such as the membership scolding the individual or individuals both privately and publicly is used. The ultimate type of enforcement would be to ostracize the nonconforming members, which might very well take the form of not communicating with them.

These are only a few of the numerous strategies which may be implemented to bring deviants back into line. Other, more severe techniques such as sabotaging the nonconformers' performance have also been utilized. It should be made clear that review and enforcement occur at the managerial levels in a form similar to that in the nonmanagerial ranks.

3. **Personalization of norms.** The behavioral patterns of people are influenced significantly by their value systems.[24] Their values in turn are influenced by the events occurring around them; values are learned and become personalized. For example, the norm of a work group may encourage group members to treat college graduates and noncollege individuals equally and courteously. This norm may be accepted by the person as morally and ethically correct. Prior to group affiliation, the member may have displayed little interest in a "fair treatment of all" philosophy. However, based on a latent feeling of fairness, the member personalizes this group-learned norm. It becomes a standard of conduct which is correct from a group as well as from a social vantage point.

In some, but definitely not in all instances, group pressures, group review and enforcement, and personalization of norms may conflict with organizational objectives such as higher production, improved quality of output, lower absenteeism, and loyalty to the firm. The emphasis here is on the word "some." It is nonsense to assume that all groups are established to resist the achievement of organizational goals.

---

[24] Litterer, *Analysis of Organizations*, p. 96.

COMMUNICATION NETWORK

In classical organization theory, the specified communication network is represented by the superior-subordinate relationships shown in the organization chart. The formal communication network follows the chain of command (Figure 9–3).

In informal groups the communication patterns are not rigidly set. In the formal organization system, the top-level executives possessing the most status direct their messages to lower-status members. However, research conducted within groups generally indicates that low-status group members direct more communication toward higher-status group members.[25]

A detailed study by Bavelas clearly illustrated some of the communication networks that can exist in groups. He was interested in the

FIGURE 9–3
Formal communication flow

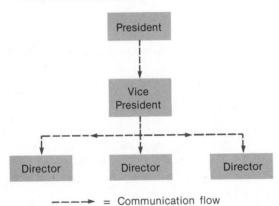

---- ► = Communication flow

efficiency with which groups completed their tasks. In the Bavelas experiments, members of a group were isolated so that no cross-communication could occur, as illustrated in Figure 9–4 (Ⓧ designates the leader).[26]

Bavelas provided some interesting insights into the effects of these four networks on leaders and problem-solving abilities. The location of a person in a central position (for example, the circled Ⓧ in the chain network of five individuals) produces group leaders. The centrally located person is in the best position to facilitate the smooth flow of information among group members.

It was also determined that when simple problems had to be solved,

[25] Harold H. Kelly, "Communication in Experimentally Created Hierarchies," *Human Relations* (February 1951), pp. 39–56.

[26] Alex Bavelas, "Communication Patterns In Task-Oriented Groups," *Journal of the Accoustical Society of America* (1950), pp. 725–30.

FIGURE 9–4
Bavelas communication networks

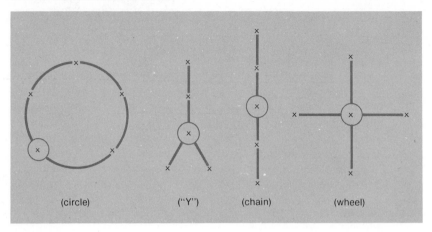

(circle)   ("Y")   (chain)   (wheel)

the wheel network was the fastest and most efficient. The members of the group provided information to the central figure, and it was acted upon rapidly. When difficult tasks had to be solved and interaction and exchange of ideas were important to task completion, the circle arrangement proved fastest.

Although the Bavelas research was conducted in a laboratory situation, it indicates clearly some of the events that may occur in small-group communication networks. The leader is at the center of the group and is a facilitator. The networks are similar to the formal organization chain-of-command pattern and enable problems to be solved efficiently.

Some examples of the four communication networks would be the following:

Circle – A committee in a manufacturing company is given the charge to study the long-range plans of the company. A department manager is appointed the chairman, (x), and four other department managers serve with him on the committee. The communication flow is circular, emanating from the appointed chairman.

"Y" – A merchandise buyer in a large clothing store is designated as (x). She is the third most important person in the organization's chain of command. She is in charge of both men's and women's clothing. Thus the president, vice president, merchandise buyer, director of men's sales, and director of women's sales constitute the "Y."

Chain — A regional sales director in an insurance company is specified as Ⓧ. He reports directly to the vice president of sales, who reports to the president of the company. Reporting directly to the regional sales director is the district manager, who has salesmen reporting to him.

Wheel — The wheel network leader could be an advertising layout manager. She reports to the director of marketing and must work closely with two other advertising layout managers who have the same authority and responsibility in the organizational hierarchy. The advertising layout manager, Ⓧ, has an assistant called an art coordinator who reports only to her.

GROUP COHESIVENESS

Cohesiveness is another important concept which must be understood if the behavioral analysis of groups is to be complete. In a simplistic definition, this concept involves the "stick-together" characteristic of groups. In a more refined definition, group cohesiveness is stated as the attraction of members to the group in terms of the strength of forces on the individual member to remain active in the group and to resist leaving it.[27]

All of the above characteristics of groups are influenced in some degree by the cohesiveness within the group.[28] For example, the greater the attraction within the group, the more likely it is that the membership will adhere closely to a group norm such as a production level.

Research findings have allowed those interested in work group cohesiveness to isolate some of the more important factors which affect it. Some of the conditions which influence cohesiveness are presented in Figure 9–5. The factors which are identified are only examples of some of the variables uncovered in research studies, but they are representative of the types of factors that can enhance or reduce cohesiveness of work groups.

Size of work group.   One of the important and necessary conditions for the existence of a group is that members interact and communicate with each other. If the group is so large that members do not get to know each other, there is little likelihood that the group will be high in cohesiveness. This is a logical assumption that would be made by those who understand the difficulties of communicating in large groups.

Research studies found in behavioral literature indicate that the logical assumption is accurate and that an inverse relationship does exist

---

[27] This definition is based upon the group cohesiveness concept presented by Stanley E. Seashore, *Group Cohesiveness in the Industrial Work Group* (Ann Arbor, Mich.: University of Michigan, Institute for Social Research, 1954).

[28] Sayles and Strauss, *Human Behavior in Organizations*, p. 101.

FIGURE 9–5
Factors contributing to group cohesiveness

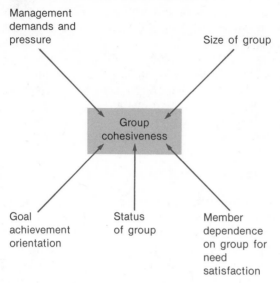

between size of group and group cohesiveness.[29] <u>As the size of a group increases, its cohesiveness decreases.</u>

Dependence of members upon the work group. As stated previously, individuals join groups because they perceive the group as a unit which can help them satisfy economic and sociopsychological needs. A group that is able to satisfy a significant portion of an individual's needs will appear attractive to that individual. Group processes such as communication and overall friendship make the group a key factor in the individual's life. Thus, what the group stands for, its norms, and its membership are bonds which relate the individual to the group. These are examples of the forces of attraction discussed by behavioralists. The greater the individual's dependency upon the group, the stronger will be these bonds of attraction.

Achievement of goals. The attainment of some set of group-established goals (for example, better production than another group) has an influence on members. For example, a work group that attains a highly desired rating for completing a task enhances the value of being a group member; individuals within the group feel a pride in being members of a work group that has performed in such a manner that they are recognized as being superior.

---

[29] Seashore, *Group Cohesiveness*, pp. 90–95. This study will be discussed in detail later in the chapter. Also see Robert C. Cummins and Donald C. King. "The Interaction of Group Size and Task Structure in an Industrial Organization," *Personnel Psychology* (Spring 1973), pp. 87–94.

Work groups that have successfully attained pre-established goals are likely to be highly cohesive units, the members tending to be more attracted toward each other because they have worked together in the past and because their efforts have resulted in achieving a desired goal. Thus, success and cohesiveness are interrelated: Success in goal achievement encourages cohesiveness, and cohesive work groups are more likely to attain preestablished goals. It is important to consider that, although group cohesiveness can lead to successful achievement of goals, that some cohesiveness can prove detrimental when group and organization goals are not congruent.

Status of group.   In an organizational setting work groups are typically ranked in a status hierarchy. An intergroup status hierarchy may develop for many different reasons, including the following:

1. One group is rated higher than another in overall performance; this is a measure of success in the organization.
2. To become a member of the group, individuals must display a high level of skill.
3. The work being done by the group is dangerous or financially more rewarding or more challenging than other work.
4. The group is less closely supervised in comparison to other groups.
5. In the past, members of the group have been considered for promotion more often than members of other groups.

These are only some of the criteria which affect the status hierarchy of groups.[30] Generally, the higher a group ranks in the intergroup status hierarchy, the greater its cohesiveness. However, the higher-status groups appear attractive only to some nonmembers. Individuals on the outside of the group very well may not want to become members of a high-status group because membership then entails close adherence to group norms.

Management demands and pressure.   The last determinant of group cohesiveness discussed in this section should not be viewed as the least significant factor because of its ranking in our discussion. It is certainly true in many organizations that management has a significant impact on group cohesiveness. The members of work groups tend to "stick together" when they are pressured by superiors to conform to some organizational norm (for example, punching in at 8:00 and not 8:05 A.M., or publishing at least 5 articles every year).

The group cohesiveness attributed to managerial demands may be a short-run or long-run phenomenon. In some cases, a group may be loosely knit (low in cohesiveness), and a company policy statement may be interpreted as a threat to the job security of group members. Conse-

---

[30] For a listing of other status criteria, see Sayles and Strauss, *Human Behavior in Organizations,* p. 102.

quently the members of the group become a more cohesive and unified whole in order to withstand the perceived management threat. After the danger is past (that is, the policy statement is rescinded), the group gradually drifts back toward low cohesiveness. In other cases, the cohesiveness may be a longer-lasting phenomenon.

INTERGROUP CONFLICT

Management prefers that groups cooperate and work toward the accomplishment of organizational and individual goals. However, conflicts often develop between groups. If the groups are working on tasks that are interdependent (i.e., department A's output flows to Department B and B's output flows to Department C), the coordination and effectiveness of working together are crucial managerial issues. The relationships can become antagonistic and so disruptive that the entire flow of production is slowed or even stopped. Cooperation is not always the most desirable result of group interaction. For example, two groups can cooperate because they both oppose the introduction of new equipment. The equipment is being introduced to improve cost control, but the groups working together can make the trial period of testing the new equipment a bad experience for management.

Determinants of intergroup conflict. There are many reasons why conflict develops between groups.[31] Some of the more important reasons relate to limited resources, communication problems, differences in interests and goals, different perceptions and attitudes, and lack of clarity about responsibilities.

Limited resources. Groups that possess an abundance of materials, money, and time usually are effective. However, when a number of groups are competing for limited resources there is a good chance that conflict will result. The competition for the limited equipment dollars or merit increase money or new positions can become fierce. Thus, when resources are limited people compete and the result can be conflict.

Communication problems. Groups often become very involved with their own areas of responsibility. Each tends to develop its own unique vocabulary. Paying attention to an area of responsibility is a worthy endeavor, but it can result in communication problems. The receiver of information must be considered when a group communicates an idea, proposal, or decision. This is often not the case, and in consequence there are misinformed receivers who become irritated and then hostile.

Different interests and goals. A group of young workers may want management to do something about the inadequate promotion

[31] Rensis Likert and Jane G. Likert, *New Ways of Managing Conflict* (New York: McGraw-Hill, 1976).

system. However, management is being accused by older workers of ignoring improvements in the company pension plan. Management recognizes the two different goals, but believes that the pension issue is the most pressing and addresses it. The groups may want management to solve both problems, but this is not currently possible. Thus, one group becomes hostile because it is ignored.

Different perceptions and attitudes. Individuals perceive differently. The groups to which they belong also can have different perceptions. Groups tend to evaluate in terms of their backgrounds, norms, and experiences. Since each of these can differ, there is likely to be conflict between groups. Most groups tend to overvalue their own worth and position and undervalue the worth and position of other groups.

Lack of clarity. Job clarity involves knowing what others expect in terms of task accomplishment. In many cases it is difficult to specify who is responsible for a certain task. This difficulty exists in most organizations. Who is responsible for losing a talented management trainee—the personnel department or the training department? Who is responsible for the increased interest in the product line—marketing or advertising or research and development? The inability to pinpoint positive and negative contributions causes groups to compete for control over those activities that are recognized.

The causes of conflict just cited are some of the more common ones. Each of them exists and needs to be managed. The management of intergroup conflict involves determining strategies to minimize such problems.

Management strategies. Management reaction to disruptive intergroup conflict can take many different forms.[32] There is typically a sequence of events. Management will first try to minimize the conflict indirectly, and if this fails it will become directly involved.

Indirect approaches. Initially managers often avoid direct approaches to solving conflict between groups. *Avoidance* is easy in the short run, since the causes of conflict are unknown, and giving attention to conflict admits that it exists. Unfortunately, avoidance does not always minimize the problem. Matters get worse because nothing is being actively done about the problem, and the groups become more antagonistic and hostile.

Another indirect strategy is to encourage the groups to meet and discuss their differences and work out a solution without management involvement. This strategy can take the form of *bargaining, persuasion, or working on a problem together.*

---

[32] Alan Filley, *Interpersonal Conflict Resolution* (Chicago: Scott, Foresman, 1975), and Louis Pondy, "Organizational Conflict: Concepts and Models," *Administrative Science Quarterly* (September 1972), pp. 296–320.

Bargaining involves the groups agreeing about what each will get and give to the other. For example, a group may agree to give another group quick turnaround time on the repairs of needed equipment if the other group agrees to bring complaints about the quality of repairs to them before going to management. Bargaining can be successful if both groups are better off (or at least no worse off) after an agreement is reached.

Persuasion involves the groups finding common areas of interest. The groups attempt to find points of agreement and show how these are important to each in attaining organizational goals. Persuasion is possible if clashes between group leaders do not exist.

A problem can be an obstacle to a goal. In order for groups to minimize their conflicts through *problem solving*, they must generally agree on the goal. If there is agreement, then the groups can propose alternative solutions that satisfy the parties involved. For example, one group may want the company to relocate the plant in a suburban area and the other group may want better working conditions. If both parties agree that a common goal is to maintain their jobs, then building a new facility in an area that does not have a high tax rate may be a good solution. Suppose that if the company does not relocate, workers will have to be laid off because of the high rate of taxes being paid by the company.

Direct approaches. Management may use *domination* to minimize conflict. It may exercise authority and require that the problem be solved by a specific date. If management uses authority, the groups may join together and resist the domination. Management becomes a common enemy, and they forget their differences in order to deal with their opponent.

Another direct approach is to *remove the key figures in the conflict.* If two individuals are in conflict because of personality differences this may be a possible alternative. Three problems exist with this approach. First, the figures who are to be removed may be respected leaders of the groups. This could lead to the groups becoming more antagonistic and in greater conflict. Second, it is difficult to pinpoint accurately whether the individuals in conflict are at odds because of personal animosities or because they represent their groups. Third, removal is not always good because there is a danger that "martyrs" will be created. The causes of the removed leaders will be remembered and fought for even though the persons themselves are gone.

A final direct strategy to minimize conflict is that of finding *superordinate goals.* These goals are desired by two or more groups, but can only be accomplished through cooperation of the groups. Studies have shown that when conflicting groups are faced with the necessity of cooperating in order to accomplish a goal, conflict can be minimized and cooperation increased.[33] For example, a companywide profit sharing plan may be used to encourage groups to work together. At the end of the year a percentage of company profits will be equally distributed to each employee. Conflict between groups can reduce the amount of profits each person receives. Thus, the superordinate goal, generating optimal profits, takes precedence.

End results: Member satisfaction and effective decisions

Two end results or consequences of group membership are the satisfaction of members and the reaching of effective group decisions. Social psychologists have, in recent years, increased their efforts to understand the causes of member satisfaction and decision making within groups.

MEMBER SATISFACTION

Perhaps the most provocative integrative analysis of work group member satisfaction is presented by Heslin and Dunphy.[34] They report on a survey of 37 studies which show specific relationships between work group member satisfaction and (1) perceived freedom to participate, (2) perceived goal attainment, and (3) status consensus.

Perceived freedom to participate. Heslin and Dunphy indicate that a member's perception of freedom to participate influences need satisfaction. The individuals who perceived themselves as active participators reported themselves more satisfied,[35] while those who perceived their freedom to participate to be insignificant typically were the least satisfied members in a work group.

The freedom-to-participate phenomenon is related to the entire spectrum of economic and socio-psychological needs. For example, the perceived ability to participate may lead individuals to believe that they are valued members of the group. This assumption can lead to the satisfaction of social, esteem, and self-actualization needs.

Perceived goal attainment. A number of studies indicate that a group member's perception of progress toward the attainment of desired goals is an important factor in member satisfaction.[36] Groups

---

[33] M. Sherif and C. W. Sherif, *Groups In Harmony and Tension* (New York: Harper and Row, 1953).

[34] Richard Heslin and Dexter Dunphy, "Three Dimensions of Member Satisfaction in Small Groups," *Human Relations* (May 1964), pp. 99–112.

[35] This was indicated in Bavelas's experiments with communication networks in Bavelas, "Communication Patterns," p. 729.

[36] Clovis R. Shepherd, *Small Groups: Some Sociological Perspectives* (San Francisco: Chandler Publishing Co., 1964), p. 101.

which progressed toward the attainment of goals indicated higher levels of member satisfaction, while members of groups not adequately progressing toward the attainment of group goals showed a lower satisfaction level.

Status consensus. This concept is defined as agreement about the relative status of all group members. Several studies reviewed by Heslin and Dunphy indicate that, when the degree of status consensus is high, member satisfaction tends to be high; where status consensus within the group is low, member satisfaction tends to be low.

It is also concluded that status consensus is more readily achieved in groups where

1. The group task specialist is perceived to be competent by the membership,
2. A leader emerges who plays a role that is considered an important group task, and
3. A leadership role emerges and is filled by an individual who concentrates on coordinating and maintaining the activities of the group.

The insightful review of Heslin and Dunphy suggests that the perceptions of the membership concerning freedom to participate, movement toward goal attainment, and status consensus significantly influence the level of need satisfaction attained by group members. Their review also clearly indicates that when an individual member's goals and needs are in conflict with the goals and needs of the overall group, lower levels of membership satisfaction are the result.

GROUP DECISION-MAKING EFFECTIVENESS

A number of research studies have raised the question of whether group decision making is superior, inferior, or equal to individual decision making. There are studies which support almost every type of claim. Maier, instead of developing an exact answer to the superiority question, discusses assets and liabilities of group decision making.[37]

Group assets. In a group there is a greater total of knowledge and information. Thus, decisions that require the use of knowledge should give groups an advantage over individuals. This additional information is helpful in reaching the best decision possible.

Many problems require making decisions that depend upon the support of other group members. Insofar as group decision making permits participation and influence, it follows that more members accept a decision when a group solves the problem than when one person solves it. A person reaching a decision must persuade others

---

[37] Norman R. F. Maier, "Assets and Liabilities in Group Problem Solving," *Psychological Review* (July 1967), pp. 239–49.

in the group who may resist being told what the best solution is for the problem. Individuals, by working on the problem, believe that they are more responsible for the solution. This feeling of shared responsibility with others is satisfying to some people.

Decisions made by an individual, which are to be carried out by others, must be communicated to those who must execute. Thus, the individual decision maker must communicate effectively before positive action is taken. The chances for communication breakdowns are reduced when the individuals who must execute the decision have participated in making it. They were involved in reaching the decision and are aware of how it was reached. Knowing the details of how the decision was reached improves the decision executors' understanding.

Group liabilities. Making a decision in a group exerts pressure on each member. The desire to be an accepted and cooperative group member tends to silence individual disagreement and favors agreement. If a majority is forceful enough, its decision will usually be accepted regardless of whether the quality is adequate.

In some groups, a dominating individual takes over. This person, because of a strong personality, organizational position, reputation, or status can dominate the group. None of these traits or characteristics is necessarily related to decision-making skill. However, they can inhibit group discussion, reduce creativity among other members, and stop members from making positive contributions.

"Stand taking" may hinder a group in reaching a good solution. Most problems have more than one possible solution, and individual group members may have personal preferences. Sometimes a member may "take a stand" on his or her preference and will feel that a defeat means loss of face. Thus the member becomes more concerned with winning than with finding the best group decision.

Group versus individual decision making. Available research suggests that better ideas emerge when a number of people work on a problem separately than in a face-to-face group.[38] These findings have been supported using groups of research scientists, managers, and students. However, another researcher, after studying 36 three-person brainstorming groups, concluded that persons in groups are not necessarily poorer decision makers than those working on their own.[39] He suggests that an inhibiting force appears to be present when people work face to face in a group.

The assets of working in a group have been noted above. These must be weighed against the liabilities of working in a group. Present

---

[38] A. Van De Ven and A. L. Delbecq, "Normal Versus Interacting Group Processes for Committee Decision Making Effectiveness," *Academy of Management Journal* (June 1971), pp. 203–12.

[39] W. R. Street, "Brainstorming by Individuals, Coacting, and Interacting Groups," *Journal of Applied Psychology* (August 1974), pp. 433–36.

knowledge suggests some important differences in decision making by individuals and groups. Groups appear to make fewer errors, take greater risks, and inhibit somewhat the generation of ideas from less vocal members. The biggest cost of group decision making seems to be the time needed to reach a decision.

A work group model

Our discussion of work groups now enables us to develop a model of work group behavior. This model is shown in Figure 9–6. The diagram has a distinct behavioral character, since it contains the "why," "how," and "when" of work groups as found in the behavioral literature. Figure 9–6 summarizes what has been discussed concerning reasons for group formation, the types of groups, the characteristics of group membership, and one of the major end results, membership satisfaction and decision making.

FIGURE 9–6
A model of work group behavior

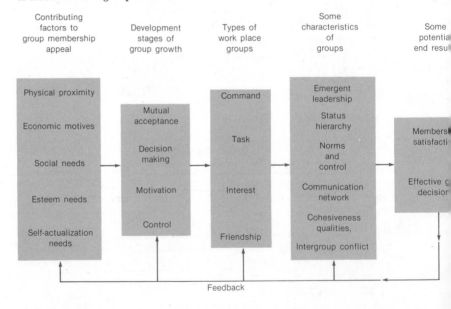

Another important aspect of the work group model is the feedback cycle. As designated in Figure 9–6, feedback on the end results of group membership influences each of the elements in the framework. For example, the perceived goal attainment in a work group influences its cohesiveness. As stated previously, groups that achieve or are moving toward success (goal attainment) have the greatest attraction (cohesiveness) within the groups.

Summary

The Behavioral School's approach to management is replete with discussions, theories, and research findings concerning work groups. This intense interest in groups is based upon premises such as that (1) groups are ubiquitous; (2) groups influence an employee's perceptions and attitudes; (3) groups influence the productivity of employees; (4) groups aid individuals in satisfying unfulfilled needs; and (5) groups facilitate communications.

The interest in groups and their dynamics has not waned and is not expected to do so. What has been and is presently being learned about group phenomena is being put to greater use in organizations. Awareness of the practical importance of groups to the continued effectiveness of an organization should generate more studies which should lead to additional understanding of group behavior and group influence in organizational settings.

Discussion and review questions

1. Some people believe that too much cooperation between groups can be a problem for organizations. Why?
2. Informal groups exist in organizations and are very important to their members. If an organization has a number of informal groups is this an indication that the company is being poorly managed?
3. Should management encourage and aid in the development of cohesive work groups? Why?
4. What would be some of the reasons for an individual to become an isolate (a member not in good standing) in a work group?
5. What factors other than those shown in Figure 9–5 could possibly lead to the development of cohesive work groups?
6. Why is it difficult to establish superordinate goals? What functions can superordinate goals serve in an organization?
7. Would behavioralists agree that the emergent leaders of informal work groups would typically utilize democratic leadership in their roles of leading the group? Why?
8. Discuss and compare the type of reward procedures that can be utilized by informal groups and by the formal organization.
9. It is generally agreed that a group influences individual behavior. Can an individual significantly influence a group's behavior? Why?
10. How can one individual dominate the discussion or activities of a group attempting to reach decisions?

Additional references

Alderfer, C. P. "Group and Intergroup Relations," in J. R. Hackman and J. L. Suttle, eds. *Improving Life at Work: Behavioral Science Approaches to Organizational Change.* Santa Monica: Goodyear, 1977.

Bucklow, M. "A New Role for the Work Group," *Administrative Science Quarterly* 7 (1966): 236–57.

Derr, C. B. "Conflict: A Neglected Resource," *The Conference Board Record* (March 1975): 39–42.

Fisher, B. A. *Small Group Decision Making.* New York: McGraw-Hill, 1974.

Hackman, J. R. "The Design of Self-Managing Work Groups," *Technical Report No. 11,* New Haven: Yale University, 1976.

Haythorn, W. W. "The Composition of Groups: A Review of the Literature," *Acta Psychologica* 28 (1968): 97–128.

Holloman, C. R., and Hendrick, H. A. "Adequacy of Group Decisions as a Function of the Decision-Making Process," *Academy of Management Journal* 15 (June 1972): 175–84.

Homans, G. C. *The Human Group.* New York: Harcourt, Brace and World, 1950.

Klein, S. M. *Workers Under Stress: The Impact of Work Pressure on Group Cohesion.* Lexington: University of Kentucky Press, 1971.

Maier, Norman R. F. "Prior Commitment as a Deterrent to Group Problem Solving," *Personnel Psychology* 26 (Spring 1973): 117–26.

Steiner, I. D. *Group Process and Productivity.* New York: Academic Press, 1972.

Stogdill, R. M. *Individual Behavior and Group Achievement.* New York: Oxford Press, 1959.

Susman, G. I. "The Impact of Automation on Work Group Autonomy and Task Specialization," *Human Relations* 23 (1970): 567–577.

Zander, A. *Motives and Goals In Groups.* New York: Academic Press, 1971.

PRACTICAL EXERCISE I
Lakeland Police Department

The mission of the Lakeland Police Department is to protect the life and property of the citizens and visitors to the city of Lakeland. Recently Bob Lukash, Chief of Police of Lakeland, has been faced with two major problems. First, there is a serious lack of understanding between residents of low-income areas and the police. This problem has generated a number of suggested solutions from politicians, community leaders, and police officers. Second, some embarrassing conflicts are occurring between the personnel department and the training division. This conflict has become so disruptive that newspaper articles about it are appearing in the *Lakeland Times*. Chief Lukash wants to resolve the problem between the units as soon as possible.

The first problem has led to charges of police brutality and discrimination. Two suggestions that the Chief is now considering for improving understanding between residents and the police are:

To train officers who work in the low-income area in human relations. The rationale behind this suggestion is that through training the officers will become more understanding.

To form a neighborhood committee, comprised of local leaders and a few police officers trained in social problems. The committee would discuss the problems and attempt to find reasonable solutions.

The Chief currently is thinking through these two alternatives and will make a decision in a few days.

The second problem involves two units in the department. The training division is responsible for police training and the investigation of applicants seeking to join the department. The division's training school offers a six-week course for new recruits twice a year. Between 10 and 12 people attend each session. The personnel unit recruits personnel through interviews, advertisements, and word of mouth. In the past year, the personnel department has been accused by the training division of not doing a good job in attracting qualified candidates.

245

The training division commanding officer Nick Tandy has met with Chief Lukash twice to voice this complaint. He asked the Chief to lean on the personnel director Martin Rossano to make him more aggressive in recruiting quality candidates.

Martin Rossano informed the Chief that the training division has suddenly raised its requirements without notifying the personnel department. He believes that this is why good candidates are lacking. The failure to communicate these changes in requirements has resulted in bad feeling between Tandy and Rossano for the past year.

The Chief has told both commanding officers that he will not tolerate this type of conflict. The newspapers have had a field day with it, and the Chief wants it stopped. He has scheduled a meeting for Monday morning and ordered both officers to attend. Tandy and Rossano have also been told to bring a suggested solution to the problem with them.

Questions for analysis

1. Which solution do you consider to be the best for improving community-police relations?
2. Why has the conflict between Tandy and Rossano become disruptive?
3. What are some feasible solutions to the conflict between personnel and training?

PRACTICAL EXERCISE II
The Lonely Keypunch Operator

Anne Martin has worked for the past eight years as a keypunch operator for the Pullman Steel Company. In the last six months she has been troubled about her relationships with the other nine keypunch operators in her work unit. Anne believes that the other members of the group are being extremely cold toward her.

Prior to the last six months, the keypunch operators would communicate throughout the day about such matters as their jobs, the company, their families, and a number of other personal matters such as problems with their children and their husbands. The ten keypunch operators were considered a very cohesive work group. The keypunch operators were women ranging in age from 25 to 55. None of the girls had a college education. They were of varied ethnic and religious backgrounds. For example, two of the operators were Italian, two were black, one was Irish, and one was English-German.

Anne was the oldest member of the group at 55. She had been well liked until about January of this year. At this time the girls no longer openly communicated with Anne, and they stopped asking her to eat lunch with them in what is referred to as "Keypunch Korner" in the cafeteria.

Over the past two years Anne has been known as one of the fastest and most accurate keypunch operators in the unit. She has had little difficulty adjusting to the new supervisors who are trained on the job in the keypunch unit. The keypunch unit has had ten supervisors since Anne began working at Pullman.

In January, the informal keypunch unit leader Phyllis Pizzuto had a heated disagreement with management about her work. The supervisor, Mary Castille, told Phyllis that her work would have to improve in both speed and accuracy. Anne liked both Phyllis and Mary and did not want to get involved in this dispute. In fact everytime Phyllis brought up the subject on the job or at lunch, Anne tried to change the subject. On a number of occasions Phyllis asked Anne, "Why are you taking the side of management?"

Since January, Phyllis Pizzuto and her best personal friend, another keypunch operator, Joy Flynn, have looked at Anne's daily production sheet. On five separate occasions Anne has seen one of them "peeking" at her output sheet.

Although none of the other operators have tried to determine Anne's productivity, they have also ostracized her. Because the group is important to her personally, Anne is trying to analyze the situation and take the best action. She is thinking about a number of alternatives:

1. Report her problem to the supervisor.
2. Request a transfer to the other keypunch unit in the plant.
3. Confront Phyllis Pizzuto and ask her why the group is cold toward her.
4. Talk to the group, excluding Phyllis and Joy, and ask them why they are cold toward her.
5. Quit her job.

Anne wants to do the best thing and really wants to get back on good terms with all of the keypunch operators. She thinks that her problems at work have carried over into her home and are affecting her relationship with her husband.

Questions for analysis:

1. What is the problem with which Anne is faced?
2. Why do you feel that the keypunch operators are a cohesive work group?
3. What course of action would you recommend for Anne? Why?

PRACTICAL EXERCISE III
Rudy Garcia's Department

The prototype-project development department of Torando Electronics Company played an essential role in the development of the product lines sold by the firm. The department consisted of 12 engineers and 35 technicians who worked on the first floor of the Baltimore, Maryland plant. Each project worked on in the department usually had at least two engineers and five technicians working together under the direction of a project supervisor.

When each project was started, the engineers submitted a written work order, and the department manager would assign the technicians to work with the engineers. Upon completion of each project a quality control assessor would inspect the work. The engineers were recognized by the top management of the company as having the expertise to submit top quality work orders and in only a few instances were their requests rejected. The engineers were college graduates and were paid on a salary basis.

Most of the 35 technicians had previously worked as assembly workers at Torando and they knew the plant operations very well. They were paid on an hourly basis and most of their pay raises were based primarily on seniority. The majority of technicians worked the day shift, although some had to work the other two shifts. Seniority was used to schedule the shift assignments.

The technicians interacted with each other off the job, through activities such as softball, bowling, card games, or professional football parties on the weekends during the season. The technicians ate lunch and took coffee breaks together.

The engineers rarely, if ever, spent any off-the-job time with the technicians. They had an engineering office where they took coffee breaks and often met after work to schedule some activity for the evening.

Rudy Garcia, the department manager, was concerned about the strained relationship that existed between the technicians and engineers. He noticed the engineers complaining about the slowness and poor quality of work being done by the technicians. These complaints were occurring regularly. The productivity of the department became a part of Rudy Garcia's performance file, and his salary increments and promotion opportunities were based on his file. It was obvious to Rudy that the production of the department was extremely low compared to other similar departments in other plants in the company.

Because of the perceived problems in the department, Rudy started to investigate the relationship between the engineers and technicians. For two weeks he talked to a number of the technicians and most of the engineers to learn more about the interaction between the groups. He found that the technicians believed that the engineers requested work orders and set up projects that were poorly developed. They also thought that their suggestions on how to accomplish projects were never followed.

Rudy discovered that the engineers believed that they were a part of the management team and needed control over the technicians. The engineers believed that the technicians were feared by management because they were unionized. In addition, the engineers thought that the technicians were "dragging their feet" and passively resisting any suggestions or recommendations initiated by the engineers.

After his preliminary investigation of the situation Rudy concluded that immediate action had to be taken. He wanted to be fair, but firm, in the steps that he needed to take to try to minimize or resolve the friction.

Questions for analysis:

1. Would you have predicted problems between the engineering and technician groups? Why?
2. What type(s) of groups are described in the exercise?
3. Is the friction among the engineers and technicians creating more or less cohesion within the groups? Why?
4. What action would you recommend that Rudy Garcia take?

10

LEADERSHIP

MANAGEMENT IN ACTION*

Largely in the past decade, scores of the country's corporations have with great fanfare set up some form of collective leadership under names like the Office of the President, Corporate Office, or the Office of the Chairman. They were touted as a reasonable response to the increasingly complex environment.

There certainly seems a need for collective leadership. Almost everyone agrees that the difficult decisions faced in a company are too complex for one person to manage. It would be better to have those top decisions handled by a select group of senior executives who have a variety of backgrounds and skills. This philosophy has motivated such firms as General Electric, Caterpillar Tractor, ITT, Borden, Nabisco, Olin, Pet, and Prudential Insurance to establish some variant of the Office of the President (OP).

In many cases, the OP has been a useful management tool, especially in widely diversified operations. General Electric has used a version of OP for more than a decade. Caterpillar Tractor's OP is also considered a success and has been in existence since 1955.

Despite the documented successes, the OP probably fails more times that it works, largely because collective leadership is at best a very tricky game to play. Most companies fail to realize that the OP requires more skillful leadership to make it work than does the traditional directive style. Because of its difficulty, individuals who are part of the Office of the President must be mature, highly knowledgeable, and very skilled in communications. They also must have complete trust in each other.

* Description of this issue is found in "How Much Room At The Top?" *Dun's Review* (March 1977), pp. 83–85.

Effective leadership is needed if an organization is to be successful and survive. Whether a leader is effective depends on the results achieved through his or her practice of leadership. The criterion of leadership success is the performance of the leader's group. An effective leader can influence followers so that they achieve the highest level of performance possible with the skills, resources, and technology available.

Interest in the subject of leading others has existed throughout the history of human groups and organizations. The behavioralists, however, have in the past 20 years scientifically analyzed leadership in organizational settings. They have found that leadership is a complex process associated with numerous theories and models. Many of the available theories and models are contradictory or overlap.[1]

In this chapter some of the more popular theories and models are discussed, and an integrative model of leadership is offered. It will become clear that there is no one best way to lead followers to achieve high levels of performance.

What is leadership?

Some writers have projected the impression that leadership is a synonym for managership. This assumption is not correct. Leaders are found not only in the managerial hierarchy, but also in informal work groups. However, the discussion in this chapter is directed toward the exercise of leadership by individuals in the managerial hierarchy.

In the management literature, there are many definitions of leadership. Listed below are a few of the more popular ones:

1. Leadership is one form of dominance, in which the followers more or less willingly accept direction and control by another person.[2]
2. Leadership is the process of influencing the activities of an organized group in efforts toward goal setting and goal achievement.[3]
3. Leadership is the process of inducing a subordinate to behave in a desired manner.[4]

---

[1] Gary Yukl, "Toward a Behavioral Theory of Leadership," *Organizational Behavior and Human Performance,* (July 1971), p. 414.

[2] K. Young, *Handbook of Social Psychology* (London: Routledge & Kegan Paul, Ltd., 1946).

[3] Ralph M. Stogdill, "Leadership, Membership and Organization," *Psychological Bulletin* (January 1950), p. 4.

[4] Warren G. Bennis, "Leadership Theory and Administrative Behavior: The Problem of Authority," *Administrative Science Quarterly* (December 1959), p. 261.

4.   Leadership is effective influence. In order to influence effectively, a leader requires on-the-job learning about his or her influence.[5]

A review of the four leadership definitions indicates that although (1) was stated in 1946 and (4) was proposed in 1976 they are very similar. The common thread running through these four definitions is that leadership is a process whereby one individual exerts influence over others. Several attempts have been made to clarify and depict the basis upon which a superior might influence a subordinate or a group of subordinates. One of the most concise and insightful approaches is offered by French and Raven.[6] They define influence in terms of power —the control which a person possesses and can exercise on others.

It is proposed by French and Raven that there are five different bases of power:

1. *Coercive power.*   This is power based upon fear. A subordinate perceives that failure to comply with the wishes of a superior would lead to punishment (for example, an undesirable work assignment, a reprimand). Coercive power is based upon the expectations of individuals that punishment is the consequence for not agreeing with the actions, attitudes, or directives of a superior.

2. *Reward power.*   This is the opposite of coercive power. A subordinate perceives that compliance with the wishes of a superior will lead to positive rewards. These rewards could be monetary (increases in pay) or nonmonetary (a compliment for a job well done).

3. *Legitimate power.*   This type of power comes from the position of a superior in the organizational hierarchy. For example, the president of a corporation possesses more legitimate power than the vice president, and the department manager has more legitimate power than the first-line supervisor.

4. *Expert power.*   An individual with this type of power is one with some expertise, special skill, or knowledge. The possession of one or more of these attributes gains the respect and compliance of peers or subordinates.

5. *Referent power.*   This power is based on a follower's identification with a leader. The leader is admired because of one or more personal traits, and the follower can be influenced because of this admiration.

Coercive, reward, and legitimate power are specified primarily by the individual's position in the organization. The first-line super-

---

[5] Chris Argyris, "Leadership, Learning, and Changing the Status Quo," *Organizational Dynamics* (Winter 1976), p. 29.

[6] John R. P. French and Bertram Raven, "The Bases of Social Power," in Dorwin Cartwright and A. F. Zander, eds., *Group Dynamics* (Evanston, Ill.: Row, Peterson, and Company, 2d. ed., 1960), pp. 607–23.

visor in an organization is at a lower managerial level than the department manager, and consequently has significantly less coercive, reward, and legitimate power than does the department manager. Upper-level managers are allowed various company facilities and resources, while managers at the lower levels cannot utilize these. The head operating room nurse has more freedom to make job-related decisions than a floor nurse. Position also affects the use of power in regard to the discipline process. A first-line supervisor can reprimand subordinates (coercive power), while the department manager can reprimand the first-line supervisor.

The degree and scope of a manager's referent and expert power bases are dictated primarily by individual characteristics. Some managers possess specific qualities (for example, skills or attributes) that make them attractive to subordinates. Managers could be considered attractive because of an ability to express themselves clearly or because they appear completely confident in performing the job. Thus, the individual superior controls the referent and expert power bases while the organization controls the coercive, reward, and legitimate power bases.

Katz and Kahn have added another concept to the power framework for studying leadership. They propose an incremental influence category in the following manner: ". . . we consider the essence of organizational leadership to be the influential increment over and above the mechanical compliance with routine directives of the organization."[7]

The incremental influence factor can be described as a combination of the referent and expert bases.[8] The essence of this influence concept is that the organizational and individual characteristics of managers are related to each other.

The leadership job: Psychological view

The psychological view proposes that the primary function of a leader is to develop effective motivation systems. The leader must be able to stimulate subordinates in such a manner that they contribute positively to organizational goals and are also able to satisfy various personal needs.

The Maslow need hierarchy could serve as a model for the leader in developing the most effective motivation system. The leader, by being familiar with the premise that "man does not live by bread

---

[7] Daniel Katz and Robert L. Kahn, *The Social Psychology of Organizations* (New York: John Wiley and Sons, Inc., 1966), p. 302.

[8] Kurt R. Student, "Supervisory Influence and Work-Group Performance, *Journal of Applied Psychology* (June 1968), pp. 188–94.

alone," but is interested in psychological growth, can develop programs that achieve optimum contribution from subordinates. A program that focuses upon the entire need spectrum — physiological, safety, social, esteem, and self-actualization — is assumed to have a higher probability for motivating successfully than a partial program.

In the psychological view, the French and Raven influence concept is an integral part. To consider only organizationally controlled power sources — coercive, reward, and legitimate — leads to the development of incomplete and often misdirected motivational programs. Leaders must also consider referent and expert power bases when developing motivation programs.

The theme stressed in the psychological view of the leader's job involves aiding subordinates in satisfying their various needs. The satisfaction of these needs in such a manner that the organization is more successful and the employees happier is the function a leader must perform. Any leader not accomplishing this complex task would be rated low according to the psychological view.

The leadership job: Sociological view

Other behavioralists perceive the leadership function as a facilitative activity. For example, the leader establishes goals and reconciles organizational conflict between followers, exerting influence by performing these activities.

The establishment of goals provides the direction which followers often require. It provides the followers with guidance so that they know what type of performance or attitude is expected for them. The goals also influence the interaction patterns that develop between followers. This leads to group characteristics such as the development of communication networks, group cohesiveness, and status hierarchies.

Conflict among followers can become so disruptive that nothing positive is contributed to the organization. When this occurs, a leader's influence must be exercised to minimize the disruptive conflict within or between groups.

The sociological view can be criticized from a pragmatic viewpoint. While it is accurate to assume that leaders facilitate the activities of followers, it is misleading to contend that leaders can always set goals and resolve conflict. These are large orders for any leader, which are once again made more difficult by differences in people, and by leadership ability and situations. In the sociological view the leader has to be a facilitator and must also perform the planning, organizing, and controlling functions.

The leadership job: A mutual sharing view

Unquestionably, the manager has the legitimate power to run a plant, establish new accounting procedures, or discard the present performance appraisal system. These rights to influence and make decisions are granted by the organization. However, influence should be viewed as a mutual exercise. In order to influence, one must be influenced to some degree. That is, the leader must be influenced by followers.

A leader who attempts to influence through coercion or fear will eventually face problems. This is not to say that the leader should be stripped of the right to discipline followers in an equitable manner. It does suggest, however, that the leader should be viewed as approachable, equitable, and considerate. The leader can exert more influence if he or she is viewed as being open to influence in some situations.

This mutual sharing view of leadership has an important message: influence can be divided or shared and both parties can gain. A leader, by sharing influence with followers, can benefit from establishing better interaction and more respect. The followers can benefit by learning more about the leader. It is been shown that managers and employees in effective organizations perceive themselves as having greater influence. The greater the total influence leaders and followers have in the organization the better seems to be the performance of the total system.[9]

The psychological, sociological, and mutual sharing views of leadership are broad-based explanations. They each call attention to the influence responsibilities of the leader. However, because they are so broad the guidelines offered managers for improving their own leadership practices are too general. In order to provide suggestions for leaders more specific theories and models are necessary.

Selected leadership theories

Recent efforts by behavioralists have shown a trend toward integrating the numerous theories of leadership. Instead of creating more theories of leadership behavior, the focus here is upon systematically organizing and categorizing what is already available. There appear to by three broad leadership theory categories. They are (1) the trait theories, (2) the personal-behavioral theories, and (3) the situational or contingency theories. Figure 10–1 illustrates that the trait and personal-

---

[9] See D. C. Pelz, "Influence: A Key to Effective Leadership in the First-Line Supervisor," *Personnel* (1952), pp. 201–21, and M. Rosner et al., "Worker Participation and Influence in Five Countries," *Industrial Relations* (1973), pp. 200–212.

FIGURE 10–1
Overlap of theories of leadership

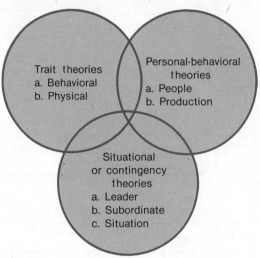

behavioral approaches can be integrated to some degree to yield the situational approach. Some of the situational theories emerging have borrowed from the trait approaches and from various personal-behavioral approaches. Therefore it is best to consider the three approaches as having many similarities and some differences.

TRAIT THEORIES

The identification of various personal traits of leaders as criteria for describing or predicting success has been used for some time. Many executives engaged in recruitment and selection of managers believe that the trait approach is as valid as any other method. However, the comparison of leaders by various physical, personality, and intelligence traits has resulted in little agreement amont researchers.

Physical traits. There are advocates of the trait theory who contend that the physical stature of a person affects ability to influence followers. For example, in an extensive review of 12 leadership investigations, Stogdill determined that nine of the studies found leaders to be taller than followers; two found them to be shorter; while one concluded that height was not the most important factor.[10] Other physical traits that have been studied with no conclusive results include weight, physique, and personal appearance.

---

[10] Ralph Stogdill, "Personal Factors Associated with Leadership," *Journal of Applied Psychology*, (January 1948), pp. 35–71.

Personality. A research study by Ghiselli[11] reports on several personality factors that are related in most, though not all, cases to effective leadership. He found that leaders who have the drive to act independently and are self-assured (for example, have confidence in their leadership skills) are successful in achieving organizational goals.

The work of Fiedler suggests that successful leaders may be more perceptive than nonsuccessful leaders.[12] He found that effective leaders are more proficient in differentiating between their best and poorest followers than are the less effective leaders. The leaders of the more effective groups maintain greater psychological distance between themselves and their followers than do leaders of less effective groups.

Intelligence. After surveying the literature, Stogdill concluded that leadership ability is associated with the judgment and verbal facility of the leader.[13] Ghiselli also concluded that an individual's intelligence is an accurate predictor of managerial success within a certain range. Above and below this range the chances of successful prediction significantly decrease.[14] It should be noted, however, that the leader's intelligence should be close to the followers. The leader who is too smart or not smart enough may lose the followers' respect.

Ghiselli has studied eight personality traits and five motivational traits.[15] The traits he has studied are:

Personality traits
> Intelligence: of a verbal and symbolic nature.
> Initiative: the willingness to strike off in new directions.
> Supervisory ability: the ability to direct others.
> Self-assurance: favorable self-evaluation.
> Affinity for the working class.
> Decisiveness.
> Masculinity-femininity.
> Maturity.

Motivational traits
> Need for job security.
> Need for financial reward.
> Need for power over others.
> Need for self-actualization.
> Need for occupational achievement.

---

[11] Edwin E. Ghiselli, "Managerial Talent," *American Psychologist* (October 1963), pp. 631–41.

[12] Fred Fiedler, "The Leader's Psychological Distance and Group Effectiveness," in Cartwright and Zander, eds., *Group Dynamics*, pp. 586–605.

[13] Stogdill, "Personal Factors."

[14] Ghiselli, "Managerial Talent."

[15] Edwin E. Ghiselli, *Explorations in Management Talent* (Pacific Palisades, Cal.: Goodyear, 1971).

The research of Ghiselli on these traits is well respected because of the scientific quality of the work. His research findings suggest the relative importance of the traits. Table 10–1 summarizes the results of Ghiselli's studies. The findings must be tempered because the traits are not totally independent from each other. However, there are some interesting pieces of information. First, intelligence and self-actualization are important for success. Second, the concept of power over others is not very important. This tends to support the Theory Y orientation. Third, the supervisory ability trait basically refers to the ability to use planning, organizing, and controlling to direct subordinates. This was an extremely important trait in the classical explanation of management. Finally, masculinity-femininity seems to have little to do with managerial success in the Ghiselli work.

TABLE 10–1
The importance of personal trait to management success

Importance	Personal trait
Very important	Supervisory ability
	Occupational achievement
	Intelligence
	Self-actualization
	Self-assurance
	Decisiveness
Moderately important	Lack of need for security
	Working class affinity
	Initiative
	Lack of need for high financial reward
	Maturity
Very little importance	Masculinity-femininity

Source: Adapted from E. E. Ghiselli, *Explorations in Management Talent* (Pacific Palisades, Cal.: Goodyear, 1971).

There are some shortcomings in the method of employing a trait approach and assuming that a manager who is confident, independent, and intelligent has a higher probability of succeeding. First, the trait theory of leadership ignores the subordinates. The followers have a significant effect on the job accomplished by the leader. Second, except for Ghiselli, trait theorists do not specify the relative importance of various traits. Should an organization attempt to find managers who are confident or those who act independently—which should be weighted more? Third, the research evidence is inconsistent. For every study that supports the idea that a particular trait is positively related to improved effectiveness there seems to be one that shows a negative or no relationship. Finally, though large numbers of traits have already been uncovered, the list grows annually, suggesting that still others will be found in the future. The cumbersome listings lead to confusion and disputes, and provide little insight into leadership.

The practicing manager searches for answers and suggestions and is not typically concerned about theoretical arguments. Perhaps the most significant limitation is that trait-related research findings do not allow us to generalize such findings from one situation to another.[16] The work of Ghiselli appears to be the best of what is available on the trait theory of leadership.

PERSONAL-BEHAVIORAL THEORIES

Personal-behavioral theories contend that leaders may best be classified by personal qualities or behavioral patterns (styles). A number of writers have presented theories of leadership which fit into the personal-behavioral (P-B) category. In all cases, however, the P-B theories of leadership focus upon what the leader does in carrying out the managerial job. Of these there is no specific style that is universally accepted.

A continuum of leadership. Tannenbaum and Schmidt postulate that managers often have difficulty in deciding what type of action is most appropriate for handling a particular problem.[17] They are not sure whether to make the decision or to delegate the decision-making authority to subordinates. To provide insight into the meaning of leadership behavior with regard to decision making, Tannenbaum and Schmidt suggest a continuum.

Figure 10–2 presents this leadership continuum. Leadership actions are related to the degree of authority used by managers, and to the amount of freedom available to the subordinates in reaching decisions. The managerial actions depicted on the left characterize managers who maintain a high degree of control, while those on the right are those of managers who delegate decision-making authority. The continuum clearly illustrates that there are a number of leadership styles. According to this theory effective leaders would be those who are adaptable, that is, who can delegate authority effectively because they consider their capabilities, subordinates' capabilities, and goals to be accomplished. Thus, Tannenbaum and Schmidt imply that leaders should not choose a strict "autocratic" or "democratic" style, but should be flexible enough to cope with different situations.

---

[16] Ibid., p. 84.

[17] Robert Tannenbaum and Warren H. Schmidt, "How to Choose a Leadership Pattern," *Harvard Business Review* (May–June 1973), pp. 162–80.

FIGURE 10-2
Continuum of leadership behavior

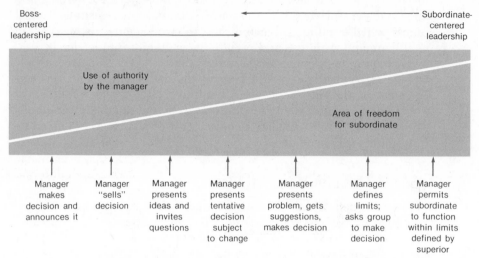

Job-centered–employee-centered leaders. Since 1947, Likert and his associates at the Institute for Social Research at the University of Michigan have conducted studies of leadership.[18] They have studied leaders in industry, hospitals, and government, obtaining data from thousands of employees.

After extensive analyses, the leaders studied were classified as job-centered or employee-centered. The *job-centered leader* structures the jobs of subordinates, closely supervises to see that designated tasks are performed, uses incentives to spur production, and determines satisfactory rates of production based on procedures such as time study. The *employee-centered leader* focuses attention on the human aspects of subordinates' problems and on building effective work groups with high performance goals. Such a leader specifies objectives, communicates them to subordinates, and gives subordinates considerable freedom to accomplish their job tasks and goals.

Likert's research shows that the majority of high-producing groups were led by supervisors who displayed an employee-centered style. In a study of clerical workers the employee-centered manager was described as a general supervisor and the job-centered manager as a close supervisor. Once again, productivity data clearly indicated that the general type of supervision (employee centered) was more effective than the close supervision style (job centered).

Based on his extensive research, Likert suggests that the type of

---

[18] Rensis Likert, *New Patterns of Management* (New York: McGraw-Hill Book Company, Inc., 1961).

leadership style significantly influences various effectiveness criteria. Such criteria as productivity, absenteeism, attitudes, turnover, and defective units were found to be more favorable from an organizational standpoint when employee-centered or general supervision was utilized. Likert implies that the choice is of the either–or variety, that is, management can be categorized and practiced as employee-centered or job-centered. His recommendation is to develop employee-centered managers whenever possible.

Two-dimensional theory. In 1945, a group of researchers at Ohio State University began extensive investigations of leadership. The central focus of their work was to study in depth the work of a leader. Their effort uncovered many provocative insights concerning leadership behavior. Perhaps the most publicized aspect of the Ohio State leadership studies was the isolation of two dimensions of leadership behavior, identified as "consideration" and "initiating structure."[19]

These two dimensions were used to describe leadership behavior in organizational settings. The researchers assessed how supervisors think they should behave in leadership roles. They also attempted to ascertain subordinate perceptions of supervisory behavior. The findings allowed the Ohio State researchers to classify leaders on "consideration" and "initiating structure" dimensions.

Leaders who were high on the "consideration" dimension reflected that they had developed a work atmosphere of mutual trust, respect for subordinates' ideas, and consideration of subordinates' feelings. Such leaders encouraged good superior-subordinate rapport and two-way communication. A low "consideration" score indicates that leaders are more impersonal in their dealings with subordinates.

A high "initiating structure" score indicates that leaders structure their roles and those of subordinates toward the attainment of goals. They are actively involved in planning work activities, communicating pertinent information, and scheduling work.

One research study attempted to compare foremen having different "consideration" and "initiating structure" scores with various performance measures.[20] The first measure was obtained from proficiency ratings made by plant management. Other measures were unexcused absenteeism, accidents, formally filed grievances, and em-

---

[19] See any of the following for excellent presentations of the two-dimensional theory: E. A. Fleishman, "The Measurement of Leadership Attitudes in Industry," *Journal of Applied Psychology* (June 1953), pp. 153–58; E. A. Fleishman and D. A. Peters, "Interpersonal Values, Leadership Attitudes and Managerial Success," *Personnel Psychology* (Summer 1962), pp. 127–43; and Abraham K. Korman, "Consideration, Initiating Structure, and Organizational Criteria—A Review," *Personnel Psychology* (Winter 1966), pp. 349–61.

[20] E. A. Fleishman, E. F. Harris, and H. E. Burtt, *Leadership and Supervision in Industry* (Columbus, Ohio: Bureau of Educational Research, Ohio State University, 1955).

ployee turnover. Indices for each of these measures were computed for each foreman's work group for an 11-month period.

Foremen who worked in production divisions were compared to foremen in nonproduction divisions on "consideration" scores, "initiating structure" scores, and proficiency ratings. In the production divisions there was a positive relationship between proficiency and "initiating structure" and a negative relationship with "consideration." In other words, the foremen who were rated by their superiors as most proficient scored high on "structure" and low on "consideration." In the nonproduction divisions the relationships were reversed.

After comparing the leadership scores and foreman proficiency ratings, the researchers compared leadership scores to the other performance measures—unexcused absenteeism, accidents, formally filed grievances, and employee turnover. In general, it was determined that high structure and low consideration were related to more absenteeism, accidents, grievances, and turnover.

A number of other studies have supported the general findings cited above, while other research findings present contradictory evidence.[21] Despite these differences, it certainly is true that the Ohio State researchers have stimulated the interest of laymen and researchers in systematically studying leadership. More effort along the lines of the Ohio State studies is needed if some of the mysteries of leadership in an organization are to be understood.

The managerial grid theory. Thus far, we have examined personal opinions and research findings concerning leadership behavior. Another P-B theory based on research findings is the managerial grid concept. Blake and Mouton propose that leadership styles can be plotted on a two-dimensional grid.[22] This grid is presented in Figure 10–3.

Five specific leadership styles are indicated in the grid. Of course these are only a few of the many possible styles of leadership that can be, and are utilized.

1,1   *Impoverished*—a minimum effort to accomplish the work is exerted by the leader.

9,1   *Task*—the leader concentrates on task efficiency but shows little regard for the development and morale of subordinates.

1,9   *Country Club*—the leader focuses on being supportive and considerate of employees. However, task efficiency is not a primary concern of this easygoing style.

---

[21] For a number of studies which dispute some of the findings of the Ohio State researchers, see Korman, "Consideration." For more supportive studies see S. Kerr and C. Schriesheim, "Consideration, Initiating Structure, and Organizational Criteria: An Update of Korman's 1966 Review," *Personnel Psychology* (Winter 1974), pp. 558–68.

[22] Robert R. Blake and Jane S. Mouton, *The Managerial Grid* (Houston, Texas: Gulf Publishing, 1964).

FIGURE 10–3
Managerial grid

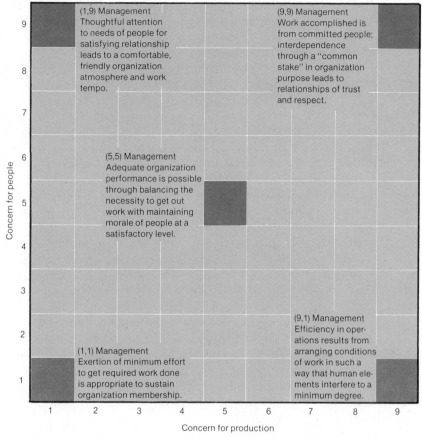

Source: Robert R. Blake and Jane S. Mouton, *The Managerial Grid* (Houston: Gulf Publishing Company, 1964),
p. 10.

5,5   *Middle of the Road* — adequate task efficiency and satisfactory
morale are the goals of this style.

9,9   *Team* — the leader facilitates production and morale by coordinating and integrating work-related activities.

It is assumed by Blake and Mouton that the leader who is a (9,9)
individual would be using the most effective style. However, defining
a (9,9) leader for every type of job is very difficult. But Blake and Mouton imply that a managerial development program can move leaders
toward a (9,9) style. They recommend a number of management development phases. It is assumed that the development experience
will aid the manager in acquiring concern for fellow employees and
expertise to accomplish task objectives such as productivity and
quality. The six phases are outlined on the following page.

Phase 1: Laboratory-seminar groups.   Typically, one-week conferences are used to introduce the leaders to the grid approach and philosophy. The training of the leaders in the conferences is conducted by line managers of the firm who are already familiar with the ideas of Blake and Mouton. A key part of the phase is to analyze and assess one's own leadership style.

Phase 2: Teamwork.   Each department works out and specifies its own (9,9) description. This phase is an extension of Phase 1, which included leaders from different departments in the conference groups. Thus, in the second phase, managers from the same department are brought together. The intent of Phases 1 and 2 is to enable leaders to learn the grid philosophy, improve their ability to assess their own leadership style, and to develop cohesiveness among the participants.

Phase 3: Intergroup interaction.   This phase involves intergroup discussion and analysis of (9,9) specifications. Situations are created whereby tensions and conflicts that exist between groups are analyzed by group members.

Phase 4: Organizational goal setting.   Goal setting on the part of the leaders in the program is discussed and analyzed. Such problems as profits, cost control, and safety are placed in a goal-setting context (for example, one participant vows to reduce direct expenses 20 percent over the next six-month period).

Phase 5: Goal attainment.   The participants attempt to accomplish the goals set in Phase 4. As in Phase 1 the participants meet, but this time the discussion focuses on organizational issues and how to accomplish the goals set in the previous phase.

Phase 6: Stabilization.   Attempts are made to stabilize the improvements brought about in the program. An evaluation of the entire program is conducted at this point.

The managerial grid approach relates task effectiveness and human satisfaction to a formal managerial development program. This program is unique in that (1) line managers, not academicians or consultants, run the program, (2) a conceptual framework of management (the grid) is utilized, and (3) the entire managerial hierarchy undergoes development, not just one level (for example, first-line supervisors).[23]

A synopsis of the personal-behavioral approach.   Examination of the various P-B theories presented in this section indicates that similar concepts are discussed, but different labels are utilized. For example, the continuum, Likert, the Ohio State researchers, and the managerial grid approach each utilize two broadly defined concepts which are summarized in Table 10–2.

---

[23] Robert R. Blake and Jane S. Mouton, "Using the Managerial Grid to Ensure MBO," *Organizational Dynamics* (Spring 1974), pp. 50–62.

Each approach summarized in Table 10–2 focuses upon two concepts; however, some differences should be emphasized. The first two theories are based primarily upon personal opinions. Although the opinions of the originators are respected, they should be supported with research evidence before more faith can be placed in each particular theory. Likert implies that the most successful leadership style

TABLE 10–2
Personal-behavioral theories

Theories	Two concepts and derivation	How theory was developed
1. Leadership continuum	1. Boss-centered and subordinate-centered; opinions of Tannenbaum and Schmidt	1. By description of authors
2. Supportive theory	2. Job-centered and employee-centered; research at the University of Michigan (Likert)	2. By field research studies
3. Two-dimensional theory	3. "Consideration" and "initiating structure"; research at Ohio State University	3. By field research studies
4. Managerial grid	4. Concern for people and concern for production; research of Blake and Mouton	4. By description and limited research

is employee centeredness. He suggests that we need look no further to find the best leadership style. The critical question is whether the employee-centered style works in all situations. Some studies dispute Likert's claim. The Ohio State researchers found that, from a production standpoint, the leader with a high "initiating structure" score was preferred by the executives of the company. Thus Likert's claim, or any other claim, that one best leadership approach has been discovered is subject to debate.

The Ohio State theory and the managerial grid approach can be integrated into an overlay of leadership, "overlay" meaning that they are merged into one.[24] Perhaps more integrative work along the lines of the overlay (Figure 10–4) would provide the student of management with a better understanding of the P-B theories of leadership. This is not to suggest that an ultimate theory of leadership has been discovered, but that the endless list of styles causes semantic difficulties by referring to the same basic leadership behavior with different terminology.

---

[24] The merging idea was originally proposed and presented by Paul Hersey and Kenneth H. Blanchard, *Management of Organizational Behavior* (Englewood Cliffs, N.J.: Prentice-Hall, Inc., 1972), p. 76.

FIGURE 10–4
Overlay of grid and Ohio State leadership theories

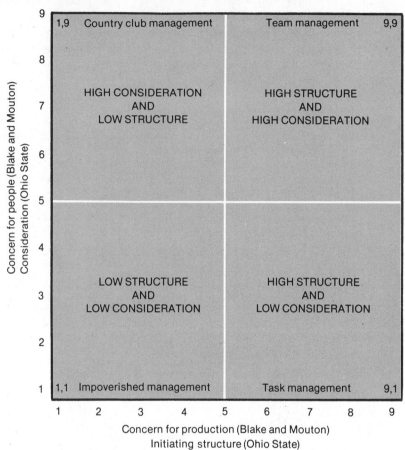

Concern for people (Blake and Mouton)
Consideration (Ohio State)

1,9 Country club management	Team management 9,9
HIGH CONSIDERATION AND LOW STRUCTURE	HIGH STRUCTURE AND HIGH CONSIDERATION
LOW STRUCTURE AND LOW CONSIDERATION	HIGH STRUCTURE AND LOW CONSIDERATION
1,1 Impoverished management	Task management 9,1

Concern for production (Blake and Mouton)
Initiating structure (Ohio State)

SITUATIONAL OR CONTINGENCY THEORIES

An increasing number of behavioral scientists are questioning the premise that a particular leadership style is effective in all situations. They believe that a manager, behaving as a democratic leader, for example, cannot be assured of effective results in every situation. As noted earlier in this chapter, the Ohio State researchers found that supervisors who scored high on initiating structure were relatively more proficient when managing production rather than non-production workers. Thus evidence exists even in the literature on personal-behavioral theories to support the view that effective leadership depends upon the interaction of the situation and the leader's behavior.

The identification of key situational factors and the determination of their relative importance are difficult undertakings. One behavioral scientist who has devoted considerable time and energy to such undertakings is Fred Fiedler.

Fiedler theory of leadership. With a considerable body of research evidence behind him, Fiedler has developed a dynamic situational or contingency theory of leadership.[25] Three important situational factors, or dimensions, are specified and are assumed to influence the leader's effectiveness.

The dimensions identified are:

1. *Leader-member relations* — This refers to the degree of confidence the subordinates have in the leader. It also includes the loyalty shown the leader and the leader's attractiveness.
2. *Task structure* — This refers to the degree to which the followers' jobs are routine as contrasted with nonroutine.
3. *Position power* — This refers to the power inherent in the leadership position. It includes the rewards and punishments typically associated with the position, the leader's official authority (based on ranking in managerial hierarchy), and the support that the leader receives from superiors and the overall organization.

Fiedler measures leadership style by evaluating leader responses to what is called a Least-Preferred Co-Worker (LPC) questionnaire. The leaders who rate their least-preferred co-worker in favorable terms (high LPC) are assumed to be people-oriented and supportive. Those leaders who give low LPC ratings are more task-oriented.

By utilizing the three-dimensional model, LPC scores, and research findings, Fiedler has specified the type of leadership style that is most appropriate in different situations. He has assembled data which relate leadership style to the three-dimensional measures of conditions favorable or unfavorable to the leader. The LPC measure of leadership style is assumed to discriminate between leaders who tend to be permissive, considerate, and foster good interpersonal relations among group members and leaders who tend to be directive, controlling, and more oriented toward task than toward people. For example, permissive leaders obtain optimal group performance in situations where the task is structured but the leader is disliked and must be diplomatic. This type of leadership style is also effective in situations where the leader is liked but the group is faced with an unstructured task.

In effect, the Fiedler model suggests that leaders who are directive and leaders who are permissive can function best in certain types of situations. Instead of stating that a leader must adopt this or that style, Fiedler identifies the type of leader who functions best in a situation.

[25] Fred E. Fiedler, *A Theory of Leadership Effectiveness* (New York: McGraw-Hill Book Co., 1967) and Fred E. Fiedler and Martin M. Chemers, *Leadership and Effective Management* (Glenview, Ill.: Scott, Foresman, and Co., 1975).

According to Fiedler we should not talk simply about good leaders or poor leaders. A leader who achieves effectiveness in one situation may or may not be effective in another. The implication of this logic is that managers should think about the situation in which a particular leader (subordinate manager) performs well or badly. Fiedler assumes that managers can enhance subordinates' effectiveness if they carefully choose situations that are favorable to the subordinates' style.

In Table 10–3 some of Fiedler's findings about the relationship of the three dimensions to leadership style for such task groups as bomber crews, management groups, high school basketball teams, and open-hearth crews are presented.

TABLE 10–3
Summary of Fiedler's investigations of leadership

	Group situation			Leadership style correlating with productivity
Condition	Leader-member relations	Task structure	Position power	
1	Good	Structured	Strong	Directive
2	Good	Structured	Weak	Directive
3	Good	Unstructured	Strong	Directive
4	Good	Unstructured	Weak	Permissive
5	Moderately poor	Structured	Strong	Permissive
6	Moderately poor	Structured	Weak	No data
7	Moderately poor	Unstructured	Strong	No relationship found
8	Moderately poor	Unstructured	Weak	Directive

A review of Table 10–3 indicates a correlation between good task performance and a *directive* style under conditions 1, 2, 3, and 8, and a correlation between good task performance and a *permissive* style under conditions 4 and 5. These results indicate that for various situations a particular leadership style achieves the best results.

An example of an effective leader under condition 1 could be the following:

> A well-liked head nurse in a university medical center who is in charge of getting the nursing team ready for open-heart surgery. The tasks which must be performed by the head nurse are very tightly structured. There is no room for error or indecision, and the duties of everyone on the nursing team are clearly specified. The head nurse has complete power to correct any personnel or performance problems within the nursing team.

A leader who is working under condition 5 shown in Table 10–3 would be the following:

> Dan Pride recently graduated from college. While in school, he took as many management courses as possible. His first job assignment was to supervise 18 technicians in a manufacturing plant in Chicago. Most of the technicians had little education past the eighth grade and had worked for more than ten years in the plant. They generally believed that college "kids" were either "wise guys" or good people, but they took their time deciding. Because they were genuine experts on their job, a formal leader had very little control over sequencing or structuring the job. The job was structured by the experts, and Dan actually concentrated on paper work, not technical work.

These two brief examples are provided to indicate that the three dimensions of leader-member relations, task structure, and position power are found in each of the eight conditions. According to Fiedler, these conditions are found throughout various organizations and directly influence the leader's effectiveness.

In various organizational settings there may be a need to "engineer" the situation to fit the leader's style, as described by Fiedler in his contingency model. Fiedler suggests some pragmatic procedures for improving a leader's relations, task structure, and position power. Some of his suggestions are as follows:

1. Leader-member relations could be improved by restructuring the leader's group of subordinates so that the group is more compatible in terms of background, education level, technical expertise, or ethnic origin. It should be noted that this would be extremely difficult in a unionized group since it may assume that this restructuring is a management plan to weaken the union.

2. The task structure can be modified in the structured or the nonstructured direction. The task can be made more structured by spelling out the jobs in greater detail. A task can be made less structured by providing only general directions for the work that is to be accomplished. Some workers like minimum task structure, while others want detailed and specific task structure.

3. Leader position power can be modified in a number of ways. A leader can be given a higher rank in the organization or more authority to do the job. A memo can be issued indicating the rank change or the authority which a leader now possesses. In addition, a leader's reward power can be increased if the organization delegates authority to evaluate the performance of subordinates.

Interestingly, Fiedler's suggestions do not include leadership training.[26] In fact, he believes that training is not an effective approach.

---

[26] Fred E. Fiedler, "The Leadership Game: Matching the Man to the Situation," *Organizational Dynamics* (Winter 1976), pp. 6–16.

Fiedler reports that his own research has shown disappointing results from training. On the average, people with much training perform about as well as people with little or no training.

Fiedler's suggestions may not be feasible in every organizational setting. Such factors as unions, technology, time, and costs to accomplish changes must be considered. For example, a unionized company that has a highly routine technology and is currently faced with intense competition in new-product development may not have the patience, time, and energy to modify the three situational dimensions so that its leaders become more effective. The real world tempers many of the logically sound and provocative suggestions offered by the contingency approach to leadership.

In effect, Fiedler has presented a theory of leadership which takes into account the leader's personality as well as such situational variables as the task to be completed and the behavioral characteristics of the group which the leader must influence. Of course, much more research is needed before the theory gains widespread acceptance or even partial agreement from among those studying leadership. There are critics who question Fiedler's methodology of measuring LPC, the subjects he uses in some of his research (for example, basketball teams, the Belgian Navy, and students), and the fact that only high and low LPC scores are considered in discussing effectiveness.[27] Despite critics and shortcomings, Fiedler has provided a starting point for leadership research in the 1970s and 1980s.

The path-goal theory of leadership. A more recent leadership approach is called the path-goal theory.[28] It proposes that the leader is a key individual in bringing about improved subordinate motivation, satisfaction, and performance. The theory suggests that four leadership styles can be and are used:

1. _Directive_ — The leader directs and there is no subordinate participation in decision making.
2. _Supportive_ — The leader is friendly and is interested in subordinates as people.
3. _Participative_ — The leader asks for, receives, and uses suggestions from subordinates to make decisions.
4. _Achievement-oriented_ — The leader sets challenging goals for subordinates and shows confidence that they can achieve the goals.

---

[27] A thorough review article that is critical of the situational or contingency model of leadership is George Craen, Kenneth Alvaris, James B. Orris, and Joseph A. Martella, "Contingency Model of Leadership Effectiveness: Antecedent and Evidential Results," _Psychological Bulletin_ (October 1970), pp. 285–96.

[28] Martin G. Evans, "The Effect of Supervisory Behavior on the Path-Goal Relationship," _Organizational Behavior and Human Performance_ (May 1970), pp. 277–298; Robert J. House, "A Path-Goal Theory of Leader Effectiveness," _Administrative Science Quarterly_ (September 1971), pp. 321–38.

The path-goal theory suggests, unlike Fiedler's theory, that these four styles are used by the *same leader* in different situations.[29]

The important key in this theory is the way the leader affects the "paths" between subordinate behavior and goals. In a sense the leader is the coach who charts out realistic paths for his or her team. The leader can affect the paths by:

1. Recognizing and stimulating subordinates' needs for rewards over which he or she (leader) has some control;
2. Rewarding goal achievement;
3. Supporting subordinates' efforts to achieve the goals;
4. Helping reduce frustrating barriers in the way of achieving goals; and
5. Increasing the opportunities for personal satisfaction for subordinates.

Basically, the leader attempts to help the subordinate find the best path, set challenging goals, and remove stressful barriers along the way.

Since the path-goal theory is relatively new, there have been a limited number of studies testing its assumptions. However, one study of ten different samples of employees found that supportive leadership has its most positive effect on satisfaction for subordinates who work on stressful and frustrating jobs. Another study determined that in three separate organizations subordinates doing nonroutine job tasks working for achievement-oriented leaders were more confident that their efforts would result in better performance.[30]

The Vroom-Yetton model. The final situational leadership model to be discussed in this section is the Vroom-Yetton Model.[31] This model attempts to identify the appropriate leadership style for a given set of circumstances, or situations. The leadership styles are defined in terms of the extent to which the subordinates participate in decision making. Thus this model is similar to the Tannenbaum and Schmidt continuum presented earlier in the chapter. At one extreme is leadership style I which specifies that the leader will make the decision; at the other extreme is leadership style V which specifies that the leader and subordinates will together arrive at a consensus decision. Three intermediate points along the continuum are also described as shown in Figure 10–5.[32]

---

[29] Robert J. House and Terence R. Mitchell, "Path-Goal Theory of Leadership," *Journal of Contemporary Business* (Autumn 1974), pp. 81–97.

[30] See Alan C. Filley, Robert J. House, and Steven Kerr, *Managerial Process and Organizational Behavior* (Glenview, Ill.: Scott, Foresman and Co., 1976), pp. 256–60.

[31] Victor Vroom and Philip Yetton, *Leadership and Decision Making* (Pittsburgh: University of Pittsburgh Press, 1973).

[32] This figure is based upon Victor H. Vroom, "A New Look at Managerial Decision Making," *Organizational Dynamics* (Winter 1973), p. 67 and 70.

FIGURE 10-5 Vroom-Yetton leadership model

Leadership style	Style I	Style II	Style III	Style IV	Style V
	Solve the problem or make the decision yourself, using information available to you at the time.	Obtain necessary information from subordinate(s), then solve the problem and make the decision yourself. The subordinates' role is to provide information, not suggest solutions.	Share the nature of the problem with relevant subordinates individually, obtain their ideas and suggestions without bringing them together as a group. Make the decision that may or may not reflect your subordinates' influence.	Share the problem with subordinates as a group, obtain their ideas and suggestions. Make the decision that may or may not reflect your subordinates' influence.	Share the problem with subordinates as a group. Together you generate and evaluate alternatives and attempt to reach agreement on a solution. Do not try to influence the group to adopt "your" solution, and be willing to accept and implement any solution that has the support of the group.

Key situational questions

Key situational questions	1	2	3	4	5	6	7	8	9	10	11	12	13	14	15	16	17
G. Is conflict among subordinates likely in preferred decisions?											YES	YES					
F. Do subordinates know the organizational goals to be attained by the solution?		YES	YES							YES	NO		NO		YES	YES	YES
E. If you make the decision yourself, is it reasonably certain that it would be accepted by subordinates?	YES	YES		YES	NO		NO		NO		NO		NO	NO	NO	NO	NO
D. Is acceptance of the solution by subordinates critical to effective implementation?	NO		YES	YES	YES	YES	YES	YES	NO	NO	YES	YES	YES	YES	YES	YES	YES
C. Is the problem such that the alternative solutions and their consequences are known with a high degree of certainty?					YES	NO	YES	NO	NO	NO	NO	YES	YES	NO	YES	YES	NO
B. Do I have sufficient information to make a high-quality decision?			YES	YES	YES	YES	YES	YES	YES	YES	YES	YES	YES	YES	YES	NO	NO
A. Is there a quality requirement such that one solution is likely to be more rational than another?	NO	NO	YES	YES	YES	YES	YES	YES	YES	YES	YES	YES	YES	NO	NO	NO	YES

The seven key questions are answered A

The appropriate style, whether I, II, III, IV, or V depends upon the combination of seven situational factors. The factors are stated in terms of questions which reflect issues related to the problem to be solved and to the subordinates themselves. These seven situational factors are designated A through G in Figure 10-5. For example, if there is only one obvious solution and if acceptance by subordinates is not critical to effective implementation, then the leader should use leadership style I; that is, he or she should make the decision on the basis of available information. But if there are several alternatives, and if acceptance of the solution by the subordinates is critical to its implementation, and if it is reasonably certain that subordinates would not accept the decision unless they were involved, then leadership style V is appropriate. Figure 10-5 shows 17 different situations and indicates for each the appropriate degree of subordinate participation in decision making. These situations are similar to the eight conditions which Fiedler identifies in his model. The important difference, however, is that Fiedler includes the leader's position power as a crucial situational factor.

Since the Vroom-Yetton model is relatively new, it needs to be researched further and developed more. The interest generated in the model among practicing managers has been significant. This approach seems to be very appealing to those who believe that one way to bridge the gap between leadership practices and performance improvement is through training in how one "ought" to lead. On this point Fiedler's assumptions and the Vroom and Yetton model and research on training do not agree with each other. Vroom and Yetton suggest leadership training, but Fiedler is skeptical about the effectiveness of such training.

An integrative leadership model

So far, the discussion of leadership has emphasized that the search for the one best way to lead has not been fruitful. Moreover, the tendency of theorists and researchers to use different terms when referring to similar concepts introduces considerable confusion. Terms such as "directive," "autocratic," "concern for production," "initiating structure," appear frequently and refer to an essentially similar form of leader behavior. At the same time it is now recognized that effective leadership behavior in one situation is not necessarily effective in a different situation. The aspiring manager is seemingly left with little established knowledge to draw on in understanding effective leadership behavior.

The authors recognize the tentative nature of all knowledge, but at the same time recognize the necessity for managers to understand

FIGURE 10–6
An integrative perspective of leadership

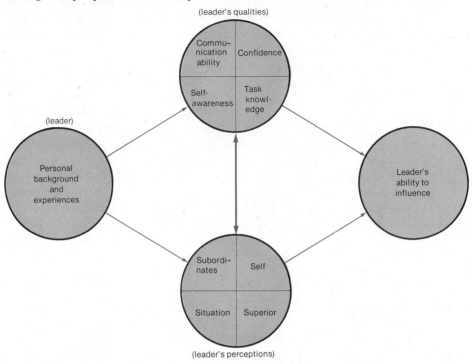

and practice leadership. With these two considerations in mind, a framework for understanding and integrating contemporary leadership theory is proposed in Figure 10–6. The framework emphasizes the effect of the leader's background and experiences on (1) qualities such as communication ability, self-awareness, confidence, and task understanding, and on (2) the leader's perceptions of subordinates, the situation, the superior, and the self. The interaction of all these factors is important for determining the leader's ability to influence others. The manner in which these variables interact and the proportionate weight of each is not known with certainty; but there is no doubt of their importance.

The leader should consider a number of important organizational and environmental variables as illustrated in Figure 10–6. In the context of the leadership framework, the effective leader is an individual who influences followers in such a manner that high productivity is achieved, high group morale exists, low absenteeism, turnover, and accident rates are the rule, and the development of followers is achieved. Figure 10–6 only specifies four personal qualities which contribute significantly to a leader's ability to influence others. This is not intended to be a complete list of relevant factors. The four qualities, however, are suited for most leadership styles and are especially compatible with the situational, or contingency, theory of leadership. They are also related to the perception factors.

AWARENESS OF SELF

One of the most important factors in the situational approach to leadership centers around leader self-awareness.[33] Leaders should be aware of their impact upon those they lead. We are not assuming that they can predict accurately in every situation how their leadership style will affect followers. However, we are suggesting that they should attempt to learn more about their influence upon others. It is assumed that leaders who know themselves are able to perform effectively such necessary functions as planning, organizing, and controlling.

Many of us maintain and develop inaccurate images of our personalities and interaction styles. For example, a leader may perceive "self" as being soft-spoken and easygoing, while subordinates consider the leader sharp-tongued and ill-tempered. This type of counterevaluation or inaccurate self-perception by the leader often reduces a leader's effectiveness.

CONFIDENCE

Leaders differ significantly in confidence they have in their ability to lead others. Leaders who lack confidence would have difficulty in diagnosing different situations and coping adequately with these situations. These difficulties result in leaders failing to perform certain functions that could lead to desirable results. For example, a leader with little self-confidence will often assume that followers cannot adequately perform their job tasks. This may lead to the leader exercising close supervision over subordinates. The closeness of supervision may prove disruptive because of the type of job being completed, the personality and type of personnel in the work group, and the size of the work group.

A lack of confidence could also result in the leader making decisions which are not adequate or are viewed as being harmful by the group members. In effect, the confidence of a leader is related to some extent to the risk-taking propensities of the leader. The leader who lacks confidence makes decisions in many instances that compromise followers' morale, rewards, and status ranking among other groups.

[33] In Chapter 11 sensitivity training will be discussed. One of the purported advantages of sensitivity training is that it improves the self-awareness of participants.

ABILITY TO COMMUNICATE

Every leader must be able to communicate objectives to followers. The leader who fails to communicate with followers may become ineffective as an influencer of others. This results because failing to communicate leads to an inability to coordinate necessary follower activities.

UNDERSTANDING OF THE TASK

The task of a group or an individual refers to what is to be done on a job. Tasks are imposed by management or self-generated by the employee. A task has physical properties and behavioral features. The physical properties are the stimuli surrounding the job. These stimuli may be a set of instructions from management or the way the employee interprets the job. The behavioral properties are the requirements or kinds of responses expected of a person doing the task.

The task may be very structured, as the job duties of a worker on an assembly line. The worker is instructed by management (stimuli), what to do with the products being processed. The goal or requirements (behavioral property) of this type of job is to produce as many units of good quality as possible.

Other tasks such as those of a research and development engineer or planning expert may be unstructured. In these jobs, the goals are not easily defined. Thus the leader may have to work hard to display "paths" and goals for the employees.

Leaders must be able to assess correctly the tasks their followers are performing. In an unstructured task situation, directive or autocratic leadership may be very inappropriate. The employees need guidelines, freedom to act, and the necessary resources to accomplish the task. Thus the leader must properly diagnose the tasks of followers so that proper leadership style choices are made. Because of this requirement, the leader must have some technical knowledge of the job and its requirements.

In Table 10–4 the integrative model is used to describe Dan Pride who was also used to illustrate condition 5 in the Fiedler model. The description of various factors provides a picture of him as a leader.

The emphasis of the authors' model is on leaders' ability to diagnose themselves and their total leadership environment. Perhaps what we are suggesting is that if leadership training programs are used, they should stress diagnostic skills. It should not be concluded that managers can be easily trained to accurately diagnose work situations and to develop appropriate leadership abilities. This type of training difficulty is summed up by Fiedler in the following manner:

> Industrial psychologists and personnel men typically view the executive's position as fixed and immutable and the individual as highly

TABLE 10–4
The integrative model and Dan Pride

Leader's characteristics (background and experience)	Leader's qualities	Leader's ability to influence	Leader's perceptions
a. 23 years old.	a. Shy—but is also impressive when he begins to communicate.	a. Performance of group will be assessed every three months by MBO review.	a. Perceives that his lack of technical knowledge could be a drawback.
b. College graduate.	b. Has confidence and ability to influence others.	b. Check of group absenteeism and turnover will be continually made.	b. Perceives group's attitudes toward college graduates as being cautious.
c. Born in Chicago.	c. Thinks that he is aggressive with others.		c. Perceives the group as being interested in quality at any cost.
d. Worked as trainee in manufacturing plant during summers.	d. Understands the tasks of followers.		

plastic and trainable. When we think of improving leadership performance, we generally think first of training the leader. Yet, we know all too well from our experience with psychotherapy, our attempts to rehabilitate prison inmates, drug addicts or juvenile delinquents—not to mention our difficulties with rearing our own progeny—that our ability to change personality has its limitations.[34]

If leaders are to become diagnostically skilled and flexible to the degree of changing their leadership style, depending upon the circumstances at hand, patience is essential. The organization must be willing to plan, and to fund development programs which are time-consuming. The approach we are suggesting is not applicable in those instances where changing the situation is less costly than changing the leader.

Summary

Inevitably, organizations require leaders to utilize the abilities of their followers so that goals may be accomplished. Although an organi-

---

[34] Fiedler, *Leadership Effectiveness*, p. 247.

zation may have the necessary requisites for the attainment of goals, if it does not have a leadership team that can influence followers, the probability is high that the organization will not survive in the long run. Consequently, it is obvious that effective leadership is the life-blood of organizational survival.

The Classical and Behavioral Schools of management have recognized the importance of leadership in organizations. This fact is disclosed by the extensive research and literature devoted to the what, why, and how of leadership. The efforts of behavioralists have resulted in numerous theories of leadership. The theories are based on concepts of influence, power, and authority. To highlight the crux of these theories, the French and Raven analysis was employed in this chapter because it focuses upon the relationship between organizational factors (for example, managerial hierarchy) and individual characteristics.

After establishing the fact that influence is the crux of leadership, a number of behavioral leadership theories were presented. The theories presented provide the reader with an indication of (1) the differences of opinion among behavioralists, (2) the different methodologies employed to study leadership, (3) the similarities between various theories, and (4) the fact that increasing research on the situational or contingency approach seem to be the current thrust.

The final note of the chapter offers the premise that there is no "one best way" to lead. It is felt that more emphasis should be given the situational approach. The key to this approach seems to be the diagnostic skill of the leader. That is, leaders who can ascertain the personality of followers, their own behavioral patterns, and understand organizational requirements are viewed as having a better chance of succeeding in influencing their subordinates.

Discussion and review questions

1. What is the difference between a normative approach to leadership and a descriptive model of leadership?

2. Reread Management in Action and decide why collective leadership would be difficult not only at the top management level but also at the first line or lower levels of management.

3. What appears to be the trend in the Behavioral School for conducting research on leadership behavior?

4. Is it feasible to alter the job so that a particular type of leader will be more effective? Discuss an actual or hypothetical situation where it would be best to alter the job to suit the leader.

5. Why is the diagnostic skill of the leader so vital to the situational approach to leadership?

6. How are "paths" and goals brought together in the path-goal theory of leadership?
7. Why should leaders be aware of their impact on followers?
8. Explain how the three situational dimensions discussed by Fiedler can be modified in an organization.
9. What do you consider to be the practical value of training in the use of the Vroom-Yetton model?
10. Which of the personal-behavioral approaches is similar to the situational theory of leadership? Why have you selected this approach?

Additional references

Bartol, K. M. "Male versus Female Leaders: The Effect of Leader Need for Dominance on Follower Satisfaction," *Academy of Management Journal* 17 (1974): 209–21.

Bowers, D. G., and Seashore, S. "Predicting Organizational Effectiveness with a Four-Factor Theory of Leadership," *Administrative Science Quarterly* 11 (1966): 238–63.

Calder, B. J. "An Attribution Theory of Leadership," in B. M. Staw and G. R. Salancik, eds. *New Directions of Organizational Behavior.* Chicago: St. Clair Press, 1977, 197–204.

Cartwright, D. "Power: A Neglected Variable in Social Psychology," in W. G. Bennis, K. D. Benne, and R. Chin, eds. *The Planning of Change.* New York: Holt, Rinehart and Winston, Inc., 1966.

Durand, D. E., and Nord, W. R. "Perceived Leader Behavior of Supervisors and Subordinates," *Academy of Management Journal* 19 (1967): 427–38.

Fiedler, F. "Engineer the Job to Fit the Manager," *Harvard Business Review* 43 (1965): 115–22.

Hill, W. "Leadership Style: Rigid or Flexible?" *Organizational Behavior and Human Performance* 9 (1973): 35–47.

Hunt, J. G. "Breakthrough in Leadership Research," *Personnel Administration* 30 (1967): 38–44.

Jago, A., and Vroom, V. H. "Hierarchical Level and Leadership Style," *Organizational Behavior and Human Performance* 18 (1977): 131–45.

Jay, A. *Management and Machiavelli.* New York: Holt, Rinehart and Winston, Inc., 1967.

Lee, J. A. "Leader Power For Managing Change," *Academy of Management Review* 2 (1977): 73–80.

McCall, W. W., Jr. "Leaders and Leadership: Of Substance and Shadow," in J. H. Hackman, E. E. Lawler III, and L. W. Porter, eds. *Perspective in Behavior in Organizations.* New York: McGraw-Hill, 1977, 375–86.

Maslow, A. H. *Eupsychian Management.* Homewood, Ill.: Richard D. Irwin, Inc., and The Dorsey Press, 1965.

Osborn, R. N., and Hunt, J. G. "An Empirical Investigation of Lateral and Vertical Leadership at Two Organizational Levels," *Journal of Business Research* 2 (1974): 209–21.

Powell, R. M., and Schlacter, J. L. "Participative Management: A Panacea?" *Academy of Management Journal* 14 (1971): 165–73.

Reddin, W. J. *Managerial Effectiveness*. New York: McGraw-Hill Book Co., 1970.

Sales, S. "Supervisory Style and Productivity: Review and Theory," *Personnel Psychology* 19 (1966): 275–86.

Sims, H. P., and Szilagyi, A. D. "Leader Structure and Subordinate Satisfaction for Two Hospital Administrative Levels: A Path Goal Analysis Approach," *Journal of Applied Psychology* 61 (April 1975): 194–97.

Stogdill, R. M. *Handbook of Leadership*. New York: The Free Press, 1974.

Vroom, V., and Jago, A. "Decision-Making As A Social Process: Normative and Descriptive Models of Leader Behavior," *Decision Sciences* 5 (1974): 743–70.

PRACTICAL EXERCISES

PRACTICAL EXERCISE I
A Leader Is Promoted

Don Langley had recently been promoted from his first-line supervisory job to the planning staff of Wheeler Manufacturing Corporation. He had been considered the best supervisor in the company and was given the promotion after only working for four years in the organization. This promotion was considered by many managers as one of the most desirable in the company.

The department under Don's leadership was exceptionally productive. It had always met its budgeted expenditures and was considered the most effective unit in the company. In addition, while other departments had major labor grievance problems, Don's unit had no grievances during his tenure of leadership.

Don's subordinates and superiors described him as task-oriented, fair, honest, sincere, and considerate. He also was considered to be a person who showed concern for other's ideas, goals, and plans for the future. Don's reputation was known throughout the company. The 35 subordinates that remained in the department were very upset that their friend and leader had been promoted from the unit. They requested that the Wheeler management reconsider the promotion decision. Don was silent and somewhat stunned by the promotion since he loved to work on the line and now would serve in a staff capacity.

Three months went by after Don took over the planning staff job and a number of problems began to appear. His former department's productivity had decreased, 15 labor grievances had been filed, and three employees had quit. Don was totally dissatisfied with the new job and was thinking about quitting. He felt that his leadership skills were being wasted in a staff job. He wanted to make his view known, but had never expressed any displeasure with Wheeler publicly. In evaluating his three month staff experience, Don concluded that he was inefficient, not motivated, and unable to perform in this type of situation.

Questions for analysis:

1. What type of leadership qualities does Don Langley possess?
2. Is Don too impatient in concluding that he is not effective in a staff job?
3. Should Wheeler's management have anticipated the problems after Don was promoted? Why?

PRACTICAL EXERCISE II
The New Accounting Unit Leader

Dabney Federated Stores, Incorporated, is one of the leading department store chains in the Southwest. The company is known for its quality merchandise and efficient service. The headquarters and general offices of the company are located in the main store in Dallas, Texas. The president of the company is Ralph Simpson and the general manager is Tony Rice. Recently, the chief accountant, Nick Maria, retired. This created a vacancy in this crucial position. Many people believed that the chief accountant is the second most prestigious and powerful person in the company.

Nick Maria had a reputation throughout the company as being an easygoing and competent accountant. He expected his subordinates to get their jobs done without being closely supervised. He wanted his subordinates to work together and know their jobs. Presently, the accounting office has nine older women, three older men, four younger women, and three younger men. All of the accounting personnel perform some type of accounting duty, which results in the preparation of reports which were used by the chief accountant in briefing Ralph Simpson and Tony Rice.

Two months ago, Joan Wesley was selected as the replacement for Nick Maria. Joan came to Dabney from the Corpon Federated Stores Company, where she was assistant director of accounting for the past seven years. She has a B.S. and an M.S. in accounting from a leading university and was thought to be the right person for the job.

The first two months Joan was on the job she had a number of frustrating experiences. She felt that these experiences had resulted in lower efficiency in her unit. Some of the experiences that she continually thought about are listed below:

1. Joan had to have cost data for the preparation of the two reports to be submitted to Ralph Simpson and Tony Rice. She requested the data from two of the younger women who asked, "What is the big rush about?" This puzzled Joan since she believed that as the chief accountant she had the right to ask for, and receive, any information she wanted.

2. Joan submitted a report to Tony Rice that had a number of errors because of faulty information one of the older men had provided. Joan was embarrassed by this and reprimanded the man at his desk in front of three other accounting department personnel.

3. One of the younger girls needed some time off during the work day to visit a lawyer. Joan discussed this with the girl and concluded that if she let the girl off, others would request time off. The girl became disgusted and a screaming bout between her and Joan ensued.

These problems and others significantly affected Joan. She wondered what she had done wrong and how she could become a more effective leader of the accounting group in the months ahead.

Questions for analysis:

1. What were the differences in leadership style used by Nick Maria and Joan Wesley?
2. As a leader, what type of influence is Joan attempting to utilize?
3. What can Joan do in the future as a leader to help reduce the frustration she is now facing in her job?
4. Analyze the situation using Fiedler's model. What type of LPC (high or low) is best suited for this exercise? Is Joan this type of leader? What variables can be modified to improve the unit's effectiveness?

PRACTICAL EXERCISE III
The Troubled Hospital Superintendent

Tyler Medical Center consisted of four buildings, had 475 patient beds, and employed 1,850 people. It was known in Illinois as a quality medical institution and a good place for medical researchers and interns to work. The superintendent of the hospital was Don Gloversmen. The Board of Trustees of the hospital relied heavily upon the judgment of the superintendent regarding the administration of the hospital.

Tyler was organized around six functionally defined areas. Each area had a head who reported to Don. The areas were:

1. Medical Services
2. Nursing Services
3. Accounting Services
4. Dietary Services
5. Plant and Housekeeping Services
6. Pharmaceutical Services

Don, as superintendent, had to handle complaints and requests from administrators in each of the areas. He was the only person in the hospital who had legitimate power to make decisions concerning administrative matters. Two areas that were extremely difficult to work with were the Medical Services and Nursing Services. Don analyzed each of the personnel components of these units in the following manner:

Medical Services—Medical doctors and laboratory technicians. Included are such individuals as physician in charge of neurology, physician in charge of pediatrics, director of surgery, director of clinical laboratories, and director of anesthesiology. The medical doctors are largely male, while the technicians are split about evenly between male and female.

Nursing Services—Primarily females in charge of providing nursing care at bedside and staffing operating rooms, delivery rooms, and nurseries. The nursing group and staff include approximately 975 employees.

Don communicated in most instances with the administrators in these two service areas. He found that his leadership style of being frank, open, and direct worked better with the Medical Services administrators than with the Nursing Services administrators. He wanted to be the best superintendent the hospital ever had, but found that his approach of being the same kind of leader for all the people he worked with was not effective.

Don reached the conclusion that he was not effective in his relationship with the nursing administrators. They seemed to be hostile toward him and the other functional areas, especially the Medical Service area. In addition, a number of patients had complained about rudeness by the nurses. The strain in his relationship with Nursing Services always seemed to peak at the monthly meeting of nursing administrators. Each month the 42 nursing supervisors who had authority and responsibility for the Nursing Services personnel met with Don. In these sessions, Don attempted to ascertain how the nursing area was performing. The nursing administrators complained that no standards for assessing performance were used to determine effectiveness. They also complained because they were being watched too closely while the Medical Services area never had discussions with the superintendent about performance.

After last month's disruptive and volatile meeting, Don decided to look at the problem. He assumed that there might be a serious flaw in his leadership ability. He also thought about what he had read about the situational approach to leadership.

Questions for analysis:

1. What are some of the causes of Don's problem with the nursing administrators?

2. As a superintendent in Tyler Medical Center, would it be necessary to consider situational or contingency leadership approaches? Why?

3. What kind of modification in the three situational dimensions — leader-member relations, task structure, and position power — could aid Don in improving his relationship with Nursing Services?

11

ORGANIZATIONAL CHANGE AND DEVELOPMENT

Organizational change[1] is a pressing problem for modern managers; and in recent years a great deal of literature has appeared which focuses on the need for *planning for change*. Some companies have instituted staff units whose mission is organizational planning.[2] The planning units are specific responses to the need for systematic, formalized procedures to anticipate and implement changes in the structure, technology, and personnel of the organization.

In this chapter the processes of organizational change and development are discussed. Before beginning, however, we must explain the manner in which we are using the terms *change* and *development*. As even the casual reader of management literature must soon realize, the term organization development (OD) connotes a variety of meanings and management strategies. In its most restrictive sense it refers specifically to some form of sensitivity training; in a larger and more encompassing sense, it refers to any systematically planned, programmatic effort to improve the effectiveness of an organization through the application of behavioral science concepts, theories, and approaches. The change effort may focus on the way in which the organization is structured, the behavior of employees, or the technology that is used in getting the work done. Therefore, OD is a method for facilitating change and development in structures and processes (e.g., relationships, roles), people (e.g., styles, skills) and technology (e.g., more routineness, more challenge).[3]

The growing realization that organizations can be changed and made more effective through managerial applications of behavioral science knowledge has created a wealth of literature.[4] This chapter presents some of the established ideas from this literature in the context of practical management. In order to provide a theme, we present the material in terms of a model which describes the important factors of the change and development process. For simplicity we will use the phrase, "the management of change," to include the concept of organization development in its broadest sense.

A model for managing change

The management of change implies a systematic process which can be broken down into subprocesses or steps. The model which describes

[1] "Organizational change" is broadly interpreted for purposes of this discussion. Some management students restrict the term to changes in the formal structure, but we will include changes in employee behavior and technology.

[2] Paul E. Holden, Carlton A. Pederson, and Gayton E. Germane, *Top Management* (New York: McGraw-Hill Book Co., 1968), pp. 66–68.

[3] Frank Friedlander and L. Dave Brown, "Organization Development," *Review of Psychology* (1974).

[4] For a sample of organizational development literature in the context of various settings, see Wendell L. French and Cecil H. Bell, Jr., *Organization Development* (Engle-

this process is illustrated in Figure 11–1 and consists of eight sub-processes linked in a logical sequence. A manager considers each of them, either explicitly or implicitly, to undertake a change program. The prospects for initiating successful change are enhanced when the manager explicitly and formally goes through each successive step. For this reason, each step is discussed in a separate section of this chapter.

It is our purpose to describe alternative change techniques and strategies, but not to propose that some alternatives are superior to others. No one change technique or change strategy can be judged superior on *a priori* grounds.[5]

The knowledgeable manager is one who recognizes the multiplicity of alternatives, and is not predisposed to one particular approach to the exclusion of all others. At the same time, the effective manager avoids the pitfalls of stagnation. The sign of decay, as Greiner has observed, is "managerial behavior that (a) is oriented more to the past than to the future, (b) recognizes the obligations of ritual more than the challenges of current problems, and (c) owes allegiance more to department goals than to overall company objectives."[6] Thus the management of change implies a flexible, forward-looking stance for the manager.[7] This attribute is essential for using the change model outlined in Figure 11–1.

The model presumes that forces for change continually act upon the firm; this assumption reflects the dynamic character of the modern world. At the same time it is the manager's responsibility to sort out the information received from the firm's control system and other sources which reflect the magnitude of change forces. The information is the basis for recognizing the need for change; it is equally desirable to recognize when change is *not* needed. But once the problem is recognized, the manager must diagnose the problem and identify relevant alternative change techniques. The change technique selected must be appropriate to the problem, as constrained by limiting conditions.

wood Cliffs, N.J.: Prentice-Hall, Inc., 1973); Larry Kirkhart and Neely Gardner, eds., "A Symposium: Organization Development," *Public Administration Review* (March–April 1974), pp. 97–140; Newton Margulies, "Organizational Development in a University Setting: Some Problems in Initiating Change," *Educational Technology* (October 1972), pp. 48–51, and Clayton P. Alderfer, "Change Processes In Organizations," in Marvin D. Dunnette, ed., *Handbook of Industrial and Organizational Psychology* (Chicago: Rand McNally, 1976), pp. 1591–1638.

[5] Jeremiah J. O'Connell, *Managing Organizational Innovation* (Homewood, Ill.: Richard D. Irwin, Inc., 1968), pp. 10, 142–45.

[6] Larry E. Greiner, "Patterns of Organization Change," *Harvard Business Review* (May–June 1967), p. 119.

[7] See Paul Hersey and Kenneth H. Blanchard, "The Management of Change," *Training and Development Journal* (January 1972), pp. 6–11, for the first of a three-part discussion of the management of change which parallels the model developed in this chapter.

FIGURE 11-1
A model for the management of change

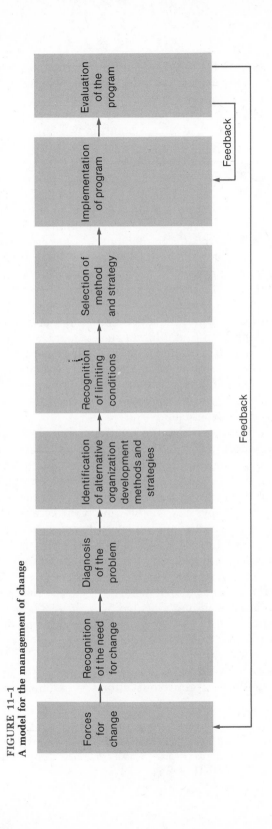

One example of a limiting condition which we have discussed in an earlier chapter is the prevailing character of group norms. The work groups may support some of the change techniques but may sabotage others. Other limiting conditions include leadership behavior, legal requirements, and economic conditions.

The fact that a change program can be thwarted underscores the fact that the choice of change *strategy* is as important as the change technique itself. One well-documented behavioral phenomenon is that people tend to resist change or at least to be reluctant to undergo change.[8] An appropriate strategy for implementing change is one which seeks to minimize resistance and maximize employee commitment. Finally, managers must implement the change and monitor the change process and change results. The model includes feedback to the implementation phase and to the forces-for-change phase. These feedback loops suggest that the change process itself must be monitored and evaluated. The implementation strategy may be faulty and lead to poor results, but prompt action could correct the situation. Moreover, the feedback loop to the initial step recognizes that *no* change is final. A new situation is created within which other problems and issues will emerge; a new setting is created which will itself become subject to change. The model suggests no "final solution"; rather, it emphasizes that modern managers operate in a dynamic setting wherein the only certainty is change itself.

The process by which the solution to one problem creates new problems is widely recognized. Blau and Scott refer to it as the "dialectic processes of change,"[9] and they illustrate the dilemma by a number of examples. They observe that assembly-line techniques increase productivity but that, at the same time, there is an increase in employee absenteeism and turnover. Assembly-line work is monotonous and routine; it alienates workers and creates discontent; morale declines and personnel problems emerge. Thus a different set of difficulties is created by the solution itself. This phenomenon must be taken into account as managers consider changes.

The thoughtful student will, no doubt, argue that many successful changes have been implemented by managers who did not consciously and systematically go through each step of the model. Indeed there are many such cases. However, these managers may not be representative of the population of managers. They may very well be intuitive managers who have the experience and judgment to guide and implement change without a conscious effort. Such men and women are the

---

[8] G. Watson, "Resistance to Change," in W. Bennis, K. Benne, and R. Chin, eds., *Planning to Change* (New York: Holt, Rinehart and Winston, 1969), pp. 488–98.

[9] Peter M. Blau and W. Richard Scott, *Formal Organizations* (San Francisco: Chandler Publishing Co., 1962), pp. 250–53.

geniuses of management. The rest of us might be well advised to follow a more systematic approach, as outlined in this chapter.

Forces for change

The forces for change can be classified conveniently into two groups, namely, external and internal forces. External forces include changes in the marketplace, technology, and environment; they are usually beyond the control of the manager. Internal forces operate inside the firm and are generally within the control of management.

EXTERNAL FORCES

The manager of a business firm has historically been concerned with reacting to changes in the marketplace. Competitors introduce new products, increase advertising, reduce prices, or improve customer service. In each case a response is required unless the manager is content to permit the erosion of profit and market share. At the same time, changes occur in customer tastes and incomes. The firm's products may no longer have customer appeal; customers may be able to purchase more expensive, higher-quality forms of the same product.

The enterprise system eventually eliminates from the economic scene those firms which do not adjust to market conditions. The isolated-from-reality manager who ignores the signals from the market will soon confront the more vocal and louder signals of discontented stockholders. By that time, however, the appropriate change may well be dissolution of the firm—the final solution.

Another source of market forces is that of the supply of resources to the firm. A change in the quality and quantity of human resources can dictate changes in the firm. For example, the adoption of automated processes can be stimulated by a decline in the supply of labor. The techniques of coal mining and tobacco farming have changed greatly during recent years because of labor shortages. We can also understand how changes in the materials and energy supply can cause the firm to attempt to substitute one material for another. Rayon stockings and synthetic rubber tires are direct outgrowths of World War II–induced shortages of raw materials. We need not catalog the whole range of possible changes in the resource markets which stimulate organizational change. The potential is great, however, and must be recognized.

The second source of external change forces is technology. The knowledge explosion since World War II introduced new technology for nearly every management function. Computers have made possible high-speed data processing and the solution to complex production problems. New machines and new processes have revolutionized the way in which many products are manufactured and distributed. High rates of obsolescence have encouraged many firms to adopt payback criteria as low as two years, so that they will not be caught with obsolete equipment. Computer technology and automation have affected not only the technical conditions of work, but the social conditions as well. New occupations have been created and others have been eliminated. Slowness in adopting new technology which reduces costs and improves quality will show itself in the financial statements sooner or later. Technological advance is a permanent fixture in contemporary society and, as a force for change, will continue to demand attention.[10]

Finally, the third external force consists of *environmental changes*. Managers must be "tuned in" to great movements over which they have no control but which, in time, control the firm's fate. The 1950s and 1960s witnessed a distinct increase in social activity. The drive for social equality posed new issues for managers, which had not been previously confronted. Sophisticated mass communication and international markets created enormous potential but also posed a great threat to those managers unable to understand what was going on. Finally, to add to the problem, the relationship between government and business became much more involved as new regulations were imposed. These pressures for change reflect the increasing complexity and interdependence of modern living. The traditional function of business is being questioned and new objectives are being advanced. No doubt the events of the future will intensify environmental forces for change.

INTERNAL FORCES

The forces for change which occur within the organization can be traced to *processes* and *people.* Process forces include decision making, communications, and interpersonal relations. Breakdowns or problems in any of these processes can create forces for change. Decisions are either not being made, are made too late, or are of poor quality. Communications are short-circuited, redundant, or simply inadequate. Tasks are not undertaken or not completed because the person responsible did not "get the word." A customer order is not filled; a grievance is not processed; or an invoice is not filed; and the supplier is not paid because of inadequate and nonexistent communications. Interpersonal and interdepartmental conflicts reflect breakdowns in the interaction between people.

Low levels of morale and high levels of absenteeism and turnover

---

[10] Thomas J. Watson, Jr., "Technological Change," in Arthur O. Lewis, Jr., ed., *Of Men and Machines* (New York: E. P. Dutton & Co., Inc., 1963), pp. 295–309.

are symptoms of people problems that must be diagnosed. A wildcat strike or a walkout may be the most tangible sign of a problem, yet such tactics are usually employed because they arouse the management to action. There is in most organizations a certain level of employee discontent; a great danger is to ignore the complaints and suggestions. But the process of change includes the *recognition* phase, and it is at this point that management must decide to act or not to act.

Recognition of the need for change

Information is the basis on which managers are made aware of the magnitude of the change forces. We noted some of the important sources of information in our discussion above. Certainly the most important information comes from the firm's preliminary, concurrent, and feedback control data. Indeed, the process of change can be viewed as a part of the control function, specifically the corrective-action requirement. Financial statements, quality control data, and budget and standard cost information are important media through which both external and internal forces are revealed. Declining profit margins and market shares are tangible signs that the firm's competitive position is deteriorating and that change may be required. Spiraling hospital costs are a sign of inefficient hospital management. These sources of feedback control information are highly developed in most organizations because of their crucial importance.

Unfortunately, the need for change goes unrecognized in many organizations until some major catastrophe occurs. The employees strike or seek the recognition of a union before management finally recognizes the need for action. Talented managers leave the organization because they are not delegated authority and responsibility. A plant is forced to close because of government fines for polluting the environment. Whether it takes a whisper or a shout, the need for change must be recognized by some means; and the exact nature of the problem must be diagnosed.

Diagnosis of the problem

Before appropriate action can be taken, the symptoms of the problem must be analyzed to discover the problem itself. Experience and judgment are critical to this phase unless the problem is readily apparent to all observers. However, managers often disagree as to the nature of the problem. There is no magic formula. The objectives of this phase can be described by three questions:

1. What is the problem, as distinct from the symptoms of the problem?
2. What must be changed to resolve the problem?
3. What outcomes (objectives) are expected from the change, and how will such objectives be measured?

The answers to these questions can come from information ordinarily found in organizations, such as financial statements, department reports, or attitude surveys. Or it may be necessary to generate *ad hoc* information through the creation of committees or task forces. Meetings between managers and employees provide a variety of points of view which can be sifted through by a smaller group. Technical operational problems may be easily diagnosed, but more subtle human relations problems usually entail extensive analysis. One approach to diagnosing the problem is the attitude survey.

Attitude surveys can be administered to the entire work force or to a sample of it. The survey permits the respondents to evaluate and rate (1) management, (2) pay and pay-related items, (3) working conditions, (4) equipment, and (5) other job-related items. The appropriate use of such surveys requires that the data be collected (usually by questionnaires) from members of an organization, analyzed in detail, and fed back to various organization members. The objective of the survey is to pinpoint the problem or problems as perceived by the members of the organization. Subsequent feedback discussions on the survey results at all levels of the organization can add additional insights into the nature of the problem.[11]

The approach which management uses to diagnose the problem is a crucial part of the total strategy for change. As will be seen in a later section, the manner in which the problem is diagnosed has clear implications for the final success of the proposed change.

Finally, the diagnostic step must specify *objectives* for change. Given the diagnosis of the problem, it is necessary to define objectives to guide as well as to evaluate the outcome of the change. The objectives can be stated in terms of financial and production data, such as profits, market shares, sales volume, productivity, scrappage, or the like. Or they can be stated as attitude and morale objectives derived from attitude survey information. They can also be stated as personal development objectives that are meaningful to the members of an organization. For example, they can focus on the personal growth or reeducation of

---

[11] Complete discussions of attitude surveys as diagnostic tools are found in Stuart M. Klein, Allen I. Kraut, and Alan Wolfson, "Employee Reactions to Attitude Survey Feedback," *Administrative Science Quarterly* (December 1971), pp. 497–514; Gary B. Brumback, "Employee Attitude Surveys," *Personnel Administration* (March–April 1972), pp. 27–34; and Diane Coryell and David Sirota, "Attitude Survey Feedback— Letting the First-Line Manager Know Where He Stands," *Personnel Administration* (May–June 1972), pp. 53–57.

one employee or a group. Whatever the objectives, they must be explicit, understandable, challenging, and meaningful.

Alternative change techniques

The choice of the particular change technique depends upon the nature of the problem management has diagnosed. Management must determine which alternative is most likely to produce the desired outcome. As we have noted above, diagnosis of the problem includes specification of the outcomes which management desires from the change. In this section, we will describe a number of change techniques. They will be classified according to the major focus of the technique, namely, to change structure, people, or technology.[12] This classification of organizational change techniques in no way implies a distinct division among the three types. On the contrary, the interrelationships among structure, people, and technology must be acknowledged and anticipated. The majority of literature on organizational change indicates the relative weakness of efforts to change only structure (e.g., job design), only people (e.g., sensitivity training), or only technology (e.g., introducing new equipment or a new computer).[13]

An important contribution of the Behavioral School is the documentation of the impact of structure on attitudes and behavior. Overspecialization and narrow spans of control can lead to low levels of morale and low productivity.[14] At the same time, the technology of production, distribution, and information processing affects the structural characteristics of the firm,[15] as well as attitudes and sentiments.[16] The fact that the interrelationships among structure, people, and technology are so pronounced might suggest a weakness in our classification scheme; but in defense of it, the techniques described below can be distinguished on the basis of their major thrust or focus — structure, people, or technology.

---

[12] See Harold J. Leavitt, "Applied Organizational Change in Industry: Structural, Technological and Humanistic Approaches," in James G. March, ed., *Handbook of Organizations* (Chicago: Rand McNally and Co., 1965), pp. 1144–68.

[13] Alderfer, "Change Processes in Organizations."

[14] Rensis Likert, *The Human Organization* (New York: McGraw-Hill Book Co., 1967).

[15] Joan Woodward, *Industrial Organization* (New York: Oxford University Press, 1967); and Frank J. Jasinski, "Adapting Organization to New Technology," *Harvard Business Review* (January–February 1959), pp. 79–86.

[16] Harriet O. Ronken and Paul R. Lawrence, *Administering Changes: A Case Study of Human Relations in a Factory* (Boston: Division of Research, Harvard Business School, 1952).

STRUCTURAL CHANGE

Changes in the structure of the organization ordinarily follow changes in strategy.[17] Logically, the organizing function follows the planning function since the structure is a means for achieving the goals established through planning. Structural change in the context of organizational change refers to managerial action which attempts to improve performance by altering the formal structure of task and authority relationships. At the same time, we must recognize that the structure creates human and social relationships which gradually can become ends for the members of the organization. These relationships, when they have been defined and made legitimate by management, introduce an element of stability.[18] Members of the organization may resist efforts to disrupt these relationships.

Structural changes alter some aspect of the formal task and authority definitions. As we have seen, the design of an organization involves the definition and specification of job content and scope, the grouping of jobs in departments, determination of the size of groups reporting to a single manager, and the provision of staff assistance. Within this framework, the communication, decision-making, and human interaction processes occur. We can see, then, that changes in the nature of jobs, bases for departmentalization, and line-staff relationships involve structural change.

Changes in the nature of jobs. The origins of changes in the nature of jobs are the implementation of new methods and new machines. Work simplification and job enrichment are two examples of methods changes. The former narrows job content and scope, whereas the latter widens them. Scientific management introduced significant changes in the way work is done through the use of motion and time studies. These methods tend to create highly specialized jobs. Job enrichment, however, moves in the opposite direction, toward despecialization.

An example of an attempted application of job enrichment was carried out in the stock transfer department of a large metropolitan bank.[19] The department was responsible for transferring the ownership of securities from one owner to another and recording the transfer. In order to remain competitive with other banks in the area, the entire stock transfer must be completed within 48 hours. At the time of the study, 300 employees worked in the department.

---

[17] Alfred Chandler, *Strategy and Structure* (Cambridge, Mass.: M.I.T. Press, 1962).

[18] R. K. Ready, *The Administrator's Job* (New York: McGraw-Hill Book Co., 1967), pp. 24–30.

[19] Linda L. Frank and J. Richard Hackman, "A Failure of Job Enrichment: The Case of The Change That Wasn't," *Journal of Applied Behavioral Science* (October 1975), pp. 413–36.

Each employee reported to a "work coordinator" who was responsible for eight to twelve employees who performed the same function. A job enrichment plan was developed in which the work of the department was divided into 13 modules. The modules focused on total responsibility for a group of corporations whose stock was handled by the bank. Under the old arrangement, employees arbitrarily handled whatever work was assigned.

It was hoped that the assignment of a specific set of corporations to each group working on a module would increase the employees' identification with and commitment to the work. These feelings were to be strengthened by allowing the workers in the module to leave work together when the security transactions from their companies had been completed.

Modules were scheduled to be introduced one at a time. The researchers collected data after each module was installed. Data on the nature of the jobs themselves, employee performance, and the change process itself were collected by use of questionnaires, interviews, company records, and actual observations.

The results suggested that almost no impact of the changes in the characteristic of the jobs was reported by employees. The researchers concluded that the type of changes in structure which, if performed, should have increased performance and effectiveness were not initiated as planned. For example, it was planned that employees would experience more autonomy in the modules than they had previously because each module would be making its own decisions. In fact, however, no structural changes were made to encourage the module members to take more responsibility. Moreover, managers continued to give orders and to supervise rather closely. In effect, management did not delegate as had been planned. And employees had the same feeling as before the modules were started — namely, that they had little autonomy.

This example illustrates the value of research on even unsuccessful job changes. In a "pure" sense, this change in the job did not take. However, it provided a valuable lesson about the interrelationships between people and structure. It also indicated that job enrichment is not always a simple solution to managerial work-related problems.

Changes in the bases for departmentalization. In the study of 30 California-based financial, service, and manufacturing firms which experienced marked growth during the period 1947–1955, McNulty found a considerable increase in the relative importance of product departmentalization relative to other bases.[20] The use of product bases indicates efforts to move toward decentralized forms of organization

---

[20] James E. McNulty, "Organizational Change in Growing Enterprises," *Administrative Science Quarterly* (June 1962), pp. 1–21.

like those found in General Motors and in General Electric. But the ambivalence of the managers in the study is demonstrated by their tendency to create "taller" rather than "flatter" organizations. With decentralization, one expects to find relatively wider spans of control. McNulty's study suggests that the problems of rapid market growth were such that management was reluctant to relinquish too much control over the situation.

Changes in line-staff relationships. These changes ordinarily include two techniques. The first and the usual approach is to create staff assistance as either an *ad hoc* or permanent solution. McNulty reported that one response of manufacturing firms to the problem of market expansion is the creation of separate staff and service units.[21] These units provide the technical expertise to deal with the production, financial, and marketing problems posed by expansion.

An illustrative case is a company which had grown quite rapidly since its entry into the fast-foods industry. Its basic sources of field control were area directors who supervised the operations of sales outlets of a particular region. During the growth period the area directors had considerable autonomy in making the advertising decisions for their regions. They could select their own media, formats, and budgets within general guidelines. But as their markets became saturated and as competitors appeared, corporate officials decided to centralize the advertising function in a staff unit located at corporate headquarters. Consequently, the area directors' freedom was limited and an essential job aspect was eliminated.[22]

A final illustration of changes in line-staff relationships is based upon the case which O'Connell described.[23] A large insurance company hired a management consulting firm to analyze the problem created by a deteriorating market position. The consulting company recommended that the firm undertake a program of decentralization by changing a staff position to a line manager. This recommendation was based upon the consultants' belief that the company must have its best personnel and resources available at the branch office level to increase premium income. Accordingly, the consultants recommended that assistant managers be converted to first-level supervisors reporting to branch managers. The transformation required a significant change in the work of assistant managers and in the work of managers throughout the organization.

These examples illustrate the range of alternatives managers must

---

[21] Ibid.

[22] See Herbert A. Simon et al., *Centralization versus Decentralization in Organizing the Controller's Department* (New York: The Controllership Foundation, 1954) for another discussion of the key issues to be resolved in the decision of where to locate staff units—in this case, an accounting unit.

[23] O'Connell, *Organizational Innovation.*

consider. Certainly we have not exhausted the possibilities. The point that should be made in concluding this discussion, however, is not that the list is incomplete, but that students and managers must recognize the interrelationships of structural parts. A change in job content does not take place in a vacuum; on the contrary, the change affects all other directly related jobs, supervisory and nonsupervisory alike. The management of structural change must be guided by the point of view that all things are connected.

BEHAVIORAL CHANGE

Behavioral change techniques refer to efforts to redirect and improve employee attitudes, skills, and knowledge bases. The major objective is to enhance the capacity of individuals to perform assigned tasks in coordination with others. The early efforts to engage in behavioral change date to scientific management work improvement and employee training methods. These attempts were primarily directed at improving employee skills and knowledge bases. The employee counseling programs which grew out of the Hawthorne studies were (and remain) primarily directed at improving employee attitudes.

Training and development programs for managers have typically emphasized supervisory relationships. These programs attempt to provide supervisors and foremen with basic technical and human-relations skills. Since supervisors are primarily concerned with overseeing the work of others, the content of these traditional programs emphasizes techniques for dealing with people problems: how to handle the malcontent, the loafer, the troublemaker, the complainer. The programs also include conceptual material dealing with communications, leadership styles, and organizational relationships. The vehicles for training include role playing, discussion groups, lectures, and organized courses offered by universities.[24] A number of programs include materials about the managerial grid, democratic leadership, and other ideas derived from the Behavioral School.[25]

Training continues to be an important technique for introducing people changes. Training has taken on quite a different form in some applications from that which developed in classical management theory.[26] Among some behavioralists a popular behavioral change approach is sensitivity training.

---

[24] Ernest Dale and L. C. Michelon, *Modern Management Methods* (New York: The World Publishing Company, 1966), pp. 15–16.

[25] See T. A. Swann and Russel C. Cox, "How Training Perked Up Morale at Maxwell House," *Management Review* (February 1972), pp. 4–11.

[26] A survey of alternative training methodologies is presented in Edward C. Ryterband and Bernard M. Bass, "Management Development," in Joseph W. McGuire, ed., *Contemporary Management* (Englewood Cliffs, N.J.: Prentice-Hall, Inc., 1974), pp. 579–609.

Sensitivity training. This change technique attempts to make the participant more aware of himself or herself and of his/her impact on others. "Sensitivity" in this context means sensitivity to self and to relationships with others. An assumption of sensitivity training is that the causes of poor task performance are the emotional problems of people who must collectively achieve a goal. If these problems can be removed, a major impediment to task performance is consequently eliminated. Sensitivity training stresses "the *process* rather than the *content* of training and . . . *emotional* rather than *conceptual* training.[27] We can see that this form of training is quite different from traditional forms which stress the acquisition of a predetermined body of concepts with immediate application to the work place.

The process of sensitivity training includes a group of managers (training group or T-group) who in most cases come together at some location other than their place of work. Under the direction of a trainer, the group usually engages in a dialogue which has no agenda and no focus. The objective is to provide an environment which produces its own learning experiences.[28] The unstructured dialogue encourages one to learn about self in dealing with others. One's motives and feelings are revealed through behavior toward others in the group and through the behavior of others. The T-group is typically unstructured. As Marrow points out in a report of his own sensitivity training, "It [sensitivity training] says, 'Open your eyes. Look at yourself. See how you look to others. Then decide what changes, if any, you want to make and in which direction you want to go'."[29]

The role of the trainer in the T-group is to facilitate the learning process. According to Kelly, the trainer's mission is "to observe, record, interpret, sometimes to lead, and always to learn."[30] The artistry and style of the trainer are critical variables in determining the direction of the T-group's sessions. The trainer must walk the uneasy path of unobtrusive leadership and be able to interpret the roles of participants and encourage them to analyze their contributions without being perceived as a threat. Unlike the group therapist, the T-group trainer is dealing with people who are not having emotional problems but who have come together to learn. The ordinarily prescribed role of the trainer is that of "permissive, nonauthoritarian, sometimes almost nonparticipative" leadership.[31]

---

[27] Henry C. Smith, *Sensitivity to People* (New York: McGraw-Hill Book Co., 1966), p. 197.

[28] L. P. Bradford, J. R. Gibb, and K. D. Benne, *T-Group Theory and Laboratory Method* (New York: John Wiley & Sons, Inc., 1964).

[29] Alfred J. Marrow, *Behind the Executive Mask* (New York: American Management Association, 1964), p. 51.

[30] Joe Kelly, *Organizational Behaviour* (Homewood, Ill.: Richard D. Irwin, Inc., 1969), p. 419.

[31] Leavitt, "Organizational Change," p. 1154.

The critical test of sensitivity training is whether the experience itself is a factor leading to improvement in task performance. It is apparent that even if the training induces positive changes in the participant's sensitivity to self and others, such behavior may be either not possible or not permissible back in the work place. The participant must deal with the same environment and the same people as before the training. The open, supportive, and permissive environment of the training sessions is not likely to be found on the job. Even so, proponents of sensitivity training would reply that it makes the participant better able to deal with the environment. We should also recognize that sensitivity training may well induce negative changes in the participant's ability to perform organizational tasks; the training sessions can be occasions of extreme stress and anxiety. The capacity to deal effectively with stress varies among individuals, and the outcome may be dysfunctional for some participants.

The research evidence to date on the effectiveness of sensitivity training as a change technique suggests mixed results.[32] A detailed review of 100 research studies found that sensitivity training was most effective at the personal level.[33] The studies reviewed compared the influence of 20 or more hours training on the participants' attitudes or behaviors. The review concluded that sensitivity training:

Stimulated short-term improvement in communication skills.

Encouraged trainees to believe that they controlled their behavior more than others.

Was likely to increase the participative orientation of trainees in leadership positions.

Improved the perceptions of others toward the trainee.

Managers should critically examine this technique in terms of the kinds of changes which are desired and those which are possible. Our model suggests the existence of conditions which limit the range of possible changes. In this light managers must determine whether the changes induced by sensitivity training are instrumental for organizational purposes and whether the prospective participant is able to tolerate the potential anxiety of the training.

The recognition that structure must be compatible with behavior and vice versa has stimulated the search for a means to relate the two. A notable contribution is that of Likert. He proposes, on the basis of

---

[32] See Robert J. House, "T-Group Education and Leadership Effectiveness: A Review of the Empirical Literature and a Critical Evaluation," *Personnel Psychology* (Spring 1967), pp. 1–32; and John P. Campbell and Marvin D. Dunnette, "Effectiveness of T-Group Experiences in Managerial Training and Development," *Psychological Bulletin* (August 1968), pp. 73–104.

[33] P. B. Smith, "Controlled Studies of the Outcome of Sensitivity Training," *Psychological Bulletin* (July 1975), pp. 597–622.

considerable research, that the most effective organizational form is
one which can be clearly distinguished from others; he furthermore
proposes that management should make a conscious effort to change
to the superior form,[34] which he terms System 4.

System 4 Organization. According to Likert an organization can
be described in terms of eight operating characteristics. They are (1)
leadership, (2) motivation, (3) communication, (4) interaction, (5)
decision making, (6) goal setting, (7) control, and (8) performance.[35]
The nature of each of these characteristics can be located on a continuum through the use of a questionnaire which members of the firm
(usually managers) complete. The arithmetic means (averages) of each
response category are calculated and plotted to produce an organizational profile. Figure 11–2 presents superimposed profiles for two
actual manufacturing plants located in eastern Kentucky.

The horizontal dimension of the organizational profile describes
four zones on the continuum for each of the eight operating characteristics which appear on the vertical dimension. Likert has labelled the
four zones as follows:

System 1—Exploitive-Authoritative,
System 2—Benevolent-Authoritative,
System 3—Consultative, and
System 4—Participative Group.

Likert no longer uses these value-laden labels since value-free descriptions of each of the systems are obviously desirable. He now defines
each system in quantitative terms on the dimensions shown in Figure
11–2.

The System 4 organization is one in which managers (1) use the
principle of supportive relationships; (2) use group methods for decision making and supervision; and (3) have high performance goals.[36]
More specific characteristics of System 4 organization are:

1. *Leadership processes* which instill confidence and trust between
   superiors and subordinates and vice versa. Subordinates feel free
   to discuss job problems with their superiors, who in turn ask for
   their ideas and opinions.
2. *Motivational processes* which develop a full range of motives
   through participatory methods. Attitudes are favorable toward the
   company and toward goals of the company.

---

[34] Likert, *Human Organizations.*

[35] A complete review of change efforts based upon the System 4–type technique is
Alfred J. Marrow, ed., *The Failure of Success* (New York: The American Management
Association, 1972).

[36] Likert, *Human Organization,* p. 47.

FIGURE 11-2
Organizational profile for two manufacturing firms

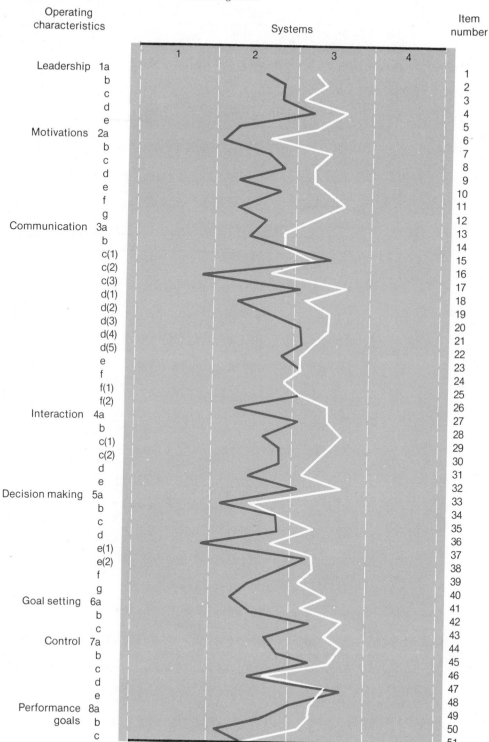

* These two profiles are based upon responses to the 51-item version of Likert's questionnaire. Copies can be obtained from the Foundation for Research on Human Behavior, Ann Arbor, Michigan. A facsimile is included in J. H. Donnelly, et al., *Fundamentals of Management* (Dallas, Tex.: Business Publications, Inc., 1971), pp. 258–72.

3. _Communication processes_ are such that information flows freely throughout the organization—upward, downward, and laterally. The information is accurate and undistorted.
4. _Interaction processes_ are open and extensive; both superiors and subordinates are able to affect departmental goals, methods, and activities.
5. _Decision-making processes_ occur at all levels of the organization through group methods.
6. _Goal-setting processes_ encourage group participation for setting high, yet realistic, objectives.
7. _Control processes_ are dispersed throughout the company with all participants seeking information to implement self-control; the emphasis of control is problem solving, not blame setting.
8. _Performance goals_ are high and actively sought by superiors who also recognize the necessity for making a full commitment to developing, through training, the human resources of the company.

The System 4 organization as described above has no counterpart in reality. Likert himself has studied a few companies which _approach_ System 4, but he has not discovered any companies which are ideally System 4. He assumes that it is an "ideal type," toward which the most successful companies are moving.

The profiles of the two firms presented in Figure 11–2 demonstrate the kinds of differences that can occur in organizational processes. In Likert's terms, the firm represented by the dotted line is clearly a System 2 organization, whereas that represented by the solid line is a System 3 organization with tendencies toward System 2. The profiles (derived from Likert's questionnaire) were used in conjunction with attitude surveys to pinpoint the nature of suspected problems. The profiles suggested the need to examine motivational, communication, and decision-making processes since the most pronounced deviations occurred in these areas. Subsequent analysis of information contained in the attitude survey and interviews with the employees confirmed these observations that problems existed in the areas of motivation, communications, and decision making. The managements of both organizations believed that efforts to move toward System 4 organization should be undertaken.

The change toward System 4 involves measuring the present state of the firm through the use of the questionnaire. Subsequent training programs emphasize the concepts of System 4 management and their application to the present organization. The use of supportive, group-oriented leadership and sustained encouragement to set goals, implement controls, and make decisions should ordinarily lead to higher earnings and productivity, according to Likert. These favorable results derive from positive changes in employee attitudes which are induced by the structural changes. As has been pointed out by others, "To obtain lasting change, one does not try to change people, but rather to change the organizational constraints that operate upon them."[37]

TECHNOLOGICAL CHANGE

This category of change includes any application of new ways to transform resources into the product or service. In the usual sense of the word, technology means new machines — lathes, presses, computers, and the like. But we should expand the concept to include new techniques with or without new machines. From this perspective, the work improvement methods of scientific management can be considered as technological breakthroughs. However, in this section only those changes which are induced by the introduction of a machine or man-machine process are discussed.

The changes in organizational efficiency brought about by a new machine are calculable in economic and engineering terms. Whether the machine is a good investment is a matter of estimating its future profitability in relation to its present cost. These calculations are an important part of the managerial control function. Here, however, we are interested in the impact of the new machine on the structure of the organization and on the behavior of the people in the organization. As some scholars have observed, technology is a key determinant of structure.[38] They tentatively conclude that firms with simple and stable technology should adopt a structure that tends toward bureaucratic organization, whereas firms with complex and dynamic technology ought to tend toward the more open and flexible System 4 structure.[39] Thus it would appear that the adoption of new technology involves a concurrent decision to adapt the organizational structure to that technology. Whether an inexorable and deterministic relationship between technology and structure exists, the fact remains that the introduction of technological innovation has far-reaching effects on the organization.

In order to catalog the impact of technological change on structure and behavior, Mann analyzed a number of actual cases and concluded that the adoption of new machines in the factory involves:

---

[37] Eliot D. Chapple and Leonard R. Sayles, *The Measure of Management* (New York: The Macmillan Company, 1961), p. 202. Stanley E. Seashore and David G. Bowers, in "Durability of Organizational Change," *American Psychologist* (1970), pp. 227–32, also report evidence that System 4-type change can be made permanent in an organization.

[38] Woodward, *Industrial Organization*, and Jasinski, *Adapting*, among others.

[39] Burns and Stalker make this point in their analysis of the ways Scottish electronic firms responded to technological change. They use the terms "mechanistic" to refer to relatively tight, highly structured organizations and "organic" to refer to relatively loose, flexibly structured organization. Tom Burns and G. M. Stalker, *The Management of Innovation* (London: Tavistock Publications, 1961).

1. Major changes in the division of labor and the content of jobs.
2. Changes in social relations among workers.
3. Improving working conditions.
4. The need for different supervisory skills.
5. Changes in career patterns, promotion procedures, and job security.
6. Generally higher wages.
7. Generally higher prestige for those who work.
8. Around-the-clock operations.[40]

The degree and extent of these observed changes in structure and behavior depend upon the magnitude of the technological change. Obviously, the introduction of a new offset printing press will not cause the great dislocations and changes which Mann observes, but the complete automation of a previously man-paced manufacturing process would include many, if not all of them.

A widespread structural adaptation to the necessity for utilizing technological innovation with minimum delay is referred to as *project* or *program management*. In this organizational form, the responsibility for achieving the goals of a short-run project is assigned to a project manager, who may then draw upon the expertise of functional experts in production, engineering, finance, or any other, as necessary. The project manager usually has complete authority over all the activities and personnel necessary to carry out the project, including personnel who ordinarily report to a functional department head. This organizational form permits horizontal communications and authority relationships necessary to complete the project but maintains the traditional and permanent vertical relationships. However, the existence of a dual authority system introduces the potential for problems associated with dual command.

The decision to adopt a technological approach to organizational change must include consideration of the potential structural and behavioral impacts. These impacts must, in turn, be reconciled with conditions which limit the scope and magnitude of the proposed change.

Recognition of limiting conditions

The selection of the change technique is based upon diagnosis of the problem, but the choice is tempered by certain conditions that exist at the time. Filley and House identify three sources of influence on the outcome of management development programs which can be

---

[40] Floyd C. Mann, "Psychological and Organizational Impacts," in John T. Dunlop, ed., *Automation and Technological Change* (Englewood Cliffs, N.J.: Prentice-Hall, Inc., 1962), pp. 50–55.

generalized to cover the entire range of organizational change efforts, whether structural, behavioral, or technological. They are the leadership climate, formal organization, and organizational culture.[41]

Leadership climate refers to the nature of the work environment which results from "the leadership style and administrative practices" of superiors. Any change program which does not have the support and commitment of management has a slim chance of success. Managers must be at least neutral toward the change. We also understand that the style of leadership itself may be the subject of change; for example, sensitivity training and System 4 are direct attempts to move managers toward a certain style — open, supportive, and group centered. But it must be recognized that the participants may be unable to adopt such styles if they are not compatible with their own superiors' styles.

The *formal organization* must be compatible with the proposed change. This includes the effects on the environment that result from the philosophy and policies of top management, as well as "legal precedent, organizational structure, and the system of control." Of course, each of these sources of impact may be the focus of the change effort; the important point is that a change in one must be compatible with all others. For example, a change in technology which will eliminate jobs contradicts a policy of guaranteed employment.

The *organizational culture* refers to the impact on the environment resulting from "group norms, values, and informal activities." The impact of traditional behavior, sanctioned by group norms but not formally acknowledged, was first documented in the Hawthorne studies. A proposed change in work methods or the installation of an automated device can run counter to the expectations and attitudes of work groups. If such is the case, the change strategist must anticipate the resulting resistance.

In a real sense, when managers evaluate the strength of limiting conditions, they are simultaneously considering the problem of objective setting. Many managers have been disappointed by change efforts which fell short of their expectations. Particularly frustrated are those managers who cannot understand why the simple issuance of a directive does not produce the intended response. Thoughtful managers will recognize that even as they operate as forces for change, other conditions are operating as forces for stability. The realities of limiting conditions are such that managers must often be content with modest change or no change at all.[42]

---

[41] Alan C. Filley and Robert J. House, *Managerial Process and Organizational Behavior* (Glenview, Ill.: Scott, Foresman and Company, 1969), pp. 423–34.

[42] Herbert Kaufman, "The Direction of Organizational Evolution," *Public Administration Review* (July–August 1974), pp. 300–307, has made a strong plea for reality-centered objectives in organizational change programs.

The implementation of change which does not consider the constraints imposed by prevailing conditions within the present organization may only make the original problem worse. Change may also prepare the ground for subsequent problems. Taken together, these limiting conditions constitute the climate for change, and this climate can be positive or negative.

The strategy for change

The selection of a strategy for implementing the change technique has consequences in the final outcome. Greiner analyzes a number of organizational changes to determine the relationship of various change strategies to the relative success of the change itself.[43] He identifies three approaches which are located along a continuum, with unilateral authority at one extreme and delegated authority at the other extreme. In the middle of the continuum are approaches which he terms shared authority.

Unilateral approaches can take the form of an edict from top management which describes the change and the responsibilities of subordinates in implementing the change. The formal communication may be a memorandum or policy statement. It is, in any form, a one-way, top-down communication.[44] Shared approaches involve lower-level groups in the process of either (1) defining the problem and alternative solutions or (2) defining solutions only after higher-level management has defined the problem. In either case, the process engages the talents and insights of all members at all levels. Finally, delegated approaches relinquish complete authority to subordinate groups. Through free-wheeling discussions, the group is ultimately responsible for the analysis of the problem and proposed solutions. According to Greiner, the relatively more successful instances of organizational change are those which tend toward the shared position of the continuum. Why would this be the case?

As has been observed, most instances of organizational change are accompanied by resistance from those involved in the change. The actual form of resistance may range in extreme from passive resignation to deliberate sabotage.[45] The objective of the strategy is at least to minimize resistance and at most to maximize cooperation and support.

---

[43] Greiner, "Patterns of Change."

[44] Greiner identifies replacement of key personnel and structural changes as two other forms of unilateral change. For our purposes, personnel and structural changes are change techniques, not strategies for implementing change. Techniques specify what is to be done; strategies specify how it is to be done.

[45] Arnold S. Judson, A Manager's Guide to Making Changes (New York: John Wiley and Sons, 1966), p. 41.

The manner in which the change is managed from beginning to end is a key determinant of the reaction of people to change,

The strategy which emphasizes share authority has the greatest likelihood of minimizing resistance to change. This is the case because it takes into account the "American culture pattern of equivalence between self-reliance and self-respect."[46] Change imposed from the top—unilateral authority—runs the danger of *creating* resistance even though the proposed change may benefit the participants in every conceivable way by any objective standard. As has been recognized by the Behavioral School, an important means for overcoming resistance to change is to involve those who will be affected by the change in the decision to make the change.

The process of shared authority is composed of six phases. According to Greiner, each of these phases accompanies each instance of reported successful change. The six phases, in logical sequence, are:

1. *Pressure and arousal.* Instances of successful change are stimulated by strong pressure on the top management of the firm. This pressure ordinarily exerts itself in the form of unmistakable and unambiguous signals that something is wrong and needs attention.

2. *Intervention and reorientation.* Because there is a tendency to seek answers in traditional solutions, the intervention of an outsider is often necessary to reorient the management away from routine approaches and toward nonroutine approaches. The outsider may be a new management appointee, a corporate staff official, or a consultant. The outsider brings a different perspective into the situation and serves as challenger to the status quo. At this point, top management must commit itself to change.

3. *Diagnosis and recognition.* The entire organization from top to bottom joins together to diagnose and specify the problem. Greiner observes that the less successful changes use either unilateral or delegated approaches in this step. The former fails because management presume that they alone know the problem and its solution and thus ignore the necessity for involving participants. The latter fails because subordinates question the sincerity of managers who totally relinquish their authority. The involvement of all concerned members of the organization and, at the same time, maintenance of the necessary authority relationships, approaches a "balance between maximized feelings of independence and the need for enforcing policy and authority."[47]

4. *Intervention and commitment.* The outsider actively encourages management and nonmanagement personnel to invent new solutions to

---

[46] Paul C. Agnew and Francis L. K. Hsu, "Introducing Change in a Mental Hospital," *Human Organization* (Winter 1960), p. 198.

[47] Agnew and Hsu, "Introducing Change," p. 198.

its diagnosed problems. All members share in this step. Through the sharing experience, a high degree of commitment to the change can be expected — provided that top management makes a commitment to the proposed new solution.

5. *Experimentation and search.* The solution is not implemented on a grand scale; rather, it is implemented on a small scale at various points throughout the organization. The objective is to test the validity of the solution on an experimental basis. This tactic avoids large errors by permitting a test run — a "shakedown" cruise.

6. *Reinforcement and acceptance.* As the experimental attempts provide positive signals that the change is proceeding as planned, there is a reinforcement effect which encourages the participants to accept the change and to enlarge, potentially, the scope of their own efforts. "People are rewarded and encouraged" by the success of the experimental changes, thus validating broader applications of the change.

The strategy for implementing change as described above involves the participation of superiors and subordinates in the entire process. But we should recognize that there is no guarantee that the strategy will work in all cases. Indeed, some very basic preconditions must exist before employees can meaningfully participate in the change process. They are:[48]

a. An intuitively obvious factor is that employees must want to become involved. For any number of reasons, they may reject the invitation. They may have other, more pressing needs, such as getting on with their own work. Or they may view the invitation to participate as a subtle (but not too subtle) attempt by managers to manipulate them toward a solution already predetermined. Perhaps they do not want to become associated with a program that is uncertain and may fail. If the leadership climate or organizational culture has created an atmosphere of mistrust and insincerity, most attempts to involve workers will be viewed by them in cynical terms.

b. The employees must be willing and able to voice their ideas. Even if they are willing, they must have expertise in some aspect of the analysis. The technical problems associated with computer installation or automated processes may be beyond the training of assembly-line workers, yet they may have valuable insights into the impact of the machinery on their and co-workers' jobs. But even if they have the knowledge they must be able to articulate their ideas.

---

[48] Based upon Judson, *Manager's Guide,* pp. 109–13. Much popular and scientific literature treats employee participation in decision making. For an example of each type, see W. L. Mandry, "Participative Management: The CIL Experience," *The Business Quarterly* (Winter 1971), pp. 80–87; and Joseph A. Alutto and James A. Belasco, "A Typology for Participation in Organizational Decision-Making," *Administrative Science Quarterly* (March 1972), pp. 117–25.

c. The managers must be secure in their own positions. Insecure managers would perceive any participation by employees as a threat to their authority. They might view employee participation as a sign of weakness or as undermining their status. They must be able to give credit for good ideas and to give explanations for ideas of questionable merit. As is evident, the managers' personalities and leadership styles must be compatible with the shared-authority approach if it is to be a successful strategy.

d. Finally, the managers must be open-minded to employees' suggestions. If they have predetermined the solution, the participation of employees will soon be recognized for what it is. Certainly, managers have final responsibility for the outcome, and can control the situation by specifying beforehand, the latitude of the employees: They may define objectives, establish constraints, or whatever, so long as the employees know the rules prior to their participation.

If any of the conditions which limit effective participation are present, the use of shared or delegated authority approaches must be viewed with caution. As we have seen, the same factors which limit the range of viable alternative change techniques also limit the range of alternative change strategies. Leadership style, formal organization, organizational culture, along with characteristics of the employees, are key variables which constrain the entire change process. It should be recognized that the nature of the problem itself affects the choice of strategy. If, for example, the problem is one which requires immediate action, a unilateral approach may be the only means since alternative approaches consume time. We can summarize by observing that the appropriate change strategy depends upon three factors: the problem, the participants, and various organizational dimensions.

Implementing and monitoring the process

The implementation of the proposed change has two dimensions — timing and scope. Timing is the selection of the appropriate point in time to initiate the change. Scope is the selection of the appropriate scale of the change. The matter of timing is strategic and depends upon a number of factors, particularly the company's operating cycle and the groundwork which has preceded the change. Certainly if a change is of considerable magnitude, it is desirable that it not compete with ordinary business operations. Thus the change might well be implemented during a slack period. On the other hand, if the problem is critical to the survival of the organization, then immediate implementation is in order. The scope of the change depends upon the strategy. The change may be implemented throughout the organization and it becomes an established fact in a short period of time. Or it may be phased into the organization level by level, department by department. The strategy of successful changes, according to Greiner, makes use of a phased approach, which limits the scope but provides feedback for each subsequent implementation.

The provision of feedback information is termed the monitoring phase. From Figure 11–1 we see that information is fed back into the implementation phase. It is also fed back into the forces for change phase because the change itself establishes a new situation which will create problems. The monitoring phase has two problems to overcome: (1) the acquisition of data which measure the desired objectives and (2) the determination of the expected trend of improvement over time.

The acquisition of information which measures the sought-after objective is the relatively easier problem to solve, although it certainly does not lend itself to naive solutions. As we have come to understand, the stimulus for change is the deterioration of performance criteria which management traces to either structural, behavioral, or technological causes. The criteria may be any number of objective indicators, including profit, sales volume, productivity, absenteeism, turnover, scrappage, or costs. The major source of feedback for those variables is the firm's usual information system. But, if the change includes the objective of improving employee attitudes and morale, the usual sources of information are limited, if not invalid. As Likert has shown, it is quite possible for a change to induce increased productivity at the expense of declining employee attitudes and motivation.[49] Thus if the manager relies on the naive assumption that productivity and employee morale are directly related, the change may be incorrectly judged successful when improved cost and profit reports become available.

To avoid the danger of overreliance on productivity data, the manager can generate *ad hoc* information which measures employee attitudes and morale. The benchmark for evaluation would be available if an attitude survey had been used in the diagnosis phase. The definition of acceptable improvement is difficult when evaluating attitudinal data since the matter of "how much more" positive should be the attitude of employees is quite different than the matter of "how much more" productive they should be. Nevertheless, if a complete analysis of results is to be undertaken, attitudinal measurements must be combined with productivity measurements.

The second problem of the monitoring phase is the determination of the trend of improvement over time. The trend itself has three dimensions: (1) the first indication of improvement, (2) the magnitude of improvement, and (3) the duration of the improvement. In Figure 11–3

---

[49] Likert, *Human Organization*, pp. 84–91.

FIGURE 11-3
Three patterns of change in results through time

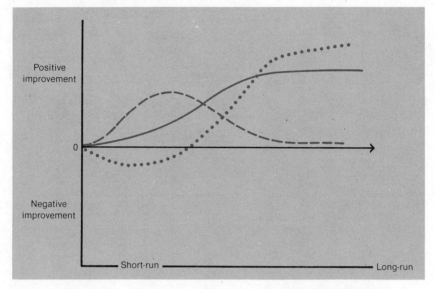

.three different patterns of change for a particular performance, behavioral, or attitudinal measure are illustrated. In the change illustrated by the solid line, improvement is slight during the early periods of time, but rises and maintains itself at a positive level. The dashed line illustrates a marked increase, but followed by a deterioration and a return to the original position. The dotted line describes a situation in which the early signs indicate a decrease, but followed by a sharp rise toward substantial improvement. The figure illustrates only three of a number of possible change patterns. A well-devised change strategy should include an analysis of what patterns can be expected. The actual pattern can then be compared to the expected.

Ideally, the pattern would consist of an index which measures all relevant variables. Figure 11-4 illustrates a model which describes the necessary information for an index measuring performance and behavioral variables. The solid line is the expected pattern through time. It shows a movement into acceptable behavior prior to a movement into acceptable performance. The expected pattern may, of course, assume any configuration. The dashed line is the plot of actual change through time. It reflects not only what is happening but also the impact of corrective action which management takes to keep the change program on course. If the expected pattern is valid as originally conceived, the management's objective is to minimize the oscillations around the planned results.

FIGURE 11–4
Expected and actual pattern of results*

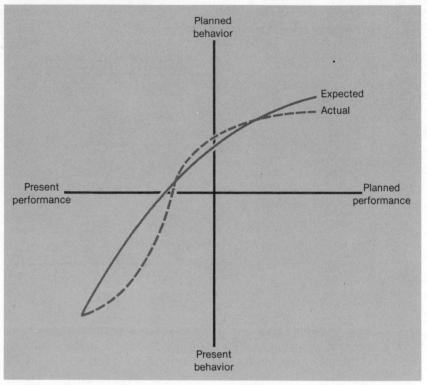

* Based upon Jeremiah J. O'Connell, *Managing Organizational Innovation* (Homewood, Ill.: Richard D. Irwin, Inc., 1968), p. 156.

In general, the monitoring phase is a specific application of management control. Before it can be effective, management must provide for a measurement of the objective, information to compare actual results with planned results, and action to correct any deviations.

Summary

This chapter concludes the discussion of the Behavioral School of management. In the context of a model which describes the process of managing organizational change and development, a number of behavioral science concepts are shown to have considerable relevance. Motivation, attitudes, work groups, and leadership style are all key concepts in an overall change framework which stresses the dynamic nature of the managerial process. Indeed, since change itself has become such a pervasive fact of the modern world, it is both appropriate and logical to cast management in a framework which emphasizes change. At the same time, the management of change certainly does not imply random and unplanned responses to a changing environment. On the contrary, we have repeatedly stressed the need for systematic analyses of all facets of the proposed change program. The literature which reports changes undertaken in various organizations indicates the critical need for planning, organizing, and controlling the change process. We have emphasized that the manner in which the change is implemented bears heavily on the ultimate outcome. In fact, we should recognize that a change technique may fail because of ineffective implementation. We have also stressed the necessity for evaluating techniques and strategies in the context of the particular organization. Thus, even though there is evidence that certain strategies (for example, shared authority) and certain techniques (for example, sensitivity training) are appropriate in many instances, their validity in the specific instance is a matter of on-site analysis.

Discussion and review questions

1. The notion of planned change is assumed to be more effective than a nonplanned approach. In fact, some state that the federal government could benefit from a planned approach in efforts to bring about changes in various agencies. Do you believe this is true? Why?

2. Diagnosing problems in organizations is time-consuming, difficult, and expensive. In addition, unless a diagnosis is correctly conducted it can cause problems. Are these factors reason enough to bypass conducting a diagnosis of problems before a change problem is initiated? Why?

3. "The successful manager is one who knows how to play the role of a change agent." Comment.

4. How can supervisors provide management with feedback information which monitors a change process? How can managers validate the correctness of such information?

5. A young manager states: "It took me 30 years to develop a set of defense mechanisms that enable me to live and function in this crazy world. I refuse to participate in any training program whose objective is to tear them down." Comment.

6. Behavioral change is difficult to measure accurately. Some changes in employee behavior subtly change over time. Why would it be difficult to measure subtle changes in behavior that may be occurring during a sensitivity training program? Should these changes, if they are occurring, be measured at all?

7. Even though structure should follow strategy, can you cite from experience any instances of structural change preceding the development of strategy?

8. What changes do you believe are necessary within your own college or university? Why do you think so? What is your evidence? What are the limiting conditions? What are the objectives? How would you evaluate your proposed changes once implemented?

9. A model can serve as a guideline for someone actually managing employees. The model used can alert managers to various constraints or issues that may appear. Would there be any value for a manager in understanding the parts of the model represented in Figure 11–1? Explain.

10. Why is the creation of staff departments such a widespread reaction to organizational problems? What are the dangers of this strategy?

Additional references

Argyris, C. *Intervention Theory and Method: A Behavioral Science View.* Reading, Mass.: Addison-Wesley Publishing Co., 1970.

Basil, D. C., and Cook, C. W. *The Management of Change.* New York: McGraw-Hill, 1974.

Bennis, W. G., Benne, K. D., and Chin, R. *The Planning of Change.* New York: Holt, Rinehart, and Winston, Inc., 1961.

Coch, L., and French, J. R. P. "Overcoming Resistance to Change," *Human Relations* 1 (1948): 512–32.

Dalton, G. W., Lawrence, P. R., and Greiner, L. E. *Organizational Change and Development.* Homewood, Ill.: Richard D. Irwin, Inc., 1970.

Kaufman, H. *The Limits of Organizational Change.* University, Ala.: University of Alabama Press, 1971.

Levinson, H., Molinari, J., and Spohn, A. G. *Organizational Diagnosis.* Cambridge, Mass.: Harvard University Press, 1972.

Patten, T. H., Jr. "Time For Organizational Development," *Personnel,* 54 March-April 1977): 26–33.

Shaw, M. E. "The Behavioral Sciences: A New Image," *Training and Development Journal* 31 (February 1977: 26–31.

Steele, F. *Consulting For Organizational Change.* Amherst, Mass.: University of Massachusetts Press, 1976.

Steelman, H. S., Jr. "Is There A Payoff to Organizational Development?" *Training and Development Journal* 30 (April 1976): 18–23.

Tichy, N. M., Hornstein, H., and Nisberg, J. N. "Participative Organization Diagnosis and Intervention Strategies: Developing Emergent Pragmatic Theories of Change," *Academy of Management Review* (1976): 109–20.

White, S. E., and Mitchell, T. R. "Organization Development: A Review of Research Content and Research Design," *Academy of Management Review* (1976): 57–73.

Is the Expert Correct?

Talk franchising, and names like McDonald's, Holiday Inns, Midas Muffler, Denny's, and Kentucky Fried Chicken inevitably come up. Everybody yearning for his or her own business would like to have bought one of these franchises years ago and ridden it into the money. Price tags on highly successful franchise outlets now can run into several hundreds of thousands of dollars. One apparently astute person who started selling Chicago-style pizza three years ago was Dana Sandell. Instead of buying a franchise, she opened her own Chicago-style pizza parlor in San Antonio, Texas.

Within three years, Dana had opened nine other parlors: three in Houston, two in Dallas, one in Galveston, one in Austin, one in College Station, and one in Amarillo. She competed with such franchises as Shakey's, Pizza Hut, and Pizza Inn in these Texas locations. Her pizzas were considered superior in taste, quality, and price over the larger franchise competitors.

The sudden expansion of her business began to cause Dana some management problems. She was just not able to oversee operations in her ten pizza parlors as thoroughly as she had with only the San Antonio outlet. Dana decided that one person could not properly manage the network of stores and that it was now necessary either to recruit new managers or to train the present store managers to handle each of the outlets. If the training program proved a success, she believed that her market standing would be maintained into the future. However, if she could not attract enough qualified people to take over store manager positions, it would only be a matter of time until her problems were reflected in shrinking profit margins.

Dana had taken a course in small business management prior to opening her first pizza parlor in San Antonio. She remembered that the instructor had discussed such concepts as control, planned change, training, and diagnosis of problems. These were obviously sound ideas and practices, but under the present circumstances Dana felt that there was little time available to diagnose problems or study a suggested change model. The problems she faced needed solution today. So she hired an organizational development consultant who was a recognized expert in sensitivity training and had developed excellent and successful programs for organizations throughout the world. After two days of observing three of the pizza parlors and discussing problems with Dana, the consultant recommended a solution.

It was proposed that the employees presently serving as store managers in the ten stores should undergo intensive sensitivity training. This would enable them to manage more effectively and provide the in-house expertise needed to compete successfully with the franchise operations. Dana was told that "sensitivity training will be the key to help you coordinate, control, and plan operations." She accepted this recommendation and felt good about having an expert on the scene directing the necessary steps to solve her management problems.

Questions for analysis

1. Is sensitivity training a potentially good solution to Dana's problem? Why?
2. Why did the organizational development consultant recommend sensitivity training?
3. What do you expect will happen after the sensitivity training program is initiated?

PRACTICAL EXERCISE II
Organizational Change in a State Department of Health

In the late 1970s the governor of a southeastern state appointed a new commissioner of health. The previous commissioner had retired from public service after spending over 20 years as the state's commissioner of health. During that time the state's Department of Health had grown from a relatively small organization employing less than 100 people to a relatively large one employing some 600 people. Its annual budget had increased from thousands to millions of dollars devoted to a wide range of personal and environmental health services. The services of the department were delivered through a statewide network of county and regional health departments, all of which received policy direction from the commissioner's office.

The newly appointed commissioner was a licensed physician with considerable experience in federal and state public health administration. He was also a member of the American Management Association and had attended many of the association's management training programs. He was a habitual reader of the management literature. His public statements and speeches typically were strongly worded appeals

for the application of management fundamentals in public health administration. His general philosophy articulated the case for strong
policy direction through the management hierarchy, with policy implemented through plans developed at the operating level—the county
and regional health departments in this instance.

At the time the commissioner took office, the organization was
structured such that 15 different division and program directors
reported directly to him. In addition to these formally established lines,
there was an informal practice of bypassing the chain of command and
going directly to the commissioner. This informal practice had been encouraged by the previous commissioner in order for him to be involved
in much of the day-to-day routine of all the divisions and programs. In
a very short period of time after assuming the office, the new commissioner found himself much more involved with routine affairs than he
thought was appropriate. Even though the wide span of control should
theoretically facilitate the development of decentralized management,
the historically defined practice was quite the opposite. Division and
program directors had simply not been permitted by the previous commissioner to exercise discretion and, as it happened, had not developed
the skills and initiative to do so.

The commissioner was generally aware of the situation when he took
office. Briefings with the governor's staff and public health experts indicated considerable dissatisfaction with the department's programs. The
consensus was that the department had not aggressively sought new
approaches and that its response to public health, particularly environmental needs, had been disappointing. Terms such as "drift" and
"indecisiveness" were generally used to describe the department's performance during the past ten years. In response to these expressions of
concern, the commissioner appointed a task force of division directors
to propose initiatives for change. The task force consisted of physicians
and engineers who had credibility within the organization and among
public health professionals. His charge to the task force was to prepare
recommendations based upon diagnosis. He reminded them that they
should approach the problem with the same scientific point of view
that buttressed their professional practices of medicine and engineering.

The task force met on many occasions during a two-month period of
time. They evaluated the solicited comments of departmental employees and clients. The commissioner himself met with the group and
offered his observations about the future direction of the Department of
Health and the appropriate organization structure and management
practices to sustain that direction.

The task force reviewed the information available to it and recommended that the commissioner make a basic change in the way the
Health Department was structured. The recommended structural
change would involve the establishment of three deputy commissioners

who would specialize in three different functions: administration, personal health, and environmental health. All the former divisions and programs would be grouped together into one of the three functions, and the managers of these units would report to them instead of to the commissioner. The recommendation stated the change would enable the commissioner to deal with broad policy matters along with the three deputies. The deputies would assume the managerial role of coordinating the divisions reporting to them and, through executive sessions with the commissioner, coordinate the three functions of administration, personal health, and environmental health. As the commissioner noted: "The recommendation of the task force is, in effect, a recommendation to move toward a System 1–type organization and away from a System 4–type organization."

The commissioner received the report of the task force and was in agreement with its recommendation. He believed, however, that it was incomplete. He stated that the proposed structure would involve more than simple changes in the organization chart. It would involve changes in the ways employees had related to one another in the past—for example, division directors would no longer go directly to the commissioner but would, instead, report to the deputy commissioners. Moreover, the change indicated that division directors would have to become more assertive in the way they dealt with their own subordinates. These new behaviors would have to be learned, he reasoned, and the task force had not addressed these issues. With these thoughts in mind and expressed to the task force members, he directed them to reconvene and develop a plan which could be implemented along with the structural change and which would train the personnel of the department to act in those ways anticipated by the change.

Questions for analysis:

1. What would be your plan for developing the new behavior required by the new structure.

2. Do you agree that the new structure tends to System 1 rather than System 4? What other evidence would you need to know fully?

3. Is there any basis for predicting whether the new structure will be more effective than its predecessor?

PRACTICAL EXERCISE III
Organizational Change in a Manufacturing Firm

The Sanitary Surgical Bandage Company recently opened a manufacturing facility in a rural area of a southwestern state. The company had been organized in 1940 by its founder and present chief executive officer. Its products were sold nationwide and were recognized for their high quality. The company had grown from very modest beginnings to become a multimillion-dollar organization. The opening of the facility in the southwest was a strategic move to locate manufacturing facilities closer to the expanding market in that part of the United States.

The company's policies and practices reflected both the manner in which surgical bandages are manufactured and the founder's idiosyncracies. For example, the company's manufacturing work force was predominantly women. This policy grew out of the historical practice of using women to make bandages by hand. Even though the company now used machinery which wrapped and packed the company's products, women were still employed as machine operators. In fact the chief executive had selected the rural location because of the availability of women in the area's labor market. The chief executive had developed personnel policies based upon what he considered to be the special needs and circumstances of women factory employees. Among these was his insistence that supervisors and foremen be men selected from the immediate locale. He did not believe that women could supervise other women, at least in a factory setting.

The chief executive was ardently antiunion and believed that the best way to keep unions out of the plant was to keep the people happy. He insisted that all the company's plants be constructed with employees in mind. The plants were air conditioned, reasonably quiet, and clean. The company's fringe benefit package was unusually generous in terms of retirement, vacation time, and medical benefits. At the same time, he believed that the company should not establish a set of work rules. Such rules are usually found in manufacturing plants and they define procedures for granting pay raises, promotions, shift assignments, and other conditions of work. The chief executive insisted that such rules tie the hands of foremen and prevent them from responding to the special circumstances of each personnel decision.

The company's executive offices were located in Cleveland. Major policy directions in sales, personnel, production, finance, engineering, and legal affairs were developed by staff specialists and issued to all the company's manufacturing and sales facilities. Local plant superintendents and sales managers had little discretion in day-to-day operations. They were expected to follow policy, meet deadlines, keep the people happy, and avoid unionization.

Bob Ivory had just recently celebrated his fifth anniversary as superintendent of the southwestern manufacturing facility when he was confronted by a group of ten irate women employees. The spokeswoman of the group stated that they were representing all the women employees and that they had requested a meeting with Mr. Ivory to discuss company policy as related to the treatment of women. The spokeswoman, Sue Taft, said that unless Mr. Ivory made some drastic changes, the women of the plant were prepared to begin discussions with a union organizer. And while the women were reluctant to proceed with unionization, they were prepared to do so if management did not respond in good faith.

Mr. Ivory was alarmed. The forcefulness of Ms. Taft's argument and the aura of hostility within the group indicated to him that the women's concerns were genuinely felt. Moreover, he recognized that the threat of unionization could be carried out since women comprised 80 percent of the total work force. His alarm was compounded by the fact that this was the first instance of employee complaint to be brought to his attention since he had become plant superintendent. When he told the group of his surprise, Ms. Taft responded, "You should get out of your office and talk to the employees. You only hear what the shift supervisors want you to hear. For that matter, I am not sure that any of the women would have told you anything anyway. Until last week we were afraid to say anything because of what they would do to us."

"What do you mean? Who are 'they'? What would they do to you?" asked Mr. Ivory. "Mr. Ivory, you seem to be a nice guy, but you really are out of it! The shift supervisors and foremen have it all their own way. They can give overtime to whoever they want to. If you get in their way or cause them trouble they will put you on the night shift." One of the other women added, "Yeah, and once you get on their list, the only way to get off of it is to play house with them!" Mr. Ivory asked if any of them had ever personally experienced such treatment. "No," said Ms. Taft, "but we know plenty who have. My foreman is always telling dirty jokes and cursing around us. Some of the girls may like it, but I don't!"

After listening to the women for the better part of the morning, Mr. Ivory asked what it was that they wanted him to do. "I can't change company policy," he said. "I can't change what the boss in Cleveland sends down. There is no way to write work rules, and he would never let me hire women as foremen. And I sure can't fire all the foremen! What can I do?" "Well," said Ms. Taft, "you better get something started or we will be organizing for a union election by the end of the week."

Questions for analysis:

1. How can Mr. Ivory determine whether a real problem exists?
2. Based upon what information is available above, what is your diagnosis?
3. What organizational change strategy should Mr. Ivory consider if the problem is primarily behavioral, rather than technological or structural?

PART FOUR

The management science school

12

FOUNDATIONS OF
THE MANAGEMENT
SCIENCE SCHOOL

This section of the book examines the third major school of thought in management—the Management Science School. In the previous section we saw that a major goal of the behavioral science approach to management is to apply scientific methodology to solving the *human problems* facing management. The major goal of the management science approach is to apply scientific methodology to solving *production and operations management problems.* The idea of applying scientific methodology to management problems is not new. In fact, the central idea can be traced as far back as the 18th and 19th centuries. At the end of the 18th century Eli Whitney, the inventor of the cotton gin, used a scientific approach to develop a mathematical model of manufacturing costs to enable more efficient use of the cotton gin. However, the recognized field of management science has only formally existed for approximately 25 years. It has been during this period that the individuals now associated with this field began to have a noticeable impact on the solution of complex military and business problems through the use of engineering and mathematical skills. During this period a new profession has come about: the "management scientist." Like the behavioral scientists, these individuals have their own professional associations, the Operations Research Society of America (1952) and the Institute of Management Sciences (1953), in addition to their own scholarly journals, courses of study in business schools and engineering schools, and large numbers of jobs within all types of organizations.

Management science and production and operations management

Probably the most important applications of management science in modern organizations has been in the areas of production management and operations management, as shown in Figure 12-1. The term *production* focuses on manufacturing technology and the flow of materials in a manufacturing plant. Indeed, the production function in a business organization is specifically concerned with the activity of producing goods, that is, the design, implementation, operation, and control of men, materials, equipment, money, and information to achieve specific production objectives. The term *operations* is broader in scope and is

FIGURE 12-1

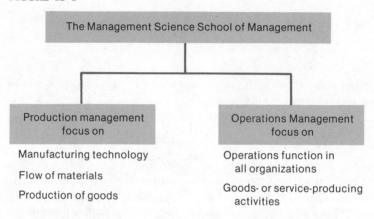

used for the goods- or service-producing activity in any organization — public, private, profit, or nonprofit. Thus a bank and a hospital have operations functions although they have nothing to do with manufacturing technology, production assembly lines, and assembled products. Operations management, therefore, is similar to production management except that it focuses on a wider class of problems and includes organizations whose technologies may be quite different from those of a manufacturing organization. There are important similarities between the flow of materials in a manufacturing plant, customers waiting in line at a banking facility or supermarket, the processing of claims in an insurance company, student registration in a college or university, and the provision of health care in a hospital.

We shall see that management science tools and models have also been applied in other functional areas such as marketing, personnel, and finance. However, *management science has probably made its greatest contribution in the areas of production and operations management.* Accordingly, the models discussed in this section of the book focus primarily on management science applications in the production and operations functions.

THE PURPOSE OF THIS SECTION

While the models of the management scientist are mathematical and specialists in this field are trained in mathematics, the basic concepts of most models can be completely comprehended and appreciated with only an understanding of very basic mathematics and arithmetic. The purpose of this section of the book is to teach potential managers *about* selected management science models, not to teach them *to be* management scientists. There is no more reason for a manager to be a technically proficient management scientist than for a physician to be a bacteriologist. However, the manager must know what to expect of management science, its strengths and weaknesses, and how to use mathematical models as *tools*, just as the physician must know what to expect of bacteriology and how it can serve as a diagnostic tool. Readers should keep this in mind as they read about management science.

Boundaries of the management science school

As is often the case with an emerging body of knowledge, there is much confusion over just what it includes. Since its early development is rarely a consciously planned effort, there may even be numerous approaches to studying phenomena which differ little except, perhaps, in name. This appears to have been the case with management science. Numerous synonyms for the term management science appear, such as operations research, operational research, operations analysis, and systems analysis. They all share in common the desire to apply scientific analysis to managerial problems in all types of organizations.

The activities of management scientists have been characterized by an emphasis on the mathematical modeling of systems. Applications by operations research specialists, mostly confined to the production segment of business firms, began after World War II. During World War II, they had successfully solved a number of military problems ranging from those of a logistical nature (equipment and troop movements) to developing strategy for submarine warfare.[1] As a result, after the war, operations research caught on quickly in some of the larger firms in the United States. Such companies as E. I. du Pont de Nemours and H. J. Heinz pioneered the use of early operations research applications. However, it was not until a few of these bolder firms had tried it with success that civilian operations research made any major headway in the United States.

---

[1] An excellent reference on this subject is E. S. Quade, ed., *Analysis for Military Decisions* (Chicago: Rand McNally & Co., 1964).

While it is difficult to place clear boundary lines around the Management Science School, it is possible to distinguish certain characteristics of its approach. It is generally agreed that most management science applications possess the following characteristics:[2]

1. A primary focus on decision making. The principal end result of the analysis must have direct implications for management action.

2. An appraisal resting on economic effectiveness criteria. A comparison of the various feasible actions must be based on measurable values that reflect the future well-being of the organization. Examples of such measured variables include costs, revenues, and rates of return on investment.

3. Reliance on a formal mathematical model. These models are actually possible solutions to the problems, which are stated in mathematical form. The procedures for manipulating the data must be so explicit that another analyst can derive the same results from the same data. This *replicability* requirement is not new to the reader who saw in the previous section that this was also a major requirement of the behavioral science approach to management. In fact, replication is the keynote of scientific analysis.

4. Dependence on an electronic computer. This is actually a requirement necessitated by either the complexity of the mathematical model, the volume of data to be manipulated, or the magnitude of computations needed to implement the model.

THE ROLE OF THE COMPUTER IN MANAGEMENT SCIENCE

Electronic computers have fostered most of the advances in the management science approach over the past two decades. In fact, it is not coincidental that computer technology developed in a parallel fashion with the field of management science. Undoubtedly there would be negligible interest right now in the field of management science (except perhaps for some applied mathematicians) if it were not for the vast data-generating capacity and computational ability of high-speed computers. The computer has gone through its own stages of development from a point where it could only process routine data to a point where it can now effectively assist in the conduct of management science studies. The increasing availability, understanding, and use of the computer have made it possible to turn heretofore theoretical mathematical models into everyday, here-and-now, practical decision aids.

Throughout this section of the book we shall examine, for illustrative

---

[2] Harvey M. Wagner, *Principles of Management Science* (Englewood Cliffs, N.J.: Prentice-Hall, Inc., 1970), p. 5.

purposes, simplified mathematical models in which all computations can be performed by hand. The reader will see that even repetitious use of these simplified models would be greatly aided by a computer, and real-world problems faced by managers in complex organizational settings are usually not amenable to hand solutions. Numerical solutions to these kinds of problems may require thousands of individual computations. A computer provides the solutions in a matter of minutes instead of weeks, with less possibility of error.

THE ROLE OF MATHEMATICAL MODELS IN MANAGEMENT SCIENCE

Mathematical models are characteristics of the management science approach. However, before defining mathematical models let us examine two points. First, in the previous section of the book we saw that experimentation is an important part of the scientific approach. However, it is rare, if ever, that a manager can perform what would be considered a bona fide scientific experiment to test the feasibility of taking a particular action. The practicalities of the real world preclude any manager from doing this. In other words, a manager cannot usually experiment with inventory to determine which level minimizes carrying costs and ordering costs, or cannot experiment with the advertising budget to determine which combination of media (for example, radio, TV, magazines) produces the most favorable sales results. However, an accurately constructed mathematical model enables the decision maker to experiment with possible solutions without interrupting the ongoing system. If the model accurately represents the ongoing system, it will provide the decision maker with the results of proposed solutions. In other words, it will react as the real system would react; and, therefore, the decision maker can simulate the behavior of the real system. It is this experimental role of mathematical models which makes them useful to managers.

Second, while there are several different types of models, the emphasis on mathematical models in the Management Science School should be clear. In order to utilize scientific analysis, one must be "quantitatively oriented," since one of the major characteristics and prerequisites of scientific inquiry is quantitative measurement. Thus the models examined in this section of the book are quantitative or mathematical in nature.

Understanding the role of mathematical models in the Management Science School, we can now define exactly what a mathematical model is: A mathematical model is a simplified representation of the relevant aspects of an actual system or process.

At this point, the value of a simplified representation may be questioned. This is why the definition includes the two words "relevant aspects." It is obvious that the value of any model depends on how well it represents the system or process under consideration. A highly simplified model that accurately describes a system or process still provides a more clearly understood starting point than a vague conception which a manager mentally creates. Such a model forces the manager to consider systematically the variables in the problem and the relationships among the variables. Thus, forcing the manager to formalize thinking reduces the possibility of overlooking important factors or giving too much weight to minor factors.

In reality, readers are probably more familiar with models for decision making than they think. The accounting equation, $A = L + C$, is a mathematical model. In fact, it is the oldest decision-making model, since it dates back to the Renaissance. It is a mathematical model showing a simplified relationship between assets, liabilities, and capital. It does not resemble the actual system physically; but it does *behave as the real system behaves*. It is an abstraction of the financial condition of a particular enterprise at a given moment of time. On the other hand, the income statement is also a mathematical model that is an abstraction of the operations of a business over a period of time.

In conclusion, instead of studying the actual system, managers can study a mathematical model or representation of the system. This enables them to manipulate variables in order to determine the effects such changes will have on the overall performance of the actual system. They are thus able to experiment using the model and predict the effect such changes will have on the actual problem.

Types of mathematical models

Before managers can understand, evaluate, and utilize mathematical models, they must be aware of the major types of these models. Mathematical models may be classified by the *purpose* of the model (descriptive or normative) and/or by the *types of variables* included in the model (deterministic or probabilistic).

PURPOSE OF THE MODEL: DESCRIPTIVE OR NORMATIVE

A *descriptive model* is one which describes how a system works. That is, *it describes things as they are and makes no* value judgments about the particular phenomenon being studied. Many times a model is constructed solely to be a description of a real-world phenomenon in mathematical terms. This model can then be used to display the situation more clearly or to indicate how it can be changed. Descriptive models display the alternative choices available to the decision maker

and, in some cases, help the decision maker determine the consequences or outcomes of each alternative. However, a descriptive model
does not select the best alternative.

A *normative (or prescriptive) model* selects the best from among alternatives based on some previously determined criteria which are
also included in the model. It tells *how the system should be in order
to achieve a particular objective.* These models are also referred to as
optimizing models and decision models since they seek the optimum
from among all the possible solutions.

TYPES OF VARIABLES IN THE MODEL:
DETERMINISTIC OR PROBABILISTIC

A model is *deterministic* when the law of chance plays no role. In
other words, the model contains no probabilistic considerations. For

FIGURE 12–2
Types of mathematical models

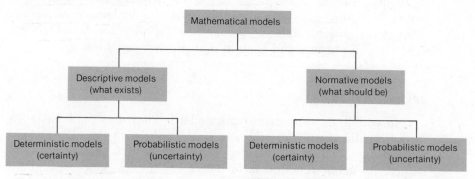

example the model, *Profit = Revenue minus Costs,* is a deterministic
mathematical model. All of the factors taken into account in the model
are exact or deterministic quantities, and the solution is determined by
this set of exact relationships. In other words, in a deterministic model,
we assume conditions of *certainty.*

Once chance or random variables are introduced, conditions of un-
certainty exist and the model is said to be a *probabilistic* model.
Probabilistic models are based on the mathematics of statistics. Conditions of uncertainty introduced in the model are often based on
observations of real-world events. For example, insurance companies
make heavy use of actuarial tables that give the probability of death
as a function of age. These tables can be considered probabilistic
models.

Figure 12–2 summarizes our discussion to this point. It indicates

athematical model may be either descriptive or normative in
 and contain either deterministic or probabilistic variables.
ime let us briefly examine some of the more popular mathe-
models in the Management Science School. Several of these
vill then be discussed in more detail in the remaining chapters
.. ... . section.

Popular management science models

DECISION THEORY MODELS

In the last two decades, the systematic analysis of decision making
has become known as "decision theory." Decision theory is firmly
rooted in the fields of statistics and the behavioral sciences and has
as its goal, to make decision making less of an art and more of a science.
Decision theory focuses upon certain elements which are common
to all decisions and provides a framework which enables a decision
maker to better analyze a complex situation containing numerous
alternatives and possible consequences. Decision theory models are
normative in purpose and contain probabilistic variables.

BREAK-EVEN MODELS

One widely used mathematical model is known as the break-even
model. While it did not originate specifically with the management
science approach, it is included here because it is mathematical in
nature. Its major function is to determine the break-even point for
the firm as a whole or any of its specific products or services. The
break-even point is that particular level of operations where total
revenue equals total cost, and profit is zero. It can also be utilized to
determine what level of profits or losses will be achieved at a particular
level of output. The break-even model is descriptive in purpose and
contains deterministic variables.

INVENTORY MODELS

Inventory models provide answers to two questions: "How much?"
and "When?" Just as the business organization is concerned with
obtaining goods to be sold at the most favorable price, it must also
be concerned with the point at which orders are placed for repeat goods
and the quantity of each order. On the one hand, enough inventory

must be available at all times to insure that there are no lost sales or loss of customer goodwill due to stockouts; but on the other hand, frequent orders result in increased costs such as the storage costs from carrying an excessive inventory. The costs of ordering and carrying an inventory behave in such a way that one increases while the other decreases. Inventory models which are normative in purpose and contain deterministic variables enable the manager to determine the economic order quantity (EOQ) and the optimum reorder point. Because they can be applied wherever inventories are kept, they have also found wide use in nonbusiness organizations.

ALLOCATION MODELS

Allocation models are used in a variety of situations in which numerous activities are all competing for limited resources. These models enable the decision maker to allocate scarce resources to maximize some given objective. The resources may in certain departments, include labor time which the production manager must allocate to several different products to maximize the objective of profit. The resource may be an advertising budget which the marketing manager must allocate over several different advertising media in order to maximize the objective of the most exposure for the product(s). In each case, the manager wishes to find the optimum way to allocate the scarce resources, given certain objectives (profit, exposure for the product) and certain constraints (available time, dollars).

One of the most widely used allocation models is the linear programming model. Linear programming expresses the objective to be achieved in the form of a mathematical function, the value of which is to be maximized (for example, profits) or minimized (for example, costs). The constraints are introduced which reduce the number of feasible alternatives. A powerful linear programming procedure known as the simplex method searches the feasible alternatives in order to find the particular one that maximizes or minimizes the value of the objective function. The linear programming model is normative in purpose and contains deterministic variables.

NETWORK MODELS

Network models are extremely useful in planning and controlling both simple and complex projects. Actually, network models are as old as scientific management. The reader will recall the discussion of the Gantt chart as a contribution of Henry Gantt and the Classical Management School. While network models are more sophisticated, both are based on the same philosophy. The two basic and most common types of network models are PERT (Program Evaluation and Review Technique) and CPM (Critical Path Method). PERT is a method of planning and controlling nonrepetitive projects—projects that have not been done before and will not be done again in the same exact manner (for example, the Space Shuttle). CPM is a planning and control technique used in projects for which some past cost data are available. Network models are normative in purpose and contain probabilistic variables.

BRAND-SWITCHING MODELS

One of the most important measuring devices used by marketing executives in determining the success or failure of their efforts is the share of the market secured by a product. Obviously, marketing managers constantly seek ways to increase their product's share of the market or to at least prevent the existing share of the market from declining. In order to do this, they must have some idea of the behavior of consumers, both in terms of their brand loyalty and their switching from one brand to another. Brand-switching models provide such information. Brand-switching models can be considered descriptive in purpose and contain probabilistic variables.

WAITING-LINE MODELS

In the production department, workers waiting in line to requisition needed tools or raw materials cost money. Their managers would like to minimize idle time, but, on the other hand, they cannot afford to provide a great number of service facilities. Thus they must strike a balance between the costs of additional facilities and worker idle time. There are many other examples of processes which generate waiting lines. These lines are often referred to as queues. As examples, people often wait in long lines in a supermarket, in a bank, and at a fuel pump in a service station. In many instances, customers become irritable when faced with long periods of waiting, and, if it becomes excessive, the business may lose customers. Waiting-line models, which are descriptive in purpose and contain probabilistic variables, enable managers to reach effective solutions to these and similar waiting-line problems.

SIMULATION MODELS

Simulation means to have the appearance or form of, without the reality. In many situations management problems are so complex that they cannot be depicted by a standard mathematical model. Simulation involves constructing a model which replicates some aspect of the organization's operation; then performing step-by-step computations with the model, thus duplicating the manner in which the actual system might perform. An individual simulation can be thought of as an experiment upon a model. Numerous trials or experiments are performed until a workable satisfactory solution, rather than an optimal solution, is reached. This experimental nature of simulation is an important advantage because the system can be studied under a wider variety of conditions than would be possible using the actual real-world system. In this respect all mathematical models involve some degree of simulation. Simulation models are descriptive in purpose and contain probabilistic variables.

Constructing management science models

In the previous section of the book we noted that behavioral scientists use certain tools and methods for obtaining information. At this point we shall discuss the steps that management scientists take to insure a logical approach for formulating and constructing mathematical models. While several general approaches are available, the following series of steps is widely accepted:

1. Define and formulate the problem.
2. Construct the model.
3. Solve the model.
4. Test the solution.
5. Develop necessary controls for the solution.
6. Implement the solution.

DEFINE AND FORMULATE PROBLEM

This first step in the model-building process lays the foundation for all of the following steps. If a problem is ill-defined or loosely formulated, any model constructed on such a weak foundation will be of little or no value. A problem that is well defined and formulated is one in which all of the elements are clearly delineated. This includes determination of the objective(s) to be achieved, identification of alternative courses of action, and all known components of the particular problem.

The types of problems faced by managers will vary in complexity. For example, some will be relatively *structured*, with easily identifiable variables which are known to behave with a high degree of certainty. Others will be *unstructured*, containing a large number of variables which behave with a high degree of uncertainty. Thus managers face problems which range from the relatively simple and structured to the complex and unstructured. Most problems will fall somewhere along a continuum between these two extremes. As an illustration, let us examine some hypothetical points on this continuum.

Structured problems. A structured problem may have a few or several variables but all of the variables are deterministic (behave with certainty).

1. *Few deterministic variables.* These types of management problems are probably in the minority. They contain only a small number of variables which behave with a high degree of certainty. Some inventory problems are of this type where all variables such as demand, ordering costs, and carrying costs are all known or exactly determinable quantities.

2. *Many deterministic variables.* These kinds of management problems contain many variables, but all of the variables behave with a high degree of certainty. Allocation problems where a number of activities are all competing for limited resources are one group of problems that usually fall into this category.

Unstructured problems. An unstructured problem may have a few or many variables but all of the variables are probabilistic (behave with uncertainty). In some extreme cases the manager may not even be able to define all the variables present.

1. *Few probabilistic variables.* Management problems of this type contain a small number of variables but they behave with a high degree of uncertainty. A banker trying to decide whether to introduce free checking accounts faces this type of problem. Although not knowing what competitors will do, the manager does know that whatever they do it is going to influence the outcome. Decision theory models have been useful for some problems of this type.

2. *Many probabilistic variables.* These kinds of management problems contain a great number of variables, and all of them behave with uncertainty. Examples of such problems are launching a new product, constructing a new hospital, and putting man on the moon. The reader can imagine that constructing mathematical models for such problems is extremely difficult even with the aid of the electronic computer. Network and simulation models can and have been used successfully for problems of this type. Table 12–1 summarizes our discussion on the types of problems faced by managers.

Unfortunately for most managers, the majority of problems they face tend to be unstructured, and very few normative models deal with this class of problem. What then does the management scientist do in order to gain the benefits of these types of models? The only alternative is to attempt to reformulate unstructured problems into more structured ones (that is, move from right to left in Table 12–1). If this can be done, then the problem becomes more definable and more easily adapt-

TABLE 12–1 ·
Types of problems faced by managers

Type of problem	Structured		Unstructured	
Number of variables.................	Few	Many	Few	Many
Types of variables.................	Deterministic (certainty)	Deterministic (certainty)	Probabilistic (uncertainty)	Probabilistic (uncertainty)
Example of useful management science technique.......	Inventory control model	Linear programming model	Decision theory	Network and simulation models

able to various management science models. Obviously this task is not an easy one because the attempt to simplify a problem may eliminate one or more important variables and assume away the problem or end up with a useless solution. Generally, there are three ways that management scientists break down complex problems into more definable ones:

a. Assume certainty. In some situations, a management scientist may assume certainty in a problem, although some of the variables may be probabilistic in nature. For example, when facing an inventory problem, the management scientist often assumes that demand for the product is known when trying to arrive at the economic order quantity (EOQ) to replenish the inventory.

b. Simplify relationships. Here the management scientist assumes that the relationship between variables is much simpler than it is in reality. For example, when utilizing the linear programming model it is assumed that the relationships among variables are linear, when in fact they probably are nonlinear.

c. Isolate operations. Management scientists can attempt to isolate a particular operation or segment of the operation. They can seek to optimize the output from that segment and assume that the remaining parts are not adversely affected. For example, in a hospital, a management scientist might try to maximize space utilization while assuming that if this is achieved, other factors will not be adversely affected (for example, morale of hospital staff, patient care, etc.).

CONSTRUCT MODEL

After the problem has been clearly formulated and defined, the model construction phase begins. This involves expressing the elements of the problem in mathematical form. Clearly, this is a vital phase. What is important here is that the model constructed responds in the same fashion as the real system. There are three basic elements of every mathematical model:

1. **Components.** These are the parts of the model. They may be firms, households, warehouses, costs, media, and other phenomena which are a part of the real system.
2. **Variables.** These relate in one way or another to the components of the model. They are often classified as *input variables* which arise outside the component and must be fed into it (for example, inventory, patients, students, raw materials); *status variables* which describe the state of a component (for example, salary, income, education, age); and *output variables* which are anything generated by a component (for example, costs, demand).
3. **Relationships.** These specify how the values of different variables are related to each other. For example, inventory models specify the relationship between ordering costs and carrying costs.

The management scientist is faced with the task of determining all of the relevant components which affect the functioning of the system under study and arriving at measurable variables to represent these factors. Finally, the relationships among the variables must be determined and expressed in mathematical form.

SOLVE MODEL

Once the model has been constructed, the next step is to arrive at a solution to the model. For a normative model, this involves mathematical techniques for arriving at the best strategy or alternative. In the case of complex linear programming problems, this may involve numerous computations. In the case of a descriptive model where usually there is no solution, the model can be termed "solved" when it accurately describes the system under study. This is arrived at by manipulating the model until this point is reached.

TEST SOLUTION

Once the model is solved, the solution should be tested before it is applied to a large segment of the organization's operations. The reason for this should be clear: Testing the solution enables management to determine the effect of the model on a small scale, and, if any errors are discovered, the model can be altered accordingly and a new solution obtained. For example, the solution to an inventory problem could be tested on a small scale using perhaps one warehouse or store. In this way one can gain some insight into the value of the solution and adjust accordingly if changes are necessary. Then and only then should the solution be applied on a full-scale basis.

DEVELOP CONTROLS

Once the model is constructed and solved, there must be a provision for *concurrent* control. In other words, the model must be carefully and continually reexamined in order to insure that the variables and relationships have not changed. Whenever there is a change in any of the variables included in the model, it may be necessary to completely revise it. There are also many forces at work which affect management decisions but over which the manager has little or no control. Thus the need for tight *monitoring* of the model is vital. The reader can imagine, for example, the impact of the fuel shortage on the models used by oil companies for allocating fuel to service stations.

IMPLEMENT SOLUTION

After the model has been solved and tested, the solution should be implemented by or recommended to the manager, in cases where staff analysts have constructed the model. In any case, the manager must be aware of the objectives, assumptions, omissions, and limitations of the model. After this is done, further reformulation of the problem may result because of some previously overlooked factor which is deemed important. Before the solution is finally implemented, all personnel who will utilize the solution produced by the model should be made aware of the basic rationale behind the model and the advantages to be gained by implementing the solution. The manager must keep in mind at all times the behavioral ramifications involved in implementing change. These were discussed in Chapter 11. A well-constructed model may not provide its true benefit if individuals in the organization resist implementation or pay only token service to the solution provided by the model. Thus behavioral factors can vitally affect the success of management science solutions and must be considered by the man-

−3

g management science models

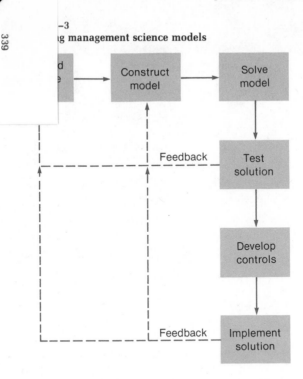

ager. The entire process for constructing management science models is illustrated in Figure 12–3.

Contributions of the management science school to the practice of management

Managers were faced with the problem of *planning, organizing, and controlling* their organizations' operations long before the advent of the electronic computer and management science models; and they would still have to perform these functions if the field of management science did not exist today. In other words, it must be recognized that management science *is not* a substitute for management. Mathematical models can be especially useful as an *aid* to the manager performing the functions of *planning and controlling production and operations.* In order to justify its existence to the practicing manager, however, management science models must provide for more efficient and effective planning and controlling.

Finally, the reader should not construe our discussions in this section of the book as implying that mathematical models can provide the entire basis for *all* management decisions. This is inconceivable. We saw in the prior section (Behavioral School of Management) that there are many kinds of management decisions that cannot rest solely on the manipulation of quantitative data. Many behavioral models are utilized in which all variables are not quantified. Also, successful implementation of a mathematical model must apply behavioral as well as mathematical science, because the resultant solution must be implemented by human beings.

Summary

Thus far in this book we have examined the Classical School of Management which was concerned, among other things, with the structure of formal organizations, the process of management, and the functions of a manager; and the Behavioral School, with its emphasis on human relations and the scientific approach to the study of human behavior in organizations. In this section the reader will be introduced to the third major block of material in the field of management, the Management Science School. We have already noted that it has probably made its greatest contribution in the areas of production management and operations management. In the following chapters, selected management science concepts and models will be discussed as well as the elements of information systems which support production and operations functions. While numerous models could be examined, we have chosen those which describe generally the contribution of Management Science to planning and controlling the production and operations functions in organizations. The management problems which relate to production and operations are primarily technical in nature. Consequently managers can use relatively straightforward engineering, statistical, and mathematical approaches which are, in essence, advanced forms of methods first developed by proponents of scientific management.

Discussion and review questions

1. "The classical bureaucratic structure is a normative model for organizing a firm." Comment.
2. Are there any similarities between the Behavioral Science School and the Management Science School?
3. Create a problem which a manager might realistically face. Now break the problem down into its subproblems.
4. "Since a mathematical model cannot include every possible variable that affects a problem, it cannot be of much value as a decision aid." What is your opinion of this statement?
5. What roles do mathematical models play in the management process of planning, organizing, and controlling?

6. After several semesters at your school, you are tired of becoming very irritated at registration time (long lines, closed courses, general havoc and bedlam). You have decided that something must be done. You contact the registrar's office and offer your services as a consultant. Since they are desperate for any help they can receive, they accept your offer. You suggest that some kind of model needs to be developed. How would you go about developing this model? What would be some of the major considerations?

7. Assume that you drive to school each morning and more than one way exists to arrive at your destination (for example, freeway or through the city). You must decide which route to take. As you analyze this problem, the process of model building is actually taking place, although it is subjective in nature. What are some of the factors that would have to be considered in order to reach an effective decision?

8. Assume you are the athletic director at your school. You have been bombarded with complaints about the distribution of tickets to students for basketball games. Tickets become available four hours before each game. This creates long lines at ticket windows and much discomfort on rainy days. In addition, crowds form in the lobby, which makes seating by game time very difficult. You have decided to try and improve this system. You decide first to construct a model of the system. What would be the components, variables, and relationships in your model? Develop some alternative solutions.

Additional references

Bierman, H., Bonini, C., and Hausman, W. *Quantitative Analysis for Business Decisions.* Homewood, Ill.: Richard D. Irwin, Inc., 1973.

Churchman, C. W., Ackoff, R. L., and Arnoff, E. L. *Introduction to Operations Research.* New York: John Wiley and Sons, Inc., 1957.

Laufer, A. C. *Operations Management.* Cincinnati: South-Western Publishing Co., 1975.

Levin, R. I., and Kirkpatrick, C. A. *Quantitative Approaches to Management.* New York: McGraw-Hill Book Co., 1975.

Mayer, R. R. *Production and Operations Management.* New York: McGraw-Hill Book Co., 1975.

Miller, D. W., and Starr, M. K. *Executive Decisions and Operations Research.* Englewood Cliffs, N.J.: Prentice-Hall, Inc., 1970.

Monks, J. G. *Operations Management: Theory and Problems.* New York: McGraw-Hill Book Co., 1977.

Paik, C. M. *Quantitative Methods for Managerial Decisions.* New York: McGraw-Hill Book Co., 1973.

Plane, D. R., and Kochenberger, G. A. *Operations Research for Managerial Decisions.* Homewood, Ill.: Richard D. Irwin, Inc., 1972.

Shore, B. *Operations Management.* New York: McGraw-Hill Book Co., 1973.

Thornton, B. M., and Preston, P. *Introduction to Management Science: Quantitative Approaches to Managerial Decisions.* Columbus, Ohio: Charles E. Merrill Publishing Co., 1977.

Vollmann, T. *Operations Management: A Systems Model-Building Approach.* Reading, Mass.: Addison-Wesley Publishing Co., 1973.

13

MANAGEMENT SCIENCE FRAMEWORK FOR DECISIONS

It is an important fact that in the final analysis the quality of the decisions managers reach is the yardstick of their performance. Effective decision making is a distinguishing feature of effective performance in all types of organizations.

Although managers are engaged in activities other than decision making, a main focus of the Management Science School is on the "how" of decisions. In the last 30 years, the systematic analysis of decision making has become known as "decision theory." The roots of decision theory are in the fields of statistics and the behavioral sciences. Its basic goal is to make decision making less of an art and more of a science. Since World War II operations researchers, statisticians, computer scientists, and behavioral scientists have sought to identify certain elements in decision making which are common to all decisions. Their goal is to provide a framework for decision makers which enables them more effectively to analyze a complex situation containing numerous alternatives and possible consequences.

Types of decisions and level in the organization

Decision making is a responsibility of all managers regardless of functional area or level in the organization. Some of these decisions may have a strong impact on the organization while others will be important but less crucial. The important point, however, is that *all* will have some effect (positive or negative, large or small) on the organization. While managers in various kinds of organizations may be separated by background, life-style, and distance, they all sooner or later must make decisions. That is, they face a situation involving several alternatives and their decision involves a comparison between the alternatives and an evaluation of the outcome. In this section we shall present a classification system into which various kinds of decisions can be placed.

TYPES OF DECISIONS

Management scientists interested in decision theory have developed several ways of classifying different types of decisions. Generally they are similar, differing mainly in terminology. We shall use the distinction suggested by Herbert Simon, who distinguishes between two types of decisions:[1]

1. Programmed decisions. If a problem or situation occurs often, a routine procedure is usually developed for solving it. Thus decisions

---

[1] Herbert Simon, *The New Science of Management Decisions*, (New York: Harper and Row, 1960), pp. 5–6.

are programmed to the extent that they are routine and repetitive and a specific procedure has been developed for handling them. Periodic automatic reorders of inventory in a business firm and the necessary grade-point average for good academic standing in a college are examples of programmed decisions.

2. **Nonprogrammed decisions.** When problems are broad, novel, and unstructured they require nonprogrammed decisions. As such there is no established procedure for handling the problem either because it has not arisen in exactly the same manner before or because it is complex or extremely important. Such decisions deserve special treatment. Examples of these problems are those of a business firm that is considering diversifying into new products and markets and a college that is considering constructing new classroom facilities.

LEVEL IN THE ORGANIZATION

While the above two classifications are broad, they do point out the importance of differentiating between programmed and nonprogrammed decisions. The managements of most organizations face many structured, repetitive problems in their daily operations. These decisions should be treated as such without expending unnecessary resources or time on them. Just as importantly, problems requiring nonprogrammed decisions must be correctly identified since it is this type of decision making that forms the basis for allocating billions of dollars in resources each year in our economy. Unfortunately, it is this type of human decision process that we know least about. Figure 13–1 illustrates the types of problems dealt with and the types of decision required at different levels in the organization. It indicates that the type of decision varies with the type of problem as well as the level in the organization where the decision is made.

Programmed decisions can be handled through rules, standard operating procedures, and the development of specific procedures for handling them. In recent years, management scientists have facilitated the handling of these types of decisions through the development of mathematical models.

Nonprogrammed decisions have traditionally been handled by general problem-solving processes, judgment, intuition, and creativity. Modern management techniques have not, unfortunately, made nearly the advances in improving managerial performance in nonprogrammed decision making as they have in programmed decision making.

Figure 13–1 indicates that the main concern of top management typically is with nonprogrammed decisions, while first-level management is generally concerned with programmed decisions. Middle managers in most organizations concentrate primarily on programmed decisions, although in some organizations they participate in non-

FIGURE 13–1

Types of problems, types of decisions, and level in organization

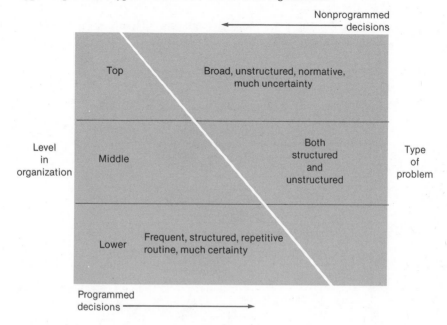

programmed decisions. What Figure 13–1 indicates, therefore, is that the nature, frequency, and degree of certainty surrounding a problem should dictate at what level of management the decision should be made.

The process of decision making

When a manager makes a decision it is, in effect the organization's response to a problem. As such, decisions should be thought of as *means* rather than ends. Every decision is the outcome of a dynamic process which is influenced by a multitude of forces. This process is presented in Figure 13–2. The reader should not, however, interpret this to mean that decision making is a fixed procedure. We present it as a sequential process rather than a series of steps to enable us to examine each element in the progression that leads to a decision. Figure 13–2 reveals that it is more applicable to nonprogrammed decisions than to programmed decisions. For example, problems that occur infrequently, are unstructured, and are characterized by a great deal of uncertainty regarding their outcome require the manager to utilize the entire process. For frequently occurring, structured problems it is not necessary to consider the entire process. If a policy is established or a specific rule or procedure developed to handle such problems it will not be necessary to develop and evaluate alternatives each time the problem arises.

The starting point in any analysis of decision making involves the determination of whether a decision needs to be made. If problems did

FIGURE 13–2
The decision-making process

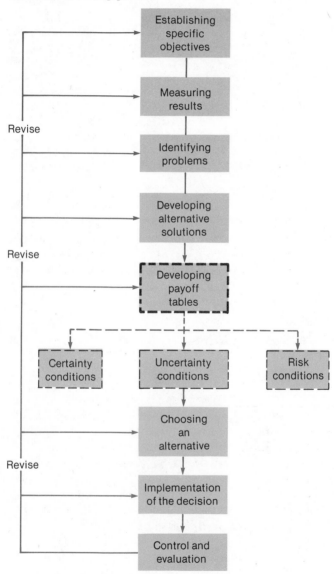

not exist, then there would be no need for decisions. For example, suppose that the marketing director of a local bank, at the beginning of the planning period, *establishes a specific* marketing *objective* of increasing the number of personal checking account customers of the bank by 10 percent. Suppose at the end of the planning period the director *measures results* and finds the objective has not been adequately accomplished. If this is the case then the marketing director must *identify the problem* and some kind of decision will be required to solve this problem. However, before making a decision, the director would *develop* a number of *feasible alternatives* (actually these are potential solutions to the problem) and consider the potential payoffs and possible consequences of each possible solution. For example, two possible solutions might be to (1) lower the service charges on personal checking accounts or (2) eliminate all service charges on personal checking accounts ("free checking").

The marketing director would consider the payoffs and possible consequences of each course of action and *choose an alternative.* However any decision is only an abstraction if it is not implemented. In other words, effective *implementation* of the chosen alternative is necessary in order to solve the problem and achieve the objective. It is possible that a "good" decision can be damaged by poor implementation. In this sense, implementation may be just as important as the actual activity of choosing. This was highlighted in the middle section of the book where we saw that a manager's job is not limited to skill in choosing good solutions, but also includes the knowledge and skill necessary to transform the solution into behavior in the organization. Finally, the solution must be *evaluated* and *controlled.* In the first section of the book we saw that the management function of control involved periodic measurements of actual results, comparing the results with the original objective, and, if deviations exist, taking corrective action.

NATURE OF OBJECTIVES

Numerous forces influence the ability of the manager to achieve specific objectives. For example, the objective of a corporate manager cannot be stated simply as maximizing profits. Although profit is a necessary objective of a business organization, it is only one of many. The decision making of corporate managers may be directed toward other important objectives such as improving market share, developing human resources, producing a quality product, acting as a socially responsible organization, and many others.

Thus, managers often face situations where they cannot optimize two objectives simultaneously. If one is *optimized,* the other is *suboptimized.* For example: If output is optimized, employee morale may be suboptimized and vice versa. Another example would be a situation in which the attainment of a short-run objective such as reducing maintenance expense may lead to long-run consequence of increased production costs. In this case, the short-run goal was *optimized* at the cost of *suboptimizing* a long-run goal. Thus, the multiplicity of objectives complicates the real world of the decision maker by giving rise to a situation where objectives may actually conflict.

VARIABLES IN DECISION MAKING

Most decision problems require that a choice be made between alternative courses which may be affected by one or more "states of nature." In decision theory the term "states of nature" designates events *beyond a manager's control that could actually happen.* States of nature are completely uncontrollable from the vantage point of the decision maker. For example, a manufacturer of children's toys knows that the accuracy of production forecasts will depend in large measure upon the state of the overall economy. Similarly, the executive of a tobacco corporation is faced with the problem of how much and what type of each of the firm's products should be produced, given the government campaign against certain tobacco products. Finally, the reaction of a competitor is also an uncontrollable variable.

The term "strategy" is used to designate the course of action selected by the decision maker to deal with the possible states of nature. The uncontrollable states of nature, plus the strategy selected, interact to yield a desirable or undesirable end-result.

UTILITY OF THE DECISION

Every outcome resulting from the interaction of a given decision alternative and a particular state of nature has some relative utility or value with respect to the objective of the decision maker. This value may be measured in quantitative units, such as time, money, and number of units produced, or it may be measured in psychological terms, such as satisfaction. Units of psychological utility are, however, difficult to assess precisely. Because the concept of relative value can be defined clearly only in terms of objective units, the utility of a particular decision outcome is ordinarily expressed in monetary units, and is called the *payoff* of that outcome.

An application of decision theory

Figure 13–2 indicates that the management science school focuses attention on developing payoff tables and analyzing decision making under conditions of certainty, risk, and uncertainty.

THE PAYOFF TABLE

The *payoff table* is a convenient way to summarize all the elements of a decision problem. An illustration of a payoff table is presented in Table 13–1. Note that the payoff table *does not* eliminate the need for a decision. It only aids us in organizing pertinent data.

The data presented in Table 13–1 deal with monetary payoffs to a

TABLE 13–1
Payoff table for Exit Oil Company

Strategies available to management	State of nature: Demand for gasoline		
	Low	Moderate	High
Centralize the distribution of gasoline	$3,000,000	$1,500,000	$2,000,000
Decentralize the distribution of gasoline	1,000,000	1,500,000	3,700,000

decision maker in the Exit Oil Company. The decision maker has two distribution strategies and faces three possible states of nature. The decision involves selecting a strategy for centralizing or decentralizing the distribution of gasoline. The demand (state of nature) for gasoline is considered under three situations—low, moderate, and high. If the decision maker selects the strategy to decentralize and a low demand for gasoline occurs, the payoff will be $1 million. A decision to centralize the distribution in a market with moderate demand will result in a payoff of $1.5 million. The payoffs shown in Table 13–1 are considered *conditional values* because they are *conditioned* on the demand for gasoline in the marketplace. They represent the value (for example, $3,000,000) if the event (low demand and centralization of distribution) should occur. The distribution alternatives are controlled by the manager, and the states of nature (demand) are *uncontrollable*. The manager must select the alternative based on what the state of nature (demand) will be.

DECISION-MAKING PROCESS: CERTAINTY

When a manager knows exactly which state of nature will occur, a circumstance of *certainty* exists. This means that the manager will be able to make perfectly accurate decisions, time after time. Of course, this type of decision-making environment is difficult, if not impossible, to find.

In reaching certainty decisions, the manager would only have to utilize a part of a payoff table and would have to examine a number of different strategies, but only the payoffs related to the one state of nature which will occur. Suppose that the decision maker at Exit Oil knows for sure that demand for gasoline is going to be high, and the objective is to generate the largest possible monetary payoff. Examination of Table 13–1 indicates that the best payoff under a condition of high demand will be achieved if distribution is decentralized. Thus, the manager will select the decentralization strategy.

The manager is fortunate because perfect information about demand is available. This is the exception. In many situations the manager will not know with certainty what state of nature will occur. The manager is forced to use *probabilities* when faced with a situation that requires making a decision under these types of conditions.

DECISION-MAKING PROCESS: RISK

In some situations the manager is able to develop estimates of the likelihood of the various states of nature occurring. This ability to estimate may be due to experience, incomplete but reliable information, or intelligence. In situations where estimates are made there is a *risk* involved, but knowledge for reaching a decision is not completely lacking. When risk is involved the situation requires the use of probability estimates.

Decision making under risk conditions, in addition to requiring probability estimates, also necessitates the use of *expected values*. Recall that the payoffs listed in Table 13–1 are conditional values because they will occur only if a specfic state of nature occurs and a specific strategy is chosen. *An expected value is the conditional value multiplied by the probability of occurrence of the state of nature.* Suppose that Exit Oil has knowledge that there is a 0.30 chance for high demand, a 0.50 chance for moderate demand, and a 0.20 chance for low demand. Management could proceed to use these probabilities in conjunction with the data shown in Table 13–1. Table 13–2 shows an unexpected value payoff table using the probability estimates.

TABLE 13–2
Expected value payoff table for Exit Oil Company

Strategies available to management	State of nature: Demand for gasoline (probability of demand)			Total expected value
	Low 0.20	Moderate 0.50	High 0.30	
Centralize the distribution of gasoline	$600,000	$750,000	$ 600,000	$1,950,000
Decentralize the distribution of gasoline	$200,000	$750,000	$1,110,000	$2,060,000

The payoffs in Table 13–2 were calculated by taking the conditional payoffs in Table 13–1 and multiplying them by the probability of a particular level of demand occurring. The calculations for the centralization alternative are:

Total expected value = Low demand probability × Conditional value + Moderate demand probability × Conditional value + High demand probability × Conditional value.

or

Total expected value = 0.20 ($3,000,000) + 0.50 ($1,500,000) + 0.30 ($2,000,000)

or

Total expected value = $600,000 + $750,000 + $600,000
= $1,950,000

The total expected value for each strategy is equal to the sum of its expected values under each possible state of nature. The $1,950,000 figure represents an *average payoff* that would be received by Exit Oil if they decided to centralize on a great number of occasions under the same conditions.

In reviewing Table 13–2 it can be seen that the total expected value if the company centralizes its gasoline distribution is $1,950,000, while a decision to decentralize yields a total expected value of $2,060,000. Using only the dollar figures, it would be best to decentralize because of the greater expected value. The difference in the total expected values is $110,000. This means that the decision should be made with caution because of small differences in the two expected values. Also remember that the probabilities are estimates that could be off target. This clearly indicates that the decision to centralize or decentralize is being reached under conditions of risk.

DECISION-MAKING PROCESS: UNCERTAINTY

A number of individuals define decision theory as focusing primarily upon making decisions and improving the decision process under conditions of *uncertainty*.[2] This is when the manager is faced with reaching a decision with no historical data concerning the probabilities of occurrence of the states of nature.

A number of different decision criteria have been proposed as possible bases for decisions under uncertainty. These decision criteria include:

---

[2] See Harold Bierman, Charles P. Bonini, and Warren H. Hausman, *Quantitative Analysis for Business Decisions* (Homewood, Ill.: Richard D. Irwin, Inc., 1973).

1. Maximizing the maximum possible payoff—the *maximax* criterion (optimistic).
2. Maximizing the minimum possible payoff—the *maximin* criterion (pessimistic).
3. Minimizing the maximum possible regret to the decision maker—the *minimax* criterion (regret).
4. Assuming equally likely probabilities for the occrrence of each possible state of nature—the *insufficient reason* criterion.

The first step in making decisions under conditions of uncertainty is to construct a conditional value payoff table like that presented in Table 13–1. The next step is the selection and application of one of the decision criteria.

Maximax criterion. Hurwicz[3] suggested that some decision makers think optimistically about the occurrence of events influencing a decision. If this philosophy is followed, the manager will select that strategy under which it is possible to receive the most favorable payoff. It is dangerous to employ this criterion because it ignores possible losses and the chances of making or not making a profit. A completely optimistic manager will examine the condition value table and seek to maximize the maximum possible gain (maximax).

Returning to Table 13–1, the manager using the maximax criterion will list the most favorable payoff for each strategy as follows:

Centralize . . . $3,000,000
Decentralize . . . $3,700,000

If maximum monetary payoff is the objective, the decision maker will decentralize.

Maximin criterion. There are managers who make decisions believing that only the worst possible outcome can occur. Wald proposed that this pessimism results in the selection of that strategy which maximizes the least favorable payoff.[4]

The pessimistic manager will examine Table 13–1 and look at the minimum payoffs for each strategy.

Centralize . . . $1,500,000
Decentralize . . . $1,000,000

These figures will result in the decision to centralize the distribution of gasoline. The decision maker has maximized the minimum payoff (maximin).

---

[3] Leonid Hurwicz, "Optimality Criteria for Decision Making under Ignorance," Cowles Commission Discussion Paper, Statistics, No. 370, 1951 (mimeographed); and R. Duncan Luce and Howard Raiffa, *Games and Decisions* (John Wiley & Sons, Inc., New York, 1957).

[4] A more complete discussion of the maximin criterion is presented in David W. Miller and Martin K. Starr, *The Structure of Human Decisions* (Englewood Cliffs, N.J.: Prentice-Hall, Inc., 1967), p. 116.

Minimax criterion. If a manager selects a strategy, and if a state of nature occurs that does not result in the most favorable payoff, regret occurs. The manager is regretful that the strategy selected did not lead to the best payoff. Savage introduced the minimax criterion to clarify the decision process which involves regret.[5]

Once the manager makes a choice and the state of nature or competitive action has occurred, the payoff is received. If the manager had known which of the various states of nature or competitive actions would occur, the strategy with no regret would have been selected.

TABLE 13–3
Regret table for Exit Oil Company

Strategies available to management	States of nature: Demand for gasoline			Maximum regret
	Low	Moderate	High	
Centralize the distribution of gasoline..........................	0	0	$1,700,000	$1,700,000
Decentralize the distribution of gasoline........................	$2,000,000	0	0	$2,000,000

Thus, *managerial regret is defined as the payoff for each strategy under every state of nature of competitive action subtracted from the most favorable payoff that is possible with the occurrence of the particular event.* For example, in Table 13–1, the most favorable payoff if the demand is high would be $3,700,000. If the manager decided to decentralize and the demand was high, he would have no regret ($3,700,000 − 3,700,000 = 0). However, assuming a decision to centralize, and high demand for gasoline exists, there would be a regret of $1,700,000 ($3,700,000 − 2,000,000 = $1,700,000).

The regret payoffs are presented in Table 13–3. The decision maker, in attempting to minimize regret, would decide to centralize. The payoff table indicates that a decision to centralize means that no matter what the demand for gasoline is the Exit Oil manager will never have a regret of more than $1,700,000. That is, centralization will minimize maximum regret (minimax).

Insufficient-reason criterion. The three preceding decision criteria assume that without any previous experience it is not worthwhile to assign probabilities to the states of nature. One well-known concept, however, is utilized in introducing probability into decision making

---

[5] L. J. Savage, "The Theory of Statistical Decision," *Journal of the American Statistical Association* (March 1951), pp. 55–67.

under conditions of uncertainty. This is referred to as the *insufficient-reason criterion*.[6] This criterion states that if managers do not know the probabilities of occurrence for the various states of nature, they should assume that all are equally likely to occur. In other words, managers should assign equal probabilities to each state of nature or competitive action.

Applying the insufficient reason criterion to the conditional values in Table 13–1 yields the following:

$$\text{Centralize Expected value} = \tfrac{1}{3}\,(\$3,000,000 + 1,500,000 + 2,000,000) = 2,166,667$$

and

$$\text{Decentralize Expected value} = \tfrac{1}{3}\,(\$1,000,000 + 1,500,000 + 3,700,000) = 2,066,667$$

The manager is faced with a close decision but will decide to centralize the distribution of gasoline.

A review of choices. The four decision criteria used for the Exit Oil decision illustrate that, depending on the orientation of the manager, different strategies will be selected. The following decisions will be made:

1. *Optimist* will decentralize.
2. *Pessimist* will centralize.
3. *Regreter* will centralize.
4. *Insufficient Reasoner* will centralize.

This example employing only two alternative choices and three demand situations indicates that uncertainty decision making is difficult. The choice of a criterion is a personalistic phenomenon. Each decision maker at different times probably acts on each of these four criteria in making decisions.

Summary

In the preceding discussion of decision-making criteria, it was easy to see that the decision theory framework can provide the manager with a systematic method for analyzing problems. This is one of the practical advantages of decision theory. *It encourages the manager to discover and enumerate potential strategies and possible states of nature.*

---

[6] This also referred to as the LaPlace criterion and Bayes's postulate. See Robert Schlaifer, *Probability and Statistics for Business Decisions* (New York: McGraw Hill, Inc., 1959), pp. 445–46.

As noted in Chapter 12, decision theory models are useful for complex-organized types of problems. Recall that these problems contain a smaller number of variables, but they behave under conditions of uncertainty, that is, they are probabilistic. Placing them in a decision theory framework (by using conditional and expected value concepts) enables the manager to give "structure" to such problems. As such, the framework enables the manager to add some organization to a situation where none existed. Thus, while a manager may not actually construct payoff tables, the disciplined process of enumerating possible states of nature is itself a benefit of decision theory models.

The Management Science School uses as its central focal point the decision-making process. Decision theory enables us to study systematically how managers think about decision making. The framework is only a step in the direction of attempting to understand how decisions are made and how decision making can be improved.

Discussion and review questions

1. Think of a recent decision made by some organization with which you are familiar—your local school system, your college or university, your state or local government, some manufacturing organization or public service agency. Discuss (1) exactly what type of problem was being confronted and (2) what objectives and choice criteria were used.

2. The stock of the Payoff Corporation has paid dividends of $1.60 per share in 13 of the last 20 dividend periods. The other seven times, it has paid $1.40. What is the expected dividend?

3. Discuss what is meant by the statement that each decision situation and outcome has a specific utility for each manager.

4. Briefly describe the type of manager that would be most inclined to employ a maximax criterion—a maximin criterion.

5. The Ace Music Company is considering two strategies for promoting the records of a new recording artist. One strategy is to concentrate entirely on television advertising, the other is to concentrate entirely on newspaper advertising. In the past, the company's profits have been influenced by general economic conditions. The profit payoffs for each strategy depend upon future economic conditions as noted in the following table.

| | States of nature | | |
Strategies	Downturn in the economy	Stable economy	Upturn in the economy
(S₁) Television advertising.......	$ 4,000	$40,000	$60,000
(S₂) Newspaper advertising......	$10,000	$20,000	$30,000

a. What would the maximax choice be?
b. What would the minimax choice be?
c. What would the maximin choice be?
d. What would the insufficient reason choice be?

6. A dairy store manager observes the daily sales of skim milk for a 100-day period and develops the table of sales presented below.

Skim milk sales

Quantities purchased	Number of days
40	20
50	15
70	15
100	30
120	20

The milk sells for $0.30 a quart and the cost to the store manager of securing the milk from the dairy is $0.20.
a. If 70 units are stocked every day, what will be the firm's expected profit per day over the long run?
b. Using the data presented in the table, what quantity (40, 50, 70, 100, or 120) should be purchased every day to maximize long-run profits?

7. Why is it difficult to assume that many business decisions are made under conditions of certainty?

8. What decision-making factors are not presented in payoff tables?

9. An analysis and forecast of next year's sales results in the following probability distribution:

Total demand	Probability
1,000 units	0.20
1,200 units	0.20
1,400 units	0.40
1,600 units	0.20

The price per unit is $58. The cost of the product is $38. If the product is not sold during the year, it is worthless.
a. Prepare a table of conditional values.
b. Prepare a table of expected values, and indicate the optimum choice if management is attempting to optimize profits.

10. Why is it necessary and advisable to consider decision making in the domain of each of the three schools of management?

11. Does the decision-making process involve the use of any principles of managing? Explain.

Additional references

Churchman, C. W.   *Challenge to Reason.* New York: McGraw-Hill Book Company, 1968.

Eilon, S.   "What Is a Decision?" *Management Science* 16B, 1969: 172–89.

Halter, A. N., and Dean, G. W.   *Decisions under Uncertainty.* Cincinnati: South-Western Publishing Company, 1971.

Hein, L. W.   *The Quantitative Approach to Managerial Decisions.* Englewood Cliffs, N.J.: Prentice-Hall, Inc., 1967.

Kassorf, S.   *Normative Decision Making.* Englewood Cliffs, N.J.: Prentice-Hall, Inc., 1970.

Magee, J. F.   "Decision Trees for Decision Making," *Harvard Business Review* 42 (1964): 72–75.

Morgan, B. W.   *An Introduction to Bayesian Statistical Decision Processes.* Englewood Cliffs, N.J.: Prentice-Hall, 1968.

Raiffa, H.   *Decision Analysis.* Reading, Mass.: Addison-Wesley Publishing Co., Inc., 1968.

Schellenberger, R. E.   *Managerial Analysis.* Homewood, Ill.: Richard D. Irwin, Inc., 1969.

Schlaifer, R.   *Analysis of Decisions under Uncertainty.* New York: McGraw-Hill Book Co., Inc., 1967.

PRACTICAL EXERCISE I
The New Airport

Jim Wilkerson has recently been appointed as head of a new section in the state's Department of Transportation. The new section was specifically charged by the Secretary of Transportation with the responsibility of selecting sites in the state for the construction of two large airports. The state had historically been a rural state with many large farms and a large scale state parks system. However, growth in the states industrial segment, an influx of population, and the growth in several nearby metropolitan areas in bordering states had necessitated creation of the new section. At the present time the state has only one airport capable of handling commercial jets. Specifically, Jim has been given two objectives:

1. Given the present and future needs for air transportation in the state, identify the two most desirable sites.
2. Consider the impact on the communities involved.

Jim is particularly concerned with the second objective. While not really an ecologist or an environmentalist, he does consider the environmental impact to be important and is also concerned about preserving the wilderness and wildlife in the state. He believes the best way to insure that such issues are considered is to conduct public hearings in all of the proposed site areas. Accordingly, for the past three months his section has actively sought and received much public input into its site studies. Jim knows that many of his peers in the Department of Transportation do not share his views and that many of them consider the public to be "uninformed" on such matters and their input to be more "emotional" than "rational." Last Monday, the Commissioner of Transportation asked Jim to come to his office. The following conversation took place:

Commissioner: Jim, I'm glad to see you and want you to know that I think you're getting this new section off to a good start.

Jim: Thank you, Commissioner. I certainly am glad to get the assignment and I must admit that I truly enjoy the work.

Commissioner: The only problem I see is that you may run short of time.

Jim: Why do you say that?

Commissioner: Jim, while I can't argue with your efforts at public participation, I must say that I believe it just won't work. You need a more objective or rational approach.

Jim: Could you explain what you mean?

Commissioner: When you've been in this business as long as I have, the one thing you learn is that you can't please everybody. Remember, one of us is going to have to defend the proposed sites before the state legislators and other politicians as well as the general public. How, for example, are you going to tell farmers that the two airports ought to be constructed on farmland instead of wilderness? Or, if it goes the other way, how are you going to explain to the environmentalists and the Department of Parks that they should be constructed in the wilderness instead of on farmland? Do you see what I mean Jim? Are you going to say, "On the basis of public opinion?" What public?

Jim: I can see your point but surely you see the impact these airports will have on the public, and aren't we here to serve the public?

Commissioner: Again I ask you: what public? All I know is we need two airport sites that will be accepted. We need a more objective approach that we can lean on instead of an emotion-based recommendation. Can't you crank up some kind of quantitative model? You can work in your environmental factors but also some economic figures and transportation costs. Believe me, the politicians like numbers. It's hard to argue with numbers, and they can lean on them when the press starts asking questions. Believe me, Jim, we're not fooling around here. We need to come up with two sites that are acceptable. We've got to be on firm ground, and numbers and economic payoffs can give it to us.

As Jim left the Commissioner's office he was unsure about what to do. The Commissioner was probably right in some respects, he thought. He decided to consider all the factors in making his decision. One thing was sure, he had seven possible sites and just two weeks to select the two final ones.

Questions for analysis:

1. What does this indicate about the process of decision making?
2. What is your opinion of the Commissioner's advice?
3. Do the values of society influence managerial decisions? Should they? Are they influencing Jim? The Commissioner?

PRACTICAL EXERCISE II
The Old Man

Ted Gray smiled as he carried some of his belongings into the huge oak paneled office which would be his on Monday. At the relatively young age of 46 he had been appointed President of Newtown Developers, the nation's largest developer of planned model cities. He was appointed three months ago when Don Stevens announced his retirement.

Stevens, or "The Old Man" as he was affectionately known in the organization, had been the only other president Newtown ever had. Most agreed he was responsible for the tremendous growth and success the company had achieved in the last two decades. Ted had worked closely with "The Old Man" for the past seven years and was his choice to succeed him.

Ted had learned all he could from Stevens. The two were very close and had spent much time together discussing management philosophies, decision making, and human relations. While they sometimes differed in opinion, the discussions were always helpful to Ted.

When he opened the top drawer in his new desk, Ted was surprised to find two old and worn pieces of paper that Don had apparently left behind. Both contained statements from Clarence Randall, formerly the head of the Inland Steel Company during the 1950s.* The first read as follows:

> Decision making is a lonely business, and the greater the degree of responsibility, the more intense the loneliness. It is human to wish to share the risk of error and to feel the comforting strength of outside support, like the flying buttresses along the wall of a medieval cathedral. But the strong man, the one who gives free enterprise its vitality, is the man who weighs thoughtfully the entire range of available opinion and then determines policy be relying solely on his own judgement.

The second piece of paper contained Randall's response to the question: "What, then are the outward attributes displayed by a man who comes to be regarded by his associates as one who may be highly trusted with the authority to say 'yes' or 'no'?" It read as follows:

The instinct for recognizing when a problem exists.

The ability to articulate the problem with clarity.

The ability to saturate himself with pertinent data.

The ability to maintain an open mind until the evidence is in.

A sense of urgency that forces him to work as rapidly as possible.

The courage not to look back after his decision is made.

Ted put the pieces of paper in his briefcase to give to Stevens the next time he saw him. Then he thought, "I'm still learning from that old goat. I bet he left them here for me."

---

* From Clarence B. Randall, "The Lonely Art of Decision Making," *Dun's Review and Modern Industry*, June 1959, p. 47.

As Ted left the building on his way home he thought, "On Monday, I'll be the Old Man." He wasn't sure now if he was glad or scared.

Questions for analysis:

1. Given today's technology, rapidly changing environment, and the increased complexities facing managers, what should Ted Gray do with the two pieces of paper? In other words, would they be of any use to him as he begins his term as President? Discuss in detail.

2. Is there anything in the statements about decision making that has changed in 20 years?

14

MANAGEMENT
INFORMATION
SYSTEMS

MANAGEMENT IN ACTION*

Recently a number of companies have begun to use computers in new ways to provide direct, personal support for managers. Known as decision support systems (DSS), these new approaches help managers retrieve, manipulate, and display information needed for making decisions.

Gould, Inc., for example, has combined a large visual display and video terminals with a computer information system. Designed to help managers make comparisons and analyze problems, it instantly prepares tables and charts in response to simple commands. IBM, working with the First National Bank of Chicago, has developed a similar system, which produces graphs and charts in color on a television screen.

Because professional judgments and insights are critical in decision making, a DSS must be designed to support a manager's skills at all stages of decision making—from problem identification to choosing the relevant data to work with, picking the approach to be used in making the decision, and evaluating the alternative courses of action. A DSS must produce information in a form managers understand, when such information is needed, and under their direct control.

* Excerpted from Eric D. Carlson, "Decision Support Systems: Personal Computing Services For Managers," *Management Review* (January 1977), p. 5.

In our discussions of the management functions of organizing the structure of organizations we noted that the modern organization consists of interrelated departments and units. In planning and controlling them, management must depend upon various sources of information, both external and internal to the organization. This has become necessary as organizations grow in complexity, thereby increasing the number of points at which decisions must be made, ranging from individual decision makers at the lowest operating levels to policy-making groups in top management.

Systems designed to provide information to managers to support the process of decision making are certainly not new developments. In fact, the accounting system was actually the first management information system. While certainly valuable, the financial accountants' statements have limited value for managers in other functional areas and other levels in the organization. The need for information for other purposes, collected from other sources, has become necessary. The goal of this chapter is to examine this growing interest in management information systems (MIS).

The need for and purpose of management information systems

Effective planning and controlling in any organization requires relevant information. We saw in the last chapter that the quality of a decision depends greatly on an understanding of the circumstances surrounding an issue and knowledge of the available alternatives, states of nature, and competitive strategies. The better the information, the better the resulting decision. Unfortunately, an organization has no memory other than the memory of the people who manage it. Because individuals come and go, managers must out of necessity develop some type of information system. The development of information systems obviously recognizes the need for information in support of managerial decisions. In fact, it is a logical extension of the emphasis in the Management Science School on decision making and quantitative tools, since both require information inputs. The need arises for (1) managing existing information and (2) utilizing the vast data-generating capacity of the computer.

MANAGING EXISTING INFORMATION

The ability of organizations to generate information is really not a problem since most are capable of producing massive amounts of information and data. In fact, the last decade has often been described as the "Age of Information." Why then do so many managers complain that they have insufficient or irrelevant information on which to base their everyday decisions? Specifically, most managers' complaints fall into the following categories.

1. There is too much of the wrong kind of information and not enough of the right kind.
2. Information is so scattered throughout the organization that it is difficult to locate answers to simple questions.
3. Vital information is sometimes suppressed by subordinates or managers in other functional areas.
4. Vital information often arrives long after it is needed.

Historically, managers did not have to deal with an overabundance of information. Instead they gathered a bare minimum of information and hoped that their decisions would be reasonably good. In fact, in some business organizations marketing research came to be recognized as an extremely valuable staff function in the 1930s and 1940s because it provided information for marketing decisions where previously there had been little or none. Today, by contrast, most managers often feel "buried" by the deluge of information and data that comes across their desks.

UTILIZING THE CAPACITY OF COMPUTERS

The means for greater production of information are certainly available. New and better computers and numerous other information—handling equipment are being developed at a rapid rate. New management science models are also being developed which improve the quality of information while at the same time reduce the cost of producing it. Still, managers complain of information losses, delays, and distortion. Apparently many managers have been so concerned about advancing technology, the abundance of new computers, management science models, and their potential that they have overlooked the planning necessary for the sale effective use of these developments. This has happened to such an extent that, for business firms, many people believe the gathering, storing, manipulating, and organizing of information for management decisions costs as much as or more than direct factory labor.[1]

Unfortunately, in some organizations computers are not being utilized effectively for providing managers with the best information

[1] There are numerous excellent articles which address this and related MIS issues. For examples, see Marshall K. Evans and Low R. Hague, "Master Plan For Information Systems," Harvard Business Review (January–February 1962), pp. 92–103; Steven L. Mandell, "MIS Is Going To Pieces," California Management Review (Summer 1975), pp. 51–57; William M. Zani, "Blueprint for MIS," Harvard Business Review (November–December 1970), pp. 94–101.

for decision making. There are many nonmeasurable (but extremely important) costs of this problem. This is because the effectiveness of most organizations is more often than not at the mercy of the information available to managers. In the dynamic environment faced by most managers, the need is great for swift and effective decisions. Thus, while the cost of managing information may be high, the cost of mismanaging it (bad decisions) is even higher.

The problem appears to be that the information requirements of today's managers have changed greatly in the past decade but the basic information arrangements within most organizations have remained essentially the same. The problem of generating the right information at the right time must now be viewed in a much broader perspective than previously. The task of generating data for managerial decisions must be viewed as the function of a *management information system* rather than as solely the function of individual managers in the various functional areas of an organization.

PURPOSE OF MIS

From the foregoing discussion the purpose of MIS should be clear. We saw in the previous chapter that one of the vital tasks performed by managers is decision making. To make decisions they must have alternatives from which to choose, authority to implement the alternative they choose, and *information*. The importance of information becomes obvious when one realizes that managers rarely work with "things" but rather with "information about things." Thus, management information systems have one primary purpose: *to provide the manager with the necessary data for making intelligent decisions.*

At this point it is important to note that some people confuse MIS with electronic data processing (EDP). This is incorrect since EDP is merely one element of MIS. Much of what comprises an organization's information system is not computerized, although the part that is, is often significant. As a result of this misconception some managers fear that the development of MIS will replace rather than support the manager. To be successful, MIS must be viewed as a management tool. Managers must recognize the necessity for better quality information and view MIS as a means to improve their performance as managers in the still nonelectronic but very human task of decision making.

Information systems can take many forms. Some may be very simple, such as reading the *Wall Street Journal* every morning or carefully filling in check stubs to maintain careful control over your checking account balance. Some contain numbers, as do accounting systems, while some do not, as in the monitoring of consumer attitudes toward a firm's product. Finally, some are very complex, with an entire bank of computers and several hundred employees.

MIS DEFINED

The term "management information system" aptly describes its function, that is: *systems for providing information to management.* More specifically, we can define MIS as:

> An organized, structured complex of individuals, machines, and procedures for providing pertinent information from both external and internal sources. It supports the planning, control, and operations functions of an organization by providing uniform information for use as the bases for decision making.[2]

Organization structure and information needs

In the previous chapter we saw that managers faced either programmed decisions or nonprogrammed decisions depending on the type of problem. It was noted that as one moved higher in the organization the problems faced became less structured, with a great deal of uncertainty, and that the procedures used for dealing with the different types of problems also varied. At this point, it should be clear that the information requirements would also vary depending on the level in the organization and the type of decision being made. Note that in every instance, however, it is vital that appropriate information flow be directed to the proper decision points. In this context, then, every organization can be viewed as an information-decision system.

THE ORGANIZATION AS AN INFORMATION-DECISION SYSTEM

When viewed as the conversion of information into action through the process of decision making, an organization can be thought of as an information-decision system. The performance of management depends largely on the availability and timely utilization of information at all levels in the organization. Information is the glue that holds organizations together.

> Information-decision systems should be considered in conjunction with the fundamental managerial functions: planning, organizing, and controlling. If organization is to implement planning and control, if organization is tied to communication, and if communication is represented by an information-decision system, then the key to success in planning and controlling any operation lies in the information-decision system.[3]

---

[2] Based on Walter J. Kennevan, "MIS Universe," *Data Management* (September 1970), p. 63; and S. Smith, R. H. Brien, and J. E. Stafford, *Readings in Marketing Information Systems* (New York: Houghton Mifflin Co., 1968), p. 7.

[3] Richard A. Johnson, Fremont E. Kast, and James E. Rosenzweig, *The Theory and Management of Systems* (New York: McGraw Hill Book Co., 1973), p. 108.

The term *information-decision system* is also used to stress the importance of generating only that information which is needed in order to facilitate effective decision making at all levels in the organization. Consider the following actual occurrence:

> If the flow of information dries up, as some brokerage houses learned in the 1970s, the organization dies. Some houses simply could not keep track of purchases or sales, or determine who owned particular blocks of stock. They didn't know when they would collect the cash they needed to pay other bills. The partners were there, and the employees and customers too, but no one was talking to anyone else any more.[4]

TYPES OF INFORMATION AND ORGANIZATION LEVEL

The types as well as sources of information will vary by level in the organization. We shall use the classification of planning information, control information, and operational information.[5]

Planning information. This type of information relates to the top-management tasks of formulating objectives for the organization, the amounts and kinds of resources necessary to attain the objectives, and the policies that govern their use. Much of this information will come from external sources and will relate to such factors as the present and predicted state of the economy, availability of resources (non-human as well as human resources) and the political and regulatory environment. This information forms the input to the nonprogrammed types of decision made at this level in the organization.

Control information. This information aids managers to make decisions which are consistent with the achievement of organizational objectives as well as to see how efficiently resources are being used. It enables middle managers to determine if "actual results" are meeting "planned-for results" (objectives). It relies heavily on internal sources of information (often interdepartmental) and involves such problems as developing budgets and measuring the performance of first-line supervisors. The nature of problems faced at this level may result in either programmed or nonprogrammed types of decisions.

Operational information. This information relates to the day-to-day activities of the organization. It includes routine and necessary

---

[4] Harold J. Leavitt, William R. Dell, and Henry B. Eyring, *The Organizational World* (New York: Harcourt, Brace, and Javonovich, 1973), p. 58.

[5] Another similar classification is strategic, tactical, and technical. See John G. Burch and Felix R. Strater, "Tailoring the Information System," *Journal of Systems Management* (February 1973), pp. 34–38. The two are similar but the one presented in this text more closely relates to the management functions. Also see Robert Anthony, *Planning and Control Systems: A Framework for Analysis* (Boston: Division of Research, Harvard Business School, 1965) and Robert Anthony, John Dearden, and Richard Vancil, *Management Control Systems* (Homewood, Illinois: Richard D. Irwin, Inc., 1965).

types of information such as financial accounting, inventory control, and production scheduling. It is generated internally and, since it usually relates to specific tasks, it often comes from one designated department. First-line supervisors are the primary users of this information. Since decision making at this level in the organization usually involves structured types of problems, many problems at the operations level can be stated as mathematical relationships. These we referred to in the opening chapter in the section as the mathematical models of the Management Science School. The mathematical models discussed in the next two chapters are examples of such problems.

Designing a management information system

An appreciation of the importance and complexity of MIS can be gained by understanding the various information flows with which we must deal as well as the various functions an MIS must perform.

UNDERSTANDING INFORMATION FLOWS

Two broad types of information flows in a management information system can be distinguished. An *external-information* flow, which is information flowing to the organization *from* its outside environment or from the firm *to* its outside environment, and an *intra-organization* flow, which is information flowing within the organization.

External information flows. Again, the external information flows proceed from the organization to its environment and from the environment to the organization. We shall label the inward flow intelligence information and the outward flow organizational communications.

Intelligence information includes data on the various elements of the organization's operating environment such as clients, patients, customers, competitors, suppliers, creditors, and the government, for use in evaluating short-run trends in the immediate external environment. It also includes long-run strategic planning information on the economic environment such as consumer income trends and spending patterns for a business organization as well as developments in the social and cultural environment in which the organization operates. This type of information has long-run significance to the organization and aids in long-range planning.

Organizational communications flows outward from the organization to the various components of its external operating environment. In the case of a business organization any advertising or other promotional efforts are considered organizational communications. Whatever the type of organization, the content of this information flow is controlled by the organization. Although an important information flow, it nevertheless is an *outward* flow with which we will not be concerned in this book.

Intra-organization flows.   When intelligence information enters the organization, it must, along with internally generated information, reach the right manager at the right time to be useful. Thus, information must flow through as well as to the organization. Unfortunately, many managers believe that somehow once information is within the organization it will find its way to the proper person at the right time.

FIGURE 14–1
Management information flows and types of information

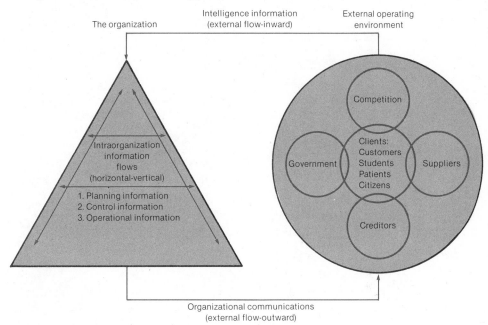

It must be recognized that within every organization there are *vertical* (both upward and downward), as well as *horizontal* information flows. The rationale of MIS is that all information flows must become part of the master plan of an MIS and not be allowed to function without a formal scheme and direction.[6] Figure 14–1 illustrates the various information flows and types of information discussed thus far.

---

[6] See Gerald S. Albaum, "Horizontal Information Flow: An Exploratory Study," *Academy of Management Journal* (March 1964), pp. 21–33 for a study of what happens to internal information in an unmanaged system. Also see Charles D. Scheive, "The Management Information System User: An Exploratory Behavioral Analysis," *Academy of Management Journal* (December 1976), pp. 577–90 for an interesting and different view of the problem.

THE FUNCTION OF AN MIS

All management information systems share several functions in varying degrees. We believe that an MIS should provide management with four major information services: determination of information needs, information gathering, information processing, and utilization.[7]

Determination of information needs. The beginning point is to attempt to answer such questions as: How much information is needed? How, when, and by whom will it be used? In what form is it needed? In other words, begin with an examination of the output requirements. One way is to classify information based on the level in the organization where it will be used as we did earlier in the chapter. Thus output requirements would be based on answers to such questions as: What information is necessary for planning and controlling operations at different organizational levels? What information is needed to allocate resources? What information is needed to evaluate performance? These types of questions recognize the fact that a different kind of information is needed for formulating organizational objectives than for scheduling production. They also recognize the fact that too much information may actually hinder a manager's performance. It is at this point that we must distinguish "need to know" types of information from "nice to know" types of information. One of the important realizations of the need for MIS is that *more information does not mean better performance.*

Information gathering and processing. The purpose of this service is to improve the overall quality of the information. It includes five component services. *Evaluation* involves determining how much confidence can be placed in a particular piece of information. Such factors as the credibility of the source, and reliability and validity of the data, must be determined. *Abstraction* involves editing and reducing incoming information and data in order to provide the managers with only that information which is relevant to their particular task. Once information has been gathered, the service of *indexing* is important in order to provide classification for storage and retrieval purposes. *Dissemination* entails getting the right information to the right manager at the right time. Indeed, this is the overriding purpose of an MIS. The final information processing service is that of *storage.* As noted earlier, an organization has no natural memory so every MIS must provide for

---

[7] These functions are briefly described in this section. However, they are the subjects of entire articles and volumes. The interested reader should consult Anthony, Dearden, and Vancil, *Management Control Systems;* Richard A. Johnson, R. Joseph Monsen, Henry P. Knowles and Borge O. Saxberg, *Management, Systems, and Society: An Introduction* (Pacific Palisades, California: Goodyear Publishing Company, Inc., 1976), Chapter 7; and Philip Kotler, "A Design for the Firm's Marketing Nerve Center," *Business Horizons* (Fall 1966), pp. 63–74. The functions discussed here are similar to those described in these works.

storage of information in order that it can be used again if needed. Modern electronic information storage equipment has greatly improved the "memory" capabilities of organizations.

③ **Information use.** How information is utilized depends greatly on its quality (accuracy), how it is presented (form), and its timeliness. This all relates to the basic need determined in the beginning. If the right questions are asked in the beginning, and the system is planned carefully, the user will be provided with relevant information. Remember that the major goal is to provide the right information to the right decision maker at the right time. This brings up the point that timeliness may take precedence over accuracy. If information is not available when it is needed then its accuracy is not important. In most cases, however, both are critical and timeliness is determined by the nature of the decisions that must be made. For example, a sales manager may find accurate weekly reports of sales for each company product to be adequate while an air-traffic controller needs accurate information every second. The functions of an MIS are presented in Figure 14–2.

In this section we have implied that a central management information unit is needed for the purpose of facilitating information flows both to and within the organization. An MIS does not focus on specific problems. Instead it monitors the external operating environment of the organization in addition to facilitating information flows within the organization. The question at this point is: How should such a unit be organized?

FIGURE 14–2
Functions of a management information system

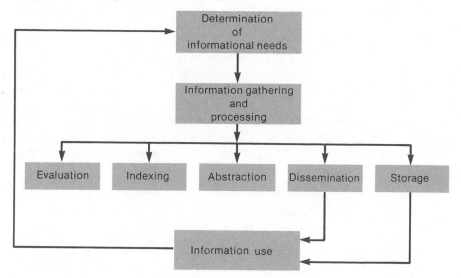

Organizing a management information system

In the past, many independent information systems have been developed for different organizational functions. Along with the development of accounting information systems, other line and staff groups in business and other organizations have developed information systems uniquely suited to their own needs. For example, in the late 1960s and early 1970s many firms were developing marketing information systems.[8] With developments in computer and communications technology it became evident that much of the information in one system should be interrelated with that in the others. Consider the following statement:

> Today the sophisticated marketing VP wants a whole range of data output so he can manage. No longer can he afford to be told that he has the territorial dollar sales volume in his files, but that the accounting department has inventory data, payroll has compensation and expense data, or the production department has scheduling data in its files in units or cartons or carloads. Nor will today's financial VP, responsible for critically forecasting cash flow, be content in having to go to marketing for sales data in dollars, to the production department for shipments, the credit department for payment records, and the accounting department for inventory in units by product by warehouse location. The information must be accessible in such form that he can search the data base, output the appropriate information, rearrange it into units, dollars, locations, and so on, then extrapolate and analyze it in terms meaningful to his department or job responsibilities.[9]

INTEGRATED INFORMATION SYSTEMS

The concept of an integrated total information system has been a goal of management for two decades or more. At last this goal is now becoming a reality as more and more private and public organizations are establishing components of information systems. Evolving systems are now in use in such business organizations as DuPont, Pillsbury, and General Electric.[10] The Planning, Programming, and Budgeting Systems (PPBS) used in many governmental agencies are examples of integrated information systems in the public sector.

The value of such an approach is apparent: Information in one area can be made available to other areas of the organization. If stored in a

---

[8] See Samuel V. Smith, Richard H. Brien, and James E. Stafford, *Readings in Marketing Information Systems* (New York: Houghton Mifflin Co., 1968) for an excellent collection of articles devoted to this topic.

[9] Irwin Kruger and James R. Miller, "Management Information Systems: Success or Failure," *Atlanta Economic Review* (November–December 1976), p. 11.

[10] The Decision Support System (DDS) discussed in the "Management in Action" excerpt at the outset of this chapter is also an example of integrated information systems.

FIGURE 14-3
Integrated management information system

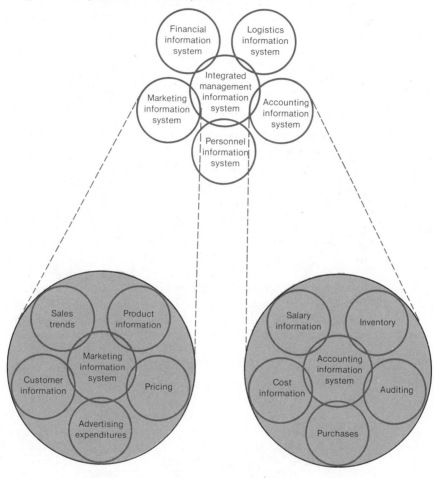

central computer, it can be utilized by all departments. Thus, sales data would not have to be kept by accounting, marketing, and production but would be available in one central data bank. This would likely increase both the accuracy and certainly the timeliness of the data. Figure 14-3 portrays the integrated information system concept illustrating two subsystems in more detail.

THE INFORMATION CENTER

If the concept of a truly integrated management information system is to become a reality, a single, separate information center must exist in the organization in order to make one individual responsible for the information. This is necessary because both users and suppliers of such information are scattered throughout the organization and some unit is needed to oversee the operation. In fact, a basic structural weakness in most organizations has been the absence of a central entity for the gathering and processing of information. As noted earlier, the information requirements of most managers have greatly changed in the past decade while the information arrangements within most organizations have remained essentially the same. Specifically, three tasks are necessary.

1. Dispersed information activities must be identified throughout the organization.
2. These activities must be viewed as parts of a whole.
3. These activities must be managed by a separate centralized information center.

This organizational unit must be responsible as a consultant, coordinator, and controller, for the functions of an MIS identified in Figure 14–2 – determining information needs, information gathering, information processing, and information use. In order to justify its existence, it must facilitate improved managerial performance through more as well as better information availability and use.

In many organizations which are "information oriented" such as those mentioned in this chapter, there has been the development of a separate, centralized, company-wide information office. It is probably more widespread in highly competitive, volatile, consumer goods industries. However, we noted earlier, the need is becoming more recognized in other areas both of private industry and the public sector. This organizational arrangement offers several advantages such as increased efficiency and more effective use of information. All computer facilities, knowledge, and storage and retrieval facilities become available to all other functions in the organization.[11]

INFORMATION AS AN ORGANIZATIONAL RESOURCE

A frequent problem in many organizations is that a great deal of information is generated for no real purpose and should be eliminated. Apparently there seems to be a tendency to generate large quantities of information on the assumption that a direct relationship exists between the amount of information and the quality of decisions. As we have seen this can only be true if the information is relevant and provided to the right decision maker – that is, is provided to

---

[11] See Steven L. Alter, "How Effective Managers Use Information Systems," *Harvard Business Review* (November–December 1976), pp. 97–104. This article examines MIS from the manager's viewpoint and concludes that computer-based information systems must be more than technological wonders.

the right person at the right time. One useful approach to the effective design and utilization of an MIS is to think of information as a basic resource of the organization as we do money, materials, personnel, and plant and equipment.[12] Thus as a basic resource, information:

1. Is vital to the survival of the organization.
2. Can only be used at a cost.
3. Must be at the right place at the right time.
4. Must be used efficiently for an optimal return on its cost to the organization.

Each user of information should consider the cost of the information relative to its utility for decision making. For example, the cost of complete information for a decision must be weighed against the expected value of a decision with incomplete information.

The future of MIS

Although some individuals still refer to MIS as a "mirage,"[13] many organizations are operating with an MIS that is very effective. These organizations have been dissatisfied with the quantity and quality of the information provided to managers and have realized that to develop an effectively functioning integrated MIS involves a great deal more than expanding or automating the data gathering process. Certainly, one of the major reasons for the increased interest in the concept of information systems has been the rapid growth in information technology. However, as we have seen throughout this chapter, *the study of information systems is not the study of computers. The study of management information systems is part of a much larger task, the study of more effective methods of managing organizations.*

Summary

Management information systems, computers, and many management science models have made it possible to reduce the number of decisions required by some managers, especially at the operations level. These are in areas where the problems are deterministic and arise with great regularity (e.g. inventory decisions) and preestablished decision rules can, therefore, be developed. However, it is difficult to

---

[12] See Robert G. Murdick and Joel E. Raso, *Information Systems for Modern Management* (Englewood Cliffs, N.J.: Prentice-Hall, Inc., 1971), chapter 5.

[13] John Dearden, "MIS Is a Mirage," *Harvard Business Review* (January–February 1972), p. 93.

foresee the elimination of the manager as the critical factor in an effective MIS. Even with the increased sophistication of computers, most decision making is, as we have noted, a human activity.

In this chapter we have seen that MIS is a logical extension of the emphasis in the Management Science School on decision making and quantitative models, since both require information. The need for quality information for decision-making purposes is certainly not a new realization. Effective planning and control in any organization has always required information. It is just that now with sophisticated information technology we are capable of generating more information, and the opportunity exists to develop more effective management of information within the organization. This goal is paramount in the development of integrated management information systems.

Discussion and review questions

1. In your own words, define a management information system. What do you think would be the characteristics of "good quality" information provided by MIS?

2. Does the organization level of managers affect their information needs? How? Explain using examples.

3. What do you see as some advantages of an integrated management information system?

4. What kinds of information would you need to make a "good" decision in the following situations:

   a. Purchasing an automobile.
   b. Operating a stereo equipment store.
   c. Developing a new course in information systems at your school.
   d. Getting married.

5. How does planning information differ from control information?

6. The study of MIS is primarily the study of electronic data processing. Comment on this statement.

7. You are provided with a great deal of information by your college or university. List as many types of information as you can. Are you doing an adequate job of managing this information? Why? Can the information be placed in categories such as information for planning, information for control? Explain.

8. What is meant by the statement, "In the area of organizational information, more is not always better"?

Additional references

Adams, C. R. and Schroeder, R. G. "Managers and MIS: They Get What They Want," *Business Horizons* (1973): 63–68.

Argyris, C. "Management Information Systems: The Challenge to Rationality and Emotionality," *Management Science* (1971): 8,275–92.

Baker, J. D. "Rational Computerization," *Business Horizons* (1972): 36–40.

Dickson, G. W. and Simmons, J. K. "The Behavioral Side of MIS," *Business Topics* (1970): 59–71.

Emery, J. C. "An Overview of Management Information Systems," *Management Review* (1974): 44–47.

Field, G. A. "Behavioral Aspects of the Computer," *Business Topics* (1970): 27–33.

Gallagher, C. A. "Perceptions of the Value of a Management Information System," *Academy of Management Journal* (1974): 46–55.

Hay, L. E. "What is an Information System?" *Business Horizons* (1971): 65–72.

King, W. R. "The Intelligent MIS – A Management Helper," *Business Horizons* (1973): 5–12.

Lloyd, J. H. "Establishing a Computer-Based MIS for the Small Business," *Managerial Planning* (1973): 14–16, 23.

Mace, M. L. "Management Information Systems for Directors," *Harvard Business Review* (1976): 14–18, 22, 166–68.

McLean, E. R. "How Effective is Your Data Processing Organization?" *California Management Review* (1973): 95–100.

Mintzberg, H. "The Myths of MIS," *California Managerial Review* (1972): 92–97.

Powers, R. F. and Dickson, G. W. "MIS Project Management: Myths, Opinions, and Reality," *California Management Review* (1973): 147–56.

Small, J. T. and Lee, W. B. "In Search of an MIS," *Business Topics* (1976): 46–55.

Soden, V. and Tucker, C. "Long-Range MIS." *Journal of Systems Management* (1976): 28–33.

Westin, A. F. "The Problem of Privacy and Security with Computerized Data Collection," *The Conference Board Record* (1974): 31–34.

Withington, F. G. "Five Generations of Computers," *Harvard Business Review* (1974): 99–108.

Wolf, A. E. *Computerized Plant Information Systems.* Englewood Cliffs, New Jersey: Prentice-Hall, Inc., 1974.

How Do We Ever Make a Decision?

Return on investment for Lobo Enterprises had not been over 7 percent for the last five years. Late last year, when it became apparent that it would not reach 5 percent for the year, top management finally decided that something needed to be done. The outcome was that one of the nation's largest management consulting firms was contracted to examine the company's operations from top to bottom.

Seven weeks later, the consultants submitted their report with numerous suggestions and recommendations. One of the strongest recommendations read as follows:

> Decision makers at the present time are relying on an inefficient, ineffective, information system. In fact, Lobo Enterprises does not have anything that resembles an information system. We strongly recommend the design of an information system to include all levels of the organization. Its major goal should be to provide decision makers with relevant, accurate, and timely information for use in making decisions in their specific areas of responsibility.

The top management agreed with the recommendation and ordered the EDP (electronic data processing) department to work with the consultants in designing an MIS. As part of the initial phase of the project, each decision maker in the organization was asked to think carefully about his or her area of responsibility and the information needed and used in making decisions related to it. Within three weeks each manager was asked to submit a report relating to information needs and the specific types and sources of information utilized on a regular basis.

Two weeks later Ralph Reeves, the chief purchasing agent for Lobo, had just completed a rough draft of his report. He called in one of his purchasing agents, Scott Reed, and asked him to take the report home for the weekend, read it, and be prepared to comment and make suggestions and recommendations for changes on Monday. Following is the report:

Information Needs and Sources of Information
for Purchasing Function

In order to make effective purchasing decisions, an industrial buyer needs a certain amount and quality of information. Primarily our information needs are related to the following:

1. Price of the items
2. Quantities to be purchased
3. Number of sources of supply
4. Urgency of the buy
5. Complexity of the items
6. Current market situation relative to the items
7. Authority over details of the purchase decision

The specific informational needs will be, for the most part, of two types: technical or quantitative. The technical needs relate to such things as dimensional prints, engineering specifications, and quality requirements. The quantitative requirements are things such as lot size, estimated prices, and terms of shipment.

A careful analysis of the purchasing task reveals numerous and diverse sources of information. Some of our most important and widely used sources are the following:

1. Engineering department
2. Research and development department
3. Production control
4. Supplier literature
5. Trade papers and magazines
6. Supplier salesmen
7. Accounting department
8. Receiving department
9. Competitors
10. Other buyers in the department
11. Production department
12. Legal department

Exhibit 1 illustrates more completely the sources of information used by a buyer prior to most procurement decisions. We in the Purchasing Department believe it illustrates clearly the need for some type of formal systemization of information.

On Monday, Scott Reed brought the report to the office of Ralph Reeves. "What do you think?" asked Reeves. "Ralph, it's excellent. I believe you have accurately detailed the information needs and sources for most purchasing decisions. I have no suggestions or recommendations for changes. One thing did cross my mind as I saw all of our information needs and numerous sources all laid out before my eyes." "What's that?" asked Reeves. There was a slight pause before Scott Reed said, "How do we ever make a decision?"

EXHIBIT 1
Sources of information used by an industrial buyer—Lobo Enterprises

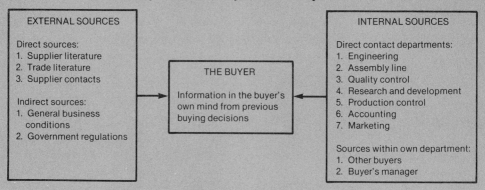

EXTERNAL SOURCES

Direct sources:
1. Supplier literature
2. Trade literature
3. Supplier contacts

Indirect sources:
1. General business conditions
2. Government regulations

THE BUYER

Information in the buyer's own mind from previous buying decisions

INTERNAL SOURCES

Direct contact departments:
1. Engineering
2. Assembly line
3. Quality control
4. Research and development
5. Production control
6. Accounting
7. Marketing

Sources within own department:
1. Other buyers
2. Buyer's manager

Questions for analysis:

1. What would be your answer to Scott Reed's question?
2. Could Figure 14–2 be of use to Lobo Enterprises? How?
3. Could the concept of an "integrated management information system" be of use to Lobo Enterprises? Why? Illustrate using specific examples.

PRACTICAL EXERCISE II
Maybe Orwell Was Right

During his 15 years as president, Bob Gentry had seen Midwestern National Bank (MNB) grow to become one of the largest banks serving metropolitan Somerset and the five-county area surrounding it. When he first joined the bank, it was catering mainly to the "old rich" in the community. By constantly seeking better ways to satisfy the changing financial needs of all groups in the community, MNB had over the last decade gained a reputation as a progressive bank among consumers. Among competitors it was known as a marketing-aggressive bank.

Gentry was reading a report from Caron King, MNB's Director of Marketing. The report focused on MNB's entrance into an important phase of electronic banking: the installation of point-of-sale terminals (POS) in local retail outlets. Probably the most advanced and complex electronic banking innovation is the use of electronic means to transfer money from buyer to seller at the time and place that a transaction occurs (the point-of-sale). In a completely developed system, the individual making the purchase authorizes the movement of money from his or her bank account to the seller's account. This transfer of funds takes place instantaneously through a combination of electronic computer equipment, terminals, and telephone communications lines. The actual location of the accounts has no bearing on the completion of the transactions, and the purchases are completed without the use of checks, money, or the issue of a monthly bill.

According to Ms. King's report, a retail merchant in Somerset participating in the POS system would be supplied a terminal connected to an electronic computer. The computer would contain the account balances and account numbers of participating customers. The computer would also have access to other computers for accounts outside the Somerset metropolitan area. The customer would be given a magnetic card, similar to a credit card, and a code number that would only be known by the customer and the computer. The card would be used when making a purchase. Inserting the card in a terminal at a supermarket counter, for example, a shopper could pay for any purchase, deposit money, or withdraw cash. The computer network would handle all transactions electronically.

Following are some excerpts from Ms. King's report:

> I believe in order to maintain our momentum in growth as well as our image as a progressive financial institution, MNB should consider entering this phase of electronic banking within the next 12 months. A busy branch bank in a large city will handle an average of 12,500 checks every business day. A very large bank with a multibranch system may process 2 million checks every business day. The nation's entire banking system processes over 30 billion checks every business day, and each must be processed by hand.
>
> While our seven branches do not process 12,500 checks each day, our studies show that the number of checks written in our trading area will double in the next decade. Despite our use of computers for record keeping, our clerical costs are mounting. In addition, we are finding it difficult to recruit enough employees for this exacting and humdrum labor.
>
> In addition, retailers are very interested in such a system because it will also reduce their cost of doing business. A typical supermarket chain, for example, will process 40,000 checks a week. For many of these the customer receives a substantial amount of change. As a result the chain not only loses the use of money while waiting for the checks to clear, but also ties up sums larger than sales receipts. Add to this an estimated $100,000 annually for labor costs involved in manually sorting and depositing them in numerous bank accounts as well as another $200,000 because banks typically charge the retailer 5¢ to 15¢ for each item handled. Finally, another $100,000 annual cost must be added for the losses on uncollected checks which average .02% of sales per year. This does not include the costs of processing returned checks that are later collected or the costs of collection efforts (e.g. letters, salaries of collectors). All in all, a typical chain's direct, accountable costs of handling checks is around ½ million dollars annually.

As he read Ms. King's report, the advantages of POS became obvious. There was no doubt in his mind that this was definitely the wave of the future. The report was excellent and he wrote Ms. King a memorandum praising her efforts and promising his total support before the Board of Directors.

Because the report was so interesting it was 8:30 P.M. before Bob Gentry left his office. As he rode the elevator he thought, "What an information system. In fact, the ultimate customer information system."

As he got into his car, however, his enthusiasm began to turn to concern as he was hit with the sudden realization that the computer could become the watchful eye that not only sees and knows all but has the capability of permanently recording every iota of information on our lives and of making these data instantly retrievable by anyone near the right button.

He thought, "From this information, or even a part, it would be a simple task to create financial dossiers on individuals. This information would be available to bank employees and of interest to credit associations and the Internal Revenue Service. Something will have to be done to limit the access to this information. Besides financial data, an extreme use of a POS terminal could be to determine the location of a person. What's going to happen to our right to privacy?"

As he drove home Gentry remembered his college course in philosophy and ethics and the professor who made the class read Orwell's 1984 about Big Brother looking over our shoulder. "I don't want one" he thought, "and I surely don't want to be one." As he entered his driveway he thought, "My God, maybe Orwell was right."

Questions for analysis:

1. When Gentry thought "the ultimate customer information system," what do you believe he had in mind? Can you think of any other uses of the kind of information stored in a POS system? Include both positive and negative uses.

2. Discuss the issue of efficiency versus individual privacy and freedom.

3. What, if anything, can be done to insure that Orwell was not right?

15

BREAK-EVEN AND INVENTORY CONTROL MODELS

Managers in both profit and nonprofit organizations are faced with cost problems which can vitally influence their organizations. Two particular management science models deal specifically with cost factors. They are the break-even model and the inventory control model. As such they are widely used in production and operations management. As is true with most of the mathematical models found in the Management Science School, both of the models have limitations. The primary objective of this chapter is to present the logic, assumptions, and limitations associated with the models.

The influence of economics and accounting

Throughout the book the reader has seen that economists and accountants have contributed principles and models to each of the three schools of management. In the area of cost-and-profit analysis, this influence is certainly obvious. Both groups have identified such important concepts as fixed costs, variable costs, total costs, and total revenue, and clarified the relationships between them. An understanding of these concepts is essential if the models are to be employed effectively.

FIXED COSTS

Some costs remain fixed regardless of the level of production or activity and are appropriately designated as *fixed costs.* The insurance on a warehouse must be paid regardless of whether or not it is being fully utilized. A public university must pay interest on bonds issued for the purpose of constructing dormitories even if student enrollments are down and the dorms are underutilized.

In some instances, fixed costs, while remaining fixed for normal variations in output, will vary if output is either exceedingly low or exceedingly high. This might occur, for example, when a retailer hires additional sales personnel during a particular busy season. Such costs are termed "semifixed" costs. When we use the term "fixed" costs we are actually thinking in terms of the short run, since in the long run all costs are subject to some variation.

VARIABLE COSTS

Costs that vary in close proportion to changes in output are known as *variable costs.* In a manufacturing plant the cost of materials used will depend on the number of units produced. Thus the costs of materials would be a variable cost. Variable costs, then, are related to the activity itself (for example, producing a product, processing a patient) rather than to creating the capacity to produce the product or process the patients.

TOTAL COSTS

Total costs are arrived at by combining fixed and variable costs to form a functional expression for the total costs associated with a particular product, set of activities, or other indicators of performance. Thus,

$$\text{Total costs} = \text{variable costs} + \text{fixed costs}$$

TOTAL REVENUE

Total revenue is calculated by using sales volume (in the case of a business enterprise) and price information. A manager forecasting total revenue would utilize the anticipated sales volume at each price level. If, however, total revenue is to be determined after the product has been sold, the exact volume and price figures are used. In any case, the total revenue, price, and volume relationship can be expressed mathematically as

$$TR = Q \times P$$

(handwritten: volume, price)

where *TR* designates total revenue, *Q* designates anticipated or actual volume, and *P* designates anticipated or actual price.

The break-even model

At the end of an operating period a business manager hopes that the revenue from sales during the period will be sufficient to cover fixed costs and variable costs, and provide some amount of profit. If revenue is sufficient only to cover costs, the firm is operating at the break-even point. The break-even point is the level of operations at which *total revenue equals total costs.*

The break-even model is a deterministic model used to illustrate the relationships between revenues, costs, and profit. The model can answer such questions as: (1) What will be the break-even point in dollars, units, or capacity? (2) What will be the profit or loss in producing and selling various quantities of a product? and (3) What level of output and sales is needed to achieve a desired level of profit?

The following symbols are generally used:

$$BE = \text{break-even point}$$
$$P = \text{selling price per unit}$$
$$VC = \text{variable cost per unit}$$
$$TFC = \text{total fixed costs}$$
$$Q = \text{number of units}$$

As we have already noted, the break-even point occurs when sales produce an amount above variable costs that equals the amount required for fixed costs. For example, if the firm sells 80,000 units annually at $10 per unit, it receives $800,000 in total revenue. If the variable cost per unit (materials, etc.) is $6, the firm obtains a margin of $4 per unit, or $320,000. If the total fixed costs for the period are $320,000, the firm has broken even.

Using the symbols cited above we can derive the break-even formula. First we define the equation for total costs:

Total costs = variable cost/unit + Total fixed costs

$$TC = VC \times Q + TFC$$

Then we define total revenue:

$$TR = P \times Q$$

Total revenue = price × volume

At the break-even point, total costs equal total revenue. Therefore, equating these two:

$$P \times Q = VC \times Q + TFC$$

Solving Q:

$$P \times Q - VC \times Q = TFC$$
$$(P - VC)Q = TFC$$
$$Q = \frac{TFC}{P - VC}$$

APPLICATIONS OF THE BREAK-EVEN MODEL

Identifying necessary level of sales. Suppose that the marketing manager of an appliance manufacturer is interested in how much the sales of one of the firm's products could decline before the product would lose money. This is necessary because a competitor is about to introduce a similar appliance. The following information is available:

Price = $20 per unit
Variable cost = $12 per unit
Total fixed costs = $80,000
Present quantity sold = 100,000

We know that

$$BE = \frac{TFC}{P - VC}$$

Thus,

$$BE = \frac{\$80,000}{\$20 - \$12}$$

$$BE = \frac{\$80,000}{\$8}$$

$$BE = 10,000 \text{ units}$$

Since 100,000 units are presently being sold annually, and sales of 10,000 units enable the firm to break even, the marketing manager knows that it can sell 90,000 fewer units without incurring a loss on the product.

Selecting a course of action. As we saw in the chapter on decision making, managers often must choose between alternative courses of action. In many cases the break-even model can be a useful aid. Let us assume that Battel, Inc., a men's accessory manufacturer, produces a gift item that it distributes through wholesalers to gift shops, tobacco shops, and variety stores. Originally the firm had planned to market the product as a novelty, but then began to consider it from a more practical viewpoint. After an extensive analysis of the potential market, the firm narrowed its distribution choice to two alternatives. The management of Battel is interested in determining what the break-even points are for each alternative. The alternatives are:

I.   Market the item to *wholesalers* who would then distribute the product to large department stores on a national basis.
II. Market the item directly to *tobacco shops* on a national basis.

Cost data for the two alternatives are presented below:

Alternative I (wholesalers)		Alternative II (tobacco shops)	
Production costs (fixed)	$20,000.00	Production costs (fixed)	$20,000.00
Production costs (per unit variable)	3.00	Production costs (per unit variable)	3.00
Marketing costs and administrative costs (fixed)	20,000.00	Marketing costs and administrative costs (fixed)	40,000.00
Marketing costs and administrative costs (per unit variable)	3.00	Marketing costs and administrative costs (per unit variable)	1.00
Battel price charged wholesalers	8.00	Battel price charged stores	6.00

By utilizing the break-even formula the following results are determined:

Alternative I

$$\text{Break-even point in units} = \frac{\$40,000}{\$8.00 - \$6.00} = 20,000 \text{ units}$$

Alternative II

$$\text{Break-even point in units} = \frac{\$60,000}{\$6.00 - \$4.00} = 30,000 \text{ units}$$

The above formulas have provided us with the break-even points for both of the alternative plans. Another way of examining the relationship between revenue, costs, and outputs is to utilize a *break-even*

FIGURE 15–1
Break-even chart for Alternative I (wholesalers)

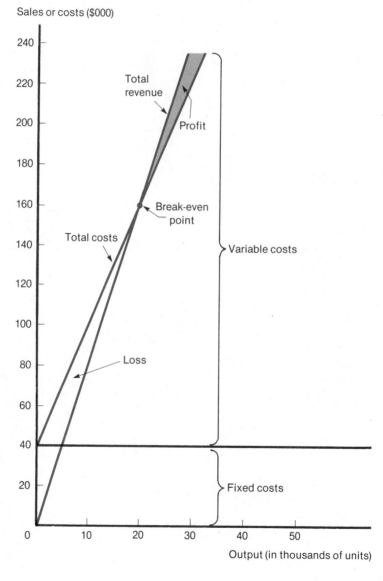

chart. The chart is used to represent graphically the relationship between the elements of the break-even model.

The relationships for Alternative I are presented in Figure 15–1. Note that the graphical analysis verifies the formulas. The break-even point is at 20,000 units or $160,000 in sales revenue. Figure 15–2 presents the same information for Alternative II. It shows that the break-even point is 30,000 units and $180,000 in sales revenue.

Note the useful information in the break-even chart. The total revenue line represents the relationship between price and volume. The area of fixed costs is shown as a horizontal line which indicates the constant nature of the fixed expenditures. The total cost line be-

FIGURE 15–2
Break-even chart for Alternative II (tobacco shops)

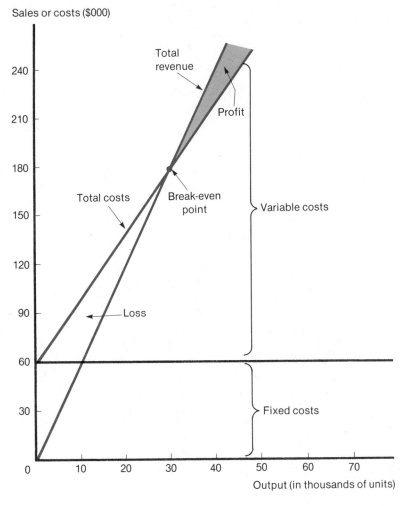

gan at the same point as fixed costs and moves upward to the right for different levels of output. This is one of the important uses of the break-even chart. It illustrates graphically the amount of loss or profit at different levels of sales.

OTHER APPLICATIONS OF THE BREAK-EVEN MODEL

The break-even model indicates the relationships between level of operation, revenue, variable costs, and fixed costs and how they all directly influence profitability. It can also be utilized to analyze the effect changes in these variables will have on profitability. As such, it has a wide variety of other uses. Let us discuss some of them briefly.

Pricing decisions. Using the break-even model, it is possible to evaluate the effects of different prices on the break-even point of the operation. Then we can estimate the probability that sales will be greater than the break-even points at these prices. In other words, we can evaluate the break-even point using different prices and consider whether sales will be sufficient to produce the revenue required to break even.

Hiring decisions. During short-run periods of peak labor, managers traditionally have had two alternatives—to schedule overtime for present employees or to hire new employees. However, the growing temporary help industry has provided a third alternative—to "rent" labor for temporary peak demand periods. The break-even model can be utilized when overtime is not feasible, to answer the question, "Is it cheaper to hire new employees or to pay an agency for temporary help when short-run demand exceeds staff capacity?"[1]

Product decisions. Deleting products from a firm's line is as vital in a changing market as adding new ones. A product that has lost appeal is likely to produce more than its share of small unprofitable orders, require short, costly production runs, take up too much management time, and tie up capital that could be used more profitably in other ventures. A common application of break-even analysis is to aid in product elimination decisions. If, at the current selling price, variable costs are being met and the product is contributing to fixed costs, it should be retained in the short run. On the other hand, in decisions to add new products, break-even analysis is used to identify the price and level of necessary sales volume.

Equipment replacement decisions. In manufacturing organizations decisions must be made on the desirability of keeping or replacing production equipment. For that purpose, the break-even model is

---

[1] For a detailed discussion see M. J. Wallace Jr., and M. Lynn Spruill, "How to Minimize Labor Costs During Peak Demand Periods," *Personnel* (July–August 1975), pp. 61–67.

used to equate the cost functions of the different pieces of equipment. Assume that a production manager is considering replacing a present piece of equipment with a new, more modern one. The break-even model can identify the level of output below which one piece of equipment will be more economical and above which the other will be more economical.

Rent or buy decisions. This application is similar to the hiring decision discussed above, except that it can involve production equipment, facilities, office equipment, planes, trucks, and automobiles. Also, in manufacturing firms, production managers often must decide whether to make items or buy them from another manufacturer. The reader should be able to see that the break-even model can be a useful aid in making these decisions.

LIMITATIONS OF THE BREAK-EVEN MODEL

In order to apply the break-even model properly to problems in production and operations management, the reader should be aware of the following:

1. Break-even analysis is useful only over relatively short ranges of output. This is because it assumes that there is a linear relationship among costs, output, and revenue.

2. Since the break-even model is a deterministic model, it is a static tool. That is, the relationships are representative of only a point in time. Therefore it is more valuable in relatively stable situations than in highly dynamic or volatile situations. It provides a simplified presentation of the relationships between cost, revenue, and output.

3. The break-even model should only be used to guide decision making. Its presentation provides a conceptual tool for understanding the relationships between costs, revenue, and output.

Despite these limitations the break-even model is widely used in production and operations management. The limitations are discussed here to clarify the conditions under which it should be used.

The inventory model

Managers are often faced with the problem of maintaining adequate inventories. This is because most organizations cannot survive without them. The basic problem is that any inventory is a drain on financial resources since it ties up funds which could be used for other purposes. At the same time, however, no organization can afford to run out of the things it needs. Thus the primary objective in inventory control is to balance the cost of carrying the inventory against the cost of running out. In this section we shall examine a management science model which aids in accomplishing this objective. It is an important tool in production and operations management.

THE INVENTORY DECISION

The seller or manufacturer of goods confronts two key inventory decisions. These mutually interrelated decisions are: (1) the size of each lot or batch of items to be purchased and (2) the time to order or request this quantity. By utilizing a basic technique (referred to as the economic order quantity model) which was developed by management scientists, the inventory decision process facing the manager can be made easier.

COST FACTORS IN INVENTORY CONTROL

In resolving inventory problems, the manager must initially identify the cost factors which affect the choices being considered. First, there are the ordering costs of getting a particular item into the actual inventory. These costs are incurred each time an order is placed. They are the clerical and administrative costs per order which also include

FIGURE 15–3
Ordering and carrying cost relationship

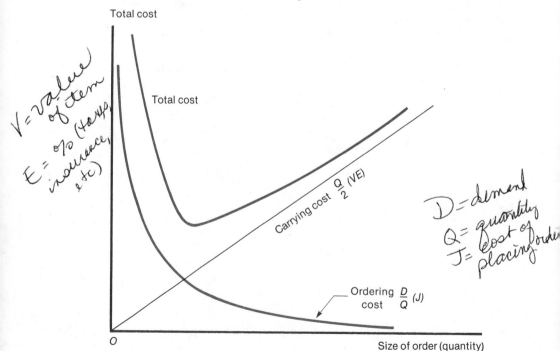

the cost of receiving and placing into inventory the goods ordered.

Second, there are the carrying costs. These include the interest on money invested in inventory, the cost of storage space, rent, obsolescence, taxes, and insurance on losses due to theft, fire, and deterioration, and protection. The carrying cost component is usually expressed as an annual figure and as a percentage of the average inventory.

To minimize inventory costs, a manager must minimize both ordering and carrying costs. Unfortunately, these two costs are related to each other in opposing directions as shown in Figure 15–3. That is, as ordering costs decrease, carrying costs increase. This is because as the size of each order increases, the number and cost of orders decreases; but since larger quantities are being ordered and placed in inventory, the cost of carrying the inventory increases.

The number of orders for a given period of time is equal to demand (D) for the period divided by the size of each order quantity (Q). The total ordering cost per period (week, month, or year) is equal to the cost of placing each order (J) multiplied by the number of orders per period, $\frac{D}{Q}$, or $\frac{D}{Q}$ (J). It should be evident now that as the order size increases, fewer orders are required to meet the demand for a period, and consequently the ordering cost component will decrease. This is illustrated graphically by the downward sloping order cost curve in Figure 15–3.

The cost of carrying an item in inventory is calculated by multiplying the value of the item (V) by a percentage figure (E), which is management's estimate of taxes, insurance, etc., per period as a percentage of the value of inventory. The total carrying costs are equal to the cost of carrying one item (VE) multiplied by the average inventory Q/2. Note that unlike ordering costs, carrying costs increase as the size of the order increases. In the illustrative problem that follows, carrying cost is shown as a straight line.

An example will illustrate why average inventory is assumed to be Q/2. Assume that an organization orders 500 items and uses 100 of them each week; at the midpoint of the first week it has on hand 450. Table 15–1 illustrates the number in inventory at the midpoint of

TABLE 15–1
Average inventory analysis

Week	Number in inventory at midpoint of week
1	450
2	350
3	250
4	150
5	50
	1,250

each week over a period of five weeks. Thus an average of 250 (1250 ÷ 5) parts are on hand over the five week period. The average (250) can also be found by utilizing the $Q/2$ formula, that is, 500/2.

TRIAL-AND-ERROR METHODOLOGY

A manager can use trial and error to determine what size of order to place. However, in attempting to select the optimal size of inventory from a cost standpoint, a number of assumptions are usually made.

1. The demand for the item over the period is assumed to be known with certainty. Thus, we are developing the economic order quantity model (EOQ) under conditions of certainty.

2. The rate at which the inventory of the item is depleted is assumed to be constant. Figure 15–4 below illustrates depletion at a constant

FIGURE 15–4
Constant depletion

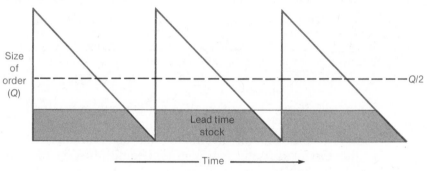

rate. The average inventory is found under conditions of constant usage (for example, selling the same amount monthly for the year).

3. The time necessary for acquiring an order of items after the order is placed is assumed to be exactly known (that is, the lead time).

These assumptions are not completely realistic, but they allow us to study in an uncomplicated manner the development of the economic order quantity model. Further sophistication of the basic model can occur only if the simplified form is clearly understood.[2]

Let us assume that a production manager is attempting to solve a lot-size problem involving a component part which is purchased from a supplier. The yearly demand, which is constant, for the part is established as 1,000. The administrative and clerical cost of placing an order is $40. The manager estimates insurance and taxes to be 10

---

[2] For examples, see Richard B. Chase and Nicholas J. Aquilano, *Production and Operations Management* (Homewood, Ill.: Richard D. Irwin, Inc., 1973), chaps. 8 and 9.

percent per year. The value of a single part is $20. Thus the variables involved are:

Demand   (D) = 1,000
Ordering costs   (J) = $40
Insurance and taxes (E) = 10 percent
Value of the item (V) = $20

The manager could utilize a tabular format to reach an inventory ordering decision that would minimize the total inventory costs. The size of inventory order and cost relationships are shown in Table 15–2.

TABLE 15–2
Trial-and-error method

Number of orders	Size of order Q	Order cost D/Q (J)	+	Carrying cost Q/2 (VE)	=	Total cost
1...........	1000	$ 40	+	$1000	=	$1040
2...........	500	80	+	500	=	580
4...........	250	160	+	250	=	410
10...........	100	400	+	100	=	500
20...........	50	800	+	50	=	850

A review of the total cost data in Table 15–2 indicates that placing four orders of 250 each yields the lowest cost. However, note that the trial-and-error method could be tedious. To eliminate the tedious nature of the trial-and-error approach, management scientists have developed a specific model known as the economic order quantity (EOQ) model.

THE EOQ MODEL

The trial-and-error method involves experimentation and manipulation of costs before the decision maker arrives at the minimum cost. Referring to Figure 15–3, we see that the minimum total inventory cost is at the point directly above the intersection of carrying cost and ordering cost. Thus, the EOQ formula may be derived by utilizing this relationship between total carrying and ordering costs. It should also be noted that for simplicity the relationship shown is linear. The first step in algebraic derivation is to set carrying and ordering costs equal to each other.

$$\frac{Q}{2}\,(VE) = \frac{D}{Q}\,(J)$$

Solving for Q yields:

$$Q(VE) = \frac{2DJ}{Q}$$

$$Q^2(VE) = 2DJ$$

$$Q^2 = \frac{2DJ}{(VE)}$$

$$Q = \sqrt{\frac{2DJ}{(VE)}}$$

The final equation is commonly referred to as the *economic order quantity* formula, and can be used to solve the inventory problem we have outlined. Using the data in our problem we can determine the economic order size, $D = 1,000$, $J = \$40$, $E = 10$ percent, and $V = \$20$.

$$Q = \sqrt{\frac{2(1000)(\$40)}{(\$20)(.10)}}$$

$$Q = \sqrt{\frac{\$80,000}{\$2.00}}$$

$$Q = \sqrt{40,000}$$

$$Q = 200$$

Reviewing the trial-and-error method shows that the least costly alternative is to place four orders to satisfy the overall demand of 1,000. However, utilization of the more exact EOQ formula suggests that placing five orders of 200 each will be least costly. Since the five-order alternative was not considered in the trial-and-error solution, the manager was not able to really minimize inventory costs.

The EOQ model can also be used to take into consideration changes in demand for a product. Let us assume that the demand is 1,000 for the first ten months of the year, and 2,000 for the last two months of the year. For the January–October period, the EOQ calculations would be as follows: $D = 1,000$; $J = \$40$; $E = 10$ percent; and $V = \$20$.

Thus,

$$EOQ = \sqrt{\frac{2(1,000)(\$40)}{(\$20)(.20)(10/12)}}$$

$$EOQ \cong \sqrt{48,000}$$

$$EOQ \cong 219 \text{ units.}$$

The November–December inventory strategy would be determined as follows: $D = 2,000$; $J = \$40$; $E = 10$ percent; and $V = \$20$.

Thus,

$$EOQ = \sqrt{\frac{2(2,000)(\$40)}{(\$20)(.10)(2/12)}}$$

$$EOQ = \sqrt{484,848}$$

$$EOQ \cong 696$$

The EOQ during the November–December peak period is approximately 696. This means that the manager must enter the decision process by determining whether two or three orders are appropriate. The human element is essential since $2 \times 696 = 1,392$ and $3 \times 696 = 2,088$, and the exact demand is 2,000. The EOQ decision for January–December was relatively clear-cut in that the demand of 1,000 could be satisfied with five orders of 200 each. The above example was used to show that despite the use of mathematical formulas, human judgment is still an important factor in many inventory control decisions.

Limitations of inventory control models

The most obvious limitation of employing the deterministic inventory control model presented is that conditions of certainty rarely exist in the real world. In our problem, we have assumed that the correct time to order is known. Many times transportation problems, order requisition difficulties, and other related problems make the lead time (time between placement of an order and actual delivery of the order) a highly unpredictable phenomenon.

The estimation of demand is another problem. Throughout our discussion, demand was stated as a specific amount. The demand for any item can at best only be roughly estimated. There are so many variables, such as competitors' prices, economic conditions, social conditions, and substitutable items, that can influence demand that stating it definitely is difficult.

Despite these limitations, the analytical approaches presented can aid the manager in reaching more effective judgments. The reader should recognize that the methods discussed are analytical approaches which attempt to yield optimal decisions. The emphasis, of course, is on the word "attempt."

Discussion and review questions

1. Under what situations would the material costs for a product not be completely variable? That is, when would material costs be semivariable?
2. Is the EOQ model able to adjust to changes in demand over a period of time? Why?

3. How can decision theory and break-even analysis be simultaneously used in analyzing cost–profit problems?

4. A student of management science is presented with the following sets of data.

Set 1	Set 2
BE units = 40,000	BE dollars = 300,000
Price = $10	Price = $15
VC/unit = $ 8	VC/unit = $12

   If a complete break-even analysis is to be conducted on Set 1 and Set 2, what piece of information is needed in each case? Show all work.

5. If you knew at what point on a graph ordering costs and carrying costs intersect, what would you also know about the economic lot size?

6. The Slag Valley Construction Corporation uses 5,000 pressure valves annually. The cost accountants ascertain that the ordering cost for securing the valves from suppliers is $60.00. Each valve costs $10.00. The carrying charge for the valves is estimated to be 20 percent per year of the value of the average inventory.
   a. Utilize the trial-and-error method to derive the economic order quantity for the following possibilities:
      Number of valves in order: 500, 1000, 2500, 5000
   b. Utilize the EOQ formula to determine the economic order size.

7. How are the following concepts related to each other?
   a. Total Cost ....Variable Cost
   b. Ordering Cost ....Carrying Cost
   c. Price ....Volume of Products Sold

Additional references

Baumol, W. J. *Economic Theory and Operations Analysis.* Englewood Cliffs, N.J.: Prentice-Hall, Inc., 1965.

Buffa, E., and Dyer, J. *Management Science/Operations Research: Model Formulations and Solution Methods.* New York: John Wiley and Sons, Inc., 1977.

Buffa, E. S., and Taubert, W. H. *Production-Inventory Systems: Planning and Control.* Rev. ed. Homewood, Ill.: Richard D. Irwin, Inc., 1972.

Starr, M. K., and Miller, D. W. *Inventory Control: Theory and Practice.* Englewood Cliffs, N.J.: Prentice-Hall, Inc., 1962.

Trueman, R. *An Introduction to Quantitative Methods for Decision Making.* New York: Holt, Rinehart and Winston, Inc., 1977.

16

LINEAR PROGRAMMING MODELS

Linear programming models are among the most widely used types of allocation models. However, the use of linear programming for management decision making is relatively new.

Since World War II, linear programming models have been used increasingly to solve management problems. With the growth of the Management Science School and the simultaneous growth of the electronic computer, complex linear programming models are now being utilized on a wide scale.

A linear programming model is an extremely useful device that has the purpose of maximizing some objective such as profits or minimizing some objective such as costs by determining what the future values of certain variables affecting the outcome should be in order to achieve the objective. The variables are ones over which the manager has some control.

The model is called linear because the mathematical equations employed to describe the particular system under study, as well as the objective to be achieved, are in the form of linear relations between the variables. A linear relationship between two or more variables is one which is directly and precisely proportional. Linear programming models are used in a variety of situations where numerous activities are all competing for limited resources. The manager must find the optimum way to allocate the limited resources given an objective and any relevant constraints.

Management's use of linear programming

Managers in all types of organizations must face numerous allocation problems. In many organizations managers have made effective use of linear programming in solving these problems.

For example, oil companies throughout the world probably have the best overall record of successfully employing linear programming models. This is because they face a large number of allocation-type problems. Most oil companies are fully integrated, which basically means that they are involved with the product through all the various stages right up to the final user. They produce oil, refine it, market it, and move it through each stage to the user. The reader can imagine how highly complex and geographically dispersed the operations of oil companies are. Managers in oil companies must make allocation decisions involving such problems as:

1. The alternative areas from which they can derive crude oil.
2. The alternative areas from which they can transport crude oil.
3. The alternative methods of transportation (for example, pipeline, trucks).

4. The alternative locations where crude oil can be refined.
5. The alternative methods of refining crude oil.
6. "Cracking" crude oil into several alternative "blending stocks."
7. Combining various blending stocks into several dozen potential products (for example, fuel oil, gasoline, kerosene).
8. Combining various blending stocks for alternative quality levels for certain products (for example, computing the right mixture of octane components in the blending of different gasolines).
9. Shipping the manufactured products from refineries into market areas.

In each of the above situations managers must allocate some scarce resource among several competing alternatives with the objective of either maximizing profits or minimizing costs. For this reason oil companies employ management scientists to construct linear programming models in order to aid line managers in planning and controlling.

THE VALUE OF LINEAR PROGRAMMING

Properly constructed linear programming models provide managers with three specific benefits:

Improved planning. Where applicable, linear programming models improve managers' planning skills because they expand their analytical ability. They enable managers to consider and evaluate a far wider range of possible allocation plans than would be humanly possible without their use.

For example, in the second section of this chapter we shall see that conventional graphical and algebraic paper-and-pencil computations can be applied in principle to very simple allocation problems involving two or three variables. However, in a real-world problem such as those noted above, such methods would be of little value. The simplex method of linear programming referred to earlier can, with the aid of an electronic computer, solve a problem containing over 500 equations and 1,000 variables in just a few hours. This is what is meant when we say that linear programming can expand the analytic ability, and therefore the planning ability, of a manager. It permits an exhaustive search of numerous alternative solutions and systematically searches for the optimum one. Previously, time constraints might have permitted examination of only a few possible alternative solutions when numerous potential solutions actually existed.

Improved decisions. Linear programming models can result in improved management decisions. Once a linear programming model is constructed there is no room for management judgment since the computer performs the computations and manipulations and provides a solution which maximizes or minimizes the stated objective within the given constraints. However, before the model is ready to be solved and after it is solved, human judgment and creativity can be used. For example, once a solution has been selected, the manager may alter or add a constraint or change the objective. The computer can then provide a new solution under the revised set of conditions. Only a manager, however, can determine which of the two solutions is best. In some cases the differences in the choices will be so slight that the manager may face an extremely difficult decision.

Improved understanding of problems. Since linear programming models are highly efficient ways of analyzing very complex problems, they also improve a manager's comprehension and appreciation of these complex problems and, by structuring a problem, enable the manager to comprehend more easily the effects of alternative assumptions. They not only provide a solution but also enable the manager to understand the problem.

SOME SPECIFIC AREAS OF APPLICATION

In this section we shall review briefly some of the specific areas in which linear programming has found wide use.

Product-mix problems. In product-mix selection, a manager must determine the levels of a number of production activities for the planning period. For example, if a firm manufactures two products, both of which must go through the same three production processes, the manager faces a problem of this nature. The two products both compete for time in the three production processes, and the task of the linear programming model in this case would be to "allocate" the limited resources (available time in the three processes) in such a way as to produce that number of each product which will maximize the firm's profits.

Feed-mix problems. Large farming organizations may purchase and mix together several types of grains for different purposes. Each grain may contain different amounts of several nutritional elements. For one situation, the production manager must blend the different grains for the purpose of producing a mixture for feeding livestock. The mixture must meet minimal nutritional requirements at the lowest cost. Linear programming can be used to "allocate" the various grains (each containing different amounts of the nutritional elements) in such a way that the resulting mixture will meet nutritional and diet specifications at the minimum cost.

Fluid-blending problems. This is a variation of the feed-mix problem. In this case, the manager seeks to blend fluids such as molten metals, chemicals, and crude oil into a finished product. Steel, chemical, and oil companies make wide use of linear programming models for problems of this type. Computing the right mixture of octane requirements in the blending of different gasolines is an example of such a problem in the oil industry.

Transportation problems. Many manufacturers and large retail chains face the following problem: Given a number of sources of supply (for example, warehouses) and destinations (for example, customers), and the cost of shipping a product from the source of each destination, select those routes that will minimize total shipping costs. The reader can imagine the complexity of the problem if the firm has many warehouses in different parts of the country and thousands of customers also geographically dispersed. Linear programming provides a means for arriving at the optimum shipping program.

Advertising media-mix problems. In most organizations, a manager must sooner or later face a media-mix problem: Given an advertising budget, how can the budgeted funds be allocated over the various advertising media in order to achieve maximum exposure of the product or service. This type of problem lends itself to the use of linear programming. There are a number of competing media (for example, five magazines) all competing for limited resources (the advertising budget). Linear programming is widely used in many advertising agencies for problems of this type.

While the above problems are probably the most popular areas of application, there are a multitude of other practical problems in which linear programming has proven its worth. For example:

1. Allocation of materials to machines in order to minimize production time.
2. Allocation of cargoes to ships and aircraft.
3. Allocation of coal to power stations to minimize shipping costs.
4. Production scheduling.
5. Personnel assignment.

There is no doubt that linear programming models improve the planning skills of managers. Linear programming models cannot, however, develop new ways of running the organization or consider possible alternatives not provided to them. Only the manager can do this. Linear programming models are tools that managers can use, nothing more.

An application of linear programming:
A product-mix problem

Assume that the production manager of the Apex Corporation has the choice of producing two different products (A and B). Furthermore, both products must go through three departments (X, Y, and Z) to be completed. Assume that Department X is production, Department Y is assembling, and Department Z is packaging. Both products require the same amount of time in Department X, but, because of special features, Product B requires twice as much time in Department Y but less time in Department Z. Product A contributes $10 per unit to profits, and Product B contributes $12 per unit. The problem the production manager faces is to determine a production "program" for the two products.

In this particular problem, the products (A and B) are the competing users and the available time in the three processes (production, assembling, and packaging) represents the limited resources. If profit is the objective, then the production manager hopes to design a program that will maximize profits. In linear programming this is formulated into a mathematical expression known as an *objective function,* the value of which can be computed when the values of all the variables are determined. Finally, the capacity of the resources is limited. That is, there is only so much time per day available in each of the three departments. If we assume that no expansion plans are called for, then this limitation is expressed as a set of constraints which restricts the values that can be assigned to the competing products.

Thus the task of the linear programming model in this case is to "allocate" the limited resources (available time in production, assembling, and packaging) among the competing users (Products A and B) in such a way as to maximize profit. To review, then, it should be clear that the linear programming model is *normative* in purpose since it selects the best alternative to optimize some objective (profit in this case) and contains *deterministic* variables since all variables are assumed to be known with certainty. Note also that in order to utilize the linear programming model it is necessary to *assume certainty* (all factors are exact or deterministic quantities) and *simplify relationships* (assume linear relationships among variables) in the problem. Let us summarize the above problem by introducing numerical values in Table 16–1.

TABLE 16–1
Apex Corporation resources

Department	Minutes required per unit		Capacity per day in minutes
	Product A	Product B	
X (production).................	6	6	300
Y (assembling).................	4	8	320
Z (packaging)	5	3	310
Profit contribution per unit	$10	$12	

A final key element of linear programming is the use of inequalities to express relationships. Equations are specific mathematical statements which are represented by an equals sign (=). For example, if profit is our sole objective in the above problem, we can express this in the following equation:

$$\text{Profit} = \$10 \text{ (number of Product A sold)}$$
$$+ \$12 \text{ (number of Product B sold)}$$

However, most problems cannot be expressed in equations such as our objective function. More often the problem may require only that minimum or maximum requirements be met. For example, in Table 16–1 it is stated that the time needed in Department X for one Product A (6 minutes) times the number of Product A's produced, plus the time required for one Product B (6 minutes) times the number of Product B's produced, must be equal to or less than the 300 minutes of available time per day in Department X. In this case, we must utilize inequalities to express the constraints. The above constraint is expressed as follows:

$$6A + 6B \leq 300$$

Any amount of time utilized which is equal to or less than 300 minutes per day would satisfy the inequality. When formulating inequalities, the sign ($\leq$) stands for "less than or equal to"; and the sign ($\geq$) stands for "greater than or equal to."

In order to develop an understanding of a typical linear programming problem we will work through this problem and solve it by the *graphic method.* We will also discuss the *algebraic method* and the *simplex method.* Of the three methods, the simplex method is the most general and powerful method. However, knowledge of the graphic method will provide a foundation for understanding the concepts and rationale of the simplex method. In addition, problems which have three or less competing candidates can be more easily solved by the first two methods.

THE GRAPHICAL METHOD

Since it is not possible to present graphically more than three variables, only problems with three or less competing candidates can be solved by this method. Since our product-mix problem presented in Table 16–1 has only two competing candidates (Products A and B), it can be solved by the graphical method.

To begin solving the problem we must restate it in mathematical form. Since the goal is to maximize profit (P) the objective function is:

$$\text{Objective Function} = P = \$10A + \$12B$$

This equation is read: Profit equals \$10 multiplied by the number of Product A produced, plus \$12 multiplied by the number of Product B produced. Assuming we produced and sold 20 of each, then profit would equal \$10 (20) + \$12 (20) or \$440.

The next step is to express constraints in mathematical form. The time used in the three departments cannot exceed the total time available per day in each of the departments. For example, the time needed to produce one Product A times the number produced, plus the time needed to produce one Product B times the number produced, must be equal to or less than the 300 minutes available each day in the production department (Department X). The constraints for all three departments can be expressed as follows:

$$6A + 6B \leq 300 \text{ minutes in Department X (production)}$$
$$4A + 8B \leq 320 \text{ minutes in Department Y (assembling)}$$
$$5A + 3B \leq 310 \text{ minutes in Department Z (packaging)}$$

Finally, every linear programming problem has a set of *nonnegativity* constraints. These are imposed to insure that any values for A and B arrived at are positive. This is obvious, since there can be no such thing as negative production (we cannot produce a minus quantity of a product). Thus, the optimal solution must have nonnegative values for A and B or: $A \geq 0$ and $B \geq 0$.

Summarizing the problem in mathematical form yields:

$$\text{Maximize Profit } (P) = \$10A + \$12B$$

Subject to the following constraints

$$6A + 6B \leq 300$$
$$4A + 8B \leq 320$$
$$5A + 3B \leq 310$$

and

$$A \geq 0$$
$$B \geq 0$$

The next step is to designate, on a two-dimensional graph, Product A on the horizontal axis and Product B on the vertical axis and plot each of the three constraint equations. Each inequality is plotted by assuming that all the available time in the particular department is devoted to one of the products. For example, in Department X, if we did not produce any of Product B, we could produce 50 units of Product A. Similarly, if we produced no Product A we would be able to produce 50 units of Product B. The calculations for each department are as follows:

In Department X (production) let $B = 0$; then

$$6A + 6B \leq 300$$
$$6A + 6(0) \leq 300$$
$$A \leq 50 \text{ units of Product A}$$

when no Product B
is produced.

In Department X let $A = 0$; then

$$6A + 6B \leq 300$$
$$6(0) + 6B \leq 300$$
$$B \leq 50 \text{ units of Product B}$$

when no Product A
is produced.

In Department Y (assembling) let $B = 0$; then

$$4A + 8B \leq 320$$
$$4A + 8(0) \leq 320$$
$$4A \leq 320$$
$$A \leq 80 \text{ units of Product A}$$

when no Product B
is assembled.

In Department Y let $A = 0$; then

$$4A + 8B \leq 320$$
$$4(0) + 8B \leq 320$$
$$8B \leq 320$$
$$B \leq 40 \text{ units of Product B}$$

when no Product A
is assembled.

In Department Z (packaging) let $B = 0$; then

$$5A + 3B \leq 310$$
$$5A + 3(0) \leq 310$$
$$5A \leq 310$$
$$A \leq 62 \text{ units of Product A}$$

when no Product B
is packaged.

In Department Z let $A = 0$; then

$$5A + 3B \leq 310$$
$$5(0) + 3B \leq 310$$
$$3B \leq 310$$
$$B \leq 103 \text{ units of Product B}$$

when no Product A
is packaged.

FIGURE 16–1
Constraint equations

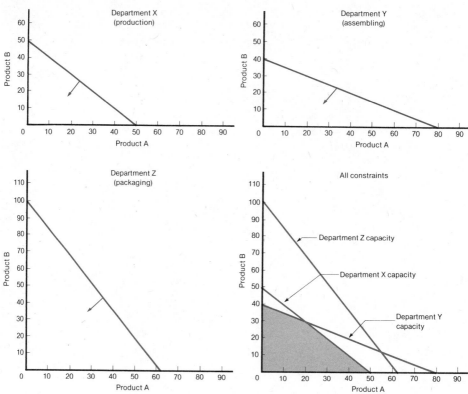

The inequalities are illustrated on separate graphs in Figure 16–1 for each department and all together on one graph. The arrow associated with each line shows the direction indicated by the inequality signs (less than or equal to) in the constraint equations. This means that any combination of Products A and B which lies in that area can be produced, assembled, or packaged without exceeding the available time in the particular department. Finally, note that the nonnegativity constraints $A \geq 0$, $B \geq 0$ restrict us to zero or more units of Products A and B.

All values for Product A and B satisfying all three constraints are shown in the shaded region in Figure 16–1. Note that any pair of values for Products A and B that satisfies the constraints in Department X and Y also satisfies Department Z. To complete one unit of Product A or B, work must be done in all three departments. Therefore, the best combination of Products A and B must fall within the shaded area in Figure 16–1. Any combination in this *feasibility space* will not exceed the maximum time in either Department X, Y, or Z.

The construction of Figure 16–1 is the first step in solving the problem by the graphical method. The goal is to locate at least one point from the shaded area in Figure 16–1 which will maximize the objective function.

FINDING THE OPTIMAL SOLUTION

The optimal solution must be guided by the objective function. If it were possible to plot the objective function in Figure 16–1 and determine the direction of maximum increase, we could then continue to move it in this direction until we reached the farthest point on the boundary of the shaded area in Figure 16–1. We would then have the optimum solution.

The problem can be solved by selecting any arbitrary profit figure and determining how many units of Product A alone or Product B alone would be needed to earn such a profit. Any profit figure will suffice, but common sense tells us to select a point within the feasibility space in Figure 16–1. Let us assume a profit figure of $300. Since Product A contributes $10 we would need 30 units in order to earn a profit of $300. If we manufacture only Product B, we would need 25 units in order to earn a $300 profit since Product B contributes a profit of $12. If we locate these two points in the feasibility space and join them we obtain what is known as a $300 equal-profit line which is nothing more than the locus of all points (all combinations of Products A and B) which will yield a profit of $300. This is illustrated in Figure 16–2 as a dotted line.

We could continue to construct these lines for higher and higher profit figures as long as we remain within the feasibility space. This is also illustrated in Figure 16–2 by dotted lines. We would be forced to stop when we reached a boundary line or corner point of the feasibility space. The highest combination still having a point in the feasibility space provides the optimal value of the objective function. When this occurs, we have found the optimum solution.

The equal-profit line farthest from the origin and still within the feasibility space would be at point H in Figure 16–2. This occurs at the intersection of the Department X and Department Y constraints. Although there are an infinite number of solutions within the feasibility space, point H provides the optimum solution.

The coordinates of the point H can be read directly from the graph if it is constructed perfectly, but they are usually found by solving simultaneously the equations of the two lines which intersect to form point H, which is the only point common to both equations. The equations to be solved are:

$$\text{Line } BC \qquad 6A + 6B = 300$$
$$\text{Line } DE \qquad 4A + 8B = 320$$

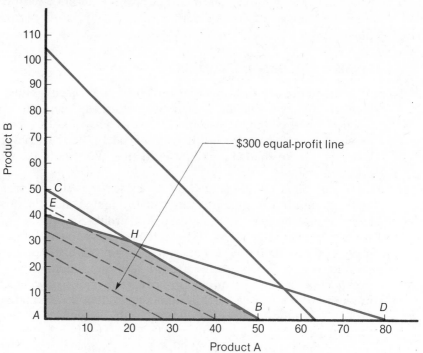

FIGURE 16-2
Equal-profit lines

To solve these equations simultaneously we
a.   Multiply the first equation by 4.
b.   Multiply the second equation by -3.
c.   Add the results.

$$4(6A + 6B = 300) = \quad 24A + \quad 24B = 1200$$
$$-3(4A + 8B = 320) = -12A + (-24B) = -960$$
$$12A \qquad\qquad = \quad 240$$
$$A \qquad\qquad\quad = \quad 20$$

d.   Substitute 20 for A in the second equation.

$$4A + 8B = 320 = 4(20) + 8B = 320$$
$$80 \ + 8B = 320$$
$$8B = 240$$
$$B = \ \ 30$$

e.   Point H is, therefore, (20, 30).

We can now test the four points that delineate the feasibility space in order to determine the highest dollar profit.

$$\begin{aligned}
\text{Point } A \quad (0,0) &= \quad 10(0) + \quad 12(0) = \$0 \\
\text{Point } B \quad (50,0) &= 10(50) + \quad 12(0) = \$500 \\
\text{Point } E \quad (0,40) &= \quad 10(0) + 12(40) = \$480 \\
\text{Point } H \ (20,30) &= 10(20) + 12(30) = \$560
\end{aligned}$$

The point that provides the most profit is point H where we manufacture 20 units of Product A and 30 units of Product B for a profit of $560.

This product-mix problem was provided only as an illustration of a linear programming model. Real applications of linear programming usually involve hundreds of constraints and sometimes thousands of variables. Obviously for such problems an electronic computer is a necessity. As we have noted previously, the graphical method cannot be used when there are more than three competing candidates. However, regardless of the number of competing candidates and constraints, the nature of linear programming is the same as was illustrated in the product-mix problem.

THE ALGEBRAIC METHOD

Where a linear programming problem has less than three competing candidates, a solution can also be more easily developed algebraically than through the use of the simplex method. The product-mix problem was stated as follows:

Maximize:

$$P = \$10\,A + \$12\,B$$

Subject to:

$$\begin{aligned}
6A + 6B &\le 300 \ \text{(Department X)} \\
4A + 8B &\le 320 \ \text{(Department Y)} \\
5A + 3B &\le 310 \ \text{(Department Z)}
\end{aligned}$$

The problem cannot be solved algebraically since we do not have equations because of the inequalities. We must first convert the inequalities to equations. The above inequalities can be transformed into equations by the addition of nonnegative variables known as slack variables (S) since they "take up the slack" and serve to form equations from the inequalities of a linear programming problem. It is possible, because of the nature of the inequalities as the "less-than-or-equal-to" type, that the optimum combination of Products A and B will not utilize all of the available time in each department. Therefore, we add to each inequality a variable which will take up the time not used in each department. Thus, we now have:

$$6A + 6B + S_x = 300 \text{ (Department X)}$$
$$4A + 8B + S_y = 320 \text{ (Department Y)}$$
$$5A + 3B + S_z = 310 \text{ (Department Z)}$$

S_x is equal to the total time available in Department X less the time used there to produce both products. S_y is equal to the total available time in Department Y less the time used there to assemble both products, and S_z equals the total available time used in Department Z less the time used to package both products. Thus, by adding slack variables we have converted the constraint inequalities into equations. The slack variables will take on whatever value is needed to make the equation hold. For example, assume that ten units of each product are manufactured.

Department X:

$$S_x = 300 - 6(10) - 6(10)$$
$$S_x = 180 \text{ minutes unused time in Department X}$$

Department Y:

$$S_y = 320 - 4(10) - 8(10)$$
$$S_y = 200 \text{ minutes of unused time in Department Y}$$

Department Z:

$$S_z = 310 - 5(10) - 3(10)$$
$$S_z = 230 \text{ minutes of unused time in Department Z}$$

Since idle time in any of the three departments can have no profit or loss, the slack variables have no money value and can be included in the objective function with zero profit contributions. Thus the problem is ready for algebraic solution as follows:

$$P = \$10A + \$12B + \$0S_x + \$0S_y + \$0S_z$$
$$6A + 6B + S_x = 300$$
$$4A + 8B + S_y = 320$$
$$5A + 3B + S_z = 310$$

We will not devote the space needed to solve this problem algebraically since that is not the purpose of this chapter. The reader skilled in algebra may wish to do so. The solution, of course, will be the same as that achieved by the graphic method. It indicates 20 units of Product A and 30 units of Product B should be manufactured, which will provide a profit of $560 and 120 minutes of unused time in Department Z. If the reader refers to Figure 16–1 it will be seen that the constraint line for Department Z is the farthest from the origin since less time was needed to package the products than to assemble or produce them. In fact, the feasibility space was formed only by the constraint lines for Department X and Y. Thus it is not surprising that Department Z has slack time.

THE SIMPLEX METHOD

The simplex method is the most widely applicable and powerful of the linear programming techniques. Both the graphical and algebraic methods are special cases of the general simplex method. The major advantage of the simplex method is that it is capable of handling any number of variables. Because of this, it usually requires a very lengthy and involved computational procedure. For our purposes it is necessary only to outline the general characteristics of the simplex method.

The simplex method is similar to the graphical and algebraic methods in that conditions of certainty and linear relationships among variables are necessary in order for it to be used. Like the algebraic method, it requires that the problem be formulated in explicit mathematical terms, stating both the objective function and the constraints. Then an initial solution is developed which satisfies all of the constraints. Modifications in the initial solution are examined and the most favorable, in terms of the objective function, is incorporated into the second solution. This is repeated until no further improvements are possible. This computational routine of the simplex method is known as an *iterative process*. To iterate is to repeat mechanical and mathematical operations. Each *iteration* brings us closer to an optimal solution because each new solution yields a larger profit or lower cost than the previous solution.

The reader can imagine the value of the simplex method in many of the real-world problems which may contain hundreds of variables. It permits an exhaustive search of the possible solutions and systematically searches for the optimum one. However, the reader should see that the basic nature is that which was illustrated in this chapter in the product-mix problem.

Summary

In this chapter, linear programming has been discussed as a powerful planning tool for the manager. It has made possible the solution of many types of allocation problems which heretofore could only be dealt with (if at all) by trial-and-error methods. In addition, however, it has forced managers to delineate more clearly the variables and relationships affecting a problem. Forcing managers to formalize their thinking on specific problems enables them to visualize the key variables in a problem, bringing organization and structure to a problem situation where little or none existed before.

The reader should not infer, however, that linear programming offers a solution for all allocation decision problems. The employment of linear programming necessitates formulation of the decision problem in mathematical terms. This means in many cases the gathering of data and extensive calculations. In such a situation, the costs incurred in using linear programming may exceed any possible gain or saving that might be obtained from its use.

Linear programming can only be used for problems in which it can be assumed that the relationships between variables are linear. This assumption cannot be made for a number of allocation problems. In addition, some allocation problems involve such a degree of complexity that their solution is not possible via linear programming.

Finally, we noted that the linear programming model is a deterministic model. This means that all variables are assumed to be known with certainty. While this is clearly a simplifying assumption, there will be many problems where such an assumption cannot be made, or, if made, the solution obtained through the use of linear programming will be of little or no value.

In conclusion, it is important for the manager to understand not only how linear programming is used, but also the conditions under which it is feasible. This is not to detract from the value of the tool but rather to strengthen the conditions under which it is used.

Discussion and review questions

1. The Lisa Ann Company makes two products. Product A contributes $20 profit and Product B contributes $12 profit. Each product must go through two manufacturing processes in order to be completed. Product A requires 12 hours in Department X and 4 hours in Department Y. Product B requires 4 hours in Department X and 8 hours in Department Y. There is a total of 60 hours available in Department X and 40 in Department Y. Find the optimum combination of the two products which would maximize total profit. Use the graphic method.

2. The Helene Manufacturers, Inc., produces two different models of professional hair dryers. Dryer A contributes $20 profit and Dryer B contributes $10. In order to be completed, each dryer must go through three manufacturing processes as follows:

	Dryer A (hours)	Dryer B (hours)	Available time in each department (hours)
Department X	4	9	180
Department Y	5	6	150
Department Z	5	14	175

Using the graphic method find the optimum combination of the products which would maximize total profit. Suppose the company could concentrate all its efforts on one model. Would this change the solution?

3. It is said that linear programming is an excellent planning tool for the manager. Referring to what you have read about planning, answer the

question, "What specifically can linear programming do in the planning function?"

4. In a very complete paragraph, describe exactly what is meant by linear programming.

5. What two conditions must a problem exhibit in order to enable the use of linear programming?

6. Can you think of an allocation problem other than those discussed in this chapter where linear programming might possibly be of some help? Describe it in a short paragraph indicating the objective and the various constraints.

7. Discuss the following statement: "Since conditions of certainty must exist in order for linear programming to be used, it is of little value to managers because conditions of certainty rarely, if ever, exist in the real world."

Additional references

Kwak, N. K. *Mathematical Programming with Business Applications.* New York: McGraw-Hill Book Co., 1973.

Levin, R. I., and Kirkpatrick, C. A. *Quantitative Approaches to Management.* New York: McGraw-Hill Book Co., 1975.

Levin, R. I., and Lamone, R. P. *Linear Programming for Management Decisions.* Homewood, Ill.: Richard D. Irwin, Inc., 1969.

Loomba, N. P. *Linear Programming: An Introductory Analysis.* New York: McGraw-Hill Book Co., 1964.

Naylor, T. H., and Byrne, E. T. *Linear Programming.* Belmont, California: Wadsworth Publishing Co., 1963.

Smythe, W. R., and Johnson, L. A. *Introduction to Linear Programming, with Applications.* Englewood Cliffs, N.J.: Prentice-Hall, Inc., 1966.

Spivey, W. Allen, and Thrall, R. M. *Linear Optimization.* New York: Holt, Rinehart, and Winston, Inc., 1970.

Wagner, H. M. *Principles of Operations Research.* 2d ed. Englewood Cliffs, N.J.: Prentice-Hall, Inc., 1975.

PART
FIVE

Future managers and their environments

Reality-centered management

17

REALITY-CENTERED MANAGEMENT

At the beginning of this book we asked the question, "What can be done in the present to prepare future managers for the future?" The result has been a book organized around the idea that tomorrow's managers should have *knowledge* about the management process and the managerial functions of planning, organizing, and controlling; about group and individual behavior; and about organizational structure. Moreover they should have skills in the use of various behavioral and quantitative techniques.

The evolving field of management is forcing each individual manager to examine, use, experiment, and discard various ideas in all of the three schools. What this means is that there is no one best way to manage. Instead, there are a variety of ways to manage appropriately. In the first section of this final chapter we shall present a framework which seeks to bring together the three major approaches to the study of management and provide a foundation for the manager of the future to formulate a reality-centered conception of the managerial process. This chapter will also attempt to project into the future some of the critical developments which will bear on the practice of management. The separate and combined effects of these developments reinforces the necessity for reality-centered management.

Reality-centered managing

The following statement aptly describes the reality-centered manager:

> ... the future executive is going to have to possess a greater breadth and intensity of knowledge than did managers past and present. The complexity of future organizations, and the confusion of society, will require that managers have a considerable knowledge of the techniques of economics and the behavioral sciences, perhaps some grasp of engineering and the physical sciences, and certainly a good conception of quantitative methodology and computer technology. More than being a mere

"tool user," however, the future manager is going to have to be a humanist as well as a technocrat. He will have to have the ability to understand people and to appraise situations and to make judicious decisions that will be followed.[1]

If the manager recognizes that useful concepts, techniques, and models exist in the three schools of management, this is a step in the direction of reality centeredness. This is not to say that experience and/or wisdom will be totally useless in the modern era of management. Instead, the need for a balance of the classical, behavioral, and management science approaches together with experience is more realistic and contemporary. Sole reliance on classical principles, or behavioral theories, or management science models, is as sterile and stagnant as relying solely on past experience. An appreciation of the schools of management and experience is what the reality-centered manager should attempt to accomplish. This kind of thinking will go far in making a manager more effective in contemporary organizations.

Integrating the three schools of management

One of the major problems that must be overcome if managers are to adopt a reality-centered approach is that they must be able to visualize what various concepts, techniques, and models can do to improve their organizations. The ideas suggested by such people as Taylor, Fayol, Urwick, Maslow, Herzberg, and Fiedler must be placed into an integrated framework. It has been suggested that each of the concepts, techniques, and models can be placed into one of two categories.[2]

The first category includes factors that focus upon greater order, systematization, routinization, and predictability. This category will be referred to as the *closed system* factors. The second category includes factors that are primarily designed to develop greater openness, sharing, creativity, and individual initiative. This category will be designated as the *open system* factors.

Both factors are valuable for the reality-centered manager. Neither set is all right nor all wrong for every management problem. It is best to view them as the extremes of a continuum along which the concepts discussed in this book can be placed.

A clearer understanding of the various techniques and models from the three schools may be obtained from Figure 17–1. The factors speci-

---

[1] Joseph W. McGuire, ed., *Contemporary Management: Issues and Viewpoints* (Englewood Cliffs, N.J.: Prentice-Hall, Inc., 1974), p. 651.

[2] This classification scheme was developed by Paul R. Lawrence and Jay W. Lorsch, *Organization and Environment* (Homewood, Ill.: Richard D. Irwin, Inc. 1969). It is appropriate for integrating the three schools of management.

FIGURE 17–1
Integrating the three schools of management

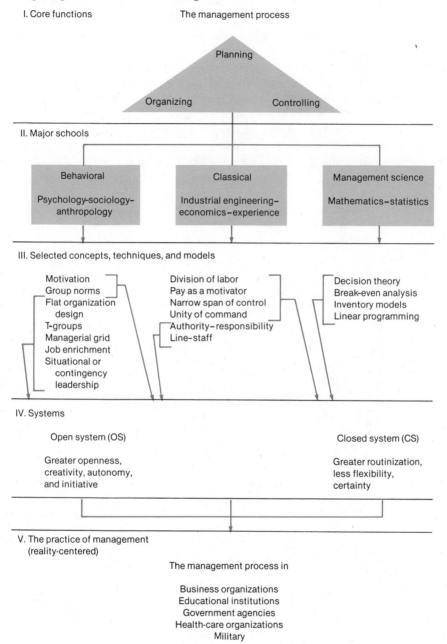

I. Core functions — The management process

Planning

Organizing — Controlling

II. Major schools

Behavioral	Classical	Management science
Psychology–sociology–anthropology	Industrial engineering–economics–experience	Mathematics–statistics

III. Selected concepts, techniques, and models

Motivation
Group norms
Flat organization design
T-groups
Managerial grid
Job enrichment
Situational or contingency leadership

Division of labor
Pay as a motivator
Narrow span of control
Unity of command
Authority–responsibility
Line–staff

Decision theory
Break-even analysis
Inventory models
Linear programming

IV. Systems

Open system (OS)

Greater openness, creativity, autonomy, and initiative

Closed system (CS)

Greater routinization, less flexibility, certainty

V. The practice of management (reality-centered)

The management process in

Business organizations
Educational institutions
Government agencies
Health-care organizations
Military

fied in the diagram are not a complete referencing of every possible approach or technique. However, the diagram does provide a guiding framework for the future manager.

Figure 17–1 indicates that at the core of the management process are the functions of planning, organizing, and controlling. Behind the application of any of the techniques and models displayed in Figure 17–1 are these core functions. They are clearly represented as the basic foundations of the field of management.

In Figure 17–1 the specific discipline that has influenced the evolution of each school is also presented. For example, the fields of statistics and mathematics have had a pronounced and obvious influence on the Management Science School. On the other hand, industrial engineering, economics, and specific management experience have significantly affected the development of the Classical School of Management.

Selected approaches from each of the three schools of management are also specified in Figure 17–1. These approaches are associated with one of the two orientations. For example, authority can be used to exercise control over a job task. This use would demand compliance and would be inflexible. However, a manager may use authority to allow subordinates to make autonomous decisions. Subordinates may be allowed to plan their own work schedules or to establish their own budgets. Therefore, authority can be interpreted as both a closed system and an open system factor, depending upon the manager and the situation.

Examination of linear programming models suggests that they are designed to aid the manager in developing a program for the optimum allocation of resources. The utilization of linear programming focuses upon predicting the optimum use of some resource. Thus, this model meets the criteria of a closed system factor.

The two major categories provide a framework for classifying the numerous concepts of the three management schools. The advantage of having this type of framework is that instead of arguing about which managerial school is most accurate, the student of management focuses upon what each concept can accomplish most effectively.

The future manager

The increasing number of concepts and techniques offered by the schools of management and the rapid pace of change require that a more sophisticated managerial cadre be called upon to make organizational decisions. Understanding the functions of planning, organizing and controlling is essential. Managers in future organizations will need to increase their technical skills, conceptual skills, diagnostic skills, awareness of social and ethical issues, and concern for human resources.

The skills and abilities required to perform effectively in future management positions will be derived from a number of sources such as: (1) educational preparation, (2) professional training and development, and (3) actual experiences on the job and in society. The education, development, and experience of managers will be a continuing process.

The specifics of the exact type of educational background, developmental process, and experience are beyond the scope of this chapter. One may anticipate, however, that knowledge of economics, the functional areas of business (for example, accounting, marketing, and production), quantitative methods, computers, and the behavioral sciences will be invaluable. This is not to say that any manager can master each of these broad areas. It is, however, feasible to assume that managers can maintain a working knowledge of the more relevant and pertinent concepts associated with each of the areas. The required comprehension is possible if the educational programs of universities and colleges, management development programs, and daily organizational activities encourage the preparation of reality-centered managers.

The reality to be managed

Managers have always been responsible for designing, directing, and evaluating organizations. That responsibility has never been particularly easy to discharge and little reason exists to believe that it will be easier in the future. In fact the evidence presently available suggests that the future realities which managers will have to deal with will pose dilemmas of even greater difficulty. We noted in Chapter 1 a number of dilemmas posed by apparent conflicts between the needs, desires, and ambitions of individuals and those of groups and organizations. We also noted the conflicts between and among governmental, economic, political, and social interests in the functioning of organizations.

In this concluding section the dilemmas of management will be projected into the future. Projections are always tentative, but not haphazard. In fact, they embody the characteristics of forecasting, a key step in the planning function. Despite the limitations of attempting to discern the future, forecasting is an absolute necessity if the future is to be managed.

INDIVIDUAL-ORGANIZATION DILEMMAS

The central focus of dilemmas which arise from the conflict between individual and organizational needs is the design of jobs. What people are expected to accomplish and the conditions under which they work have been analyzed since the earliest efforts of Classical Management. Scientific management and classical organization theory dealt primarily with issues related to the efficient use of humans in work organizations. Through motion and time study and work simplification techniques these early writers introduced the means by which efficient and productive jobs could be designed.

Then, as we now know, the Behavioral School criticized the classical writers for ignoring the human element. Human relations and behavioral science writers believe that the design of jobs must include opportunities to satisfy upper-level needs such as esteem, achievement, and self-actualization. A variety of techniques and programs such as job enlargement, job enrichment, management-by-objectives, and participative management have evolved to improve the quality of worklife (QWL).

The exact meaning of QWL is still being worked out by management practitioners and scholars. A recent review of the status of QWL applications notes: "The absolute *essential* component of any QWL program is real and ever-present opportunity for individuals or task groups at any level to influence their working environments, to have some say over what goes on in connection with their work."[3] This meaning stresses the importance of self-control and individual participation as aspects of high-quality worklife.

A broader meaning of high-quality worklife notes seven characteristics.[4]

1. Jobs are interesting, challenging, and responsible.
2. Workers are rewarded through fair wages and recognition for their contributions.
3. Workplaces are clean, light, quiet, and safe.
4. Supervision is minimal but available when needed.
5. Workers are involved in decisions which affect them and their jobs.
6. Jobs are secure and promote the development of friendly relationships with coworkers.
7. Organizations provide facilities for personal welfare and medical attention.

These characteristics pertain to QWL programs implemented in such organizations as AT&T, General Electric, General Foods, Motorola, Proctor and Gamble, and General Motors.

It is reasonable to believe that the pressure for improving the quality of worklife will continue in the future. This projection is

---

[3] Edward M. Glaser, "State-of-the-Art Questions About Quality of Worklife," *Personnel*, (May–June 1976), p. 39.

[4] Tom Lupton, "Efficiency and the Quality of Worklife," *Organizational Dynamics* (Autumn 1975), p. 68.

supported by the evidence currently available. For example:[5] (1) the supply of second-class labor is already diminishing in this and other Western countries. Traditional sources of cheap and docile labor such as rural outmigration, children, and women are drying up; (2) the mix of jobs is changing from predominantly blue-collar to white-collar; (3) legislation and judicial decisions have created greater and greater obligations on work organizations to deal directly with quality of worklife issues such as health and safety; (4) the level of education and literacy has risen and will continue to do so for all segments of society.

The net effect of these changing conditions is that future managers will have to deal with increasingly educated and aware individuals. Their attitudes and values will emphasize autonomy, growth, and self-development. And many of their interests will be protected and promoted by law.

At the same time, however, the future manager will be forced to pay even closer attention to efficient use of resources. The sources of energy are also drying up. Yet as a noted management expert states: "There is no direct connection between the quality of worklife and business efficiency."[6] The difficult issue is knowing and recognizing the conditions within which improving QWL also improves efficiency. Contingency theories of organizational design, leadership, and motivation all suggest similar conclusions. Environmental factors such as characteristics of the labor supply, trends in society, conditions in the economy, and stability of the environment have been associated with outcomes of QWL programs.[7] The managerial dilemma, then, comes down to deciding between efficiency and quality of worklife in those environments when the two outcomes are inversely related.

ORGANIZATION-ENVIRONMENT DILEMMAS

It is common today to read articles or hear speeches calling for more "people consciousness" or "social responsibility" on the part of managers in every type of organization. In considering the meaning of these demands, it is important to note that this movement is only one part of a much broader and more pervasive change in the values of people in our society. It is no coincidence that demands for more social awareness among the managers of large organizations, the concerns of the younger generation, minority group protests, the

---

[5] Stanley E. Seashore, "The Future of Work: How It May Change and What It May Mean," Industrial and Labor Relations Report (Fall 1975), p. 14–16.

[6] Lupton, "Efficiency and the Quality of Worklife," p. 68.

[7] Noel M. Tichy and Jay N. Nisberg, "When Does Work Restructuring Work? Organizational Innovations at Volvo and G.M." Organizational Dynamics (Summer 1976), p. 68.

consumerism movement, women's rights, discontent on the nation's assembly lines, concern about ecology, and problems in the nation's prisons have all occurred almost simultaneously. The last few years have been characterized by such phrases as "the meaning of work," "the quality of life," "the environment," "power to the people," and numerous others. The common ingredient of each of these co-called movements is *people*, and each of them will profoundly influence every type of organization—public and private—in our society during the next decade.

The demands for more social awareness and responsibility from the nation's managers is only one part of the overall attempt of our society to make all institutions—business, government, educational, medical —more responsive to human needs. The managers in these organizations will be called upon to react to these demands. Earlier in the book we indicated the necessity of monitoring the organizations' external environment for important inputs to the management process. As society's values and needs change, they must influence the management process. These needs and changing values must be reflected in the alternatives considered and the priorities assigned by managers.

Some expected changes in managerial practices in business organizations in the foreseeable future are described in Table 17–1. Examination of the table reveals that most of the expected changes reflect the ferment within our society and our evolving "people-oriented" values. While Table 17–1 is concerned specifically with business organizations, most of the changes are pervasive, reflecting changes in societal values, and will extend far beyond business managers to those in every type of organization in our society. It is also interesting to note that many of the forecasted changes reflect a more open-system orientation.

Business organizations and social responsibility. During the last decade society has been placing increased demands on large business organizations for greater social responsibility—that is, business involvement in solving both social and ecological problems. Some executives have replied, "Why us?" while others have agreed. Some firms commit resources to social action programs; others agree they should but, as yet, have not; and still others believe that they meet their social responsibilities by being profitable, providing employment, and paying taxes. The problem is a very real and complex one with which business organizations and our society will be forced to come to grips during the next decade.

In early history the wealthy and the powerful have often assumed responsibility for the welfare of those less fortunate around them. It is probably the lingering survival of this paternalistic belief that today demands from the large business organization the kind of social responsibility that has throughout history been expected of wealth and power. In the context of present times these expectations fall in such areas as

TABLE 17-1
Past versus future managerial practices*

Past	Future
Assumption that a business manager's sole responsibility is to optimize stockholder wealth	Profit still dominant but modified by the assumption that a business manager has other social responsibilities
Business performance measured only by economic standards	Application of both an economic and a social measure of performance
Emphasis on quantity of production	Emphasis on quantity and quality
Authoritarian management	Permissive/democratic management
Short-term intuitive planning	Long-range comprehensive structured planning
Entrepreneur	Renaissance manager
Control	Creativity
People subordinate	People dominant
Financial accounting	Human resources accounting
Caveat emptor ("let the buyer beware")	Ombudsman
Centralized decision making	Decentralized and small-group decision making
Concentration on internal functioning	Concentration on external ingredients for company success
Dominance of economic forecasts in decision making	Major use of social, technical, and political forecasts as well as economic forecasts
Business viewed as a single system	Business viewed as a system within a larger social system
Business ideology calls for aloofness from government	Business-government cooperation and convergence of planning
Business has little concern for social costs of production	Increasing concern for internalizing social costs of production

* George Steiner, presidential address before the American Academy of Management (Minneapolis, August 15, 1972).

educating the young, policing the streets, cleaning up polluted air and water, teaching disadvantaged citizens how to earn a living, rebuilding ghettos, and providing management expertise for city governments.

As problems such as these continue to mount, business managers of the future will be more than ever faced with reconciling their responsibilities to two groups of people: stockholders and society in general. In addition to the belief that power implies responsibility, there are other reasons why the modern corporation will be looked to for help in solving society's problems. For example, more and more citizens are realizing that in addition to having the power, the modern business corporation also has the technical know-how to aid in solving the nation's problems. The federal government itself holds a similar viewpoint and has begun actively to solicit the aid of the large corporation.

While there are strong arguments *for* social responsibility by business organizations, there are also some powerful arguments *against* it. For example, there are those who maintain that the large corporation administers a wealth that it does not own and, therefore, should not be forced to develop a social awareness over the use of assets that are owned ultimately by private citizens. Others seriously question whether it is proper to place public problems on the shoulders of corporate managers. They point out that persons who are highly skilled in business matters may not be so in matters of politics, the humanities, and the social sciences. They also note that such persons are in no way accountable to the voters for their decisions and could, in determining what is best for society, turn into paternalistic rulers.

One of the major problems surrounding the entire issue appears to be that of clearly defining what social responsibility is as well as deciding what society should reasonably expect from the business firm in this area. Notwithstanding this problem, as well as the debates pro and con, it appears that demands for socially responsible business behavior will continue and probably increase. While the direction and extent of these demands cannot be known at this time, many business organizations are responding to the present challenges. Following are some specific instances in which business has taken on responsibilities that can be considered social in nature:

1.   The city of New York called in McKinsey and Company to analyze the city's air pollution problems, and the Traffic Commission invited Sperry Rand, and later IBM, to "help solve the city's growing traffic headache."[8]
2.   The governors of Alabama, California, Nebraska, and other states have borrowed business executives, whose salaries continue to be paid by their respective companies, as consultants in seeking ways to trim the costs of state government.[9]
3.   A large western bank has, since 1971, sponsored a tennis program (using professional instructors and company employees) for disadvantaged youth.
4.   A supermarket chain in the West has, since 1970, conducted a continuing, multifaceted program for encouraging and aiding food consumers in becoming more ecologically effective as individuals, as well as altering certain internal practices of the firm in the interest of ecology.

---

[8] See Hazel Henderson, "Should Business Tackle Society's Problems?" *Harvard Business Review* (July–August 1968), p. 78.

[9] Ibid., p. 79.

5. A large eastern firm, newly located on the shores of a heavily polluted lake, instituted an ongoing program of research studies and seminars as well as internal operational changes with the goal of reaching workable solutions to the critical pollution problem.

The manager's social responsibility dilemma. Managers find themselves on the horns of a dilemma. When they attempt to become involved in society's problems they may be faced with a group of angry stockholders who maintain that companies have no legal right to retain earnings for such uses, and that the stockholders should decide how the money is spent since they are the rightful owners. On the other hand, when managers attempt to maximize profit for the stockholders they may be faced with the wrath of other citizens who claim that corporate managers have no respect for the needs of society as a whole and are failing to safeguard the environmental conditions that provide for the survival and growth of the business organization.

The root cause of the conflict over social responsibility appears to lie in the irreconcilability of two theories of the corporation—the theory of the *traditional corporation* on the one hand, and the theory of the *metrocorporation* on the other.[10] Both theories express extreme viewpoints.

The *traditional corporation* is an instrument of a single group—the shareholders—and has one clearcut purpose: to conduct business for profit. The prior claim of the stockholders on earnings after taxes is unquestioned, and management has to do no "balancing" of interests in distributing the earnings. This traditional view recognizes no social responsibilities except for legal ones and leaves the public interests to the care of the state. As we noted previously, the view has been attacked as being shortsighted and ultimately self-destructive.

The opposite model of the traditional corporation is the *metrocorporation*, which assumes limitless social responsibility. In this type of corporation, managers accept an accountability to many different segments of society. This type of corporation is a major social institution with comprehensive aims, and it is far removed from the strict, limited objective of the traditional corporation: profit for the stockholders. The metrocorporation emphasizes its rights and duties as a "citizen" in its relationships with the various groups in its environment. The negative aspects of this model were also previously pointed out: undue power for managers and the danger of their becoming paternalistic rulers; incompetence in areas such as humanities and politics; and the suboptimization of corporate economic goals and functions.

Obviously, the above descriptions represent two opposite extremes. The business manager of the future will undoubtedly find a middle

---

[10] This discussion is based upon Richard Eells and Clarence Walton, *Conceptual Foundations of Business* (Homewood, Ill.: Richard D. Irwin, Inc., 1961), pp. 468–76.

ground between these positions. The following statement should aid in establishing this position.

> The large business corporation is here to stay. It is an indispensible instrument for getting done some of the things that people want done. It is neither the exclusive instrument of one class of interests nor an indiscriminate roster of "social" interests. Like other large organizations, the corporation has to be tempered to the times; and as a viable instrument it must adapt to the changing requirements of our free, complex, and interdependent society.[11]

Thus it is necessary to find a position somewhere between the extremes of the traditional corporation and the metrocorporation which will take into account public expectations and not be in conflict with management's responsibilities to the stockholder. This model has been referred to as the *well-tempered corporation*.[12] This viewpoint holds that the claims of stockholders and creditors will more likely be met if a firm develops a position as a socially responsible company. This can only be done if management integrates the factors of production with respect to the primary interests of the owners and the prevailing norms and values of society. Since the values of our society are changing rapidly, so is the definition of a socially responsible firm. The following statement reflects a realistic response to the difficult question, "What is a socially responsible firm?"

> The answer to this question will change and eventually must be answered by society itself. It may be best to define the socially responsible firm as one that anticipates what the public will expect from it and attempts to meet these demands before the public focuses its criticism upon it. In a nutshell, the socially responsible firm is one that is responsive to (even anticipates) the demands of society, not only economic ones, but social and environmental ones as well.[13]

This will be a major task facing the managers of the future.

A postscript

Issues of social responsibility, ecology, the meaning of work, the quality of worklife, minority employment, sex discrimination, etc., have very important "value" implications for management. Contemporary managers will be forced to weave these value changes into their own concept of what a manager should do and be. This process

---

[11] Ibid., p. 474.

[12] Ibid.

[13] R. Joseph Monsen, *Business and the Changing Environment* (New York: McGraw-Hill Book Co., 1973), p. 121.

cannot be learned through reading a textbook since it extends far beyond the classroom.

It is inconceivable to imagine that a society can be confronted with critical shortages, insufficient natural resources, and ecological pollution without experiencing a change in values. During the past several decades managers operated for the most part in an environment characterized by abundance and a societal commitment to growth. If the next decade is characterized by shortages and a societal commitment to conservation, then conflicts will undoubtedly arise with which managers will be forced to deal. In fact, some individuals see our society shifting from a "things first-people second" orientation to one of "people first and things second."

Such a reorientation of our societal values will have a profound impact on future management practice in every type of organization. What it will mean is that the manager of the future will not be able to act as an isolationist with respect to society because the measure of an effective manager in the future will likely be more than effective performance alone.

Discussion and review questions

1. If you were asked to describe the field of management in a one-page essay, what would you say?

2. It is generally assumed that computer experts still do not have much influence on the policy makers in organizations. Do you believe that their status and power within the organization will change in the future? Why?

3. Many management scholars believe that new functions will be found in the organization chart of the future. These functions will be additions to the traditional functions such as finance, marketing, public relations, and production. Do you foresee any new areas on the organization chart of tomorrow? What will be some of the responsibilities of the executives heading up these new areas?

4. Develop a figure which will enlarge upon and extend the schools of management and the concepts presented in Figure 17–1.

5. Assume that all corporations take on added social responsibilities. Whom do you feel will bear the additional costs—stockholders, employees? Or will prices increase?

6. A man calls at your home and represents himself as conducting an educational survey. When you admit him to your home, he proceeds to ask a few questions about the children in school and then begins a sales talk about encyclopedias. Do this and other types of activities by business firms have any relationship to social responsibility?

7. A corporation in your city has just announced that it will contribute $25,000 to the Department of Marketing at your school to be used to study

consumer buying habits in your state. How do you view this act? Is it altruistic? Is it motivated by a desire for profit?

8. What are the interrelationships between the dilemmas of improving the quality of worklife and meeting social responsibilities?

9. Which of the three schools of management will provide the techniques for achieving more efficient use of natural resources? Why?

10. In a historical context, is the present and future conflict between quality of worklife and efficiency different in any significant way from the conflict between work-related and people-related management activities?

Additional references

Ackerman, R. W. *The Social Challenge to Business.* Cambridge, Ma.: Harvard University Press, 1975.

Anshen, M., and Back, G. L., eds. *Management and Corporations, 1985.* New York: McGraw-Hill Book Company, 1960.

Cavanagh, G. *American Business Values in Transition.* Englewood Cliffs, N.J.: Prentice-Hall, Inc., 1976.

Davis, K., and Blomstrom, R. L. *Business, Society, and Environment: Social Power and Social Response.* New York: McGraw-Hill Book Company, 1971.

Eells, R. *Global Corporations.* New York: Free Press, 1976.

Eppen, G. D., ed. *Energy: The Policy Issues.* Chicago: University of Chicago Press, 1975.

Estes, R. *Corporate Social Accounting.* New York: John Wiley and Sons, 1976.

Gordon, F. E., and Strober, M. H., eds. *Bringing Women into Management.* New York: McGraw-Hill Book Co., 1975.

Gruber, W. H., and Niles, J. S. *The New Management: Line Executive and Staff Professional in the Future.* New York: McGraw-Hill Book Co., 1976.

Kreps, J., and Clark, R. *Sex, Age, and Work.* Baltimore, Md.: Johns Hopkins University Press, 1976.

Livingstone, J. M. *The International Enterprise.* New York: John Wiley and Sons, 1975.

Luthans, F., and Hodgetts, R. M. *Social Issues in Business.* New York: The Macmillan Company, 1972.

Madden, C. H. *Clash of Culture: Management in an Age of Changing Values.* Washington, D.C.: National Planning Association, 1976.

Massie, J. L., and Luytjes, J. B. *Management in an International Context.* New York: Harper and Row, Publishers, 1972.

McGuire, J. W. *Contemporary Management: Issues and Viewpoints.* Englewood Cliffs, N.J.: Prentice-Hall, Inc., 1974.

Negandi, A. R., and Estafen, B. D. "A Research Model to Determine the Applicability of American Management Know-How in Differing Cultures and/or Environments," *Academy of Management Journal 8* (1965): 309–18.

Seidler, L. J., and Seidler, L. L. *Social Accounting.* Los Angeles: Melville Publishing Co., 1975.

Sethi, S. P. *Up Against the Corporate Wall: Modern Corporations and Social Issues of the Seventies.* Englewood Cliffs, N.J.: Prentice-Hall, Inc., 1974.

Sethi, S. P., ed. *The Unstable Ground: Corporate Social Policy in a Dynamic Society.* Los Angeles: Melville Publishing Company, 1974.

Steiner, G. A., ed. *Issues in Business and Society.* New York: Random House Inc., 1972.

Stone, C. D. *Where the Law Ends: The Social Control of Corporate Behavior.* New York: Harper and Row, 1975.

Viola, R. H. *Organizations in a Changing Society: Administration and Human Values.* Philadelphia: W. B. Saunders Co., 1977.

Walton, C. C. *Ethos and the Executive.* Englewood Cliffs, N.J.: Prentice-Hall, Inc., 1969.

INTEGRATIVE PRACTICAL EXERCISE

National Motor Parts Company*

The National Motor Parts Company is one of the five largest firms in the basic auto parts industry. It has nine operating divisions and a total work force of over 80,000 employees. Its extensive staff organization provides specialized skills at the corporate, divisional, and plant level. At each of these levels, the cost accounting and industrial engineering groups exert a considerable amount of interest over the development and execution of corporate policy. Though individual divisions are operationally autonomous, division officials generally follow the policy suggestions made by the cost accounting and industrial engineering staffs. A partial organization chart is shown in Exhibit 1.

One program recently advocated by Phil King, corporate director of industrial engineering, was a review of work standards on all jobs which had not been checked or audited within the previous two years. King's request arose from the fact that he had seen several instances of what appeared to him to be goldbricking during a tour of plants in several of National's operating divisions. Upon his return to the central office, Mr. King met with two of his staff engineers, and after careful deliberation, an audit plan was drawn up. This plan was subsequently approved by the executive vice president in charge of manufacturing operations.

The audit plan suggested by King used a technique known as work sampling to check on the idle time present in individual job standards. In essence, the approach taken relied on the fact that a series of short, random observations, if taken often enough over an appropriate time period, could give an accurate picture of the operations performed in each job. The work sampling results would be used to determine which jobs were not requiring the employees to work for an entire day to meet their stated output standards. By the same token, those jobs which were demanding a full day's work to meet existing standards would also be recognized. Though work sampling was to be used to identify standards which were loose (i.e., standards which did not require a

EXHIBIT 1

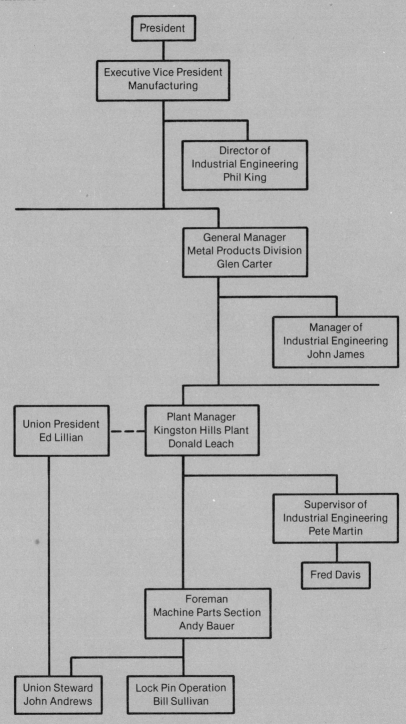

full day's work to meet standard output requirements for that day), King's proposal included the further suggestion that looseness, when detected, should be checked in detail by the use of stopwatch time study and a thorough motion study of the job in question.

To launch his program, Mr. King held a series of meetings with the heads of divisional industrial engineering groups. Though objections were raised about the cost and time considerations inherent in the proposal, the division engineering managers agreed that the plan was technically sound and agreed to put it into effect as soon as possible.

One of the more receptive listeners to Mr. King's standards audit procedure was John James, manager of industrial engineering in National's Metal Products Division. This division employs 21,000 people in five plants. James, who holds degrees in both industrial engineering and mathematics, thought that King's plan was both technically sound and eminently practical. He returned to division headquarters in Kingston, Michigan, and drew up procedures to implement the plan in the Metal Products Division's five plants.

Within a month after the corporate staff meeting, James offered his own version of the audit plan to Glenn Carter, the division manager. Carter, who had come to respect James' technical ability and practical know-how, accepted the plan readily and agreed to present it at the next weekly meeting of his plant managers. Carter suggested that he should merely outline the plan to his plant managers and that James should be available to fill in details and to answer questions.

In the subsequent meeting, each of the plant managers agreed that such an audit was sound, and each, in turn, suggested that James contact the heads of their plant industrial engineering departments to explain the details of his plan. Three plant managers who had formerly been in charge of industrial engineering groups in the National hierarchy offered to provide additional clerical and engineering help on a temporary basis in order to get the program moving quickly.

After gaining the support of Mr. Carter and the five plant managers, James met with the heads of industrial engineering in each of the division's five plants. Though the familiar objections were raised about the time and cost of such a program, all five men stated that the audit procedure was practical and they agreed to put it into effect immediately. Within this group, the plan was embraced most enthusiastically by Pete Martin, the industrial engineer in charge of the Kingston Hills plant.

The Kingston Hills plant shared the same plot of land as the headquarters of the Metal Products Division. It employed more than 5,000 workers and was generally considered to be the most modern and most efficient of the division's plants. Donald Leach, the plant manager, was one of the three men in the division who rose to his present position from a supervisory job in the industrial engineering hierarchy. Leach's plant was equipped with the latest advances in automated equipment, and it was, according to division records, the most profitable plant in the division. Leach prided himself on his ability to attract and retain good managerial talent and he was particularly proud of the work done by Pete Martin in developing new methods of work and in adapting mathematical techniques and procedures to fit the needs of the operations at the Kingston Hills plant. Thus, when Martin suggested the adoption of an audit program, Leach agreed readily and offered Martin additional clerical help to work on the details of setting up the program.

Pete Martin went to work on the program immediately, and within a week the first audit reports were completed. After one month, audits had been completed on seventeen operations. Sixteen of these audits indicated that very little idle time was evident in the operations studied, but the audit performed on one job, the production of a tiny metal lock pin used in automatic transmission units, seemed to show an unusual amount of idle time. The job in question was performed by Bill Sullivan, an experienced long-service employee. Sullivan set up, tended, and performed certain minor maintenance tasks on an automatic screw machine. Because the products he worked on were varied, the original standards had been measured quite carefully.[1] Since the time when the original standards were set, changes had occurred which caused the standards to become loose. Materials changes, changes in tolerance limits on the various machined parts, the time and methods used to set up the various runs, the actual length of machine runs, and the adoption of a more standardized parts line had all occurred in recent years; and since several of these changes had apparently not been reflected in adjustments in the affected output standards, it was a rare day when Sullivan failed to obtain his expected or standard output.

The looseness of Sullivan's standards was no revelation to several of his immediate co-workers. One worker, for example, when conversing with Pete Martin about the audit, stated, "If your audit doesn't pick up that soft touch Sullivan's got, you'd better toss the whole thing down the drain." Few of the workers were bitter about Sullivan's "gravy train" job, however, since the looseness of his standards give him no wage advantages over his fellow workers. In other National plants where payment was tied directly to output through the use of incentive payment plans, the relative looseness of standards had frequently caused bitter disputes because of the wage inequities it generated. In the Kingston Hills Plant, the failure of management to detect a loose standard meant that workers accrued leisure time benefits, not higher wages. Though workers objected to such "unfair" work loads, no

---

[1] Sullivan's standard at this time was .33734 minutes per piece, or approximately 180 units of output per hour.

grievance had ever been filed to ask management to correct such inequities.

The second phase of the audit procedure entailed a review of Sullivan's job by Fred Davis, one of Martin's most competent engineers. In this study, Davis compared the previously set standard with the newly calculated time required to perform the operation under changed conditions. This, in turn, showed a tentative idle time of four hours per shift.[2] Davis's stopwatch time study of the screw machine operation confirmed the results of the initial audit, and a detailed methods study of the job turned up substantial changes in the original working conditions including changes in materials and methods of operation. Mr. Leach, when confronted with this information by Martin and Davis, ordered them to take steps to correct what he believed was an inequity in the basic work load structure.

After several weeks of study, Davis devised a plan where, with certain layout changes and some methods improvements, Sullivan would operate not one, but two machines. Davis's methods study showed that the time allowances were adequate enough to allow Sullivan to complete the requirements of the revised job if he worked a full eight-hour day. Davis showed his plan to Pete Martin, and together they presented it to Mr. Leach. Leach approved the plan and directed the purchasing department to acquire another automatic screw machine. He thereupon called in Andy Bauer, Sullivan's immediate supervisor, and informed him that Sullivan should be told of the impending change.[3] Bauer, who had worked with Mr. Davis on the methods study, agreed to tell Sullivan that management intended to exercise its contractual right "to make changes in methods, equipment, materials, and conditions of work in order to obtain greater efficiency and to adjust existing work standards to reflect such changes." The labor contract further stated that "in case of such methods change only those elements of the standard will be changed which are affected by the change in methods, etc." One other section of the contract spelled out the fact that "standards will be set on the basis of fairness and equity and that they shall be consistent with the quality of workmanship, efficiency of operation, and reasonable working capacities of normal operations." In the National Motors contract, as in most others in the basic auto industry, the resolution of work standards disputes can be solved only by dealings between management and the

---

[2] Though a four-hour idle time may seem to be so high as to be almost unbelievable, engineering studies performed elsewhere in National Motors uncovered similar looseness. Experts in the industrial engineering field concede that this situation can arise in even the best-managed plants.

[3] The new standard called for a time of .1664 minutes per piece, or approximately 360 units per hour.

labor union. Arbitration is specifically prohibited as a means of settling disputes over work standards.

Two months later, the new machine was installed at the work place along with several minor changes in layout and work flow. Foreman Bauer instructed Sullivan in his new duties, and Sullivan, though he was unhappy about the new layout, started to work with the two machines. During the day, John Andrews, the union steward, stopped by to check on the new job.[4] Sullivan complained violently that he was the victim of a "speedup." Andrews, after listening to the details of the shift from one to two machines, suggested that Sullivan file a grievance.

That evening Sullivan wrote a grievance and, shortly before starting work the next morning, turned it over to John Andrews. Andrews, following the normal procedure for processing such grievances, presented it to Andy Bauer for discussion and possible solution. Because of the technical nature of the grievance, Bauer called upon Pete Martin and Fred Davis to explain the nature of the change to Andrews. When Martin and Davis showed their detailed methods studies to Andrews, he stated, "What your guys have done here is to blow up a big smoke screen to hide the fact that you're pulling a speedup on Sullivan's job." The net result of the meeting was that the grievance, still unsettled, moved to the second step in grievance procedure. This step involved discussion between the head of the local union, Ed Lillian, and Donald Leach, the plant manager.

Mr. Leach, when presented with Bill Sullivan's grievance, immediately called Pete Martin into his office to discuss the problem. Together they reviewed the methods study and the subsequent standards revisions. The approaches and the figures shown by Martin seemed correct and reasonable to Mr. Leach, and he believed that the contractual clause allowing him to "make changes in methods equipment, materials, and conditions of work in order to obtain greater efficiency and to adjust existing work standards to reflect such changes" justified the introduction of the second machine. He stated, "It's my duty to my work force to maintain an efficient operation so that the job security of all the workers will be protected." Leach also said, "The only way we can continue to grow and prosper and provide steady employment for our workers is to push for more efficiency in all of our plant activities." In his upcoming meeting with Ed Lillian, Leach planned to use this reasoning as the basis for his insistence on the introduction of the second machine. He also intended to allow Lillian to review any

[4] One of the main duties of a union steward is to represent the worker in presenting grievances to management. He is usually elected to this office by fellow workers. Stewards hold regular jobs in the plants where they perform their duties, and they receive no extra pay for their union activities.

and all of the data used as the basis for changes made on the disputed job.

Ed Lillian, on the other hand, expected to rely heavily on John Andrews to present the union side of the dispute. Lillian told Andrews that he would support him fully if the company's actions were in violation of the labor contract.

The feelings of the parties prior to the grievance meeting are summarized below:

Bill Sullivan: All of a sudden I'm expected to turn out three thousand pieces per day where I used to have to do fourteen hundred.[5] If this isn't a speedup I don't know what the hell it is. I've got rights and I expect the union to protect them.

John Andrews: The company hasn't done a thing to change methods here. They've just come in and made changes to correct their mistakes from the past. Their actions violate the fairness and equity clauses relating to revisions of work standards which exist in the labor contract.

Pete Martin: We've made good studies of Sullivan's job and we know that the lock pin standard is loose. It's not unfair to ask him to put in a fair day's work in order to earn a fair day's pay.

Ed Lillian: Even though Don Leach is sometimes tough in his dealings with us, he's been fair and consistent. On this issue, however, I'm not sure he's really right.

Donald Leach: I believe that I'm both contractually and economically correct when I take the stand that the second machine should be maintained on this operation. After all, if we don't have efficiency in this plant the workers won't have any job security.

Glenn Carter: The real issue here is whether or not managers have the right to run their own plants. If we have to subsidize inefficiency in our operations we won't be in business very long.

The grievance meeting scheduled to resolve this dispute was affected by at least two other factors:

1. Strikes over production standards are legal during the life of the labor contract. Though other issues (wages, hours, working conditions, etc.) can be grieved, no strikes can be called legally on these matters until the existing contract expires.

2. Though one more step remained in the division's grievance procedure, Mr. Carter had written a note to Ed Lillian which stated that he "would not, under any circumstances, alter the stand taken by Mr. Leach in the plant level negotiations." Since the dispute cannot be arbitrated, the parties are faced with the problem of devising some other strategy to solve (or to "win") the disagreement.

---

[5] In actuality Sullivan was required to turn out 1,440 pieces per day before the audit. After the methods change and subsequent standards revision, Sullivan's quota rose to 2,880.

In a front-page editorial on the day before the grievance meeting, the local *Kingston Daily Record* asks the disputants to act with "caution and care." The *Record's* editorial recalls that "the steel industry became embroiled in a similar issue which evolved into a strike lasting six months."

Questions for analysis:

1. Each of the parties to the disagreement has feelings about the causes of the dispute. Analyze the bases for each person's feelings in terms of unstated assumptions and values.

2. Which ones of the parties to the dispute appear to be analyzing the causes of the dispute in terms of *work-related* as distinct from *person-related* management activities? Explain.

3. What in your judgment are the underlying causes of this dispute? What do you believe should be the solution to the dispute? How can similar disputes be avoided in the future?

4. What solution would a manager propose who understands only Classical and Management Science Schools principles and methods? What solution would be proposed by a manager who understands only Behavioral School principles and methods?

5. Analyze the causes of the dispute in terms of the causes of intergroup conflict. What would be the appropriate strategy for managing the conflict during the grievance meeting?

GLOSSARY
OF TERMS

GLOSSARY OF TERMS

Acceptance theory of authority A theory of authority that Barnard proposed according to which the ultimate source of authority is the decision of the subordinate to accept the superior's orders.

Accountability The process by which a subordinate reports the use of assigned resources to a designated superior.

Administrative duties The 16 guidelines that Fayol believed should direct the manager in carrying out the organizing function. There is considerable overlap between his 16 Administrative Duties and his 14 Management Principles.

Allocation models This type of management science model is used in a situation where several possible candidates or activities are all competing for limited resources. It enables the user to allocate scarce resources in order to maximize some predetermined objective.

Anthropology Examines all the behaviors of man that have been learned. This includes social, technical, and family behaviors. It is often defined as the study of man and his works.

Authority The legitimate right to use assigned resources to accomplish a delegated task or objective. The right to give orders and to exact obedience. The legal bases for formal authority are private property, the state, or a Supreme Being.

Behavioral change Planned change in the attitudes, skills, and knowledge of organizational personnel.

Behavioral motivation theory The Behavioral School of Management advocates the pluralistic view of motivation which emphasizes that many different types of needs influence behavior, and that man is motivated by the desire to satisfy many needs.

Behavioral School of Management A body of literature which is characterized by its concern for human behavior in the work environment. The school's primary means for acquiring knowledge is the scientific method with emphasis upon research. The Behavioral School of Management thought followed the Classical School. Its first phase may be identified as "human relations" theory. This phase became popular in the 1940s and early 1950s. Its second phase was the "behavioral science" approach which came into popular use in the early 1950s.

Behavioral science approach This approach to the study of management can be thought of as the study of observable and verifiable human behavior in organizations, using scientific procedures. It draws especially from psychology, sociology, and anthropology.

Brand-switching models This type of management science model provides the manager with some idea of the behavior of consumers in terms of their loyalty and their switching from one brand to another.

Bureaucracy A form of organization which has many of the characteristics of the classical organization design, that is, is highly structured and centralized, with narrow spans of control.

Carrying costs These are the costs incurred by carrying an inventory. They include such costs as the taxes and insurance on the goods in inventory, interest on money invested in inventory and storage space, and the costs incurred because of the obsolescence of the inventory.

Case study This type of research design attempts to examine numerous characteristics of a person or group over an extended period of time. Since the results achieved by a case study are usually based on a sample of one, the user cannot be certain as to their generality. Most case studies raise questions for future research.

Certainty decision A decision in which the manager is certain about the state of nature or competitor action that will occur. Thus, the probability that a particular event will occur is 1.00.

Classical management motivation theory The classical approach to motivation emphasized monetary incentives as prime means for motivating the individual. This approach was undoubtedly strongly influenced by the classical economists who emphasized man's rational pursuit of economic objectives.

Classical School of Management A body of literature which represents the earliest attempts to define and describe the field of management. The school's main focus is on formally prescribed relationships. Its primary means for acquiring knowledge are personal observation and case studies.

Closed system (CS) factors Management concepts and techniques which focus upon greater order, systematization, routinization, and predictability. Most of the management science techniques and many classical concepts fall into this category.

Coercive power Power of a leader that is derived from fear on the part of the follower. The follower perceives the leader as a person who can punish deviant behavior and actions.

Command group The command group is specified by the formal organization chart. The group of subordinates who report to one particular supervisor constitutes the command group.

Components These are the parts of a management science model. They may be firms, households, warehouses, costs, or any other factor which is part of the system or process being modeled.

Concurrent control Techniques and methods which focus on the actual, ongoing activity of the organization.

Contingency organizational design This is the view that the internal functioning of organizations must be consistent with the demands of the organization task, technology, and external environment, and the needs of its members if the organization is to be effective. Contingency design focuses on what is best for a particular organization.

Contributed value   A measure of efficiency which relates value added to sales or profit.

Controlling function   All managerial activity that is undertaken to assure that actual operations go according to plan.

Decentralization   This concept can be viewed as the pushing downward of the appropriate amount of decision-making authority. Each organization practices a certain degree of decentralization.

Decision theory model   This type of model focuses upon certain elements in decision making that are common to all decisions and provides means to enable a decision maker to better analyze a complex situation that contains numerous alternatives and possible consequences. Strongly rooted in the fields of statistics and the behavioral sciences.

Defense mechanisms   When a person is blocked in attempts to satisfy needs, one or more defense mechanisms may be evoked. Some of the most common are withdrawal, aggression, substitution, compensation, repression, regression, projection, and rationalization.

Departmentalization   The process of grouping jobs together on the basis of some common characteristic; typically, the basis is product, client, location, process, or function.

Descriptive model   This type of model describes how a system works. It describes things as they are and makes no value judgments about the particular thing being studied. It may display the alternative choices available to the decision maker, but it does not select the best alternative.

Determinants of personality   The formation of the human personality is influenced by the mutual interaction of many factors. Four general classifications of factors must be considered: constitutional determinants, group-membership determinants, role determinants, and situational determinants.

Deterministic model   The word "deterministic" refers to the type of variables included in the model. A model is deterministic when the law of chance plays no role. All the factors taken into account in the model are assumed to be exact or determinate quantities.

Dialectic process of change   Any change which management implements in reaction to a particular problem will create new problems; the solution to a problem creates the environment within which new problems will emerge.

Direction   A subfunction of control which refers to the manager's act of interpreting orders to a subordinate.

Discounted rate of return   The rate of return that equates future cash proceeds and the initial cost of the investment.

Diverse environment   An environment which consists of many markets tending to have different and conflicting needs and demands.

Econometric analysis   A technique which involves the specification of relationships among many variables and the verification of relationships through statistical techniques.

Emergent leader   The leader who emerges from within the group. This person embodies the group's attitudes, values, beliefs, and opinions.

EOQ model   The economic order quantity model. It is used to resolve size of order problems. A manager concerned with minimizing inventory costs could utilize the *EOQ* model to study the relationships between carrying costs, ordering costs, and demand.

Equal profit line Used in graphic solution, traces the path of the objective function across the feasibility space, for an arbitrary profit (cost) level. The level which passes through that point of the feasibility space which is farthest to the right and upward is the profit at optimality.

Expectancy motivation model One of the more recent models of motivation which expands upon those developed by Maslow and Herzberg. It views motivation as a process governing choices and explains how the *goals* of individuals influence their *effort*.

Experiment This type of research design contains two key elements, namely, manipulation of some variable by the researcher and observation or measurement of the results.

Expert power The power which individuals possess because followers perceive them to have a special skill or special knowledge or special expertise.

Feasibility space Only takes on meaning in a graphic solution, and then only in the two-dimensional case. Defines area which contains all combinations of all variables which satisfy the inequalities. Bounded by lines representing the structural constraints.

Feedback control Techniques and methods which analyze historical data to correct future events.

First-line management The lowest level of a hierarchy; managers at this level coordinate the work of nonmanagers but report to a manager.

Fixed costs These are costs that remain fixed regardless of the level of sales generated or the number of units produced. Costs such as property taxes, depreciation, and insurance premiums are considered fixed.

Flat pyramid structure An organization type that reduces the layers of management, widens the span of control of managers at various levels, and is often more decentralized with regard to decision-making autonomy.

Forecasting Projections of the future from which management derives budgets and plans.

Friendship group A group that is established in the work place because of some common group characteristic (for example, the members like professional football), and that extends the interaction of members to include activities outside the work place.

Frustration This occurs when individuals are unable to satisfy their needs. Frustration may result in constructive problem-solving behavior or defensive behavior.

Functional foremanship The application of division of labor at the foreman level, as suggested by F. W. Taylor. It involves splitting the task of the foreman into eight subtasks and assigning each subtask to a separate individual.

Goal priority The relative importance of goals, in both the short and the long run.

Goal structure Refers to (1) the delegation of authority to pursue subgoals and (2) the relationship among multiple goals.

Graicunas' law A mathematical formulation of the relationship between the number of subordinates (N) and the number of potential superior–subordinate contacts (C), that is to say,

$$C = N\left(\frac{2^N}{2} + N - 1\right).$$

Group cohesiveness The attraction of members to the group in terms of the desirability of group membership to the members. The "stick-togetherness" of a group.

Group decision A decision that is reached within the structure of a group by the membership.

Hawthorne Studies Provided the impetus for the human relations approach to management. The studies were conducted by a group of researchers from Harvard University at the Chicago Hawthorne Plant of Western Electric. The general progression of the research took place in four phases: (1) Experiments in Illumination, (2) Relay Assembly Test Room Experiment, (3) Interview Program, and (4) Bank Wiring Observation Room Experiment.

Hierarchy of needs A widely adopted pluralistic framework of motivation. Developed by psychologist A. H. Maslow, the theory stresses two ideas:
1. Only needs not yet satisfied can influence behavior.
2. Man's needs are arranged in a hierarchy of importance. When one level has been satisfied, a higher level need emerges and demands satisfaction.

Maslow also distinguishes five general classes of needs: physiological, safety, social, esteem, and self-actualization.

Horizontal specialization of management The process by which the natural sequence of a task is broken down into specialized subgroups and a manager is assigned the authority and responsibility for coordinating the subgroups.

Hostile environment An environment which is risky and poses constraints on managers' freedom of action.

Human relations approach This approach to management emphasized the important role that individuals play in determining the success or failure of an organization. It embarked on the critical task of compensating for some of the deficiencies in classical theory. Basically, it took the premises of the Classical School as given. However, it showed how these premises were modified as a result of individual behavior and the influence of the work group.

Incremental influence This concept refers to the influence of a leader over and above the influence base bestowed because of position in the organization.

Inequality A functional relationship which allows latitude in variable values. Expresses either an upper or lower limit that combined variable values may take on.

Informal group A group that develops apart from official management plans and operates as a subculture within the organization.

Informal group norms The agreement among group members to adhere to a level of production, a group attitude, or a group belief.

Insufficient-reason criterion   If a manager is operating under conditions of uncertainty, it is assumed that there is an equal probability that each of the possible states of nature or competitive actions may occur.

Intelligence information   Data on the various elements of the organization's operating environment such as clients, competitors, suppliers, creditors, and the government, for use in evaluating short-run trends. It also includes long-run strategic planning information on the economic environment such as consumer income trends and spending patterns for a business organization as well as developments in the social and cultural environment in which the organization operates.

Interaction analysis   The technique developed by R. F. Bales to study group interaction. Through the observation of groups working on solving a case, Bales determined that task and human relations specialists emerge. Based upon observing the group interactions and answers to questions as to what occurred within the group to solve the case, Bales developed an interaction profile.

Intergroup conflict   A form of conflict that exists between groups because of such issues as limited resources, communication problems, or different perceptions of their members.

Interest group   A group that forms because of some special topic of interest. Generally, when the interest becomes weaker or a goal has been achieved, the group disbands.

Intraorganization flows   When intelligence information enters the boundaries of the organization, it must, along with internally generated information, reach the right manager at the right time to be useful. Within every organization there are *vertical* (both upward and downward), as well as *horizontal* information flows.

Inventory models   This type of management science model answers two questions relating to inventory management: "How much?" and "When?" It provides the manager with the point at which orders should be placed for repeat goods and the quantity of each order.

Investment decisions   Decisions which commit present funds in exchange for potential future funds. These decisions are controlled through a capital budget.

Job depth   The relative freedom that a job holder has in the performance of assigned duties.

Job enlargement   A form of despecialization in that the number of tasks performed by the employee is increased. The increase in tasks theoretically makes the job more interesting and challenging and consequently work becomes more psychologically rewarding.

Job enrichment   Suggested formally by Herzberg, this involves building into individual jobs greater scope for personal achievement, recognition, and responsibility. It is concerned with strengthening the motivational factors and only incidentally with maintenance.

Job rotation   The procedure of moving a worker from one work station to another to minimize boredom.

Job scope   The relative complexity of the assigned task as reflected by its cycle time.

Leader-member relations This is a dimension of leadership (Fiedler) that refers to the degree of confidence which followers have in their leader.

Leadership A much defined, yet nebulous, term. In the context of the behavioral school the term refers to the ability of a person to influence the activities of followers in an organizational setting. The emphasis is on the fact that the leader must interact with his followers in order to be influential.

Legitimate power The power which a leader has in the managerial hierarchy because of rank. For example, the department manager, who is ranked higher than the foreman in the managerial hierarchy, possesses more legitimate power.

Line function Activities which contribute directly to the creation of the organization's output. In manufacturing, the line functions are manufacturing, marketing, and finance.

Maintenance factors Distinguished by Herzberg in his "two-factor" theory of motivation. Maintenance factors are those conditions of the job which operate primarily to dissatisfy employees when they are not present. However, their presence does not build strong motivation among employees. Herzberg distinguished 16 of these factors (for example, salary, job security, work conditions).

Management The process of coordinating individual and group activity toward group goals.

Management by objectives A management technique which consists of the following major elements:
1. A superior and a subordinate meet to discuss goals and jointly establish attainable goals for the subordinate.
2. The superior and subordinate meet again after the initial goals have been set to evaluate the subordinate's performance in terms of the preestablished goals.

Management functions The activities which a manager must perform as a result of position in the firm. The text identifies planning, organizing, and controlling as the management functions.

Management information systems An organized, structured complex of individuals, machines, and procedures for providing pertinent information from both external and internal sources. It supports the planning, control, and operations functions of an organization by providing uniform information for use as the basis for decision making.

Management science school A body of literature characterized by its use of mathematical and statistical techniques to build models for the solution of production and operational problems. The school's primary means for acquiring knowledge is mathematical deduction.

Managerial performance The extent to which a manager achieves coordinated work through the efforts of subordinates; coordinated work results from appropriate use of relevant planning, organizing, and controlling techniques and methods.

Market survey A set of techniques which enables the manager to estimate the attitude of consumers toward aspects of a product or service.

Mathematical model A simplified mathematical representation of the relevant aspects of an actual system or process.

Maximax criterion The optimistic manager believes that only the most favorable result will occur, and decides to maximize the maximum payoff.

Maximin criterion The pessimistic manager believes that only the least favorable result will occur, and therefore decides to maximize the minimum payoff.

Metrocorporation The corporation seen as having unlimited social responsibilities, with its managers holding themselves accountable to several groups in society. This view of the corporation is the opposite of the traditional one in which managers are mainly accountable to the stockholders.

Middle management The middle level of an administrative hierarchy; managers at this level coordinate the work of managers and report to a manager.

Minimax criterion The manager believes that once a decision is made and an outcome occurs, there will be some regret, and selects that strategy which results in the least regret.

Mooney's theory of organization A theoretical statement based upon Mooney's personal experience and his analysis of the forms which organizations have taken throughout history. According to Mooney, the underlying principle of all organizations is *coordination*, which is implemented through the *scalar* process. The result is a system of specialized tasks which Mooney terms the *functional* effect.

Motion study The process of analyzing work in order to determine the preferred motions to be used in the completion of tasks. Motion study is a major contribution of scientific management, principally through the efforts of Taylor and Gilbreth.

Motivation The inner state that activates or moves. It can be described as all the inner striving conditions such as drives, desires, and motives.

Motivational factors Distinguished by Herzberg in his "two-factor" theory of motivation. Motivational factors are those job conditions which, if present, operate to build high levels of motivation and job satisfaction. However, their absence does not prove highly dissatisfying. Herzberg distinguished six of these factors (for example, achievement, recognition, advancement).

Moving budgeting A form of budgeting which involves periodic updating through time.

Multinational firm A firm with branches, divisions, and subsidiaries in foreign countries. It is currently estimated that approximately 5,000 American firms operate in foreign nations.

Normative model This type of model is specifically constructed to select from among alternatives the best alternative based on some previously determined criteria, which are also included in the model. It tells how the system should be in order to achieve a particular objective.

Nonprogrammed decisions When problems are broad, novel, and unstructured they require nonprogrammed decisions. There is no established procedure for handling them either because they have not arisen in exactly the same manner before or because they are complex or extremely important.

Objective function Expression of the sole objective of the problem, to maximize if profit, to minimize if cost, made up of a linear summation of the products of the quantity of each variable and the respective unit profit (cost).

Open system (OS) factors Management concepts and techniques which focus upon developing greater openness, sharing, creativity, and individual initiative. Most of the behavioral concepts and many classical concepts fall into this category.

Operational planning A planning process which deals with short-range goals and activities.

Ordering cost A major cost component that is considered in inventory control decisions. Each time the firm orders items for inventory, it must formally contact the supplier. This preparation usually includes some clerical and administrative work in placing the order and labor to put the items in inventory. The clerical, administrative, and labor costs make up the ordering cost element in inventory control models.

Organizational change The process of diagnosing and implementing changes in the structural, behavioral, or technological components of an organization.

Organizational communications Information flow that moves outward from the organization to the various components of its external operating environment. Whatever the type of organization, the content of this information flow is controlled by the organization (e.g., advertising in business organizations).

Organizational performance The extent to which an organization achieves the results society expects of it. Organizational performance is affected in part, but not entirely, by managerial performance.

Organizational psychology The study of behavior and attitudes within an organization, including the effect of the organization upon the individual and the individual's effect upon the organization.

Organization structure The formally defined framework of task and authority relationships. It is analogous to the biological concept of the skeleton.

Organizing function All managerial activity which results in the design of a formal structure of tasks and authority.

Participative approach A technique advocated by behavioralists which stresses the idea that employees throughout the firm should be allowed to participate in decision making.

Path-goal leadership An approach to leadership in which the leader indicates to followers the "paths" to accomplish their goals.

Payback period The length of time that it takes for an investment to pay for itself out of future funds.

Payoff table A two-dimensional array of data which indicates in tabular form the payoffs for various strategy, state of nature, or competitive action combinations.

Performance evaluation A feedback control technique which focuses on the extent to which employees have achieved expected levels of work during a specified time period.

Personal-behavioral theories A group of leadership theories that are based primarily on personal and behavioral characteristics of leaders. Included in this category are theories based on opinion and on extensive research in actual organizations.

Personality   The general sum of traits or characteristics of an individual. It is a very important determinant of individual behavior and motivation.

Person-related managerial activities   The actions of managers which involve them in relationships with their subordinates, peers, and superiors.

Planning function   All managerial activities which lead to the definition of goals and to the determination of appropriate means to achieve those goals.

Preliminary control   Techniques and methods which attempt to maintain the quality and quantity of resources.

Principles of management   In classical management theory, rules of conduct which should guide managers' behavior, or underlying laws of nature which determine the structure of organizations.

Probabilistic model   Model based on the mathematics of statistics. Conditions of uncertainty are introduced in the model often based on observations of real-world events.

Profitability measures   Measurements of efficiency in the business firm; may be the ratio of net profit either to capital or to total assets or to sales.

Programmed decisions   If a problem or situation occurs often, a routine procedure is usually developed for solving it. Thus, decisions are programmed to the extent that they are routine and repetitive and a specific procedure has been developed for handling them.

Rate of return   A general concept which refers to the ratio of annual returns to the initial cost of the investment.

Reality-centered management   A view of management which recognizes a need for a balance of classical, behavioral, and management science approaches, as well as experience. Reality-centered managers would seek to blend both experience and the schools of management and recognize that in order to be effective in the contemporary organization they cannot rely solely on one approach.

Referent power   The power of a leader based on attractiveness. That is, the leader is admired because of certain personal qualities and the follower identifies closely with these characteristics.

Reward power   The power generated by the perception of followers that compliance with the wishes of leaders can lead to positive rewards (for example, promotion).

Risk decisions   Decision situations in which managers do not know for certain the probability of occurrence of the state of nature or competitive actions. However, they have some past experience and/or data upon which they can rely to develop probabilities. These probabilities are used with conditional values to determine expected values.

Sample survey   Collection of data from a limited number of units which are assumed to be representative of the entire group.

Scalar chain   The graded chain of authority through which all communications flow.

Sensitivity training   A form of educational experience which stresses the process and emotional aspects of learning.

Simulation model A model which replicates some aspect of the firm's operation. By performing step-by-step computations with the model, one duplicates the manner in which the actual system might perform.

Slack variable Variable introduced into constraint inequalities in order to form equalities. Their unit profit (cost) is zero.

Social psychology Branch of psychology dealing with the behavior of individuals as they relate to other individuals.

Social responsibility During the last decade, society has been placing increased demands on large business organizations for greater social responsibility—that is, business involvement in solving both social and ecological problems.

Sociogram A diagram which illustrates the interpersonal relationships existing within a group. By use of the sociogram it is possible to trace communication patterns within a group.

Sociology The science that seeks to isolate, define, and describe human behavior in groups. It strives to develop laws and generalizations about human nature, social interaction culture, and social organization.

Sociometric analysis The use of self-reports to find personal preference and repulsion patterns of members of work groups.

Soldiering A term used during the scientific management era to refer to the observed practice of output restriction. That is, workers were observed to be producing at a lower rate than what would ordinarily be expected.

Staff functions Activities which contribute indirectly to the creation of the organization's output. Ordinarily, staff personnel advise line personnel.

Status consensus The agreement of group members about the relative status of members of the group.

Status hierarchy The ranking of group members within the group, that is, the prestige rank order of group members.

Strategic planning A planning process which deals with long range goals, selection of activities to achieve those goals, and the allocation of resources to those activities.

Structural change Planned changes in the formally prescribed task and authority relationships.

Structure (in group context) The term "structure" refers to relatively stable relationships among members of a work group. It is basically the group culture which influences the group's reward system—norms, among other things.

Suboptimization The objectives which a manager is attempting to achieve are often dependent. Thus, the optimization of one can result in a lower degree of attainment for at least some of the multiple objectives. This lower degree of attainment is known as suboptimization.

Supervision A subfunction of control which refers to the oversight of subordinates' work activity.

System-4 organization An organizational type which stresses open, supportive leadership and group methods for decision making and goal setting.

Tall pyramid structure A structure which fosters narrow spans of control, a large number of management levels, and more centralized decision making.

Task group   A formal group of individuals working as a unit to complete a task.

Task structure   The degree of structure imposed on a job. The job may be routine or nonroutine. If the job is routine it will be spelled out in detail. An inspector on the assembly line has a structured task, while the job of the research scientist has relatively little task structure.

Technically complex environment   An environment which consists of technologically advanced opportunities and constraints.

Technological change   Planned changes in the use of techniques and knowledge appropriate for the organization's purpose.

Theory X   A set of assumptions about the nature of man which, according to Douglas McGregor, underlies the classical management theory. The assumptions stress the indolent characteristics of man.

Theory Y   An approach to management which is based on assumptions which are exactly the opposite of Theory X. They are:
1. Workers do not inherently dislike work.
2. Workers do not want to be controlled and threatened.
3. Workers under proper working conditions seek out additional responsibility.
4. Workers desire to satisfy other needs besides those related to job security.

Time series analysis   A statistical technique for analyzing the relationship between a specified variable and time.

Time study   The process of determining the appropriate elapsed time for the completion of a task or job. It was part of F. W. Taylor's effort to determine a fair day's work.

Top management   The top level of an administrative hierarchy; managers at this level coordinate the work of other managers, but do not report to a manager.

Traditional corporation   The corporation viewed as an instrumentality of a single group—the shareholders—and as having one clear-cut purpose: conducting business for maximal profit. This view recognizes no public responsibilities except legal ones, and leaves the public interest to the care of the state.

Trait theory   The trait theory attempts to specify which personal characteristics (physical, personality, mental) are associated with leadership success. It relies on research that relates various traits to success criteria.

Turbulent environment   An environment which tends to change regularly and rapidly. Such environments pose great problems to managers because of the absence of reliable information about the magnitude and direction of the changes.

Uncertainty decisions   Decision situations in which no past experience or historical data is available. Any one of a number of criteria are employed depending upon the personality of the manager.

Unity of command   A management principle which states that each subordinate should report to only one superior.

Unity of direction   The process of grouping all related activities under one superior.

Unsatisfied need The starting point in the process of motivation. It is a deficiency of something within the individual that provides the spark which leads to behavior.

Variable budgeting A form of budgeting which targets expected costs at various potential output levels.

Variable costs Costs that vary closely with changes in production. For example, as the number of units produced increases, the amount of material used also increases. Thus the cost of material used to produce a product would be an example of variable costs.

Vertical specialization of management The process by which the right to command is delegated downward so as to create a hierarchy of positions graded by degrees of assigned authority.

Vroom-Yetton model A situational model of leadership which attempts to identify the appropriate leadership style for a given set of circumstances, or situations. The leadership styles are defined in terms of the extent to which the subordinates participate in decision making.

Waiting-line models Waiting-line models enable the manager to reach optimal decisions in facilities planning. They help in striking a balance between the cost of additional facilities and some other factor such as idle time or customer ill will.

Well-tempered corporation The corporation viewed as lying between the two extremes of the *traditional corporation* and the *metrocorporation*. This type of corporation takes into account public expectations, but with full regard for management's responsibilities to the stockholders. Its supporters hold that the claims of stockholders and creditors will more likely be met if a firm develops a position as a socially responsible company.

Work-related managerial activities The actions of managers taken to achieve specific task outcomes; examples include decision making, problem solving, paperwork processing, and budgeting.

Zero-based budgeting A form of budgeting which requires justification of all requested expenditures for a program or activity (termed a "decision center"), not simply the increases in expenditures.

INDEXES

NAME INDEX

A

Ackerman, R. W., 434
Ackoff, L. R., 85
Ackoff, R. L., 342
Adams, C. R., 378
Agnew, Paul C., 309 n
Albaum, Gerald S., 371 n
Alderfer, Clayton P., 244, 288 n, 295 n
Alter, Steven L., 376 n
Alutto, Joseph A., 310 n
Alvaris, Kenneth, 270 n
Anderson, Donald N., 61
Anshen, M., 434
Ansoff, H. I., 85
Anthony, R. N., 85
Anthony, Robert, 369 n, 372 n
Aquilano, Nicholas J., 396 n
Aram, John D., 10
Argyris, Chris, 174, 252 n, 316, 379
Aristotle, 6
Arnoff, E. L., 342
Asch, Solomon E., 229
Ashford, N. A., 34

B

Back, G. L., 434
Baker, A. W., 118, 151
Baker, J. D., 379
Bales, R. F., 215–17, 452
Barnard, Chester I., 40, 49, 57–58, 60, 167, 174
Barry, John R., 190 n
Bartol, K. M., 279
Basil, D. C., 316
Bass, Bernard M., 221–22, 299 n
Baumol, W. J., 400
Baur, R. A., 85
Bavelas, Alex, 231–32, 239 n
Belasco, James A., 310 n
Bell, Cecil H., Jr., 287 n
Benne, K. D., 279, 290 n, 300 n, 316
Bennis, Warren G., 221 n, 251 n, 279, 290 n, 316
Berelson, Bernard, 170 n, 177
Berger, Chris J., 114 n
Berke, Jules, 95

Bernstein, Leopold A., 141 n
Bierman, Harold, 85, 136 n, 342, 353 n
Birnberg, Jacob G., 145 n
Blake, Robert R., 262–64
Blanchard, Kenneth H., 288 n
Blau, Peter M., 290
Blomstrom, R. L., 434
Bonini, Charles P., 342, 353 n
Borgatta, Edgar F., 218 n
Bowers, David G., 118, 279, 305 n
Boyd, Thomas, 141 n
Bradford, L. P., 300 n
Branch, M. C., 85
Brandeis, L. D., 60
Brech, E. F. L., 43 n
Brien, Richard H., 368 n, 374 n
Brigham, Eugene F., 138 n
Brown, A., 119
Brown, L. Dave, 287 n
Brumback, Gary B., 294 n
Bucklow, M., 244
Buffa, E., 400
Buffa, E. S., 400
Bunge, Walter R., 78 n
Burch, John G., 369 n
Burns, Tom, 305 n
Burtt, H. E., 261 n
Byrne, E. T., 417

C

Calder, B. J., 279
Cammann, Cortlandt, 141 n
Campbell, John P., 191 n, 200, 301 n
Campbell, Maureen E., 22 n
Carey, Alex, 164 n
Carlson, Eric D., 364
Carroll, Stephen J., 73 n
Cartwright, Dorwin, 218 n, 252 n, 279
Cass, E. L., 34
Cavanagh, G., 434
Chamberlain, Neil W., 66 n
Chandler, Alfred, 296 n
Chapple, Eliot D., 305 n
Chase, Richard B., 396 n
Cheit, E. F., 14
Chemers, Martin M., 267 n

SUBJECT INDEX

Y–Z

This book has been set in 10 and 9 point Melior, leaded 2 points. Part numbers are 54 point Weiss Roman and part titles are 24 point Melior Bold. Chapter numbers are 54 point Weiss Series II and chapter titles are 20 point Melior Bold. The size of the maximum type page is 30 picas by 47 picas.

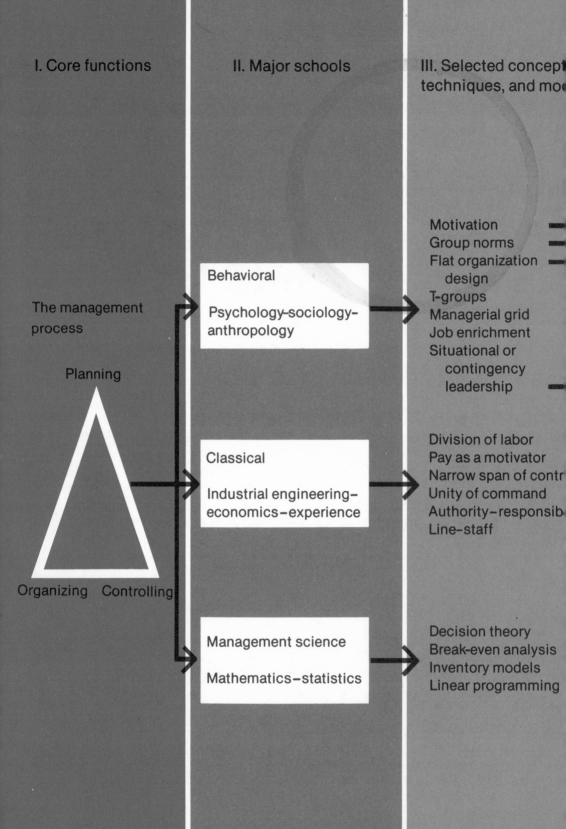

I. Core functions

The management
process

Planning

Organizing   Controlling

II. Major schools

Behavioral

Psychology–sociology–
anthropology

Classical

Industrial engineering–
economics–experience

Management science

Mathematics–statistics

III. Selected concept
techniques, and mod

Motivation
Group norms
Flat organization
   design
T-groups
Managerial grid
Job enrichment
Situational or
   contingency
   leadership

Division of labor
Pay as a motivator
Narrow span of contr
Unity of command
Authority–responsib
Line–staff

Decision theory
Break-even analysis
Inventory models
Linear programming